AURAL/ORAL DRAMATURGIES

This book focuses on the 'aural turn' in contemporary theatre-making, examining a number of seemingly disparate trends that foreground speech and sound – 'post-verbatim' theatre, 'amplified storytelling' (works using microphones and headphones), and 'gig theatre' that incorporates live music performance.

Its main argument is that the dramaturgical underpinnings of these works contribute to an understanding of theatre as an extra-literary activity, greater than the centrality of the script that traditionally dominated many historical discussions. This quality is usually expressed in terms of the corporeality in dance and physical theatre, but the aural/oral turn gives an alternative viewpoint on the interplay between text and performance. The book's case studies draw on the ways in which a range of theatre companies engage with the dramaturgy of speech and sound in their work. It is further accompanied by a specially curated collection of digital resources, including interviews, conversations, and presentations from artists and academics ('Lend Me Your Ears' on www.auralia.space).

This is a key text for scholars, students, and practitioners of contemporary performance, and anyone working with dramaturgies of orality and aurality in today's performance environment.

Duška Radosavljević teaches at the Royal Central School of Speech and Drama, University of London. She is the author of the award-winning monograph *Theatre-Making: Interplay Between Text and Performance in the 21st Century* (2013), and editor of *Theatre Criticism: Changing Landscapes* (2016) and *The Contemporary Ensemble: Interviews with Theatre-Makers* (2013).

AURAL/ORAL DRAMATURGIES

Theatre in the Digital Age

Duška Radosavljević

LONDON AND NEW YORK

Cover image: East London Workers Party Silent Disco (2016) by ZU-UK.
Photo by: Ludovic des Cognets

First published 2023
by Routledge
4 Park Square, Milton Park, Abingdon, Oxon OX14 4RN

and by Routledge
605 Third Avenue, New York, NY 10158

Routledge is an imprint of the Taylor & Francis Group, an informa business

© 2023 Duška Radosavljević

The right of Duška Radosavljević to be identified as author of this work has been asserted in accordance with sections 77 and 78 of the Copyright, Designs and Patents Act 1988.

All rights reserved. No part of this book may be reprinted or reproduced or utilised in any form or by any electronic, mechanical, or other means, now known or hereafter invented, including photocopying and recording, or in any information storage or retrieval system, without permission in writing from the publishers.

Trademark notice: Product or corporate names may be trademarks or registered trademarks, and are used only for identification and explanation without intent to infringe.

British Library Cataloguing-in-Publication Data
A catalogue record for this book is available from the British Library

Library of Congress Cataloging-in-Publication Data
A catalog record has been requested for this book

Names: Radosavljević, Duška, author.
Title: Aural/oral dramaturgies : theatre in the digital age/Duška Radosavljević.
Description: Abingdon, Oxon ; New York, NY : Routledge, 2023. | Includes bibliographical references and index.
Identifiers: LCCN 2022019582 (print) | LCCN 2022019583 (ebook) | ISBN 9780367560768 (hardback) | ISBN 9780367560744 (paperback) | ISBN 9781003096337 (ebook)
Subjects: LCSH: Theater--Sound effects. | Theater--Production and direction. | Drama--Technique. | Technology and the arts.
Classification: LCC PN2053 .R26 2023 (print) | LCC PN2053 (ebook) | DDC 792.02/33--dc23/eng/202206-09
LC record available at https://lccn.loc.gov/2022019582
LC ebook record available at https://lccn.loc.gov/2022019583

ISBN: 978-0-367-56076-8 (hbk)
ISBN: 978-0-367-56074-4 (pbk)
ISBN: 978-1-003-09633-7 (ebk)

DOI: 10.4324/9781003096337

Typeset in Bembo
by KnowledgeWorks Global Ltd.

CONTENTS

Preface   *viii*
Acknowledgements   *xv*

1 Introduction(s): The Difficult Second Album   1

   Side A: Literature Review 1
   Track 01: Overture: Premises 1
   Track 02: Context: The Aural/Oral Dramaturgies (A/OD) Project 3
   Track 03: Changing Trends 4
   *Track 04: Research Methodology: A Long View of Institutional
      Knowledge Production 6*
   Track 05: Intersections: Dramaturgy, Speech, and Sound 13

   Side B: Methodology 24
   Track 06: Methodology: A Genealogical Retro-Articulation 24
   Track 07: Embracing Contradictions 28
   Track 08: Relational Ethnography 32
   *Track 09: Towards a Dramaturgical Research Methodology: A Close
      View 35*
   Track 10: How to Read This Book 38
   Hidden Track: COVID-19 Coda 40

2 Post-Verbatim   61
   *Genealogies of Verbatim Theatre: A Brief Recap and an Ethnographic
      Addendum 63*
   Reconfiguring Critique through Performative Ethnography 66

Counterpoint: A Performative Intervention 69
Towards Post-Verbatim Theatre: Holding onto Contradictions 73
Polyphonic Insights 81

3 Amplified Storytelling   91
   Exposition 91
   Emplotment: From Gusle to Gestalt 94
   Culmination: Form vs Content 100
   Peripeteia: Exploding the Narrative 107
   Resolution 114

4 Gig Theatre   121
   Gig Theatre: The Term 124
   Historicising Gig Theatre 1: Storytelling, Punk, and Genre 129
   Historicising Gig Theatre 2: Rock Against Racism 134
   Historicising Gig Theatre 3: DIY and Dramaturgy 139
   Gig Theatre and Dramaturgy 142
   Gig Theatre and (Rave) Culture 147

5 Conclusion(s): Aural/Oral Dramaturgies in the Digital Age   160
   The A/OD Case Studies: Notes on a Polyphonic Methodology 162
   Paradigmatic Questions 165
   'Bottom Up': Dramaturgy of Layering 167
   The Disruption of Closure: Dramaturgy of Methexis 168
   Enmeshment vs Immersion: Dramaturgy of Intersubjectivity 170
   Epilogue: Liminalities 172

Appendices   *179*
   Appendix 2.1 Anna Deavere Smith: Notes from the Field *179*
   Appendix 2.2 SKaGeN: Pardon/In Cuffs *181*
   Appendix 2.3 Dead Centre: Lippy *182*
   Appendix 2.4 Milo Rau: Five Easy Pieces *183*
   Appendix 2.5 Lola Arias: Minefield *185*
   Appendix 3.1 Kieran Hurley: Heads Up *187*
   Appendix 3.2 Kieran Hurley: Beats *188*
   Appendix 3.3 Nassim Soleimanpour: Blind Hamlet *189*
   Appendix 3.4 Rachel Mars: Our Carnal Hearts *189*
   Appendix 3.5 Ontroerend Goed: World Without Us *190*
   Appendix 3.6 Dead Centre: Chekhov's First Play *191*
   Appendix 4.1 RashDash: Another Someone *194*
   Appendix 4.2 Lucy McCormick: Triple Threat *194*
   Appendix 4.3 Lucy McCormick: Post-Popular *196*

Appendix 4.4 Beatbox Academy: Frankenstein *197*
Appendix 4.5 nabokov: Symphony *198*
Appendix 4.6 Wildcard Theatre: Electrolyte *199*
Appendix 4.7 RashDash: Two Man Show *200*
Appendix 4.8 Unfolding Theatre: Putting the Band Back Together *202*
Appendix 4.9 Taylor Mac: A 24-Decade History of Popular Music: The First Act *203*

Lend Me Your Ears Collection   *206*
Index   *215*

PREFACE

Between the ages of four and six, I was fascinated by the idea of writing. In my birth country Yugoslavia, we used to start school at seven, so this self-instruction predated my formal education. I had an old school primer – 'bukvar' – in which each letter was laid out on individual pages, with matching illustrations and lines to practise their cursive forms, and then somewhere towards the end – all 30 characters of the Serbian 'azbuka' neatly laid out on the right-hand side of the picture of an old man with a red fez hat and long moustache.

The old man was called Vuk – literally 'wolf'. But his slightly intimidating name and demeanour were of no concern, especially given that the other key cultural figure of my childhood, the author of the most ubiquitous children's poetry in Serbia, had the nickname 'Zmaj' – 'Dragon'. The Enlightenment among the South Slavs was a formidable project.

Born in 1787, Vuk – full name Vuk Stefanović Karadžić, but I'll stay on first name terms thanks to the privilege of befriending him in childhood – was named after the wild animal by his illiterate peasant parents, who had lost numerous babies beforehand, in order to ward off evil spirits and keep this child alive.

As it happens, Vuk did not only survive but he gained immortality through his contributions to Serbian and South Slav culture. His work happened in the 19th century in the spirit of national reawakening and the pan-Slavic struggle for liberation from the Austro-Hungarian and Ottoman empires. An auto-didact himself, Vuk fought to reform and simplify the official written language, based on the Church Slavonic, in order to bring it closer to the vernacular and make literacy available to the masses. His contemporary Ljudevit Gaj (1809–1872) was undertaking similar efforts in Croatia, the result of which was an alignment of the standardised Croatian Latin alphabet and the Serbian Cyrillic. Both alphabets now had 30 directly corresponding letters, each of which also corresponded to a single sound, making them fully phonetic. These efforts later led to the official language of the state of Yugoslavia (1929–1991), Serbo-Croatian, being the only language in the world with two official alphabets. Not only did this make literacy more attainable, but we could also code-switch in writing if we wanted to.

Vuk followed me throughout my school life as I collected a string of 'Vukova diploma' certificates for academic achievement all the way through to high school graduation. But more importantly, I retained the love of writing, while increasingly perhaps taking Vuk's role in it for granted.

When I graduated from high school in 1993 and left the warzone that remained of Yugoslavia, the culpability of Serbian nationalism in the ongoing war made me deeply ashamed of my ethnic origins. As I learnt to write more fluently in English and dedicated myself to the study of theatre, I never needed Vuk again either, and he paled into oblivion. Or so I thought.

There was an interesting moment in the course of putting the finishing touches to my PhD thesis in 2002 that took me on a long journey back to Vuk. Dealing with the overarching and in many ways fundamental research question of my PhD, 'Why is there so little knowledge or interest in the Yugoslav and Serbian theatre, literature and culture in the English-speaking world?', I came across the largely forgotten work of the American linguists Milman Parry (1902–1935) and Albert Lord (1912–1991), who spent the early 20th century researching the so-called oral literature of the South Slavs. On the basis of their field research, which involved phonographic recording of the extemporaneous performances of often illiterate folk singers from the Balkans, Parry and Lord developed the 'oral-formulaic theory'. Its main premise was that oral composition contained a systematic use of patterns and rhythms within a specific meter, which retroactively also revolutionised academic understanding of Homeric verse authorship. At exactly the same time, I coincidentally went to the cinema to see Curtis Hanson's film *8 Mile*, featuring Eminem, and in watching a rap battle scene, I realised I was watching the compositional process described by Parry and Lord as taking place in the extemporaneous performance of those Balkan singers.

Fast Forward the length of someone else's whole childhood, I am reading Vuk again. I am still experiencing some unease around looking at content classed as 'Serbian', but on this occasion, my main point of interest is my own positioning as a researcher – the fact that despite having lived the majority of my life in the UK, I am aware that my cultural lens and my cultural foundations have been initiated elsewhere. Additionally, I am aware of my ongoing responsibility to challenge the pre-existing workings of Western canon-creation and continue the ambassadorial work on behalf of my culture.

*

The following is foundational knowledge for anyone who grew up in Yugoslavia, but for the benefit of the non-Yugoslav readers, I need to preface this book with a brief snapshot of Vuk's work for the purpose of contextualisation and to free up space later for matters concerning aural/oral dramaturgies directly.

Between 1814 and 1864, in addition to numerous other books, Vuk published nine volumes of Serbian oral poetry, some of which he initially recalled from memory but much of which he personally recorded in writing 'from the mouths of the singers'. Over the years of their publication, these songs attracted the attention and admiration of the European cultural giants, including the brothers Grimm (1785–1863 and 1786–1859), Johann Wolfgang von Goethe (1749–1832), Prosper Mérimée (1803–1870), Walter Scott (1771–1832), Alexander Pushkin (1799–1837), and others, many of whom engaged in translating these works. Jacob Grimm believed that 'the most significant literary event of his time was the discovery of the traditional poetry of the Serbs' (Low 1922: xiv).

Partly responsible for this fame was the song 'Hasanaginica' ('The Hasan Aga's Wife'), an Italian translation of which had been included in the 1744 travelogue *Viaggio in Dalmazia* by Alberto Fortis. The song had also independently caught the attention of Goethe, who made it famous in his own German translation, and later even reportedly inspired Sir Walter Scott's literary interest. By 1827, a full volume of *Serbian Popular Poetry* appeared in English, translated by Sir John Bowring (1792–1872).

Vuk's own ethnographic endeavour was ignited in 1813, when he encountered Goethe's translation of 'The Hasan Aga's Wife' thanks to his Slovenian mentor in Vienna – Jernej Kopitar (1780–1844). This prompted Vuk to make available not only the songs of the South Slavs to Europe but also the language and the culture as a whole. As a result, Vuk published the first Serbian-German-Latin dictionary in 1818 and the first Serbian grammar book in 1824.

The internet makes it possible to retrieve scanned copies of some original 19th-century volumes – for example, *Narodne srpske pjesme: Knjiga prva u kojoj su različne ženske pjesme* (*Popular Serbian Songs: Volume One Containing Various Female Songs*), published by Breitkopf and Härtel in Leipzig, also in 1824. This book alone contains 406 items. Its Introduction, written by Vuk, offers numerous insights into the inception and the nature of these creations. Many aspects of these descriptions – that the songs are divided into epic and lyrical, that they are performed to the accompaniment of the one-string instrument gusle, and that they are often carried around by travellers and outlaws – are well known, but the act of reading Vuk's words directly, and from this temporal and spatial distance, allows new levels of insight.

I am drawn to the detail of Vuk signing his introduction off on Christmas Day 1823. At this point, Vuk is 36 years old and has been married for five years to Anna Maria Kraus from Vienna – a marriage that will be blessed with 13 children, many of whom will have died young. The book cover of the *Popular Serbian Songs* states that the author, a Doctor of Philosophy, is also a member of the learned societies of St. Petersburg and Krakow.

In the Introduction, Vuk notes that his previous collection of songs was recalled from his memory and that he had changed some words to fit with the current literary standards of the day, but on this occasion, he says, he has 'corrected' these 'improvements', noting down instead the words as he heard them from the singers. For reasons of categorisation, he offers the taxonomy of 'heroic' and 'female' (or 'women's') songs, explaining that the former are often sung by men to the musical accompaniment of the gusle, and the latter, contrary to their taxonomic designation, are sung, he says, not only by women, but often by young men, too.

Although this taxonomy later changed to 'epic' and 'lyric' songs, respectively, the original 'terminological imbalance' identified by Celia Hawkesworth (2000: 34), and the relative value implied in the gender affiliation, has remained and been reinforced by subsequent scholarship. Heroic or epic songs are longer and more dramatic and have traditionally been seen to have greater value as they also constitute a form of historiography, while the lyric or female songs are often short and linked to specific rituals (change of season, communal tasks, rites of passage). In respect of trying to redress the value imbalance between the two genres, Hawkesworth also notes the work of Yugoslav academic Hatidža Krnjević in the 1980s, which was focused on giving the lyric songs more prominence for their assumed older age of composition and longer lasting anthropological significance: 'Heroic times are the past, the lyric is always the present' (in Hawkesworth 2000: 37).

Looking directly at Vuk, one can discern that, notwithstanding the gender biases of his own time, he is more interested in the rural/urban divide than the gender divide. In the rural areas, all men and many women can sing to the gusle, he notes, while in towns, it is mostly just the blind who use it as a means of earning a living. A particularly interesting characteristic of the so-called 'ženske'/female songs, in the context of performance studies, is that they are intended to be dialogic, collectively performed, and participatory, while the epic songs are intended to be delivered to an audience by a solo performer. Moreover, Vuk further notes that there are some songs that cannot be sorted into either of these two categories because they are long like the epic songs, but they are neither delivered to the musical accompaniment of the gusle nor sung like the lyric songs; instead, they are simply told. It is interesting that this third genre, which Hawkesworth refers to as 'Ballads and Romances', concerning individuals and their destinies, is distinguished by Vuk by means of their performance mode.

Though I will problematise the issue of oral performance later in the book, it is useful to give a couple of paragraphs to Vuk's singers here. Hawkesworth highlights a list of women singers that Vuk collected some songs from including Blind Živana (Živana Antonijević of Zemun) and her apprentice Blind Jeca (Jelena Marković). Although these singers never thought of themselves as authors but rather as tellers of existing stories, there were, according to Hawkesworth, notable stylistic differences between their individual versions. Hawkesworth's analysis identifies that, by comparison to some others, Živana's versions are characterised by more complex, dramatic plots, 'striking emotional colouring', and 'tenderness between individuals' (2000: 56–7) linked to notions of moral justice.

Meanwhile her apprentice Jeca's songs are characterised by their conciseness and, like Živana's, a greater prominence given to female characters.

Vuk also has much to say about the process of composition. He recalls the ways in which these songs were composed in his childhood around real-life events, such as weddings, and often as humorous retellings of things gone wrong – the wedding guests having a fight, etc. He notes that the same process applies to the composition and transmission of more serious songs concerning historical events. However, the notion of authorship itself is quite interesting for the reason of its seemingly devalorised status:

> That it is impossible to find out who was the first to make up each new song (let alone the old ones) is no wonder, but it is a surprise that no one among these ordinary people considers it masterful or glorious to make up a new song, and not only does no one want to take credit for it but everyone (even the one who deserves it) pushes it away and says that he has heard it from another.
>
> (Karadžić 1824: xxxi, my translation)

Vuk stresses that this is particularly the case with local songs and the songs concerning recent events, by contrast to those that are older or that come from more distant places. Another interesting aspect is the existence of different versions of the same song testifying, according to Vuk, to the malleability of these songs which change as they are passed on 'from mouth to mouth', 'growing and becoming more ornamental, and sometimes diminishing and becoming of poorer quality' (Karadžić 1824: xxxii). Like Hawkesworth, Vuk also notes that the individual singers do inflect particular renditions according to their own style, and that this is normal practice.

Finally, Vuk makes a distinction I find particularly interesting between those singers who are very meticulous about the 'sequence and the thoughts', capable of repeating the song consistently and clearly, as opposed to those who are better singers and improvisers, and therefore seemingly more concerned with the performance than the text. Subjected to the regimes of writing, Vuk expressed personal preference towards the former as they made his job of recording songs easier – and he gives the example of Tešan Podrugović, an outlaw – 'hajduk' – who 'could not (or did not want to) sing at all, but was instead telling the songs as if he was reading from a book' (Karadžić 1824: xxxiii). Hawkesworth notes that much more biographical detail is known about Vuk's male singers than female ones because they often had more dramatic lives and this is illustrated well at this point, where Vuk also informs us how Podrugović had once killed a Turk in self-defence which put an end to his life as a merchant and forced him into exile.

There are important insights contained within the story of Vuk Karadžić concerning the issues of ideology and canon construction. Vuk's work coincides with the moment of European Romanticism and nationalist European projects of the 19th century. On one level, this impulse is harnessed to positive ends as part of the Illyrian movement aimed at liberating the South Slavs from the Austro-Hungarian and Ottoman empires and bringing them together. Additionally, the work is deeply emancipatory for the locals, as pointed out by Maximilian Mügge: Vuk's effort raised 'the language of the common people, from the position of a despised slang to that of the standard literary language' (1916: 30). On another level, Vuk's work can be perceived to have inadvertently led to a local traditionalism and stultification of values, and to the Western exoticisation or othering of the culture(s) of the South Slavs. In relative terms, the European interest in the Serbian culture was a kind of colonialist flash in the pan.

★

There is another important aspect of my personal interests and formative influences to account for in the context of this book. I was born in socialist Yugoslavia and grew up in the late 1970s and early 1980s, a time and place characterised by the country's unique positionality between the communist East and the liberal West. We grew up with relatively unrestricted access to Levi's jeans, Hollywood films, and MTV music videos, enjoying a brand of 'communist consumerism' that ensured full immersion in the contemporary Western popular culture. While Yugoslav socialism did not offer political pluralism until the introduction of the multi-party election in 1990, the breadth of choice in cultural consumption accounted for all tastes, from hard rock to hip hop, comics to PC games, Macedonian Darkwave to Neue Slowenische Kunst. In 1989, I went to a gig that determined the musical allegiance of my teenage years as firmly belonging to Yugoslav post punk. A whole other book is required to properly encapsulate the troubled political significance of that moment when as a young person I euphorically witnessed the beginning of the end – the elevating promise of the Yugoslav alternative being defeated by rampaging nationalism and a tragic finale.

Ekatarina Velika (EKV), nowadays described as 'the most lyrical and musically accomplished band' of the Yugoslav new wave (Bousfield 2021), was at the time a fringe act by comparison to those who filled out football stadiums. Their reputation in the mainstream was not helped by the fact that on turning up to receive a music award in 1992 in a live broadcast on state TV, the frontman Milan Mladenović asked instead for a minute of silence for the victims of the ongoing Yugoslav wars (https://www.youtube.com/watch?v=04vf3d00ZUc). Two years later, Mladenović himself died of cancer at age 35, and many of his associates also died young. EKV however made a crucial contribution to my identity formation in many inarticulable ways. One of particular relevance in this context is the impact that the 1989 gig made on my appreciation of music and live performance. Although my musical enthusiasm did to some extent involve the customary record collecting, it was far more importantly characterised by committed attendance of concerts (which, in a naïve attempt at documentation perhaps, I strived to capture on portable dictaphones). EKV had a focused performance style uninterested in banter or the stirring up of crowd behaviour; in one interview they gave in the 1980s, their keyboard player Margita Stefanović, who was also a trained architect, described their concerts as 'imaginary cities'. I credit this formative influence for the cultivation of my theatrical predilections, and for being an important factor in arriving at the point of writing this book.

★

I wrote the opening paragraphs of this Preface in January 2020. At the time, my children were exactly four and six years old – an age when I could now witness as a parent the emerging fascination and grappling with the difficulties of writing that I was recalling from personal experience while embarking on the Aural/Oral Dramaturgies research project. In January 2020, none of us knew that our lives were about to change abruptly, on a global scale. The move of our everyday lives to the digital realm, caused by Covid-19, was a civilisational disruption which would bring about categorically new memories of encounters with literacy, cultural heritage, and history in the making.

The layered structure of this Preface signals the desire of this book to account for themes that emerge from foundational contradictions and unlikely juxtapositions. One of the themes that emerges from the above is the theme of survival: What ensures the survival of a cultural legacy? How to survive a crisis? Or to paraphrase a song lyric: 'How to protect oneself from change–only through change?'

This book will not have answers to such big questions, only perhaps some apposite stories – but, in the context of Aural/Oral Dramaturgies, that might in fact be the point.

Duška Radosavljević
April 2022

Bibliography

Bousfield, Jonathan (2021). '40 years after the New Wave: the story of the music that changed Yugoslavia'. https://www.calvertjournal.com/features/show/12495/yugoslav-new-wave-1980s-music-40-years-on

Hawkesworth, Celia (2000). *Voices in the Shadows: Women and Verbal Art in Serbia and Bosnia*, Budapest, London: Central European University Press.

Karadžić, Vuk Stefanović (1824). *Narodne Srpske Pjesme: Knjiga Prva*, Lipisca: Brejtkopf i Eršl, https://books.google.co.uk/books?id=jccGAAAAQAAJ&printsec=frontcover&source=gbs_ge_summary_r&cad=0#v=onepage&q&f=false.

Low, D.H. (1922). *The Ballads of Marko Kraljević*, Cambridge: Cambridge University Press.

Mügge, Maximilian A. (1916). *Serbian Folk Songs, Fairy Tales and Proverbs*, London: Drane's Danegeld House.

ACKNOWLEDGEMENTS

My thanks are due to the AHRC, Royal Central School of Speech and Drama, Battersea Arts Centre, Digital Theatre, and Victoria & Albert Museum for supporting the Aural/Oral Dramaturgies project (AH/S010750/1) with institutional and financial resources. Special thanks to Bethany Haynes, Tarek Iskander, Talia Rogers, and Simon Sladen for their initial belief and enthusiasm that ensured this project got off the ground, and to various anonymous readers and peer reviewers for their encouragement and approval.

At the Royal Central School of Speech and Drama, I owe my thanks to Sally Baggott, Maria Delgado, and Tony Fisher for reading and commenting on the various drafts of the AHRC application; to Elaine Henry for steadfast administrative support throughout; to Dan Heatherington for his helpful oversight; to Wayne Burgess and Hayat Hassan for help with technical issues; and to Sally Mackey, Broderick Chow, Ellen Pruyne, Kate Elswit, and to Bryce Lease for their practical contributions to the project delivery. I thank Lynne Kendrick, Ross Brown, Adelina Ong, and Farokh Soltani for their camaraderie and expert contributions, and to Steve Farrier for patience, understanding, and support with organising my workload. Nohar Lazarovich, David Shearing, and Diana Damian Martin also have my thanks for their collegiality that facilitated aspects of this work.

I would like to thank my students at Central for what they have taught me, and particularly the postgraduate researchers for informing and stimulating my thinking, especially Maja Milatovic-Ovadia, Hara Topa, Clio Unger, Alma Prelec, and Laura Kressly.

I could not have wished for better people to work with on this project than Flora Pitrolo, Beatriz Cabur, Jane Boston, Deelee Dubé, Tim Bano, Juan Salazar, Ken Mitzutani, Nick Awde, Tom Colley, Samantha McAtear, Kalina Petrova, Saskia Craft-Stanley, Jonathan Rogerson and Matt Powell. Each one of them has been an irreplaceable source of joy, inspiration, hard work, and expertise. I am honoured to have had this chance to collaborate with and learn from all of them. This also goes for our resourceful and supportive Advisory and Steering Board, and for all of 90+ contributors to Lend Me Your Ears (www.auralia. space), spearheaded by our Artists in Residence: Gracefool Collective, sair goetz, Silvia Mercuriali, SK Shlomo, and Sleepwalk Collective.

I owe extra thanks to Gay McAuley, Trish Read and David Roesner for their generosity and care which exceeded their call of duty throughout this eventful time.

In addition, I offer my gratitude to everyone who took part in the special issue of *Critical Stages* 24 that also forms part of the Aural/Oral Dramaturgies project – working with such an impressively international group of people all the way up to the winter festivities of 2021 was a true celebration. Special thanks to Savas Patsalidis for always saying 'yes' to our various requests, and also to Yana Meerzon for accommodating and taking forward a number of our suggestions.

A number of people have helped the development of this book by inviting me to speak about the work at various workshops and events; my thanks for this go to Ildikó Ungvari Zrínyi, Petra Bjelica, Alexandra Portmann & Peter Boenisch, Fernando M. Oliveira & Vânia Rodrigues, and Esa Kirkkopelto.

For helpful comments on drafts, I owe drinks and chocolates to Demetris Zavros, George Rodosthenous, Silvija Jestrovic, Ben Spatz, Patrice Pavis, and Alexandra Portmann, and to Kasia Lech and Caridad Svich for their generous endorsements.

Finally, for interminable correspondence about photographs and for relevant permissions I must thank Christopher Brett Bailey, Beckie Darlington, Jemima Yong, Nic Green, Abbi Greenland, Shelly Campbell, Kieran Hurley, James Meteyard, Biddy Hayward, Debbie Chinn, and especially Jorge Lopes Ramos whose personal archive yielded the front cover photograph. The providential magic of social media must be acknowledged here too for incidentally bringing me into contact with photographer Michael John Bowring – descendent of one of the first translators of Serbian epic poetry into English, Sir John Bowring – who now lives in Serbia and whose photograph of gusle is featured in Chapter 3.

I'd like to thank *The Theatre Times*, *Exeunt*, *The Stage*, *Total Theatre*, and *Theatre Guide London* for publishing my work over the years and ultimately helping to shape the content of this book.

At Routledge, I wish to thank Ben Piggott and Steph Hines for their faith in this project and timely communication, as well as Michele Dimont and Meeta Singh for their patient support throughout production.

None of this would have been possible without the unwavering love and patience of my family, particularly Dragan and Dragana Radosavljević for letting me go out to theatre and concerts in those formative years, and to Tobias, Joakim, and Katarina Krojer for letting me stay in to write this book when we should have been hanging out together. I dedicate this work to them.

1
INTRODUCTION(S)
The Difficult Second Album

SIDE A: LITERATURE REVIEW

Track 01: Overture: Premises
Track 02: Context: The A/OD Project
Track 03: Changing Trends
Track 04: Research Methodology: A Long View of Institutional Knowledge Production
Track 05: Intersections: Dramaturgy, Speech, and Sound

Track 01: Overture: Premises

First and foremost, this is a book about dramaturgy. This declaration seems necessary for several reasons. One is disciplinary clarity. At the beginning of the 21st century, the academic field around the intersection of Sound with Theatre and Performance Studies is becoming so significant in its own right (Ovadija 2013, Curtin 2014, Home-Cook 2015, Kendrick 2017, Bennett 2019, Brown 2020a), that I can only claim the status of an immigrant in it. I come to this project without pre-existing expertise in sound, but with a deep curiosity about the provenance of an emerging set of trends perceived in the process of theatre-going, and with a primary and all-encompassing disciplinary interest in theatre-making. Writing this book represents a process of discovery. Secondly, this statement is necessary as a means of ensuring continuous commitment to my primary academic and professional affiliation as the titles of my previous books do not always make this explicit.

If we take dramaturgy to mean a dynamic theoretical-practical system of reflection on how theatre and live performance are made – and how in turn they generate socio-political, critical, epistemic, and creative engagement – all my academic work so far (including publications on ensemble theatre, mums and babies' theatre, and theatre criticism) has been about dramaturgy. Furthermore, given the ever-growing field of Theatre and Performance Studies, it seems important to state the disciplinary allegiance in order for the work to enter relevant discussions. Finally, even though it is concerned with speech and sound, and ultimately technical innovation in the digital age, this book is about theatre dramaturgy rather than radio, podcast, or new media dramaturgy per se. That said, theatre is here conceived of in its broadest sense, as not confined to purpose-built venues or proscenium arch-framed performer-audience relationships, but also, importantly, as not excluding the ocular dimension suggested by the etymology of its Greek root – θέατρον (play, spectacle).

In this respect, it also seems important to state some underlying assumptions:

The main drive of my work as a dramaturg, teacher, and academic for over 20 years has been the constant necessity to highlight the core idea that theatre is ontologically not a literary form.

This will sound obvious to many theatre professionals, academics, and students of Drama, Theatre, and Performance, including those who consider themselves primarily playwrights or writers of performance texts, but as this book will show, that which is obvious is not necessarily always fully apprehensible. Somehow we continue to operate with deep-seated beliefs which perpetuate the supremacy of the written word. Not intended to patronise, this statement rather aims to gesture towards the centuries-long historical imbalance in the Western culture which has, due to the materiality, circulability, and eventual hegemony of the written word, enthroned in our minds a semantic shortcut between theatre and its most readily available document – the written text.

No matter how committed we might be to the ontological idea of theatre as primarily performance – and therefore kinaesthetic, visual, spatial, ephemeral – the appeal of potential immortalisation contained within the promise of the written word, might eventually trap us in.[1]

Fortuitously, through concurrent efforts of decolonisation, the time has come for renewed resistance to the pervading authority of the written word in theatre and performance (and possibly even dominant modes of academic knowledge production too). The irony of writing about this is not lost on me, but few more appropriate, academically significant, original, and rigorous[2] options exist at this early point of attempting to redress the balance. Additionally, this represents a challenge to myself as a researcher as I too am someone more comfortable with written expression. The fact that this book is complemented by web-based audio-visual materials – the Lend Me Your Ears (LMYE) collection on www.auralia.space[3] and the special issue of the *Critical Stages* journal (https://www.critical-stages.org/24/) – is at least a move in this new direction of finding a more suitable form of output for the research focused on the non-writing-based compositional practices.

In terms of the object of research, this book is about works of theatre and performance that begin their life not necessarily as texts, or movement pieces, or works devised in response to an abstract concept or a concrete stimulus, but the works privileging the dramaturgical potential of speech and sound to intersubjectively engage the audience in a shared experience.

To suit the form to the content, this introductory essay is structured as a concept album,[4] named 'The Difficult Second Album' mostly as a way of noting the relationship of this work to my previous monograph *Theatre-Making* (2013a). One reason is to break through the formal difficulty of conceptualising a book project that emerges within multiple intersections of lineage, subject matter, methodological considerations, and unforeseen circumstances. Another reason is to allow multiple points of entry into the subject matter of the book, hence the plurality of introduction(s). As per the favoured listening experience in the digital age, the tracks can be shuffled. The unique potential of the fragmentary nature afforded by the individual tracks to constitute an overarching concept is deployed in the interest of contextualisation. Side A represents a multi-track literature review, and Side B is concerned with articulating a research methodology that emerges across my work and shapes/is shaped by this research project.

Track 02: Context: The Aural/Oral Dramaturgies (A/OD) Project

This book is an outcome of the AHRC-funded project 'Aural/Oral Dramaturgies: Post-Verbatim, Amplified Storytelling and Gig Theatre in the Digital Age' (AH/S010750/1).

In the English language, both 'aural' and 'oral' are pronounced the same – /ˈɔːr(ə)l/, so in speech, it is enough to just say 'Oral Dramaturgies' or 'Aural Dramaturgies' to imply both meanings, both ends of the spectrum, and a simultaneous emphasis on the range of dramaturgies that can occur between the mouth and the ear. This homonymity is one of the reasons why these terms were selected over a number of other possibilities (sonic, sonorous, audio, auditory, audio-lingual, acoustic), most of which have been theorised elsewhere. In writing, however, it is necessary to use both these words to capture the specificity of the intersection – hence 'Aural/Oral Dramaturgies' or 'dramaturgies of speech and sound'. As a non-native English-speaker, I am obliged to notice that this convenient homonymity does not necessarily translate into other languages.

To ensure clarity, depth of enquiry, and relevance to live theatre and performance, this project focuses on the intersection of the aural and the oral (aural/oral) rather than the full breadth of the oral-aural spectrum. The notion of 'aural' as one that contains oral also evokes Tim Ingold's idea of 'earsight' – 'a kind of seeing with the ear' in apprehension of language (2000: 248) – explored by Lynne Kendrick alongside Don Idhe's 'auditory aura' for the potential of 'aura-lity' to become a 'political move' (2017: 18) – and also George Home-Cook's idea of 'atmosphere' as 'central to the theatrical phenomenon' (2015: 172).[5] However, in this work, I am explicitly interested in both terms rather than the 'aural' that subsumes or merely implies the 'oral'.

At the core of this project is an interest in live performance that places watching and listening in a dynamic, sometimes technology-aided, relationship within the theatre auditorium, and therefore potentially overturns, supersedes, or reconfigures the previously dominant dramaturgical maxim of 'show rather than tell'. Such works frequently require altered terms of audience engagement and feature various degrees of audience immersion. However, their multiple modes of conceptual and creative generation and formal manifestation require a plural designation – 'dramaturgies'.

Throughout the book, these dramaturgies are sometimes referred to more informally as the 'dramaturgies of speech and sound' or the 'theatre of speech and sound'. The collocation 'speech and sound' is a deliberate and necessary choice intended to signal a decentring of the written word in theatre, within the wider context of decolonisation.[6]

Aural/oral dramaturgies – or dramaturgies of speech and sound – are therefore defined here as audience-oriented, relational dramaturgies[7] that use speech and sound as fundamental to the processes of performance-making, rather than as incidental, auxiliary,[8] or decorative means, deemed secondary to the textual, corporeal, or visual elements of theatre and performance.

Notwithstanding the fact that several authors have traced historical lineages of these dramaturgies – Adrian Curtin (2014) and Mladen Ovadija (2013) have both independently connected the dramaturgy of sound to the historical avant-garde, for example – the current investigation considers the shaping of these dramaturgies through the ongoing significance of 'technicity' in the digital age (Stiegler 1998, Broadhurst and Machon 2012, Worthen 2020). Aural/oral dramaturgies in theatre exist within a wider paradigm, alongside such phenomena as 'Twitter's oral culture' (Tufekci 2011), TED talks, podcasts, and speech-activated personal assistants; and the aural/oral turn is also to be found in museums and art galleries – most notably the David Bowie (2013), Pink Floyd (2017), and the Opera (2017) exhibitions in the Victoria & Albert Museum in London (see Bailey et al. 2019).

Since much of the integral research for this book has been conducted under the conditions of the COVID-19 global pandemic, the findings of the A/OD project are a result of the additional circumstantial parameters as much as they are a response to the initial design. However the Research Questions outlined at the outset of this project,[9] still illuminate this book's central concerns with compositional strategies (RQ1), conceptual framing (RQ2), and the role of technology (RQ3).

Track 03: Changing Trends

The A/OD project emerges out of the findings of my book *Theatre-Making* (2013a) about the changing notions of theatre authorship in the 21st century. In this context actors are freed up from the playwright's authority to assume an authorship position for themselves; playwriting is no longer conceived of as a literary activity but also as a kinaesthetic, designerly, and/or a musical one; the performance script is an increasingly unstable entity, a structure deliberately open to and contingent on the audience input rather than serving as a blueprint for performance. Directors increasingly position themselves as enablers and equal members of ensembles rather than as leaders or cult figures. The fourth wall is removed, the audience are actively involved within the process of making. As a result, theatre-making brings about heterarchies in the place of former hierarchies, stripping the notion of authority of its connotations of power (see Radosavljević in Boenisch and Williams 2019).

A specific offshoot from *Theatre-Making* growing into the current research project is the insight cited by several contemporary playwrights in the interviews they gave me that their writing practice is deeply influenced by musical compositional processes (Adriano Shaplin, Simon Stephens) and/or their musical band membership (Chris Thorpe). Since the book's publication, the form of 'gig theatre' has gradually distinguished itself in British theatre, and theatre-making trends that similarly emphasise the immersive potential of live music are also discernible in other cultural contexts. It seems important to note that these forms are not merely music gigs but hybrid forms that feature elements of speech and/or storytelling in a dramatic (Middle Child, RashDash) and sometimes post-dramatic vein (Christopher Brett Bailey). 'Gig theatre' is also not an isolated hybrid performance form capitalising on the use of speech and sound. Others include 'headphone theatre' (Klich 2017) and 'karaoke theatre' (Parker-Starbuck 2017) which I consider under the label of 'amplified storytelling', and various postdramatic derivations of verbatim theatre designated here as 'post-verbatim'. Although verbatim theatre had been previously framed as part of the political and ethnographic theatre as 'dramaturgy of the real' (Martin 2010), the A/OD project observes a gradual disaggregation of verbatim speech from documentary theatre and its increased theatricalisation in the works of Valentijn Dhaenens, Lola Arias, and Nic Green, for example. Here the oral begins to draw attention to itself as part of the aural and requires a new theoretical framing alongside a greater 'turn to listening'. Consequently, I perceive these changing trends as part of a paradigm shift.[10]

This paradigmatic perception is further invoked by an apparent shift from the emphasis on corporeality and physical theatre which pre-dominated in Western theatre in the late 20th century and which was itself a reaction to the prevalence of text-based theatre-making practices. Some of the physical theatre companies, who in the 1980s represented an alternative to the text-based mainstream, have more recently turned to text and verbatim theatre themselves. DV8 completed the third decade of its existence as a dance company in the United Kingdom with not one but three verbatim pieces – *To Be Straight With You* (2007), *Can We Talk About This?* (2011), and *John* (2014). Similarly, Canadian director Robert Lepage – famed for his striking visual and multimedia theatre – dedicated his ten-hour-long *Lipsynch* in 2008 to the exploration of voice, speech, and language. Simon McBurney of Complicite, following decades of Jacques Lecoq-influenced corporeal theatre-making, also arrived in 2015 at a more engaged exploration of sound in his one-man show *The Encounter* and in *Beware of Pity*, an adaptation of Stefan Zweig's novel he directed in the same year at the Schaubühne, Berlin. By all accounts, this notably amplified prominence of speech and sound on stage after decades of physical theatre, could also be perceived as a return of the repressed.

Tracing the genealogies of Performance Studies in the United States, Shannon Jackson suggests that, in seeking to prioritise the marginalised, the interdisciplinary, and the corporeal, Performance Studies initially defined itself as a field by opposition to the dramatic and oral literature which it saw as aligned with the canonical (2004: 24). Similarly, Konstantinos Thomaidis notes that 'voice - conventionally seen as speech – might have fallen victim to its close association with spoken text and sung lyrics in theatre practices' (2017: 10). This conflation of the oral and the textual/literary prompts a re-examination of the Western processes of authorship and knowledge production which is also tackled in this book.

Ultimately, where my previous research into forms of theatrical authorship explored collaboration to reinvestigate the relationship between text and performance,[11] the A/OD project moves the discussion beyond this binary by focusing on *the inextricability of text from performance* characteristic of various manifestations of aural/oral dramaturgy.

Research methodology consequently emerges as a key contextual consideration for the A/OD project for three reasons. First, building on the methods deployed in the previous research, the primary purpose here is an exploration of the creative strategies of the selected artists rather than the critical study of the finished works (although critical viewing of contemporary performance was foundational in scoping the project and is documented in the appendices). Secondly, the circumstantial effect of the COVID-19 lockdown necessitated an explicit methodological rethinking of the project.[12] Finally, the ontological focus on speech and sound at the core of the selected artworks, additionally resists conventional critical contemplation (as shown in Track 05) and raises questions about the suitability of existing research methodologies in Theatre and Performance. For this reason, it is necessary to historically frame methodological innovation as part of the Introduction(s).

Track 04: Research Methodology: A Long View of Institutional Knowledge Production

Academic research represents pursuit of new knowledge through systematic methodologies designed to produce evidence for specific claims and hypotheses.[13] This distinguishes knowledge gained through research from subjective beliefs or speculations based on the so-called anecdotal evidence.[14] Evidence-based epistemology is part of a legacy of the European age of Enlightenment and the subsequent 19th century turn away from a theological view of the world towards a scientific, empirical one, subject to critical thinking. This overview re-articulates some implicit principles of institutional knowledge production in order to appropriately contextualise the innovatory methodological orientation of the A/OD project.

Whereas scientific methodology pertaining to hard sciences is possible to summarise in generic terms,[15] standards of 'academic rigour' and what represents 'research methodology' are less easily articulated in the field of Theatre and Performance, or the Humanities more broadly, where academics are customarily trained by acculturation through 'communities of practice' (Wenger 1998). This discrepancy might be partially understood by reference to the long view of the institutional histories of knowledge production in Western European universities which originally evolved in the medieval ages as a way of legitimating and codifying the professional practices of Law, Medicine, and Theology. The present-day university model which includes a greater variety of fields is a result of the development of the so-called 'research university' in the 19th century, primarily in Germany, spearheaded by Wilhelm von Humboldt (1767–1835), and by extension, in the United States, whose growth of the university sector, influenced by the German model, coincided with the professionalisation needs of the industrial age.[16] In considering relevant research methodologies for Theatre and Performance in the 21st century, it is important to discern the ways in which 'knowledge production' – itself a clearly industrialist term – has been socially constructed, and that the discipline-specific protocols of Theatre and Performance are entrenched in these intellectual histories.

Up until the late 19th century, theatre had been primarily a craft whose training by transmission – or acculturation – did not necessitate university legitimation. Theatre and performance initially entered academia not as a subject discipline in their own right but as an incidental object of interest in Philology, Literature, History, Anthropology, and Folkloric Studies.[17] In that respect, any relevant material concerning theatre and performance would have been subjected to the epistemic regimes of other subject disciplines. One example of resulting epistemological problems was the English Language departments' conceptualisation of Shakespeare's plays primarily as literature rather than as performance documents or with any reference to the materialities of theatre-making.

By comparison to other academic disciplines, Theatre and Performance Studies did not formalise distinct native research methodologies, but they initially inherited analytical, critical, and hermeneutic methodologies from other fields that previously encompassed theatre or drama.

In terms of theoretical framing of Theatre and Performance, it is possible to chart three influential intellectual genealogies in early 20th-century Europe, which have been foundational for the field, sometimes in intertwined ways: (1) structuralist/poststructuralist/deconstruction – rooted in the studies of linguistics;[18] (2) phenomenology – a branch of philosophy concerned with structures of experience and consciousness;[19] and (3) critical theory – rooted in the critical philosophical tradition of Humboldt and Immanuel Kant (1724–1804), and evolving most influentially through the Frankfurt School (founded 1929).[20]

The formalist/structuralist intellectual tradition exerted possibly the strongest early influence on the training systems in theatre- and film-making in Europe and eventually also in Hollywood. The subsequent poststructuralist ideas of the 'death of the author' (Barthes 1967) and the 'author function' (Foucault 1969), which redress the balance between the author and the reader in favour of the latter are also complementary with the intrinsically hermeneutic tasks of theatre vis-à-vis the playtext as blueprint for performance. Similarly, the Marxist hermeneutics of the Frankfurt School were useful even if its proponents were predominantly concerned with the ideological significance of the cultural products, rather than the processes of their creation. The core method of critique, augmented also by the simultaneous influence of psychoanalysis, evolved and generated other important critical lenses of feminism, postmodernism, queer theory, postcolonialism, and more recently intersectionality. At the same time, the phenomenological focus on embodiment, experience, and affect entered the scene with the advent of Performance Studies as a discipline in the United States in the second half of the 20th century and has been more recently re-invigorated through the 'experiential turn' in performance-making itself (including the emergence of performance works which prioritise the audience experience, such as immersive theatre, one-to-one, and interactive or site-specific performance).[21]

Following the period of German intellectual hegemony in the 19th century, anglophone academia has asserted leadership in reconfiguring methodologies of training and research in the 20th century, sometimes through interventions in the institutional production of knowledge. This is specifically relevant to the field of Theatre and Performance Studies which was conceived in this context. In the United Kingdom, a significant early methodological innovation was the Frankfurt School-inspired Cultural Materialism of Raymond Williams (1921–88) who moved the analytical focus from literature towards the cultural conditions of drama in performance.[22] The introduction of the independent degree subject of Drama at Bristol University in 1947 was another significant step which combined historical and textual study with experiential learning through the practical staging of plays. The first Drama Department in the United States, founded in 1924 at Yale University, was geared towards professional training. The beginnings of Performance Studies as an intellectual discipline were prompted by a combination of factors, including according to Jon McKenzie the social events of the 1960s, which led sociologists to borrow theatrical metaphors to explain social phenomena. As such, McKenzie notes that despite the intersection of many fields of study within the matrix of Performance Studies, the 'passageways between theatre and anthropology are the ones most often cited as generative of the paradigm' (2001: 35). Since its formal inception,[23] Performance Studies scholars both in the United States and beyond have expanded the epistemic field of the subject and the associated research methodologies by frequently deploying an interdisciplinary approach and bringing together insights, frameworks, and concerns from visual arts, philosophy, political theory, linguistics, digital humanities, education, psychology, and hard sciences into the field.[24] In Central Europe, practical professional training occurs in conservatoires while the study of drama/theatre/performance remains largely theoretical with few notable exceptions combining theory and practical teaching such as the universities of Giessen and Hildesheim in Germany, and Aarhus in Denmark. More pertinently in this context, it is worth noting that the questions around research methodology in the field of Theatre and Performance are inevitably complicated further by inherent ontological, epistemological, and disciplinary instabilities and their interrelations as illustrated by Kershaw and Nicholson (2011), who arrive at the conclusion that the field of Performance Studies can be more 'productively' designated as a 'quasi-discipline' (2011: 8).[25]

In long historical terms, the advent of Theatre and Performance Studies therefore highlights the implicit hierarchy between episteme and technē – the two aspects of knowledge present in classical Greek philosophy and therefore fundamental to the Western epistemological tradition. While episteme refers to scientific, mathematical, axiomatic, theoretical knowledge or 'know why', technē refers to 'know how' or craft.[26] 'Technē' ('craft') – alongside 'phronesis' ('practical wisdom')[27] – is contrasted to the certainties of 'episteme' ('scientific knowledge') as being related to contingent aspects of knowledge. 'Technē' is linked to making ('poeisis') and is a means to an end, while 'phronesis' is linked to doing ('praxis') and ethical judgment and is an end in itself (https://plato.stanford.edu/entries/episteme-techne/). Such nuancing notwithstanding, the hierarchy implicit to Aristotle's epistemological framework has persisted over the centuries with the academic study consistently privileging episteme over technē. This inherited imbalance creates insecurity for the field of Theatre and Performance, which intrinsically values making and doing as a source of knowledge and is by no means subject to epistemic certainties. It also creates a gap of ambivalence between the academic study of drama/theatre/performance and the actual theatre-making sector in the English-speaking world: practitioners rarely take interest in the research emerging from Theatre and Performance departments, and the academics are perceived to take interest in practice only selectively or in instrumentalising ways.

A distinct methodological tradition worth noting here for its potential challenge to the Aristotelian hierarchy is Practice as Research (PaR). PaR instituted itself in Theatre and Performance studies in the United Kingdom, having started, incidentally also at Bristol University, as a Practice as Research in Performance (PARIP) initiative (2001–2006) led by Baz Kershaw. Contextually, this initiative can be seen as related to the rethinking and re-examination of research in the 1990s, which according to art and design researcher Christopher Frayling was a 'pragmatic result of decisions about government funding of higher education' (1993: 1) in the United Kingdom. Frayling redefines research in his field as (1) 'research into' (closest to the existing university research methodologies concerning contexts, histories, theories, and aesthetic issues), (2) 'research through' (concerned with action research and emphasising documentation of process), and (3) 'research for' (embodied in the artefact as the main outcome). The latter comes closest to PARIP's definition that 'certain epistemological issues can only be addressed in and through practice, rather than through traditional critical writing based research' (PARIP website http://www.bris.ac.uk/parip/faq.htm).[28] In this respect, both PaR and Frayling's 'research for' entail a certain form of epistemological conceptualisation that exceeds verbal communication. Consequently, PaR has been a methodology deployed primarily by artist-researchers.[29]

In 2018, education academic Carol Costley and public health specialist John Fulton compiled an edited collection on *Methodologies for Practice Research* aimed at students pursuing professional doctorates – for example, in Education (EdD), Business Administration (DBA), Professional Studies (DProf) – and attempting to transform their field of practice rather than the field of theoretical knowledge as envisaged by traditional PhDs. Costley and Fulton rooted their notion of Practice Research in Frayling's propositions and their volume is driven by a desire to valorise practice as a pertinent epistemological framework that multiple fields can refer to, thus expanding the focus of Practice Research beyond Arts and Humanities.[30]

Although Costley and Fulton's interest in new practice-based research methodologies could perhaps be seen as an adverse effect of the neoliberalisation of universities (Seal 2018, Maisuria and Helmes 2020, Fleming 2021) generating greater numbers of PhD graduates than can fill the available positions in the higher education sector, their efforts imply a re-conceptualisation of PhD study outside its Humboldtian remit as a qualification for a research career. Similarly, the dissolution of repertory theatres in the United Kingdom in the 1980s has resulted in an increase of the numbers of freelance theatre artists pursuing postgraduate studies to enhance their career prospects or refine their area of specialisation. Hence, the foundational Humboldtian values and the critical research methodologies originally geared towards expanding the pool of academic knowledge, may no longer cater for the individual objectives of all artists/researchers. This results in another ongoing paradigm shift concerning the very purpose of postgraduate studies now geared towards employability rather than research. This change raises the question if the epistemic heritage of the 19th century may in fact need to be re-examined? Or in the words of French sociologist of science Bruno Latour (2004): '[…] has critique run out of steam?'

In the 2004 essay, in which he also questions the very foundations of his career as a social constructionist, Latour, who has transitioned towards New Materialism, makes the point that has become particularly obvious in the aftermath of COVID-19: that the tools of social critique can be appropriated by conspiracy theorists and turned against scientific knowledge itself. His aim is not to abolish critique but to prompt rethinking of its practice with more care. Similarly, Rita Felski's idea of postcritique, in part inspired by Latour, is a call for a critical methodology that transcends the existing ones characterised by Paul Ricoeur as the 'hermeneutics of suspicion' (1965) and/or by Eve Kosofsky Sedgwick as 'paranoid reading' (1997/2003). Drawing on psychoanalysis, Sedgwick has offered the possibility of 'reparative reading' (1997/2003) as a counteractive strategy, and a similar impulse could be traced back to Susan Sontag's *Against Interpretation* (1966). The fact that these had been lone (predominantly female) voices for a long time is explained by Elizabeth Anker and Rita Felski (2017) through the political entrenchment of critique within universities as the main form of leftist resistance to neoliberal capitalism and that any attempt at questioning the protocols of critique itself automatically implied political conservatism, co-optation, or anti-intellectualism on the part of the questioner. Anker and Felski's introductory essay to their edited volume is a helpful and comprehensive charting of the functions and workings of critique (diagnosis, allegory, and self-reflexivity), as well as its limitations (its own move to a hegemonic position, Eurocentric bias, rationalism which precludes engagement with epistemological paradigms of the global South, elitism, dogmatism, and mistrust of ordinary language, and its perceived political inefficiency and impotence). As Felski (2015) had previously argued, postcritique is about finding new ways of understanding the workings of politics and the agency of texts within them. Writing from the position of literary critics, Anker and Felski call for 'new models and practices of reading that are less beholden to suspicion and scepticism, more willing to avow the creative, innovative, world-making aspects of literature and criticism' (2017: 20). This echoes Bruno Latour's call for a new critic as 'the one who assembles' rather than the one who debunks, 'the one who offers participants an arena in which to gather' and 'the one for whom, if something is constructed, then it means it is fragile, and thus in great need of care and caution' (2004: 246). The implied emphasis of both of these perspectives reads to me as a call for new forms of knowledge production.

Although Latour and Felski's ideas meet across the Atlantic, it is necessary to acknowledge that their respective thinking evolves within distinct institutional contexts. In a highly polemical account of the 'political history' of the Digital Humanities, Allington et al. (2016) locate the birthplace of this field at the School of English, University of Virginia which is, incidentally, also the academic home of Rita Felski. They characterise this institutional context as traditionally reactionary due to its association with Fredson Bowers' authority-reinforcing textual studies, E.D Hirsch's canon-defending popular hit *Cultural Literacy* (1987), and eventually with Felski's postcritique. Whether or not Felski's ideological bias follows in this vein ought to be separately established, however, this article certainly throws light on Felski and Anker's claims about the significance of ideological feuds in American universities. In no uncertain terms, Allington et al. characterise digital humanities as an opportunistic and reactionary institutional movement, whose ability to attract research funding, in combination with 'post-interpretative, non-suspicious, technocratic, conservative, managerial, lab-based practice[s]' serves to perpetuate and empower the neoliberal university:

> In the academy and outside of it, the privileging of technical expertise above other forms of knowledge is a political gesture, and one that has proved highly effective in neutralizing critique of established power relations.
> (Allington et al. 2016)

As a European reader, I am surprised by the radicalism of these claims and specifically the implication that 'technical expertise' functions primarily as an emblematic representation of capitalism and privilege – associated with the Silicon Valley status structures – and as an anti-political or at least depoliticised epistemology. Though it is important to take the ideological implications of this context into account, the article also reveals an entrenchment of unhelpful binaries in politicising and valorising different epistemologies, which in turn risks rendering critique itself as a conservative force, resistant to innovation.

The combined effects of the COVID-19 pandemic and the anti-racist protests of 2020, together with a wider move towards alternative – decolonial, posthumanist – epistemological paradigms, have certainly issued a series of challenges to the pre-existing order. Regardless of the future of (post)critique itself, the continued relevance of the digital humanities can no longer be so easily dismissed. Allington et al.'s critique of digital humanities also overlooked some of the ongoing efforts to resolve the perceived ideological problems of the field. For example, James E Dobson's book *Critical Digital Humanities* (2019), which aims to address the perceived gap between critique and digital humanities, invokes Alexander Galloway's (2014) historicisation of the field as ultimately relational in its methodological approach[31] as a result of the changing notions of knowledge. According to him, the field of digital humanities emerges from a 'moment in history when knowledge becomes production, when knowledge loses its absolute claims to immanent efficacy' (Galloway in Dobson 2019: 12). Subsequently Roopika Risam (2018) has also made a valuable contribution by scoping the field of postcolonial digital humanities. Crucially, Dobson's work locates potential for new ideas within the very limitations of the digital humanities' nascent focus on text and reading processes shaped by the written word.

However, by virtue of its disciplinary focus on the extra-textual, visual, and corporeal, the field of Theatre and Performance had already generated alternative modes of 'reading' or relating to data, which do transcend the written text. David Saltz (2004) charts a number of ways in which the field of Theatre and Performance had ever since the 1980s utilised digital technology for teaching and research purposes (including navigation of archival records of performances, digital simulation for historical reconstruction as well as the use of computerisation in live performance). More recently, Christopher Balme (2019) has shown how digitisation of archives has made it possible for entirely new historical narratives to emerge through materialisation of digital links between previously unconnected or invisible elements of data.

An interesting marker of the advances in thinking around the digital methodologies in Theatre and Performance Studies is available in the interdisciplinary article co-authored collaboratively by performance studies scholar Maaike Bleeker, screen cultures scholar Nanna Verhoeff, and digital and game studies scholar Stefan Werning 'Sensing Data' (2020), which proposes a 'creative humanities' approach to knowledge production. The process here is not so much concerned with utilising digital technologies in order to study aspects of theatre and performance research problems, but conversely, with utilising creative artefacts (which they call 'knowledge objects') derived from data sonifications, 3D materialisations, and data-driven interactives – and more generally the 'performativity of knowing' drawn from the creative arts – in order to 'presentify' and enable sensorial relation to abstract data generated through, for example, oceanography, meteorology, electroencephalogramatic (EEG), or demographic statistics. In other words, they place artistic creation and artefacts at the centre of knowledge production to facilitate sensorial perception/cognition of abstract data.

Though this is not a model that is directly deployed in the A/OD project, Bleeker et al.'s 'performative' notion of knowledge related to how the creative artefacts 'bring about rather than represent ways of knowing' (2020: 17) can be discerned as being at the core of this project's assumptions regarding the potential for knowledge production within creative performance practice. Furthermore, Bleeker et al. take inspiration from Karen Barad's radically relational posthumanist approach to knowing as agential 'entanglement' (Barad 2007) – not dissimilar from Bruno Latour's own agent-network theory (ANT) (2005) – between the knowledge objects and the knowers; an approach that ultimately also has the potential to undo some of the existing Western-centric hierarchies. Similarly, though somewhat more modestly in this context, the A/OD project places the artist's creative process – including its material and immaterial entanglements with technologies and networks of influence – at the centre of its research enquiry.

The main aim of this research is to take forward the idea implicit to practice research that artistic process represents a form of epistemology. The project's distinct contribution, however, is to show that an artist can act as a potential producer of knowledge when involved in innovatory arts practice even when they are not engaged in processes of academic research. Artistic process as an epistemology is here understood to create scope for a coalitional model of arts-based research between an academic and an artist. This collaborative act is hereafter referred to as 'knowledge-creation' to avoid the industrialist implications of the term 'knowledge production'.

This methodological proposition will find further justification in an ontological and epistemological consideration of the intersections between dramaturgy, speech, and sound.

Track 05: Intersections: Dramaturgy, Speech, and Sound

I place my work in the area of dramaturgy as a subsection of Theatre *and* Performance rather than within either one of these fields individually. This is because – as many academic efforts have already shown including Turner and Behrndt (2007), Trencsényi and Cochrane (2014), and Eckersall et al. (2017) – dramaturgy is no longer concerned with only drama or text. Its fundamental processes of conceptualisation also pertain to the works of performance in the broadest sense. Having gradually expanded its remit at the end of the 20th century beyond the written text into devised theatre, dance, street theatre, circus as well as event management and public relations (Romanska 2015), architecture (Turner 2015), ecology (Woynarski 2020), and the digital (Masura 2020), dramaturgy has also, inevitably, faced the need to reconsider its own operative and research methodologies in the process.

An interesting gap emerges in relation to the dramaturgies of speech and/or sound due to the sound's fundamentally 'invisible' presence in theatre and performance-making. Sound is rarely to be found in the contents pages or indexes of the mentioned dramaturgy books, although Turner and Behrndt do note the kinship between dramaturg and sound designer (2007: 101, 102, a theme that quietly continues in Turner 2015), and Trencsényi and Cochrane feature an interview with John Collins, founder and artistic director of Elevator Repair Service (ERS) also famous as the Wooster Group's sound designer.[32]

Eckersall et al. do offer a substantial chapter on the matter of Acoustic Dramaturgy in an attempt to 'locate the specific materiality of sound in the superfield of NMD [New Media Dramaturgy]' (2017: 154). More specifically they are concerned with the relation between sound and audience and the possible forms of listening entailed in a process beyond the idea of sound as 'an emotional trigger for the drama' in order to 'think instead about the agency of sound in switching on and off receptors in the human body' to facilitate interactive and immersive effects (2017: 136). In this process, they bring the field of dramaturgy into a productive dialogue with the only other existing works on the dramaturgy of sound at the time (Brown 2005, Ovadija 2013, Home-Cook 2015).[33] Even though in his 2019 book *A Theory of Dramaturgy*, Janek Szatkowski briefly acknowledges the sonority of spoken language in theatre (2019: 136), he largely reiterates the traditionally-held Western hegemonic view of the logocentric function of language in meaning-making in theatre. Hence, the nexus between the fields of dramaturgy, speech, and sound remains relatively under-researched, although tangentially, we can also find relevant considerations of the dramaturgies of speech and sound in the context of music theatre (Roesner 2014, Verstraete 2011), theatre aurality (Home-Cook 2015, Kendrick 2017), intermediality of theatre and performance (Balme; Chapple; Boenisch in Chapple and Kattenbelt 2006), and by extension in the context of digital theatre and performance (Chatzichristodoulou et al. 2017).

Aural/oral dramaturgies can be more specifically designated as forms of postdramatic dramaturgy.[34] Hans-Thies Lehmann (1999/2006) indeed frequently mentions 'sound spaces' and the materiality of sound, or the sound of language in his seminal book, though the closest he gets to its theorisation is under the heading of 'Musicalisation'. Catherine Bouko (2010) considers this an insufficiently developed 'mention' (2010: 75), which she takes as a cue for her notion of 'postdramatic musicality' framed by reference to text as a material 'that is no longer the core of the performance' but a source of musicalised enunciation (2010: 77–8). David Roesner too has developed the notion of 'musicality' as a 'model, method and metaphor' inherent to both making theatre and watching theatre (2014: 13), and Sven Bjerstedt has contributed further to the thinking around the 'conceptual loans' between music and theatre in defining their respective ontologies by reference to each other (2021: 4). Though the latter two works are not restricted to postdramatic musicality, the relevance of Lehmann's 'flexible paradigm' (Bouko 2010) will be impossible to avoid in this book.

In this track, I am particularly interested in how selected long historical perspectives on speech and sound – specifically in the way they eventually intersect with Lehmann's long historical view of dramatic theatre striving towards the postdramatic – reveal new significance and creative and political potential for contemporary dramaturgy/ies. The main advantage of the long historical approach – the 'longue durée' – as shown in the previous track, is that it can reveal entrenched beliefs and values, whose emergence might have been contingent on a specific time and space, but whose hegemonic position might have ensured their unquestioned perpetuation and an occlusion of alternatives. It is a historiographic method considered to have a decentring and decolonial potential (see Keita 2005, for example).

Particularly relevant to aural/oral dramaturgies will be Adriana Cavarero's (2005) intervention in the Western philosophical tradition, which advocates for an anti-platonic, anti-metaphysical, embodied, 'relational ontology of plural uniqueness' as a way of rethinking politics. Cavarero understands the act of speaking as relational and thus fundamentally political, not because of what is said but in the Arendtian sense of speaking being a form of political action, as well as an act of 'shar[ing] an interactive space of reciprocal exposure' (Cavarero 2005: 190).[35] The main target of Cavarero's intervention is '[t]he metaphysical machine, which methodologically negates the primacy of the voice' (2005: 15), because Platonic tradition privileges logocentrism, videocentrism, and thought over sound, listening, and relationality. In this respect, she also makes an important distinction between thinking and speaking which refutes Plato's belief that speaking equals 'thinking expressed outloud' or 'an acoustic substitute for thinking' (2005: 174).

I will return to Cavarero and the topic of speech below, via the more encompassing topics of sound and listening.

The primary concern of theatre scholars interested in sound has been to understand its ontology, cultural history, and theoretical acumen in relation to contemporary cultural production. Alongside this, and similarly to Home-Cook's phenomenological enquiry into aural attention in theatre, a number of works in the field have begun to engage with the theme of listening, including, for example, Rajni Shah's 2021 monograph *Experiments in Listening*, Helena Grehan's ethical idea of 'slow listening' (2019), and Deirdre Heddon's ecological idea of 'entangled listening' (2017) inspired by Jean-Luc Nancy. In addition to the notable work of Salomé Voegelin on listening as a socio-political practice (2010, 2014, 2018), there is also the fascinating *Hungry Listening* (2020) by Dylan Robinson engaging with listening from both Indigenous and settler perspectives in a bid to contribute a decolonial, performative, and relational perspective to the predominantly white field of Sound Studies.

A source that helps elucidate the inherent cultural and theoretical 'invisibility' of sound throughout history is the 2019 edited collection *Sound Objects*, by literary scholars James Steintrager and Rey Chow. In their introduction, the authors trace the absence and presence of sound in philosophical thinking. Much like I do in my long view of research methodologies (Track 04), they start with the aim to re-articulate the familiar. The essay opens with a perceived rift between the mid-20th-century mainstream philosophical approaches of phenomenology/existentialism on the one hand and critical theory on the other. In among other factors, they trace the noted marginalisation of sound from philosophical discourse back to Immanuel Kant's hierarchy of arts which places poetry at the top, painting in the middle, and music at the bottom. Another significant factor is the idea that sound is conceptually and categorically distinct from the notions of theory, contemplation, and visuality – and one might add 'theatre' (θέατρον – play, spectacle).

Steintrager and Chow:

> Calling for a theory (or, more pluralistically, theories) of the sonic ought to acknowledge the terminological misfit, at least in etymological terms: sound objects are not contemplated at all they are apprehended in ways other than the visual – the very framework and rhetorical resonances of 'theory' are potentially misleading and inadequate – and that theory itself must also proceed otherwise, with sound.
>
> (2019: 6)[36]

In signalling the need for a different methodology, they use their edited volume as an opportunity to forge an interdisciplinary and intermedial encounter between thinkers across the disciplines of 'sound studies' and 'auditory cultures'. They aim to 'probe' a perceived 'reluctance to think sound theoretically' (2019: 14) while also embracing the limitations, paradoxes, and contradictions of 'applying a term anchored in contemplation to audition' (2019: 15). Even though critically conscious of the often re-iterated origin myths around Sound Studies as a discipline, this, like many other texts dealing with histories of the field, includes a genealogy comprising Pierre Schaeffer (1910–95),[37] R Murray Shafer (1933–), Jacques Attali (1943–), Michel Serres (1930–2019), Don Ihde (1934–), Michel Chion (1947–), Friedrich Kittler (1943–2011), and, notably, historian Jonathan Sterne (1970–) whose book *The Audible Past* (2003) is seen as a foundational text for the field.

Many of these names are also featured in Susan Bennett's book *Theory for Theatre Studies: Sound* which she characterises as a 'sonic history' bound together with both technological and an evolution of 'knowledge about how sounds are made and heard' (2019: 10). This interest in sound is also conceptually linked to Bennett's long-standing academic interest in theatre audience (conscious of a shared etymological root): 'Audiences by virtue of their presence, are contracted to listen and, inevitably, become producers of sound themselves' (2019: 5). Bennett is certainly not the only scholar to take a historical approach to the topic. However, while Ovadija and Curtin, respectively, focused on tracing the significance of sound in contemporary theatre back to the historical avant-garde specifically, Bennett's long view spans millennia. It is divided in three sections, including classical sound (the architectures of ancient Greek, Roman, and early modern Elizabethan theatres), the avant-garde sound (the early participatory experiments of the futurists, the highly influential inventions of the telephone, the radio, and the tape recorder), and the experiential sound linked to the inventions of the late 20th-century mobile technologies. This last mode is also profoundly linked to the 'co-compositional role' of the audience (Neumark in Bennett 2019: 104) or the 'listening participation' required to create meaning (2019: 113). Bennett's volume concludes, therefore, in a thematic confluence with a topic she had previously established as her area of expertise – theatre audiences (see Bennett 1990) – establishing and reinforcing the need to understand sound 'multimodally and interactively' rather than as a 'discrete category' (2019: 112). It is via the topic of listening that Bennett arrives at an acknowledgment of a Western-centric approach to the currently existing theories and understanding of sound, and in her Coda about 'sound across the world' invites an expansion of sonic epistemologies by echoing the call of ethnomusicologists/anthropologists David Samuels and colleagues (2010) for a 'sounded anthropology' which re-examines methodologies and the politicity of recording with an emphasis on the inclusion of diverse cultural voices, rather than treating the field recording as only a source of data.

The cited Samuels et al. article 'Soundscapes: Toward a Sounded Anthropology' is a useful attempt at a re-examination of disciplinary history and advocates a move away from an 'anthropology about sound' to 'anthropology in sound' which, not dissimilarly to Practice Research methodologies, foregrounds non-literary – 'sounded' and possibly non-Western – 'ways of knowing' (2010: 339). In other words, acknowledging the 'entwinement' of anthropology's own history with the histories of technology, aesthetics, and mediation, the authors urge their disciplinary community to attend to the issues of sound, recording, listening and the culturally contingent 'politics of aurality' (ibid.). This evokes anthropologist Steven Feld's concept of 'acoustemology' which he had introduced in the 1990s as a means of investigating 'sounding and listening as knowing-in-action: a knowing with and knowing-through the audible' (Feld in Novak and Sakakeeny 2015: 12). Crucially, Feld defines acoustemology as 'aligned with relational ontology' (2015: 12–3), and underlines its paradigmatic compatibility with the thinking of New Materialist philosophers such as Donna Haraway and Bruno Latour, posthumanists and decolonial theorists. In his 2015 definition, Feld also offers a political explanation as to why the coining of the term was necessary over choosing some of the more common phrases in existence (including the 'anthropology of sound' and R. Murray Schafer's 'acoustic ecology' or 'soundscape'), and, more importantly, he traces the emergence of the theoretical concept back to his anthropological practice and ethnographic work. The notion of acoustemology as a way of knowing through sound emerged specifically out of a deep 25-year-long immersion into the culture, worldview, and conception of listening of the Bosavi people in Papua New Guinea; however, its abstraction and application to other contexts are not only possible but deemed imperative.[38] In his 2020a volume *Sound Effect: The Theatre We Hear*, Ross Brown deployed the apparatus of acoustemology in conducting his own long-view study of a '250-year Western cultural history of hearing', whereby Feld's rainforest as a site of acoustemological research is replaced by the Western theatre auditorium (exemplified initially by Shakespeare's Globe). In an interesting development of Feld's concept, Brown proposes his own idea of the 'audimus' – a socially produced space, which

> takes the first person-plural of [Latin] audire, to hear, to describe the collective auditory habitus (set of learned auditory techniques, dispositions and habits) of the *we* which theatre convenes
> (2020b: 20, manuscript version, original emphasis)

Brown's audimus makes it conceivable for communities to have shared understanding or interpretations of sonic references, experiences, and more broadly, acoustemologies, in the context of 21st-century theatre-going. Thus understood, ultimately, according to Brown, there is no such thing as sound per se, only the 'sound effect'.

It is appropriate to align this with the work of Julian Henriques (2011) who situates his research enquiry into 'thinking through sound' outside of the Western genealogies by contextualising it within the Jamaican reggae sound systems culture. Interestingly, even though he also perceives the 'thinking through sound' as 'distinct and different' to thinking through images, or even music, he claims it is also distinct from 'thinking about' anything. Instead, 'thinking through sound is a *way* of thinking, a process of knowledge, and a gnosis' (2011: xvii, original emphasis), compared in a footnote to 'thinking through craft', an idea by American art historian Glenn Adamson which seeks to re-uphold technē as a viable epistemology. Henriques further delineates his object of research as not an object at all, but a 'process or event, not a coded representation but medium, not a thought but a feeling', and thus his book *Sonic Bodies* 'mounts an auditory investigation, rather than only an investigation of audition' (ibid) in relation to the sound systems culture. In this process, he deploys Charles Sanders' Pierce's method of 'abduction'[39] which leads Henriques to a rhetorically powerful and enticing theoretical consideration of 'sounding' as a dynamic model for 'raising questions about the world – as distinct from the way the trope of the visual image is often used to settle them' (2011: xviii).

By being rooted in the Caribbean cultural tradition, Henriques's idea of thinking through sounding also entails the 'orientation towards the spoken word' (2011: 8), as exemplified by the rhetorical figure of the MC in sound systems culture. This is a suitable cue for a relevant examination of speech and orality.

In his 1962 volume *The Gutenberg Galaxy*, controversial Canadian philosopher and progenitor of the field of Media Studies, Marshall McLuhan (1911–80) famously departed from the premise that our evolution as a species is characterised by a process of substitution of many of our natural faculties with artificially created tools – running with vehicles, bodily strength with weapons, etc. In this vein, McLuhan argues that language is also a human invention intended to store experience (1962: 5). Exploring the effect of the printing press on our cognitive and political evolution – at the risk of techno-determinism[40] – *The Gutenberg Galaxy* introduces the idea that the development of literacy has encouraged a visual mode of perception and augmented processes of individuation, isolation, and abstraction, leaving behind the more holistic modes of perception characteristic of the oral cultures.

The opening lines of *The Gutenberg Galaxy* make an explicit reference to the empirical work of the Harvard classicists Milman Parry (1902–35) and Albert Lord (1912–91) which had taken place in the then Yugoslavia between the 1930s and 1960s, advising that McLuhan's book should be read as a companion piece to Lord's *The Singer of Tales* (1960). By studying a living folkloric tradition of epic verse performance in Serbo-Croatian, Parry and Lord developed a theory of 'oral-formulaic composition' with which they revolutionised the field of Homeric studies. According to the oral-formulaic theory, the key element of epic verse composition is a system of specific 'metric, melodic, syntactic and acoustic patterns' (Lord 2000: 33) which the singers/composers deploy in extemporaneous performance. In other words, each singer will render a well-known narrative differently depending on their own use of specific patterns which they have internalised during long years of apprenticeship and practice. By focusing on the exigencies of performance as the primary factor in composition, Parry and Lord inverted the paradigmatic Gutenbergian assumption of textual primacy thus altering the existing ideas about the authorship of Homeric verse. Crucially for scholars of Theatre and Performance, this work drew attention to the fact that the way in which a narrative is rendered can be determined by a performer rather than a pre-existing textual author.

Though the influence of McLuhan, Parry, and Lord had ceased for a number of decades, Danish scholar Thomas Pettitt has more recently applied this methodology of 'oral formulaic composition' to his study of Early Modern English drama. Arguing that the pre-Early Modern 'cultural system' was more fluid in its conception of cultural production as opposed to the regimented 'cultural system' of the Gutenberg age, Pettitt is more specifically interested in the ways in which particular theatrical tropes (such as a woman crying over a corpse, or an interrupted procession, or particular clowning motifs) recur within a broad body of dramatic works from the period. Thus he uses the oral-formulaic theory in order to illuminate our understanding of the nature of authorship in Elizabethan England '[lying] athwart the opening of the Gutenberg parenthesis' (2010: 10).[41]

In the digital age, this line of thought is interminably attractive, but not without its problems. In a groundbreaking 2011 essay, Jonathan Sterne critiques the work of Walter Ong (1912–2003), McLuhan's colleague at the Toronto School of Communication Theory, who in 1982, famously published the book *Orality and Literacy*. A long-view investigation of language as a tool for storing experience, Ong's book used the term 'secondary orality' to encapsulate the non-print, broadcast media (TV and radio) mode of communication and cognition, considered, however, distinct from the pre-literate, 'primary orality'. Even though Ong proposed his notion of 'secondary orality' well before the advent of the internet, he credited the 'electronic age' for actually drawing our attention to the categorical distinction between orality and literacy.[42] By orality, he was interested in the human condition that existed not only pre-Gutenberg, but pre-literacy and, interestingly, he considered writing to be a 'pre-emptive and imperialist activity that tends to assimilate other things to itself' (2002: 11).

Jonathan Sterne's fascinating and methodologically instructive piece of historiography uncovers the provenance of Ong's ideas in a Christian spiritualist tradition, informed by his initial training as a theologian.[43] Sterne traces the book's precepts – the sound-sight, spirit-word, Hebreic-Greek binaries that underpin his thinking – to Ong's earlier studies of the sacred texts' translations. Specifically, Sterne speculates that 'in the tradition of Christian spiritualism, Ong sought a way to commune with the spirit of God' (2011: 214) and that the development of an electronic oral-aural consciousness ('secondary orality') gave him hope in the possibility of hearing the word of God upon his second coming (2011: 219). But how appropriate, asks Sterne, is this model for secular cultural theory today?

Re-reading Ong's and McLuhan's ideas with references to the contingencies of their own ideological contexts, Sterne uncovers further inherent problems, for example, the hegemonic assumption of white Western historical progression over non-Western cultures' location in the historical past as a cultural default, and the implicit denial of coeval existence of different cultures.[44] Sterne is careful to note that his intention is not to target individuals for racial ignorance, but to 'trouble the paradigm' (2011: 220), thus placing the responsibility for dominant views more appropriately on the paradigmatic consensus-formation. Ultimately Sterne's aim is to argue for a 'reconstruction of deep communication history' (2011: 209) and to celebrate the intellectual curiosity of the Toronto School of Communication. His rousing finale opens up valuable new avenues:

> What if the invention of writing and its stabilization in print were not the single most important turning points in communication history, but only one of many technological turning points? What if scholars—whose lives' work is dedicated to the written word—have overestimated its world-historical importance? We want to believe Plato that everything changed with writing. We are inclined to imagine writing as the moment that consciousness first allowed itself to be externalized in physical form. But what would happen if we instead submitted the history of communication technology to the rigours of the broader history of technology?
>
> (2011: 221)

Recalibration of historical material can go in both directions. Unlike Ong whose reassessment by Sterne introduces the need for post hoc reservation, aspects of Marshall McLuhan's work, initially dismissed by his contemporaries, have more recently been judiciously rehabilitated by critics. In a 2015 re-review of McLuhan's now classic 1964 title *The Medium is the Message*, Barry Sandywell retrospectively bestows on McLuhan seminal importance in anticipating the work of Jean Baudrillard, Jacques Derrida, Gilles Deleuze, Bernard Stiegler, Mark Hansen, Jean-François Lyotard, and N. Katherine Hayles – 'a current of thought' advancing the idea of originary technicity (2015: 1411).[45]

This brings me to the work of Jacques Derrida which should have a crucial place in a literature review about speech and language for its challenge to the tradition of logocentrism in Western philosophy. Derrida perceives the Western tradition as holding writing as exterior and therefore subordinate to speech (a notion more specifically termed 'phonocentrism'), which he aimed to emancipate from this subordination, most famously in his seminal 1967 text *Of Grammatology*. Fundamentally opposed, therefore, to McLuhan and Ong's notions of orality as a kind of civilisational promise, Derrida's efforts are intensely devoted to defence of writing as more imperative. Even though Derrida and McLuhan's work is occasionally considered side by side, and Derrida is sometimes claimed to have been influenced by the work of McLuhan (as in Sandywell above), there are very few occasional references to his work in Derrida's writing. In a summary to his address at the Montreal conference on Communication in 1971, Derrida stated their ideological differences:

> We are witnessing not an end of writing that would restore, in accord with McLuhan's ideological representation, a transparency or an immediacy to social relations; but rather the increasingly powerful historical expansion of a general writing, of which the system of speech, consciousness, meaning, presence, truth, etc., would be only an effect, and should be analyzed as such. It is the exposure of this effect that I have called elsewhere logocentrism.
> (Derrida 1972/1988: 20)

It is possible, as Samuel et al. claim, that the hugely influential publication of Gayatri Spivak's translation of Derrida's *Of Grammatology* in English in 1976 – 'which heralded a disciplinary turn away from voice and sound […] toward a focus on textuality and inscription' (Samuel et al. 2010: 331) – has also had the effect of temporarily eclipsing some of the key synchronous ideas regarding sound or even more broadly the interest in speech and orality. Nevertheless, this has started to change in recent years with new significant works on the subject such as, most notably, Cavarero's 2005 feminist reappraisal of the Western logocentric tradition (containing a critique of Derrida) *For More Than One Voice*, Mladen Dolar's 2006 *A Voice and Nothing More*, rooted in a Lacanian tradition but also dealing with Derridian 'phonocentrism', or Brandon LaBelle's 2014 multifaceted critical exploration *Lexicon of the Mouth*.

Another important concept drawn from Derrida is the above-mentioned idea of 'technicity' (Sandywell 2015, Bradley 2011). In its designation as 'originary technicity', the term refers to the mechanism of life itself but in its more specific sense 'technicity' is explored initially by Derrida as a means of exteriorisation of memory through writing in 'Plato's Pharmacy', an essay published in 1969 and aimed at challenging the elevation of the metaphysical over the technical in the Western philosophical tradition. Though Bradley sees Derrida's deconstruction as 'nothing other than the deconstruction of the historic opposition *between* thought and technics' (2011: 18, original emphasis), the more explicit and substantial engagement with technicity is available in the work of Derrida's disciple Bernard Stiegler in his series *Technics and Time 1–3* (1994–2001), and then further on in the ever-unfolding spectrum of posthumanist theory.

Recognising how Western philosophy has since its inception by the ancient Greeks repressed technicity as an object of enquiry (by separating technē from episteme as noted in Track 04), Bernard Stiegler seeks to redress this balance, especially in the wake of the industrial age and by reference to how technicity is also constitutive of the human notion of temporality and of our own sense of being human. Stiegler places technical objects – the 'inorganic organized beings' as a 'third genre of being' in 'between the inorganic beings of the physical sciences and the organized beings of biology' (1998: 17), and thus problematises the relationship between the subject and object vis-à-vis the humans and technology.

It is not surprising that such revalorisation of technicity, prosthesis, and technē itself has appeal for the field of Theatre and Performance.[46] In 2020, Shakespearean scholar W.B. Worthen deployed Stiegler's technicity as a means of understanding the apparatus of theatre as a technology in itself or as a prosthetic for the humans' exteriorisation of memory. It is important to state that understanding theatre by reference to its technicity or its status as a technology is not a matter of considering ways in which it deploys technologies, but the way in which it is itself a tool in the anthropological endeavour of understanding ourselves as a species. This generates a number of epistemological advantages not just for a historian seeking to redress or adjust the imbalance between (Shakespearean) text and performance, but also in the process of understanding formal innovations in 21st century, as is expanded upon in the A/OD project.

In the context of researching the emergent dramaturgies of speech and sound, the dominant theoretical frameworks and critical-hermeneutic research methodologies do not suffice. However, rather than proposing radical alternatives, the A/OD project situates itself within an intersection of long-historical perspectives on theatre, speech, sound, and knowledge creation. Three important strands will be taken forward from the contextualising literature review of Side A: (1) the idea of relationality – fundamental to Bleeker et al.'s epistemological framework, Cavarero's conception of vocal ontology, and other decolonial and posthumanist epistemologies – which in turn supports agential entanglement of the artist in the production of knowledge,[47] (2) the epistemological dignification of technicity of theatre as an object of research via Stiegler and Worthen, and (3) decolonising potential of 'thinking through sound' (Henriques), also exemplified by Feld, Cavarero and others, when considering the prevailing significance of aurality/orality in the digital age.

To this end, I symbolically end this section with a quote from Ngũgĩ wa Thiong'o concerning orature in African tradition, a form of oral literature not dissimilar from the tradition studied by Parry and Lord in the Balkans, which Ngũgĩ envisages in its future manifestation as 'cyber-orature born out of cyber-ture (cybernurture)':

> Performance is the central feature of orature, and this differentiates the concept of orature from that of literature. Performance involves performer and audience, in orature this often being a participatory audience; and performance space, in orature this being anything from the fireside, the village square or market place, to a shrine. But whatever the combination of location, time and audience, orature realizes its fullness in performance. [...] In the electronic space, or the virtual space, orality in general and orature in particular are coming back.
>
> (Ngũgĩ 2007: 7)

SIDE B: METHODOLOGY

Track 06: Methodology: A Genealogical Retro-Articulation
Track 07: Embracing Contradictions
Track 08: Relational Ethnography
Track 09: Towards a Dramaturgical Research Methodology: A Close View
Track 10: How to Read this Book

Track 06: Methodology: A Genealogical Retro-Articulation

(I dedicate this number to PhD students out there.)

Being bespoke to each particular project, one's research methodology in Arts and Humanities is notoriously difficult to articulate and frequently becomes evident only in retrospect. This is partly a matter of pragmatic priorities whereby the intrinsic tools of discussion and argument are necessarily occluded in the process of advancing the argument. Secondly, research methodology's inherent technicity has historically rendered it of lesser epistemological importance. Either way, in academic writing, researchers deploy assumptions, beliefs, and knowledges they have internalised as part of academic training and acculturation to the extent they are no longer easily discernible.

A notable instance of retroarticulation of methodology exists in the work of Michel Foucault who wrote *The Archaeology of Knowledge* in 1969 with the aim of examining the historiographic methodology he had deployed in his previous works *Madness and Civilization* (1961), *The Birth of the Clinic* (1963), and *The Order of Things* (1966). His stated aims were to 'uncover the principles' within the field of historical knowledge (1972: 15), to eschew 'the categories of cultural totalities' (1972: 16), and to define 'a method of historical analysis'. Acutely contextual to Foucault's stated aims is his explicit desire to challenge and depart from the hold of the structuralist analysis predominating at the time of his writing (i.e. the categories of 'cultural totalities'). Instead, Foucault's genealogical approach, being developed here for the first time, is concerned with tracing the history of the present in a manner that problematises and/or reverses the traditional linear, cause and effect, chronological approach. In the appendix 'The Discourse on Language', Foucault elaborates on 'genealogy' as an analytical method to be used in conjunction with the 'critical method' for uncovering constraints (limitations, exclusions, appropriations) and 'instances of control' in the history of discourse (or more fundamentally 'speech'). While criticism deploys discursive processes, genealogy is concerned with 'their formation, at once scattered, discontinuous and regular' (1972: 233). Foucault also introduced his notion of the 'author-function' in this piece, his definition of authorship that is no longer concerned with the author as an individual but 'the author as the unifying principle in a particular group of writings or statements' (1972: 221). It could be claimed that since 1969, the Foucauldian genealogical method – like the author-function – gradually became so prevalent that it has been customarily internalised as a viable method by multiple generations of scholars.[48] This includes, perhaps, Sterne who implicitly deploys it in his reading of Ong (Track 05), but also by myself when I resort to genealogical analyses in *Theatre-Making* (2013a). This is not to say that Foucault's precepts and legacy should continue to be perpetuated blindly, especially given the changing political, ideological, methodological, and ethical contingencies of our time some 50 years hence.[49] However, the notion of the necessarily retroactive articulation of research methodology is directly related to the task at hand here.

As noted in Side A, the A/OD project is methodologically as well as in terms of its subject matter embroiled in a continuity with my previous research, but more importantly, it necessitates a methodological approach that conceptually suits the dramaturgies of speech and sound as its object of study. Echoing Foucault, this is a good opportunity to 'uncover the principles' and attempt to 'define the [underlying] methods' as a means of articulating a genealogy of the methodological approach pertaining to the A/OD project.

Comprising of a specific combination of research methods (analysis, interview, archival, or practice-based) and individually internalised ideological/discursive/rhetorical strategies on the part of a researcher, research methodology in the Arts and Humanities is necessarily idiomatic and project-specific. It goes without saying that the articulation of methodological approach I undertake here is not intended to be prescriptive. I am also not proposing any radically new ideas. In retroactively eliciting and articulating the research methodology that underlies *Theatre-Making* (2013a), I focus on the specificities of my methodological approach, shaped by my own networks of influence and processes of acculturation as a researcher.

1. The first aspect of my research idiom could be characterised as quasi-ethnographic in nature, as it does not come from ethnographic training but is linked to my positionality as a bicultural and bilingual partial outsider,[50] a position of liminality which entails a continuous code-switching between the insider/outsider and the privileged/marginalised perspective in questioning the historicities of underlying assumptions or the uses of specific vocabularies. For example, in *Theatre-Making*, this led to an investigation of the emergence of the term 'devising' within the United Kingdom and its relationship of both similarity and distinction to its central European closest semantic equivalent 'improvisation'. Therefore, a continued emphasis is placed on a full contextual understanding of the terms by reference to their cultural and historical contingencies – with a necessary provision for a Foucauldian genealogical understanding of historiography – rather than a linear carrying over of meanings across time and across cultures. Analogously, in the context of my dramaturgical/academic investigation of the relationship between text and performance, an argument is made in favour of translation as necessarily an act of transformation, reconfiguration, and semantic relationality rather than equivalence (2013a: 28–34).

2. The second inter-related aspect of the research methodology intrinsic to my previous work is a conviction that an artist's potential for knowledge creation is equal to that of a scholar, but that the two types of epistemology are expressed in different 'languages'.[51] This does not presuppose a categorical binary between the artist and the academic, especially given the possibility of a liminal positionality of an artist/academic noted earlier, but mainly different priorities in the respective domains of artistic practice and academic knowledge creation. The research therefore seeks to collaboratively engage with the artist's innovatory epistemological processes and potentially generate their rendering in an academic context, rather than merely critique the work or exploit the celebrity potential of the artist as a vehicle for the promotion of academic work. The artist's testimony is obtained as part of this work, ideally without a pre-existing thesis or critical agenda – and, conversely, without uncritical adulation – but with a clear knowledge-seeking remit, deep listening, and readiness for methodological improvisation. Additionally, the artist and their testimony, although perceived in relation to their specific genealogies, are not treated in isolation. These insights are subsequently related to and corroborated by testimonies of other artists who share similar ways of working, spheres of influence, or aesthetic and methodological considerations. The individual artists/companies can be perceived as constituting/belonging to incidental networks of influence with discernible ethical and methodological similarities even if they work in distinct and unrelated cultural contexts unaware of each other's work (for example, the work of Tim Crouch is analysed in parallel with the works of Croatian Shadow Casters and Belgian Ontroerend Goed in Chapter 5 of *Theatre-Making*, even though they do not operate within a shared cultural community or context). Individual artists can be perceived as forming incidental communities of practice for the purposes of the research even if – and maybe even more productively so, when – they are not actually aware of each other's work.

3. Thirdly, the focus is often on an artist/company with whom I as a theatregoer, critic, or researcher can be sure to have a continuity of familiarity that spans at least two or three productions. The significance of this is illustrated by the example of how the reading of Kneehigh's *Cymbeline* at the RSC varies depending on the critic or audience member's route towards this work (Chapter 2 of *Theatre-Making*), but it is most effectively illustrated in Chapter 5 of *Theatre-Making* on the example of Tim Crouch's *The Author* (2009) the full understanding of which entirely depends on a wider understanding of the artist's oeuvre and of their methodology developed across a number of works influencing each other sequentially.[52] I refer to this composite notion – entailing the author function, the works' agential entanglements, the trajectories, and articulations of a distinct artistic methodology – as the artist's 'performance idiom'. I further define my methodological approach as distinct from the critical methodologies which extract individual works out

of the context of the artist's 'performance idiom' to place them at the service of a theoretical hypothesis.
4. Finally, it is important to consider how the data collected in this way is processed – in this case, in the form of written analysis and argument. Both *Theatre-Making* and the current research project begin with a diagnosis of an emerging trend (e.g. 'theatre-making', 'gig theatre') often proposed via the culturally embedded perspective of arts journalists. The project is then to understand this observed trend or critical mass paradigmatically, by reference to its cultural, economic, political, methodological context(s), and potential genealogies of its emergence. Although *Theatre-Making* uses the term 'paradigm (shift)' as adopted from Thomas Kuhn, one can also usefully apply Hans-Thies Lehmann's redefinition of it to indicate 'the shared negative boundary demarcating the internally highly diverse variants' of the same trend 'widely recognised – albeit not always welcomed – as an authentic testimony of the times' (1999/2006: 24). In this respect, my research methodology frequently resorts to the critical and discursive work contained within the (digital and non-digital) public sphere as an important point of reference. Case studies drawn from the empirical research are then used to corroborate and augment the findings further, bringing the artists' work and performance idioms into a network of relations – with each other, with their contexts, means of emergence, modes of documented reception, and existing hermeneutic readings of their work – before eliciting new insights, alternative possibilities, and cumulative arguments.

In talking about the artist's 'performance idiom' and my methodological/rhetorical 'research idiom', it might be necessary to devote a few words to the choice of terminology. The term 'idiom' implies a linguistic or philological bias; however, it is also a term that most accurately encapsulates various levels of my intellectual interest in inarticulable aspects of methodology (both pertaining to performance-making and research). According to the Cambridge Dictionary, the term 'idiom' has two specific levels of meaning: (1) 'a group of words in a fixed order that have a particular meaning that is different from the meanings of each word on its own', and (2) 'the style of expression in writing, speech, or music that is typical of a particular period, person, or group' (https://dictionary.cambridge.org/dictionary/english/idiom). The first aspect of meaning (also known as the non-compositionality principle) mirrors the notion I frequently encountered in my ensemble research that ensemble work was perceived as being 'greater than the sum of its parts' (Radosavljević 2013b). It also usefully conveys the problem of untranslatability of an idiom by means of 'word-for-word translation', or direct semantic equivalence, and the requirement for a deeper contextual and integrative (figurative or metaphorical) engagement with the object of semantic contemplation. The second level of meaning also usefully conveys the notion of form (not excluding content) or style of a particular working methodology. In the artistic context, this notion of style pertains to the formal characteristics of a particular artist's body of work that help distinguish it from the others, while in research methodology, this aspect is also commonly known as rhetoric (or a style of persuasion).

Track 07: Embracing Contradictions

Worth declaring in this context of methodological articulation is my more fundamental commitment to the dialectical method in reasoning.[53] A relevant example to delve into here would be the notion of (de)professionalisation which is at the core of *Theatre-Making* (2013a) but which I have not yet explicitly problematised before. The emergence of the multi-skilled theatre professional – the theatre-maker[54]– still pertains to the A/OD project, particularly in relation to Gig Theatre's hybridisation of professionalities and deprofessionalised working practices (Chapter 4).

Based on an empirical investigation, *Theatre-Making* perceives the late 20th-century emergence of the new profile from British universities, as well as its integration in the cultural sector and in the public critical discourse, as an inherently constructive process of 'deprofessionalisation'.[55] Deprofessionalisation is understood here not as a valorisation of dilettantism but as a re-examination of the demarcated divisions of labour established in the 19th-century repertory theatres in Europe and coinciding with the professionalisation needs of the industrial revolution. Although Simon Shepherd has noted a case of 'British exceptionalism' whereby the ideas of S.W. Taylor about the principles of scientific management had a slower uptake in the United Kingdom compared to Germany (Shepherd 2012: 87), British theatre industry does operate this prevailing division of labour: writer/director/actor/designer etc. However, by de-emphasising production values in favour of process and experimentation, British practice-based, predominantly left-leaning university degrees can be seen to have organically generated new ways of creative collaborative working and enabled graduates to bypass the professionalised gatekeeping processes within the theatre industry. The arts funding system in the United Kingdom and the programming politics of the theatre sector, fortunately, do not discriminate against self-declared theatre-makers on the grounds of vocational credentials.

A starkly different taxonomic and philosophical perspective around the processes of professionalisation and deprofessionalisation is available in the field of sociology. This trend, also referred to as 'new professionalism' in the United States, problematises an increased bureaucracy, managerialism, and reduced autonomy for the professionals as well as the insidious workings of the market logic to the detriment of professions (Bourdieu 2002: 183–4). While this process is rightly seen as deleterious by sociologist Eric Hoyle (2008), his end-of-career article on the subject of deprofessionalisation in education symptomatically arrives at a necessarily ambiguous stand on the phenomenon that acknowledges simultaneous needs for both autonomy and control. Hoyle highlights the notion of a 'dilemma' as foundational to his research methodology – a stance also amounting to a dialectic.

Deprofessionalisation can be understood as a disempowering neoliberal trend for those previously affiliated to professions with a historic hegemonic advantage (see Demially and de la Broise's fascinating empirical study of postal workers, academics, and psychiatrists in France in 2009). At the same time, as shown by empirical evidence of my previous research, it can be perceived as an emancipatory opportunity to enter the workplace for those with innovatory ideas, relevant knowledge, and political consciousness but without vocational training or preordained pathways towards formal professional affiliations. In the context of knowledge creation, we should be able to cognitively accommodate and examine both implications without one automatically excluding or diminishing the significance of the other. Relationality is necessarily dialectical.

Importantly, the implications of deprofessionalisation are different for members of different cultural contexts which is additionally why a relational understanding of the phenomenon is necessary. When it comes to theatre, deprofessionalisation will not have the same positive appeal in funding systems which favour institutions over freelance artists (such as much of central Europe). De-institutionalisation of the theatre artists in the English-speaking world can certainly be linked to the free-market economy model prompted by Thatcherism and Reaganism in the 1980s United Kingdom and United States, respectively, and thus also to the advent of neoliberal capitalism. However, this rather obvious association between deprofessionalisation and neoliberal capitalism is easy to make, and I worry that in making such critical associations by default, we perhaps miss the opportunity to examine full implications of the perceived phenomenon.

The critical gesture that would rightly and irrefutably perceive deprofessionalisation as a manifestation of neoliberal capitalism, can at the same time occlude and foreclose the possibilities to perceive this development more 'reparatively' (Sedgwick 2003, Kondo 2018) as a potential act of emancipation, or with a view to formal innovation, and other positive changes to the theatre ecologies that freedom from the old hegemonies makes possible. These critical perspectives are, in my view, further compounded by the customary exclusion of the artist's own agency from the critical discourse.

One reason why it is difficult to perceive alternatives is because Western academia is beholden to critique as the most reliable, the most rigorous, and essentially the most powerful (and empowering for the critic) research method in the arts and humanities, and by extension, also in the relatively young field of Theatre and Performance studies. Debunking hidden workings of neoliberal capitalism, unmasking the mechanisms of ideology, conducting 'hermeneutics of suspicion' (Ricoeur 1965) have ever since the Frankfurt School served as failsafe tools for reflecting on cultural production. In addition, the poststructuralist denunciation of authorial intent as a relevant parameter of analysis – although freeing and deeply necessary in 1968, as persuasively argued by Barthes and Foucault – has since then rendered the author/artist quite insignificant in the eyes of the academic enquiry.[56] Besides, aesthetic concerns with form rather than content are frequently devalorised as apolitical, uncritical, or culturally conservative.

It is indeed also paramount to resist a-critical, anti-critical, a-political, or anti-political approaches to Theatre and Performance studies. The field must not ignore or minimise the insidious workings of neoliberal capitalism. Thus, in the spirit of dialectic enquiry, it is necessary to reach towards a synthesis beyond the critical/post-critical binary. This is a call for a diversification and augmentation of the methodological range implied by Foucault as consisting of the 'analytical' and the 'critical' methods. The A/OD project shows that the academic field of Theatre and Performance, in collaboration with the critical and political acumen of diverse creative artists themselves, harbours additional epistemological, creative, and political means of dealing with the multi-faceted challenges of our time.

In this specific context, and by further extension of the principle of embracing contradictions, it is also necessary to acknowledge the critically problematised notions of 'immersivity', 'relationality', and 'collaboration' prompted by the emergence of works that alter the terms of audience engagement. Such works are often noted to deploy the more prominent immersive role of sound (Home-Cook 2015, Kendrick 2017) and some of them can also be explored by reference to the relational capacity of orality and voice to engender communities (Cavarero 2005), and will therefore form the object of research in this book.

Probably one of the most authoritative early texts on immersive theatre[57] has been Adam Alston's article 'Audience Participation and Neoliberal Value' in which he persuasively argues that the privileging of hedonistic and narcissistic desire rendered immersive theatre 'susceptible to co-optation by profit-making enterprises' (2013: 13). Alston problematises the question of the politics of participation in immersive theatre and usefully introduces the notion of 'entrepreneurial participation' to qualify its form of spectatorship.[58]

My coterminous investigation of theatre authorship (2013) settles on a corpus of work involving the audience as co-author, which, influenced by Bourriaud, I called 'relational new works'.[59] I specifically excluded the 'immersive theatre' of Punchdrunk on the grounds that this company's relationship with the audience was constrained by a gaming-inspired dynamic I qualified as a 'dramaturgy of anxiety' (2013: 151).[60] I was primarily interested in the fact that these new works, which featured significant formal similarities and communitarian strategies, emerged concurrently in disparate cultural contexts indicating a paradigmatic departure of European theatre from the 19th-century theatre conventions (e.g. the 'fourth wall') and divisions of theatrical labour.[61]

Like Alston, Bojana Kunst (2015), was sceptical about the emancipatory efficacy of the works perceived by Bourriaud as relational or that they led to anything but an exploitation of the audience (2015: 65). Within a Marxist critical paradigm, Kunst's position is strongly critical of the resulting 'fetishisation' of collaboration, whose compulsive repetitive invocation indicates to her a lack of criticality, an 'anxiety of subjugation', and an 'inability to inflict change' (2015: 82).

It is interesting that these terms privileging the experiential, bottom-up dimension – 'deprofessionalisation', 'immersion', and 'collaboration' – all generate dialectical tension. What seems to be at stake is a threat to criticality that comes with the assertion of the affective.

George Home-Cook:

> Helplessly set adrift within a sea of clichés, bathed by self-affirming yet homogenising presuppositions, and enveloped within a seemingly impenetrable atmosphere of authenticity, the notion of 'immersion' has become a convenient means of bypassing the rigours of reason, and, hence, critical reflection at large.
>
> (2015: 195)

Likewise, Lynne Kendrick (2017) emphasises the importance of conceiving of theatre aurality as a 'critical field', possibly due to the risks to criticality contained in the affective experience of attending sound-based performance. Its 'critical reach can become a little restricted', explains Kendrick, due to the tendency of sound to 'conceal itself in its effect' (2017: xxi).[62] Alston perceives a methodological problem for a critical theorist vis-à-vis the affective co-optation the artwork requires of its audience in order to function as intended, but without a loss of critical engagement, the theorist requires in order to do their work. Upon reviewing several options, Alston settles on a critical methodology that requires 'conjugation' on a case-by-case basis with 'first hand experience [forming] a sensible place to begin a critique' (2016: 26). Kendrick, on the other hand, observes that immersive theatre is 'directed' ('as well as utterly absorbing') and that the authorial intent behind the design of the experience can ensure that immersion is not an 'uncritical experience in which subjectivity is lost' (2017: 67). These conclusions in their different ways intuit a move towards a relational epistemology that is developed further below.

Relationality, as deployed by Cavarero (2005), Barad (2007), and Feld (2015), implies a focus on the multiple specificities of 'plural uniqueness' (Cavarero 2005) rather than necessary exclusions that the critical analytic processes of abstraction require. Similarly, decolonial notions of relationality, emerging from various Indigenous metaphysics, emphasise agentic understanding of the non-human world. For example, trawlwulwuy scholar Lauren Tynan defines relationality by opposition to 'extractivism' (2021). My own, prevalently European – though not exclusively Western European – worldview remains inextricably founded on a dialectical approach which I want to take forward as a complementary form of relationality.

My contention is that, in knowledge creation, an ability to embrace apparent contradictions will be paramount: an innovation can be both a product of neoliberalism and emancipatory, collaboration can be both coercive and generative, and immersion does not have to preclude criticality. Diverse up-to-date corroborations of the dialectic principle are available in the concepts of 'trialectics' offered by Edward de Soja to account for the spatial dimension, 'globalectics' by Ngũgĩ wa Thiong'o (2012) intended to 'pluralize the linearity of dialectics' (McEachern Yoon), or 'tidalectics' coined by Kamau Braithwaite to account for an 'oceanic worldview' (Hessler 2018). For the pragmatic needs of this study, which goes on to consider (de)professionalised theatre-making in the digital age, I remain committed to the generative tension of contradiction itself – i.e. the inherent ambiguity of liminality, the simultaneity of affect and critique, and the significance of entangled subjectivity within the process of immersion.

Track 08: Relational Ethnography

Immersivity can be perceived as a shared characteristic of specific contemporary performance trends, the ontology of sound, and the research discipline of ethnography, whose deployment in the design of the A/OD project warrants further investigation.

In recent years, the methodology of ethnography has been systematically deployed in relation to Theatre and Performance research (McAuley 2006, 2012, Flynn and Tinius 2015, Kondo 2018, Tinius 2020). This work emerges out of a longer lineage of the intersection between sociology/ethnography and Theatre and Performance which includes, among others, sociologists Erving Goffman (1922–82) and Norman Denzin (1941–) as well as artists such as Anna Deavere Smith (explored further in Chapter 2). Similarly, the work of the pioneering Performance Studies theorist Dwight Conquergood (1949–2004) contains much contextualising relevance here. It is possible to claim that Conquergood's inherently relational (in a Cavarerian sense)[63] approach to ethnography is identifiable in his research idiom throughout his career, namely through the key formative emphases on speech, listening, embodiment, and performance itself.[64] In 1991, in an essay entitled 'Rethinking Ethnography', Conquergood explicitly challenged the ocular-centrism and texto-centrism[65] of ethnography advocating 'speaking and listening, instead of observing', in order to challenge 'the visualist bias of positivism' (Conquergood and Patrick, 2013: 87):

> The communicative praxis of speaking and listening, conversation, demands copresence even as it decenters the categories of knower and known. Vulnerability and self-disclosure are enabled through conversations. Closure, on the other hand, is constituted by the gaze.

Knowledge is frequently at the centre of Conquergood's work. Towards the end of his life, in 2002, Conquergood published another key article expounding on his radically interventionist methodology to confront the 'apartheid of knowledges' in academia (2002: 153) that privileges thinking over doing, interpreting over making, conceptualising over creating, and ultimately text over speech – thus silencing the oppressed. In this process, Conquergood is careful to avoid an adversarial, binarist approach. Inspired by Zora Neal Hurston's example of how the oppressed can use texts as a subversive strategy against the oppressor, as well as Ngugi wa Thiong'o's non-binarist idea of orature, he proffers the maxim that could be fundamental here too that: 'textocentrism – not texts – is the problem'

(2002: 151).⁶⁶ Although this speaks directly to the dramaturgies of speech and sound, Conquergood's maxim, in conjunction with his understanding of the 'communicative praxis of speaking and listening', can be understood as a rejection of hegemonic privileging itself in favour of the fine balance of co-presence.⁶⁷ This idea informs the thinking in this book.

In its design, the A/OD project originally integrated Gay McAuley's idea of 'rehearsal ethnography'. McAuley's methodology has its roots in her initial interest in performance space and semiotics and was eventually shaped by a combination of sociological ideas including Margaret Mead's 'balance between empathic involvement and disciplined attachment' (in McAuley 2012: 9), Clifford Geertz' concept of 'thick description' (2012: 9), and Randall Collins and Emile Durkheim's ideas of collective sociality (2012: 10). McAuley's foundation of Rehearsal Studies at the University of Sydney and the associated methodology of rehearsal ethnography form a significant contribution to the field of Theatre and Performance. It also coincides with other relevant inquiries into rehearsal as a historical object (Stern 2000), creative process in contemporary performance-making (Harvie and Lavender 2010, Mermikides and Smart 2010), and artistic practice as a site of political practice (Buchmann et al. 2016, Hunter 2019).

While Gay McAuley's rehearsal ethnography is contextualised by the '[post-modern shift] in interest from the reified art object to the dynamic processes involved in its production and reception' (1998: 75), the rehearsal process is largely understood as the continuous period between day one of professional theatre production and the opening night some weeks later.⁶⁸ McAuley is resolute about the discipline required for a comprehensive ethnographic recording of the entire process (through note-taking and audio-visual means); however, it is also important to note how this practice is limited by the existing methodological and ideological constraints of ethnographic practice itself. Dorinne Kondo, for example, reminds us that ethnography's constituent element – immersion – 'is never politically innocent' and that anthropology more broadly 'has confronted the politics of appropriation, colonizing empathy, and imperialism that can animate immersion' (2018: 110).

Sociologist Matthew Desmond, on the other hand, critiques the conventional ethnographic focus on 'static entities delimited by location or social classification' (2014: 550) which presupposes homogenous and neatly delineated bounded objects and where relations between people are artificially severed in order to study places or groups in relative isolation. McAuley does note that rehearsal is a 'bounded event' (1998: 79) defined by the time and space of rehearsal. Further, she observes that crucial creative decisions can actually happen in the heads of the relevant artists before the rehearsal process starts, or in the 'marginal spaces' of coffee breaks, lunchtimes, or dressing rooms (1998: 79). Therefore, even the most disciplined application of the existing protocols of ethnography can be insufficient in capturing some relevant insights. In her subsequent work, McAuley continues to refine her methodology with a view to the problems of disciplinary rigour, epistemological purpose, the calibration and implications of the insider/outsider perspective, power-balance, and the issue of selection and interpretation of fieldwork data. A moment I find particularly striking and productive for further exploration is the description of an instance whereby the ethnographer returns to the observed community with an edited version of the initial video documentation for further discussion and meta-documentation of the way in which the document is perceived by the participants. Although this protocol too carries its own limitations that require critical awareness (such as the relationship between personal memory and the document), it forfeits immersion for a relationality (between the ethnographer observer, the document, and the informants) that redresses the power balance and redefines the object of research in favour of the process rather than the bounded group, place, or event.

Matthew Desmond advocates the notion of 'relational ethnography' (2014) in order to account for objects of research not defined by the static concepts of group or place. Additionally, relational ethnography is focused on complexity, in that it 'incorporates fully' into the ethnographic sample 'at least two types of actors or agencies occupying different positions within the social space and bound together in a relationship of mutual dependence or struggle' (2014: 554). Similar to McAulay's ethnographer and informants coming together around an ethnographic record of a shared experience for further discussion and documentation, participants in a relational ethnography are 'engaged with one another' and 'dissimilar from one another' (2014: 554–55) and, importantly, they are 'enmeshed' with one another within a dynamic concept of a 'field' understood as an 'objective space of relations between positions occupied by agents or institutions' (2014: 555). Desmond's recommendations for constructing the relational object of analysis include the focus on: '(1) fields rather than places; (2) boundaries rather than bounded groups; (3) processes rather than processed people; and (4) cultural conflict rather than group culture' (2014: 562). He provides an illustrative example of his own study of urban poverty, focusing not on the urban poor, but on multiple perspectives involved in a specific case of evictions in a low-income housing market in Milwaukee, which involved not only landlords and tenants but also lawyers, ex-boyfriends, pastors, and dope suppliers.[69]

In designing the A/OD project, I was instinctively interested in creating a sample consisting of several smaller case studies rather than focusing in depth on a single substantial one. This had the potential to establish, if not a 'field' of A/OD, hypothetically speaking, then at least some of its co-ordinates, and to generate a multiplicity of processes for comparative analysis. I was happy to sacrifice the comprehensive oversight of a full rehearsal period recommended by McAuley, in favour of having four comparably circumscribed week-long 'scratch performance' processes.[70] As a result of the COVID-19 lockdown, sustained observation became altogether impossible, and I opted instead for a considerably greater number of conversations, interviews, and commissioned presentations from artists in order to get a more substantial representation from the 'field'. The recorded interviews, conversations, and presentations were collected and curated in a single web-based database – Lend Me Your Ears (LMYE) on purpose-built website www.auralia.space. Although the database does not provide scope to study 'relations' in the sense of interactions between different individuals and companies represented in the sample – and this is in fact not the point – the amassed sample of testimonies provides opportunities to establish relations between themes, motifs, points of convergence, divergence, consonance, and dissonance within the sample. Furthermore, the digital conception of the 'field' redefines different aspects of the ethnographer's relations to it. Here, the sociological and methodological framework of the actor-network theory (ANT) proposed by Bruno Latour (2005) becomes directly relevant to this ethnographic work, especially given its conception of the 'social' as necessarily imbricated in 'associations' with technology, innovation, and the non-human elements (or 'actors').

Latour's ANT is a method for 'situations where innovations proliferate, where group boundaries are uncertain, when the range of entities to be taken into account fluctuates' and more importantly the situations where 'the last thing to do would be to limit in advance the shape, size, heterogeneity, and combination of associations' (2005: 11). The researcher's task in this context is 'no longer to impose some order, to limit the range of acceptable entities'; instead one has to follow the ANT slogan – 'to follow the actors themselves' (2005: 11–12). Similarly, the A/OD project is primarily concerned with processes of making live performance and not necessarily only from the perspective of reverse engineering of the finished product, but primarily from the perspective of a creative and methodological departure into the unknown.

Track 09: Towards a Dramaturgical Research Methodology: A Close View

Writing from the position of literary critics, Anker and Felski call for new models of reading 'willing to avow […] world-making aspects of literature and criticism' (2017: 20). Sound and theatre scholars' recent work too invokes the world-making capacity of these arts: Salomé Voegelin's conception of the contingent materiality of sound is understood by reference to 'worlding' (Voegelin 2014), and Dorinne Kondo's *Worldmaking* (2018) is an ethnography of a theatre industry which explores 'reparative creativity' in the work of minoritarian theatre artists. While Voegelin's inspiration is drawn from the phenomenological thinking of Martin Heidegger (Voegelin 2014: 177, 187), Anker and Felski and Kondo, respectively, respond to Eve Kosofsky Sedgwick's taxonomy of 'paranoid' and 'reparative' theoretical strategies rooted in the psychoanalytical theory of Melanie Klein. Anker and Felski pursue reparative strategies via the notion of 'postcritique', whereas, unwilling to forfeit critique's potential to uncover power relations, Kondo offers 'reparative critique'. Kondo's specific offering is actually named 'dramaturgical critique' – a practice not antithetical to care or activism, but one that uses critique as 'a step toward the reparative' (Kondo 2018: 44).

As a practising dramaturg, I fully subscribe to Kondo's proposition; however, my task here is to identify a reparative artist-centred research methodology that can be deployed by an academic studying artistic process and is conceptually suited to the dramaturgies of speech and sound – a model that modifies, complements, and expands the critical apparatus, ideally in coalition with the artist(s).

In order to qualify the relationship between the academic and the artist in this context further, I settle for the term 'coalition' and 'alliance' drawn from Kondo's own considerations of the 'politics of affiliation'. Following Kondo, these notions remove the imperative of 'harmony' from the pursuit of social justice and allow for the incidence of 'reparative conflict' in theatre-making.[71] Coalition, alliance, and affiliation in the context of knowledge creation are intended to imply simultaneous inclusivity, solidarity, incommensurability, and difference while also circumventing the potentially transgressive connotations of 'collaboration' (Kunst 2015) or 'community' (Nancy 1991). I opt for these terms in qualifying the emergent A/OD research methodology not as a means of generating branding but as a means of qualifying the technicity of this research (although at the same time this book retains the use of the term 'community' in order to denote instances of incidental, bottom-up and temporary community-building characteristic of theatre attendance). Thus I do not have single a catchy name for the reparative, relational, coalitional, artist-centred research methodology I am describing here – and I wish to resist the imperialist impulse to name it – other than to follow the example of Kondo above in qualifying it as simply 'dramaturgical'. Maybe by the end of this study, the aural/oral dramaturgies as an object of research will generate the principles of an A/OD research methodology too. Or maybe that work will exceed the limitations of this book.

I can say with more certainty that the main thrust of the research methodology applied in the A/OD project stems from the conviction that the work of the artist contains the capacity to make contribution to the creation of knowledge. This is not claimed from my position as a dramaturg, or from the position of an artist engaged in Practice Research, or an ethnographer of rehearsal, but from the position of an academic and an ally. The project aims to redress the imbalance caused by rendering the work of the artist to the perennial position of the object of criticism and the consequent removal of epistemological agency from creative work. As implied by much theoretical work and the legacy of Western philosophy, the object of discussion in this book lies at the intersection of the categories frequently perceived as oppressed in various (binary) hierarchies – art (vs science), technicity (vs metaphysics), sound (vs vision), speech (vs literacy) – and, in this sense, it is concerned with reparation too.

I am troubled by how little value seems to be bestowed on theatre and performance research. This negligence is true not only of research users outside of the field but also of the theatre artists and the theatre and performance researchers themselves who frequently look to other research disciplines to corroborate their claims, thus easily overlooking or devalorising knowledges available within the field. A rare example to the contrary is available in Karen Savage and Dominic

Symonds' 2018 book *Economies of Collaboration in Performance*, premised on the idea that 'arts organisations and communities can teach us a great deal about the economies of collaboration' (2018: 6). One of the particularly interesting arguments in the book is the notion that forms of collaborative labour found in theatre and performance produce models as yet not recognised by the economic theory. Hence artistic collaborations have been 'ahead of the game in turning to collaborative economies far earlier and far more fundamentally than the systems of economic machinery' such as states, global enterprise, and corporate organisations (2018: 6). Yet it is the latter agencies that subsequently imbued collaboration with the neoliberalist agendas, the outcome of which is critiqued by Kunst.

The A/OD project began with the intention to study a selection of four representative artistic processes through rehearsal ethnography but unexpectedly ended up convening a digital space for ethnographic study – a network of documents providing insights into dozens of different artists' processes, as well as relevant academic dialogues and ideas. Following both Desmond and Latour (discussed in Track 08), I am predominantly interested in conjunctions, intersections, and knots within the networked ecology of the field of contemporary theatre and performance-making. I am interested in studying the relational nature of authority itself, the way in which an individual artist's creative agency can be understood as a dynamic and enmeshed entity contingent on networks of influence and (incidental) communities of practice. The relational approach ensures that the researcher sees the work of the artist on its own terms in relation to its conditions of emergence rather than selectively as a means of upholding a pre-existing thesis the researcher/critic brings to the analysis. The rigour of this approach is therefore not contained in the sharpness of the critic's tools but in creating the conditions to fully apprehend the contingencies of the artist's idiom making epistemological insight possible, and to effectively co-articulate the epistemic contribution of the artist's work. Furthermore, rather than positioning the object of study necessarily in relation to an ethnically and geographically defined culture, it is possible instead to perceive the work as part of an ecology of a theatre and performance-making 'field' delineated in terms of a shared paradigmatic creative concern.

Research is a process, and the A/OD project also partially unfolds in the writing of this book. The methodological principles I outlined earlier – regarding the ethnographic code-switching, coalition with the artist in knowledge-creation, the imperative of long-view in determining the trajectory of development of an artist's performance idiom, and a paradigmatic circumscription of a networked ecology (determining an entangled positioning of the artist in relation to their influences, contexts, tools, and incidental communities of practice)[72] – will still pertain to the methodological principles emerging by the end of this book. They will have been shaped in the ensuing discussion of the dramaturgies of speech and sound. The dramaturgies of speech and sound and their specific innovatory manifestations in theatre are indeed the object of this research project, so the specific matters of research methodologies and decolonial epistemologies will remain relatively implicit to the ensuing discussion and may form basis for future work.

This book is a meta-conversation with the multitude of voices, testimonies, and discussions generated and curated throughout the A/OD project as well as the theoretical works that frame the discussion. Rather than focusing on each individual case study, which would be impossible to accomplish within the limited space of a single chapter or even a single book, the aim is to tease out resonant findings and running themes that might be helpful in advancing the argument. Each chapter investigates a distinct body of artistic work pre-defined by means of its emphasis on the use of speech (post-verbatim), technology (amplified storytelling), popular music (gig theatre) – although all of these themes run fugue-like across all of the chapters.[73]

As I prepare for sample analysis I return to Adriana Cavarero:

> The thinker, including the platonic Socrates, knows his own thoughts beforehand. [...] Speaking, on the contrary, is always bound to time. It does not know in advance where it is going, and it entrusts itself to the unpredictable nature of what the interlocutors say. In short, thought is as solitary as speech is relational.
>
> (2005: 174)

In Cavarero's terms, relationality contained in the act of speaking presupposes a temporal and interpersonal contingency, communication of a kind of sonic idiom she refers to as vocal 'uniqueness', as well as improvisatory spontaneity – or simply being fully present in a shared space together. This can be linked to Conquergood's emphases on co-presence, vulnerability, and self-disclosure 'enabled through conversations' as opposed to ocular-centricity's valorisation of closure (2013: 87).

In continuation of the themes seeded in the Preface, and in the interest of further conceptual and methodological self-disclosure, the above also brings to mind a dictum by Vuk Stefanović Karadžić designed to replace the archaic official written language of the South Slavs with the everyday speech of the illiterate majority: 'Write as you speak, read as it's written'. My own writing, in turn, has often been described by readers as resembling the way I speak, as conversational, or in some rare, cherished moments, as music. As I write this paragraph, in the aftermath of completing the majority of the current book's chapters, another methodological principle emerges that I can retroactively articulate here. Much of this book is written in the vein of speech articulated by Cavarero above: without always knowing in advance where the discussion is going, in a relatively continuous burst of time, and in anticipation of further conversations.

Track 10: How to Read This Book

This book should be read in conjunction with the collection of recordings of interviews, conversations, and presentations about the dramaturgies of speech and sound, Lend Me Your Ears (LMYE), which is available in two forms: as permanently archived individual items on Figshare (https://rcssd.figshare.com/

account/home#/projects/75384) and as a fully searchable website www.auralia. space (available until 2032). Each recording has an accompanying transcript which is scrollable or downloadable on the website and on Figshare. In the main discussion, I refer to each recording by citing the name of the person interviewed, the category and issue number of LMYE the recording belongs to, the year of publication, and, where relevant, the page number of the accompanying pdf (e.g. McCormick in LMYE Gallery#1 2020: 3).

Although the Figshare-generated citations give the names of all of the authors involved (for formal referencing), I have truncated these citation formats for discussion purposes here using only the names of the cited artists and scholars, to save space, to make the cross-referencing easier, and, primarily, to foreground the artist's ownership of their contributions to this coalitional research.

Additionally, the book comes with appendices which contain reviews of performances under the discussion in the book which I saw in the period 2010–20 and wrote about for a variety of web-based publications. The reviews are included in full for illustrative purposes because the main discussion does not allow space for performance analysis in detail. These reviews, which represent another layer in the network of relevant documents informing the A/OD project, also evidence how some initial ideas underlying this book were formed and how the process of seeing these performances helped to scope this project.

The book has five chapters. This first introductory chapter serves the multiple purposes of elucidating the provenance and the research context of the ideas explored in the book, providing an intersecting literature review about speech, sound, dramaturgy, ethnography and methodology, and of ultimately articulating the principles of the methodological approach underlying this research. It is possible to read the fragmented Introduction(s) chapter in a non-linear way, though this is not crucial. Bookended by the Introduction(s) chapter, and the Conclusion(s) chapter is an in-depth chapter-by-chapter discussion of the three trends identified as forming part of the paradigm shift of the dramaturgies of speech and sound: post-verbatim, amplified storytelling, and gig theatre. This intervening discussion constitutes analysis of the 'fieldwork' by reference to relevant theoretical and contextual sources.

Chapter 2 on Post-Verbatim analyses Anna Deveare Smith's *Notes from the Field* and Nic Green's *Cock and Bull* to chart a move away from documentary procedures of verbatim theatre towards a more contrapuntal relationship between text and its performance. Ideas of polyphony and counterpoint are considered in terms of their technicity in creating scope for engendering an act of collective affective critique among the audience.

Starting with the example of the Unspoken Project's polyphonic use of biological speech and AAC technology in theatre-making, Chapter 3 on Amplified Storytelling considers the technicity of technology in dramaturgical expression. This chapter draws on the politically problematic legacy of the Serbian orature and its remediation in the music video of Rambo Amadeus's 1991 hit 'Smrt popa Mila Jovovića' to explore how technology can intervene to facilitate and/

or amplify an intersubjective relationship between the artwork and the audience. It draws insights from the fieldwork about the significance of tools such as microphones and software but also of the associated compositional innovations such as layering and sampling. Crucially it contextualises the dramaturgical workings of speech and sound within the multi-modality of theatre.

Chapter 4 offers a polyphonic history of Gig Theatre, and a qualification of this postdramatic form in terms of its juxtapositions of the musical and the visual content, the genre and the frame, the affect and critique, music and its cultural context. The chapter focuses on the use of gig theatre in Wildcard's *Electrolyte* (2018) for postdramatic representation of mental illness. It questions to what extent gig theatre is a UK culture-specific phenomenon.

Chapter 5 summarises the polyphonic workings of the book and the A/OD project as a whole. It notes the boundaries of the conducted enquiry, elicits the notions of the 'dramaturgy of layering', the 'disruption of closure', enmeshment vs immersion, and the digital liminalities which keep space open for further study.

Hidden Track: COVID-19 Coda

It seems important to devote a few pages to the description of the empirical aspect of the A/OD project and outline how the research was shaped by the circumstances of COVID-19.

The scoping and formulation of the research questions underpinning the A/OD project emerge out of the process of documented theatre attendance (see Appendices). The notions of 'gig theatre', 'amplified storytelling', and 'post-verbatim' have emerged through a variety of local and international works I encountered at the Edinburgh Fringe and in London theatres in the period 2010–20.

The AHRC project proposal additionally envisaged a prospect of engaging with the creative processes of selected artists through rehearsal ethnography. In a partnership-defining conversation with Battersea Arts Centre (BAC), and specifically producer Bethany Haynes, we determined a mutual benefit in combining my research aims with the BAC-specific commissioning model known as 'scratch'.[74]

This model enabled me to contemplate commissioning more than one artist under the remit of A/OD to accommodate variations of creative practice. Scratch commissions – engaging a selection of artists for a week of rehearsals and leading up to a short public presentation – while contributing seed funding for the artists' future commissions, represented a more viable model for rehearsal ethnography purposes over commissioning a full performance. The reduced scale increased the manageability of the documentation process envisaged by Gay McAuley (1998, 2006, 2012) around a conventional six-week rehearsal in a professional theatre. McAuley's methodology strongly advocates for a meticulous, deep, and systematic engagement, and its planned outcome is documentation intended for an ethnographic archive and further academic analysis. In the A/OD project, the object of research was not the entirety of the staging process, but rather the composite insights drawn from a multiplicity of performance authorship models foregrounding speech and sound as a point of departure. Idealistically perhaps, the prospect of commissioning a number of artists whose individual projects represented different takes on 'post-verbatim', 'amplified storytelling', and 'gig theatre' entailed a promise of a sample, a field, or a group of artists and methodologies to be studied. Further prospects included the project conference/festival at BAC, a 12-part research podcast to be produced by Tim Bano and hosted by Digital Theatre Plus (DT+), a journal issue, and a workshop package to be developed with voice specialist Jane Boston.

Although an Artists Call Out released by BAC in October 2019 generated 120 applications approaching the topic from a number of unanticipated perspectives (spoken word, live art, disability arts, installation, sound art), in the selection process, Haynes and I gave priority to proposals most directly responding to the key terms in the project title. Additionally, we applied the criterion of a discernible 'performance idiom', or evidence that the artist had found their 'voice'. For fairness, in this context, my methodological principle of longitudinal familiarity with the artist's output was less important than the direct thematic relevance of the proposed project. (Instead we requested evidence of some pre-existing relevant documentation of the artist's work that would be available for contextual study.) Despite the presence among the applicants of artists whose work I had known, the final selection included four artists whose work I had mostly not seen previously.[75] The selected A/OD Artists in Residence were: Silvia Mercuriali (with a headphone piece for swimming pools), beatboxer SK Shlomo (with an autobiographical solo show about overcoming mental illness), Gracefool Collective (with a site-specific dance piece about climate change), and San Francisco-based intermedial artist sair goetz (with a work about gender fluidity and neo-ventriloquism).

The project officially began in January 2020 and the postdoctoral research associate Flora Pitrolo was appointed in March 2020. The COVID-19 lockdown in the United Kingdom was announced on 16 March 2020, one day before we were due to enter the rehearsal room with SK Shlomo. As a result, Flora and I were confronted with the necessity to redesign various aspects of the empirical research and the planned outputs. Remote interviewing was a possibility so we began with the selected Artists in Residence and then expanded the list to include other relevant artists and companies whose work fitted the remit of the project. As the prospect of the project conference became increasingly unviable, we proceeded to convene a number of asynchronous academic conversations between invited scholars, artists, and activists on Zoom with a view to editing them into individual podcast episodes. The originally planned 12-part podcast Lend Me Your Ears in which each episode had been envisaged as consisting of mixed content drawn from various aspects of the project, unfolded instead into an open-ended collection of individually edited recordings.

This prompted the need for a project website as a space where all the generated materials would be curated. The 'space' would consist of different 'rooms' for different categories of recordings: the Gallery ('interviews with artists') and the Salon ('conversations about sound') accommodated the initial audio recordings; the Laboratory ('creative practices'), and the Library ('oral introductions') were later introduced for video recordings. The Zoom-generated Laboratory documentaries focused on the making of individual pieces of performance, and the Library profiled authors and their academic books about speech, sound, dramaturgy, and methodology.

I will briefly outline the emergent methodological rationale and associated issues arising with each of these distinct forms of recordings. The Gallery interviews followed the principles of interviewing I had already developed in *The Contemporary Ensemble*, whereby, interested in the developmental journey of the artist's performance idiom, I traced their training histories, formative artistic influences, and methodologies of working across a number of performances. Whereas these principles had previously been intrinsic to the conversation, this time I was foregrounding them as the aims of the conversation, and as a result, the interviewed artists were able to help clarify when certain aspects of their journeys unfolded in non-linear ways. Additionally, many artists observed that it was useful to them to be asked to articulate their methodology in this way. The Gallery interviews were published as audio only, partly because audio interviews had been envisaged from the outset as conceptually suited to the remit of the project, and partly because video recordings only came about through embracing Zoom as a recording methodology during the lockdown.[76]

Retroactively, it might be speculated that the focus on sound-only in these interviews helped to more consciously focus on the processes of *listening* and the *articulation* of the artist's performance idiom unimpeded by any limitations or distractions the visual aspect might impose. Compared to video editing, sound editing also made it easier to remove distractions characteristic of speech (such as hesitations, coughs, filler words, false starts, non-sequiturs, and unfinished sentences), which, even though they are often considered to have dramaturgical value in verbatim theatre-making (as Chapter 2 shows), were an obstacle to academically valued semantic clarity and coherence.

As an editor, I had previously only processed the recorded interviews on paper, which posed no constraints on lightly editing transcribed content in the interest of clarity and flow for the anticipated reader. As part of the editorial process involving audio, I encountered limitations in what was possible to cut or rearrange, but I was also able to usefully discover the categorical imperatives of speech and its resistance of the regimes of writing. Even the most articulate speakers were unconsciously compelled to maintain a sense of continuity by frequently starting their sentences with 'And' or 'So'. In sound-only, this is not an obstacle as we are all used to mentally editing out these incidentals in favour of meaning when listening; however, these speech characteristics become more incongruous when transcribed. The regimes of writing, civilisationaly internalised over centuries, do not accommodate a sense of spontaneity, uncertainty, and temporality observed by Cavarero as pertaining to speech. Having decided to append accompanying transcripts to all audio-visual materials for accessibility reasons and for subsequent analysis/teaching purposes, we also had to make the decision to what extent we wanted our transcripts to be literal and to what extent we wanted them to be reader-friendly. As part of our ethical procedure, we ran all transcripts past our interviewees and even when they had no corrections, I often encountered a general expectation of editorial intervention in the interest of coherence.[77] The balance we struck was hopefully somewhere in the middle: we sparingly edited some of the speech-specific elements that disrupt coherence but kept the transcripts as close as possible to what was said. What I am describing in this section are the pragmatic decisions made for purposes of enabling the research to meet the public in the most accessible form possible; however, many aspects of these decisions could be problematised further, not least the question of why it still seemed academically indispensable to commit to having the written records of the audio-visual recordings. Certainly, the editorial attention given to the transcripts of the recordings (including stylistic standardisation of conventions, transcribing, paper editing, proofreading, visual layout, and presentation) far outweighed any other single aspect of the academic labour in that phase of the project.

The second category of materials – the Salon – was intended as substitution for the project conference which was conceived in the AHRC project proposal to privilege spoken presentation (over the more common academic practice of reading pre-written papers). In developing the invitation for participation in the Salon, Flora Pitrolo and I had some newfound freedoms to envisage these academic contributions differently. For a start, this became a curatorial exercise rather than one warranting an open call. The format was partly circumstantially determined – we aimed for an hour-long conversation between two, possibly three interlocutors, as an optimum length of time to maintain concentration on Zoom during the pandemic. In order to pass on the authorial and editorial control to the participants, we decided that the Salon conversations would be unmoderated by us, and remunerated (using repurposed conference funding). Flora proposed the particularly generative dramaturgical idea to build into the Salon conversations the requirement of the 'sonic cues' that the interlocutors would be asked to bring along to their encounter. These sonic cues could take any form ranging from personal recordings to commercial footage (though the latter presented a copyright issue which we dealt with separately), and their intended function was two-fold: to help along in the structuring of the conversation and to stimulate the listener's engagement. Our role was to provide the space and to keep the time.

Although we were careful to follow the institutional ethical procedures of the Royal Central School of Speech and Drama regarding consent of our interviewees,[78] the empirical process raised two more procedural and ethical questions that required some further thinking and standardisation: (1) the question of remuneration, and (2) the question of selection criteria for contributors. The first question had already been considered in the early stages of conceptualising the podcast for the purposes of writing the grant application. Based on Tim Bano's experience of working for the BBC, we adopted the standard industry rule that remuneration would not be offered for recordings that constituted promotion of the guest's work, but if the contributors were commissioned to deliver their expertise on a specific subject or if additional preparation was required, they would be offered a fixed fee. It logically followed that the Salon guests should be offered remuneration, whereas the Gallery interview represented promotion of work. However, this sat uncomfortably with me under the conditions of the pandemic when many artists were out of work while many academics were still on payroll, and this ethical problem led to envisaging another strand, the Laboratory, where selected artists would be commissioned to deliver a more substantial contribution in exchange for a fee.

As for the question of selection, the Gallery strand was relatively easy to curate. In addition to the Artists in Residence selected through the call, other interviewees were approached on the basis of the researchers' pre-existing familiarity with their work as well as the willingness and availability of the invited artist to be interviewed. We kept an extended wish list and although we did not get to work through it all, we did interview 39 artists in addition to the Artists in Residence, generating 27 edited Gallery interviews.[79] The selection of contributors to the Salon was less circumscribed by pre-existing factors and parameters, as we were able to draw on a wide range of disciplines and interdisciplinary possibilities dealing with the issues of speech, sound, dramaturgy, and methodology. Partly determined by the design of the AHRC project proposal, the selection process for the Salon was combined with the convening of an Advisory Board for the project, whereby specific Board members were also invited to convene a Salon conversation with an interlocutor of their choice. In rare cases, we helped with creating the match (Johnson & Beswick), and in some cases, we convened the conversations beyond the Advisory Board membership, on the basis of the chosen topic of conversation (Double & Long and Mandic & Ramshaw).

The conception of the Laboratory was partly shaped by my desire to find substitution for the rehearsal ethnography element of the research. Under the constraints of the pandemic, I became particularly interested in how the artists were using their computers at the time when the significance of the digital tools became so overwhelmingly paramount.[80] Additionally, I continued to be fascinated by the metadiscursive perspective exemplified by McAuley's ethnographer returning to the observed community with a document for further discussion. Seeing Oliver Zahn's *In Praise of Forgetting II* as part of the GIFT Festival on 2 May 2020 – a piece of desktop theatre made as a pandemic substitute for a live performance using archive materials – was a crucial breakthrough in envisaging the Laboratory format. It crystallised the idea that the way I wanted to engage with the work of specific artists was via the screen-share function of Zoom, curating a guided tour of their personal documentation of a creative process leading towards a particular already completed piece of work. We briefed the artists that their presentation should be organised around five pre-planned headings and up to one hour long, but, in a set up that reconfigures the conventional artist–document–ethnographer relationship, the artist was fully in control around what they wanted to share with us about their process and how to engage in a reflection about it. This represents a relinquishing of 'thick description' in favour of a set of insights offered by the artist that carried the potential to be subsequently related to the rest of the sample.

The Library strand promoting the work of academics was conceived to provide symmetry to the Gallery strand which promotes the artists' work, and to complement the two strands of respective commissions from academics (The Salon) and artists (The Laboratory). The Libraries feature a preset Q and A format with academics speaking to camera for 20 minutes and orally summarising a specific book or Practice Research project they authored. This idea was linked to the foundational principle of the A/OD project foregrounding the affordances of speech over writing in knowledge-creation. There were seven set questions intended to trace the genealogy of the ideas explored in the book, to consider the book's organisational principles, as well as to demystify the processes of authorship. Once again, we had a long wish list of books we wanted to feature but the final selection was determined by the limitations of time and availability.

The concept of Lend Me Your Ears allows for open-ended accretion of relevant data in different strands; however, the project was ultimately limited by the time and funding constraints. In several months of Zoom field work, the scope of the project had far exceeded the original idea of a podcast series. We were in fact moving away from a linear way of thinking about the production of material and towards a spontaneous layering of different audio-visual formats around the five different topics of the planned monograph structure: Introduction(s), Post-Verbatim, Amplified Storytelling, Gig Theatre, and Liminal/Digital Auralities.[81] The overall data was adding up to a 'field' or an ecology, or an incidental community of artists and thinkers whose contributions would provide an opportunity for an immersive, acoustemological enquiry.

The website www.auralia.space was designed by Beatriz Cabur, a playwright/director in her own right and original founder of the global theatre portal *The Theatre Times*. This ensured that dramaturgical thinking was also at the core of the presentation of the material itself and its navigational potential.

The immersion in the various facets of the primary research has aided our intellectual engagement with the data, the process, and the key questions in a number of useful ways which will unfold in the course of this book. On the sensory level, a certain number of unanticipated key terms began to reverberate across the sonic pathways of the networked digital space and have entered our academic register: 'layering', 'instinct', 'improvisation', 'DIY', 'software', 'sampling', 'collage', 'archives', 'identity' etc. Having decided to tag each post with relevant keywords for easier navigation, we also created a tag document for the collection as a whole, which, in the process of editing the transcripts, allowed us to also trace these patterns of resonance. Methodological innovation resulting from the COVID-19-induced improvisation has allowed us to diversify and add to the repertoire of existing oral history research methods and artefacts. In addition to free-form interview aimed at tracing the genealogies of the artist's 'performance idiom', which I have now taken further by working more explicitly towards *articulation* in an audio mode, we have also created scope for reflection on the notions of *conversation*, *dialogue*, and *improvised co-authorship* as research methods in the Arts and Humanities (based on the Salon strand), *reversed engineering*, *making-of presentation* and *guided tour of personal computer archive* (based on the Laboratory strand), and *oral summary of a book by its author* (in the Library) replacing written blurb and book review. I hope to develop these methods further in future work.

In addition to the collection of data available as Lend Me Your Ears (LMYE), which also now includes a podcast training course on 'Decolonising the Voice' by Jane Boston and Deelee Dubé, Flora and I have also curated a special issue of Critical Stages (https://www.critical-stages.org/24/), assembled through an open call, in order to diversify modes of conversation and expand our polyphonic inquiry. This book is polyvalently and substantially enmeshed with these other discursive companions.

Notes

1 This includes books authored as documentation of performance (Marina Abramović's *The Artist Body* 1998 and *The Cleaner* 2017), documentation of theatre works (Oberon collections of works by Third Angel in 2019, Ontroerend Goed in 2019 and 2015, and Les Enfants Terribles in 2011), and numerous handbooks, memoirs, general interest books by theatre-makers, for example.
2 The United Kingdom-based Research Assessment Framework (REF), uses 'originality, significance and rigour' as the key criteria for assessing outputs in relation to international research quality standards. See page 7 here: https://www.ref.ac.uk/media/1450/ref-2019_02-panel-criteria-and-working-methods.pdf.
3 The recordings are also individually archived on Figshare (https://rcssd.figshare.com/account/home#/projects/75384) for long term preservation.
4 I made this decision before I became aware of Daphne Brooks's fascinating volume *Liner Notes for the Revolution* (2021), which even more elegantly fuses academic content and form in this way. Thanks to Flora Pitrolo and P.A. Skanze for bringing Daphne Brooks's work within the orbit of the A/OD project as LMYE Salon#4.
5 Walter Benjamin's idea of the 'aura' of the work of art in relation to technology (discussed in the seminal essay 'The Work of Art in the Age of Mechanical Reproduction, (1936) might also be usefully re-considered in relation to aurality as pointed out by Curtin (2014: 69–70).
6 In using this term, I observe the warnings from Moosavi (2020) regarding reductionism, essentialisation, overlooking of the marginalised voices, nativism and tokenism associated with this term. I align to this my own positionality as a person from the Balkans as outlined in my previous works, particularly Radosavljević 2012 and Radosavljević 2020.

7 Although this notion has been variously defined and theorised by Peter Boenisch (2012) and by the Relational Dramaturgies research group at Utrecht University (https://transmissioninmotion.sites.uu.nl/dramaturgy/), I primarily refer here to the understanding of relationality in theatre which I explored with reference to Nicolas Bourriaud and Jean-Luc Nancy in *Theatre-Making* (2013).
8 An example of the auxiliary status of speech is contained in the voice training of actors concerned with technical performance rather than the dramaturgical potential of voice (see Thomaidis 2017). Similarly, in performance-making, sound is often thought of as 'incidental' or an 'effect' (see Brown 2020).
9 The Research Questions were as follows: (1) What compositional strategies underpin the performance-making which foregrounds orality/aurality in the 21st century?; (2) How do we adequately scope and theoretically frame aural/oral dramaturgy as an emerging interdisciplinary field of enquiry?; and (3) What potential correlation can be discerned between: a) technological developments, b) increasing cognitive bias towards the oral/aural in our daily life, and c) contemporary performance-making practices; and how can this understanding help improve the effectiveness of our aural/oral composition and presentation skills? (https://www.auralia.space/research/).
10 This term is being applied with due reservations pointed out by Lehmann (1999/2006), for example, about the distinction between art and science and inherent limitations in the ability of art to 'conform to the developmental logic of paradigms and paradigm shifts' (1999/2006: 24).
11 This was the AHRC-funded Fellowship 'The Role of Ensemble Theatre in Redefining 'Playwriting' and 'Writing for Performance' in the 21st Century' AH/J003522/1.
12 My contribution to the crowd-sourced documented compiled by Vida Midgelow (2020) testifies to these considerations: https://collective-encounters.org.uk/wp-content/uploads/2020/06/Doing-Arts-Research-in-a-Pandemic.pdf.
13 Science is the pursuit and application of knowledge and understanding of the natural and social world following a systematic methodology based on evidence. ('Our definition' https://sciencecouncil.org/about-science/our-definition-of-science/).
14 'Scientific knowledge refers to knowledge of a person that must be based on the methods and procedures of science rather than on subjective belief or unsupported speculation. The person must have good grounds for his/her belief'. ('Scientific Knowledge Law and Legal definition' https://definitions.uslegal.com/s/scientific-knowledge/).
15 A summary of scientific research methodology is available here: https://sciencecouncil.org/about-science/our-definition-of-science/ and a variation of the above here: https://definitions.uslegal.com/s/scientific-knowledge/.
16 Gerald Graff offers an interesting statistic that in 1850 there were only 8 graduate students in all of United States; in 1875, one year before the foundation of John Hopkins as the first American research university, there were 399, 'whereas by 1908 there would be almost 8000' (1987: 26).
17 As shown by Shannon Jackson (2004), in the United States, the relatively young discipline(s) of Theatre Studies and Performance Studies resulted from a gradual disciplinary emancipation of Drama from Literature and Philology.
18 This included the structural study of language through Russian Formalism, the Prague School, Structuralism, Semiotics and Narratology, eventually leading to the antithetical ideas of Poststructuralism (Roland Barthes 1915–1980, Michel Foucault 1926–1984) and Deconstruction (Jacques Derrida 1930–2004). Linguistic concerns that are fundamental to Structuralism and Semiotics via Ferdinand de Saussure (1857–1913), have also led to a very different kind of formative influence on Performance Studies through the work of British philosopher of language J.L. Austin (1911–1960).
19 Significant proponents of Phenomenology included Edmund Husserl (1859–1938), Martin Heidegger (1889–1976), Hans-Georg Gadamer (1900–2002), Maurice Merleau-Ponty (1908–1961), Emmanuel Levinas (1906–1995), and Paul Ricoeur (1913–2005).

20 The Frankfurt School members Walter Benjamin (1892–1940), Max Horkheimer (1895–1973), Herbert Marcuse (1898–1979), Theodor Adorno (1903–1969), and others, laid important foundations for a Marxist analysis of culture whose influence expanded in multiple directions internationally, partly through these individuals' forced displacement and migrations during the Second World War.

21 The 'experiential turn' can be traced back to the performative works emerging in galleries, museums, and the visual arts, but also in another direction back to community theatre practices.

22 Alongside Jamaican-born British sociologist Stuart Hall (1932–2014) and English scholar Richard Hoggart (1918–2014), Raymond Williams is credited as a key influence on the British school of Cultural Studies, which was founded in 1964 at the Birmingham Centre for Contemporary Cultural Studies and led by Hall (1969–1979). Williams was also the Professor of Drama at Cambridge University (1974–1983), even though he taught in an English department.

23 Significant dates include the renaming of the New York University's Graduate Drama Programme in 1980 as Performance Studies and the foundation of the research association Performance Studies International in New York in 1995.

24 Jackson (2004) and Carlson (1996) offer comprehensive overviews of the genealogies of the field in the US. Alternative historiographies of the field of Theatre and Performance studies have emerged in other cultures too, for example, in the German context, Erika Fischer-Lichte's *The Transformative Power of Performance* (2004/2008).

25 They examine three pre-defined trifecta concerning the field and draw a fourth one from their collection concerning 'skills/methods/methodologies' to emphasise the necessary 'creativity' and the heart of Theatre and Performance research.

26 Stanford Encyclopaedia of Philosophy makes an interesting point that in translating 'episteme' as 'scientific knowledge' which is often the case, it must be noted that this concept excludes the idea of experimentation which is a necessary feature of contemporary science, and that episteme should be understood in terms of 'certainty'.

27 Aristotle in *Nicomachean Ethics* expands the definition of knowledge to include five 'virtues' of thought: technē, episteme, phronesis, sophia, and nous. Phronesis and sophia are two different kinds of wisdom (practical and theoretical) and nous is basic understanding through perception.

28 Similarly in 'research for', 'the goal is not primarily communicable knowledge in the sense of verbal communication, but in the sense of visual or iconic or imagistic communication' (1993: 5).

29 Promotion of PaR in the early days led to misunderstandings prompting practicing artists within academia to think any creative practice which yielded insights could constitute practice as research if it was retrospectively articulated as such. Robin Nelson (2013) articulated a protocol for helping artists transition to practitioner-researchers through careful delineation of their endeavour as academic research led by a research question – or 'research inquiry' – which necessarily leads to new knowledge. Nelson includes case studies of similar research projects taking place in other cultural contexts, sometimes under the names of 'practice-led' or 'artistic research'.

30 Since a HEFCE-funded interdisciplinary symposium at Goldsmith College in 2015, the syntagm 'Practice Research' has gained currency in Theatre and Performance too as a way of embracing nuances of correlation including variations of practice 'as'/'through'/'-based' research. Thanks to Rachel Hahn and Ben Spatz in bringing the significance of this event to my attention in a public Facebook discussion on 5 August 2021.

31 '[A] student or scholar must internalize the many options and enact them appropriately given the task at hand; this method for that problem, followed by a new method for the next' (Galloway in Dobson 2019: 12).

32 It is interesting that when asked about working with a dramaturg, Collins encapsulates the 'whole practice' of ERS as a company as being the 'work of dramaturgy': 'And everyone, to a greater or lesser extent, has the expectation that they will do that kind of work' (2014: 122).

33 Both Ovadija and Home-Cook's books are versions of their respective PhDs. I note the provenance of these monographs not to diminish their status but on the contrary to amplify their significance in breaking new ground.
34 I note the seemingly self-contradictory nature of this wording, however it stands in relation to the expanded idea of dramaturgy outlined earlier and also in the context of Lehmann's own definition of 'postdramatic' as theatre that does not eschew drama or text but on the contrary defines itself in relation to it.
35 'The speakers are not political because of what they say, but because they say it to others who share an interactive space of reciprocal exposure. To speak to one another is to communicate to one another the unrepeatable uniqueness of each speaker. According to Arendt, speech falls under the political name of action' (Cavarero 2005: 190).
36 My thanks to PhD student Hara Topa at the Royal Central School of Speech and Drama for drawing my attention to this quote, although she takes her specific engagement with this work in a different direction.
37 Schaeffer introduced a number of key concepts into the disciplinary vocabulary including the notion of 'sound object' itself which inspires the title of the Steintrager and Chow volume.
38 Anthropologist Tom Rice (2018) has subsequently traced 'multiple acoustemologies' whereby the methodology has been applied to studies of incarceration, history, and hospitals, for example. He also traces ways in which the concept has been theoretically expanded to accommodate technological developments (see Porcello 2004), and, more significantly, beyond the deaf-hearing dichotomies to accommodate potential non-sonocentric acoustemologies (see Friedner and Helmreich 2012).
39 Abduction is distinct from induction or deduction, but intended to 'generate theories which may then later be assessed' https://plato.stanford.edu/entries/abduction/peirce.html).
40 Technological determinism is a critical concept that is traceable back to Karl Marx's ideas around the role of technology in socio-political progress, however the invention of the term is attributed to American social scientist Thorsten Veblein (1857–1929) who, together with his followers promoted the ideas that technology itself had agency that could outweigh human agency. This resulted in technological determinism being seen as a reductionist theoretical view that can lead to flawed ideas and arguments. Posthumanist notions of networked agency and agential entaglement, however, move this discussion in a direction that transcends concerns about technological determinism.
41 The 'Gutenberg parenthesis' is a term coined by Pettitt's colleague Lars Ole Sauerberg. Pettitt is not alone in his speculation that the oral tradition still held considerable, if not superior, cultural value in the 17th century and beyond. Book historian Martha Woodmansee (1992) recalls an instance of a deliberate fabrication of a Gaelic epic bard Ossian by poet James Mcphereson who claimed to have translated his work into English in order to raise the value of his own literary endeavour. This incident took place as recently as 1760.
42 While the age of the printing press had prompted individuation in the use of tools to 'translate' experience (books authored by individuals were consumed by individuals), the age of the new technologies promoted a collectivity and a connectivity not dissimilar to the pre-literate one, or to McLuhan's idea of the 'global village'. One could further observe that what 'secondary orality' in the digital age seems to be dialectically producing is an increased interest in sensorial experience itself: experiential learning, experience design and 'experiential theatre', for that matter.
43 Thanks to Annie Goh for drawing my attention to this paper and to her response (Goh 2016).
44 Sterne also quotes an important cautionary observation by Lorna Roth (2005) that 'by depoliticizing communication as apolitical technology, McLuhanite approaches to media colluded with existing institutional prejudices to keep First Peoples (especially the Inuit) out of Canadian media policy until the mid-1970s' (Sterne 2011: 220).
45 This is also traced by Arthur Bradley (2011) from Marx and Freud to Bernard Stiegler and Jacques Derrida.

46 In 2012, Sue Broadhurst and Josephine Machon published an edited volume that thematised technicity at the intersection of their interest in identity, performance, and technology.

47 Relationality is also used by Philip Auslander as a means of addressing and resolving the charge of technological determinism as part of his definition of 'digital liveness'. He uses the phenomenological perspective of Hans-Georg Gadamer to help him resolve this problem through a construction of a relation between technological and spectatorial determinism: 'The experience of liveness results from our conscious act of grasping virtual entities as live in response to the claims they make on us' (Auslander 2012: 10).

48 Tony Fisher and Kélina Gotman (2020) have relatively recently collated the first collection of articles articulating the inherent theatricality of Foucault's own author function and the explicit relevance of his work to the field of Theatre and Performance.

49 At the time of writing, ethically compromising accounts about Foucault's personal life have emerged which represent grounds for some reservation 'French philosopher Michel Foucault abused boys in Tunisia' *The Times*, 28.03.2021, https://www.thetimes.co.uk/article/french-philosopher-michel-foucault-abused-boys-in-tunisia-6t5sj7jvw. However, such mainstream media reports have also been taken with some more rigorous scepticism elsewhere. See Kelly, Mark G.E. (2021) 'Must We Cancel Foucault?', http://www.telospress.com/must-we-cancel-foucault/; with thanks to Tony Fisher for pointing me to this source. Foucault's work must be perceived as contingent on its own historical and ideological context.

50 My positionality could be more usefully determined further by qualifying my native cultural affiliation with an entity largely unclassifiable by the most commonly existing cultural hegemonic structures and criteria. I was born and raised in the Socialist Federal Republic of Yugoslavia, a state that dissolved in the early 1990s in an interethnic civil war. Yugoslavia was a single-party socialist state, which was however not part of the Eastern Bloc during the Cold War. It operated a liberal internal political system of 'self-management' and its foreign politics promoted anti-imperialism and decolonisation most notably by leading the way in the formation of the Non-Aligned Movement with member states from Asia and Africa in 1961. After the end of Yugoslavia, colonial stereotypes of Balkanism (a manifestation of Dorinne Kondo's 'affective violence' 2018) have once again been retroactively applied to the region I come from. I left Yugoslavia aged 19 and settled in the United Kingdom where my cultural assimilation process was always limited by my name, accent and memory of different cultural possibilities. In ethnographic terms I could most closely declare myself as a perpetual immigrant rather than a detached academic observer (a figure traditionally originating from a culturally privileged Western academic context). This implies inherently different hegemonic positions too. Additionally, I also occupy the multiple professional roles of dramaturg, theatre critic, academic, teacher, and many of those roles entail the position of liminality.

51 This is not a unique position, but may stem from the philological (structuralist and semiotic) provenance of Theatre Studies as a field. Melissa Trimingham also notes that insights drawn from artistic practice in Practice as Research need to be 'translated into analytical language' (Trimingham 2002: 54).

52 Even though Crouch's *My Arm* (2002), *An Oak Tree* (2005), *England* (2007), and *The Author* (2009) are not conceived of or presented as a tetralogy in the way that the work of ensembles such as Shadow Casters and Ontroerend Goed explicitly are, methodological lines of progressive interrelation within the series of works are claimed by all of these artists as corroborated in the interviews they gave me. Understanding the genealogy of Crouch's performance idiom in this way in the run up to *The Author* (2009) definitely serves to provide additional hermeneutic access to this work. See interview with Crouch in *Theatre-Making* (2013), and also interviews with Shadow Casters and Ontroerend Goed in *The Contemporary Ensemble* (2013) for additional perspectives on methodological interrelations between individual artistic works.

53 This has been internalised as part of the European intellectual tradition, and more specifically through a Marxist dialectic materialist tradition underlying my early education.
54 Self-proclaimed 'theatre-makers' are distinguished from actors by critic Lyn Gardner (in Radosavljevic 2013b) primarily by means of their training backgrounds. While they emerge from British university drama/theatre/performance studies departments where they study the subject in a multidisciplinary way, the industry-ready professional personnel of actors, directors, designers, producers more frequently graduate from tailored Drama School courses.
55 In *Theatre-Making*, I used the term 'multiprofessionalisation' rather than 'deprofessionalisation', however, I did opt for the latter as one of the tenets of the 21st century theatre-making in a public-facing summary of the book in *Exeunt* magazine (http://exeuntmagazine.com/features/ten-traits-of-theatre-making-in-the-21st-century/). Similarly, the term with its positive connotations can be found in the field via the broad spectrum approach of performance studies in the United States or more specifically in relation to applied theatre and the inherently social value of theatre and performance (see for example Schininà 2004: 17–31).
56 I say the 'eyes' in reference to the ocular-centric approach embroiled with the notions of both theory and theatre.
57 Although the syntagm 'immersive theatre' was introduced by specific artists (Punchdrunk) and amplified by newspaper criticism, it quickly entered the academy (see White 2012, Worthen 2012, Machon 2013).
58 Gareth White's 2013 book too opts for 'participation' as a preferred term, coming in the aftermath of important, sometimes clashing, contributions on spectatorship, relationality, participation, and the social turn in the arts made respectively by Jacques Rancière (2007), Nicolas Bourriaud (1998/2002), Clare Bishop (2006a, 2006b), and Shannon Jackson (2011).
59 The choice of the term 'new works' was influenced by the Arts Council England Theatre Policy 2007 term 'new works' used to designate works of theatre and performance that did not constitute 'new writing' per se.
60 Like White and Alston, perhaps – though unaware of their work being written at the same time – I was interested in works that engendered a more efficacious and equitable relationship with the audience. However, I did include the work of Ontroerend Goed (co-classified by Alston with Punchdrunk as guilty of neoliberalisation) as well as Tim Crouch's *The Author*, and the Croatian company Shadow Casters.
61 Additionally, the explicit communitarian agenda of Shadow Casters' participatory trilogy *On Togetherness*, which was one of my key case studies, led me to somewhat idealistically frame the impulse of these works – via Jean-Luc Nancy's idea of community as divested of the Western essentialism (1991).
62 Further, Kendrick elaborates: 'Aurality encompasses sound and its reception in comingled ways that often means the two cannot be separated—nor should they be. It makes no sense to refer to sound without hearing it, and voices cannot be talked about without engaging the ears upon which they fall' (Kendrick 2017: xxii).
63 In her tribute to Dwight Conquergood, Lisa Merrill has drawn connections between Adriana Caverero's notion of 'sonorous materiality', Walter Ong's claim that 'the spoken word forms human beings into close-knit groups', Roland Barthes' notion of 'the grain of one's voice' and the performance ethnography work of Dwight Conquergood himself in that it 'highlights such embodied community-building by oppressed persons as well as acknowledges the performative and strategic oral code-switching oppressed persons are often enjoined to perform' (Merrill in Conquergood 2013: 323).
64 Conquergood's initial base as a PhD scholar in the 1970s was the School of Speech (formerly School of Oratory) at Northwestern University in Chicago, which later became the home of the strain of Performance Studies rooted in Oral Interpretation identified by Shannon Jackson (2004) as crucial in the formation of the field alongside the New York University's anthropological strain. Conquergood's PhD was in medievalist linguistics on the topic of the Anglo-Saxon 'boast speech' in Beowulf, and this was where, according to Joseph Roach, Conquergood found his 'voice' (in Conquergood 2013: 328–31).

65 For example, Clifford Geertz textocentric idea of culture as an 'ensemble of texts' (1973) which Conquergood criticises again in later works.

66 Conquergood's mission has in many ways inspired the origins of the work presented here too as it also lies at the foundation of my thinking about dramaturgy (Radosavljević 2009).

67 Dorinne Kondo has more recently rejected the notion of 'power-free conversation' in the context of contesting 'power-evasive pluralism' (2018: 40), however, I need to dwell a bit more on the potential of 'disclosure' that Conquergood offers.

68 McAuley also admits that her initial interest that led her to rehearsal ethnography was an interest in the 'genesis of key performance decisions' and that she was 'essentially product- rather than process-oriented' (1998: 78).

69 This process is documented in Desmond's book *Evicted: Poverty and Profit in the American City* (2016), and also in the *Guardian* article: https://www.theguardian.com/books/2016/mar/11/matthew-desmond-the-problem-raging-in-our-cities-milwaukee.

70 Battersea Arts Centre's invention of the form of a 'scratch performance' or 'scratch night' goes back to 1996 when it emerged as a programming idea developed between the then Artistic Director Tom Morris and Improbable theatre (Battersea Arts Centre, 2015).

71 The term was originally proffered by radical feminists of colour as an alternative to the white feminists' totalising notion of sisterhood (Fowlkes 1997) and has been deployed in solidarity by white scholars such as Judith Butler in a range of works from *Gender Trouble* (1990) to *Notes Toward a Performative Theory of Assembly* (2015).

72 I note that I am here opting for the more systematising terms 'network' and 'community' rather than the unruly 'agential entanglement' drawn earlier from Barad and Bleeker et al.. These designations feel more accurate as terminology drawn from my previous work (e.g. the use of 'community' via Jean-Luc Nancy in *Theatre-Making*), while still retaining the idea of agential entanglement at their core and relevance to the current project.

73 For a more formally accomplished example of fugue-like academic thinking under the remit of the A/OD project, see Solakidi (2021).

74 The original idea of scratch performance was linked to developing Improbable's improvised piece *Animo* (1996) in small sections by continuously changing the piece in response to collected audience feedback. Having developed this programming model further, in 2000 BAC presented the first Scratch Night consisting of several short samples of work-in-progress. Famous works developed at BAC over the years which started their lives as ten-minute scratch performances include Richard Thomas and Stewart Lee's *Jerry Springer the Opera* (2003), Kae Tempest's *Brand New Ancients* (2013), and Little Bulb's *Orpheus* (2013). Since then scratch has become a creative methodology widely used by artists, programming venues and festivals in the United Kingdom. BAC has developed and adapted the scratch model to other aspects of their work as a creative organisation, including redevelopment of their building, their education and community work, and their expansion into the digital domain (Battersea Arts Centre, 2015). BAC's scratch has also found application in the museum sector. David Jubb, former producer at BAC who took over the artistic leadership of the organisation (2004–2020), is quoted as defining scratch as 'a way of approaching problems, activities, even organisational structures. It gives you the freedom to fail, the capacity to experiment. It is also an essentially shared and communal process. It allows participants to constantly evaluate their activities and provide critical feedback' (https://creativemuseums.bac.org.uk/content/43478/scratch/scratch, now defunct).

75 The only exception was Silvia Mercuriali's headphone piece *etiquette* made as part of Rotozaza which I had experienced once, seven years previously, in Prague.

76 With our sound producer Tim Bano we considered various recording platform possibilities. The more podcast-appropriate Squadcast and Zencastr were attractive, but I settled for the potentially lesser audio quality of Zoom because of this software's more comprehensive documentation capacity including video and transcript-generation (even though subsequently we determined that human transcription was actually necessary in all cases).

77 From my previous experience of interviewing public figures, I also learnt that it mattered to those I interviewed that their statements came across as coherent and articulate in writing, more so than that they were conveyed verbatim.

78 After careful consideration we decided it was more appropriate to engage our interviewees in a more long-term relationship than to simply get them to sign away their consent as the conventional ethical protocols dictate. For ethical reasons we began by sending each interviewee the Zoom recording and the Zoom-generated transcript and, as promised at the outset of each conversation, we gave the chance to the contributors to retrospectively excise any of the content they wished to remove for whatever reason after the recording was completed. In this way, the contributors were able to contribute to our paper editing process before we arrived at the final cut. As we moved through the process, we found that various contributors were increasingly happy to grant carte blanche on completion of the recording. However, we then also sent each contributor the final edited version of the recording and the transcript of their contribution on the mock up pages of the website when they were nearly ready for publication and invited them to review the materials at this point to suggest any last minute corrections. In each case, we allowed at least four weeks and often more for any feedback from contributors to be collected and implemented before the final version of the material was published and the website officially launched in the week commencing 12 April 2021.

79 Not everybody we approached was willing or available to take part. Some recordings were not taken to the final stages of post-production for various reasons including the artists' consent and quality of the recording, and some contributions, though fascinating in their own right did not resonate with the rest of the sample. For example, the interview with Théâtre sans frontières' co-founders John Cobb and Sarah Kemp about their work with multiple languages and with Robert Lepage on *Lipsynch* (2008) was atypical in its structure because it focused on Lepage more so than on the artists' own work. Consequently, this interview was strategically left aside for inclusion in further research. Similarly, the interviews with Aris Biniaris, Bobo Jelčić, and others, though not featured on the website for technical reasons, do inform the thinking behind this book.

80 At one point, I fantasised about a piece of software that could be built into the artists' computers to record their work-in-progress as a direct replacement for the intended continuous recording and thick description of the creative processes in the rehearsal room. This is of course ethically problematic as it would amount to anxiety-inducing surveillance. We also considered simply featuring samples of creative practice in the Laboratory section of the website, although this too was difficult to circumscribe in terms of selection, qualification, quantification, remuneration, programming politics, etc.

81 This structure was retroactively imposed on the generated material. It is important to note that despite this parallel logic, there is no direct correlation between the materials contained in each themed issue of Lend Me Your Ears on www.auralia.space and the corresponding chapter in this book. This is because I would like to reserve the right to use the process of writing as a process of discovery and further development of ideas. In this respect some bleeding through and across the boundaries of each issue/chapter is bound to occur. In keeping with some of my earlier ideas around methodology, the relationship between the thematically organised primary material and the written publication is therefore one of transformation rather than 'word for word' translation.

Bibliography

Allington, Daniel, Brouillette, Sarah, and Golumbia, David (2016). 'Neoliberal tools (and archives): A political history of digital humanities', LA Review of Books; https://lareviewofbooks.org/article/neoliberal-tools-archives-political-history-digital-humanities/.

Alston, Adam (2013). 'Audience participation and neoliberal value: Risk, agency and responsibility in immersive theatre', *Performance Research: A Journal of the Performing Arts*, 18:2, 128–38, https://doi.org/10.1080/13528165.2013.807177

Alston, Adam (2016). *Beyond Immersive Theatre: Aesthetics, Politics and Productive Participation*, Cham: Palgrave Macmillan.

Anker, Elizabeth S., and Felski, Rita (eds) (2017). *Critique and Postcritique*, Durham and London: Duke University Press.

Auslander, Philip (2012). 'Digital liveness: A historico-philosophical perspective', *PAJ* 102, 3–11.

Bailey, Kate, Broackes, Victoria, and de Visscher, Eric (2019). '"The longer we heard, the more we looked": Music at the Victoria and Albert Museum', *Curator the Museum Journal*, 62:3, 327–41.

Balme, Christopher (2006). 'Audio theatre: The mediatization of theatrical space', in Chapple, Freda and Kattenbelt, Chiel (eds), *Intermediality in Theatre and Performance*, Amsterdam/New York: Rodopi.

Balme, Christopher (2019). *The Globalization of Theatre 1870–1930: The Theatrical Networks of Maurice E. Bandmann*, Cambridge: Cambridge University Press.

Barad, Karen (2007). *Meeting the Universe Halfway. Quantum Physics and the Entanglement of Matter and Meaning*, Durham, NC: Duke University Press.

Barthes, Roland (1967/1977). 'Death of an author', in *Image Music Text*, Fontana Press, London

Battersea Arts Centre (2015). 'Scratch 15', Google Arts & Culture, https://artsandculture.google.com/story/pAVRQ-DJIxwA8A

Bennett, Susan (1990). *Theatre Audiences: A Theory of Production and Reception*, London and New York: Routledge.

Bennett, Susan (2019). *Theory for Theatre Studies: Sound*, London, New York: Methuen.

Bishop, Claire (2006a). 'The Social Turn: Collaboration and Its Discontents', Artforum, 178–85.

Bishop, Claire (2006b). *Participation*, London: Whitechapel Gallery; Cambridge, MA: The MIT Press.

Bjerstedt, Sven (2021). *Storytelling in Jazz and Musicality in Theatre: Through the Mirror*, London: Routledge.

Bleeker, Maaike, Verhoeff, Nana, and Werning, Stefan (2020). 'Sensing data: Encountering data sonifications, materialization, and interactives as *knowledge objects*', *Convergence: The International Journal of Research into New Media Technologies*, 26:5–6, 1–20 (online-generated pdf). doi: https://doi.org/10.1177/1354856520938601

Boenisch, Peter (2006). 'Mediation unfinished: Choreographing intermediality in contemporary dance performance', in Chapple, Freda and Kattenbelt, Chiel (eds), *Intermediality in Theatre and Performance*, Amsterdam/New York: Rodopi.

Boenisch, Peter (2012). 'Acts of spectating: The dramaturgy of the audience's experience in contemporary theatre', *Critical Stages*. https://www.critical-stages.org/7/acts-of-spectating-the-dramaturgy-of-the-audiences-experience-in-contemporary-theatre/

Boenisch, Peter, and Williams, David (eds) (2019). *The Director's Theatre*, London: Macmillan International.

Bouko, Catherine (2010). 'Jazz musicality in postdramatic theatre and the opacity of auditory signs', *Studies in Musical Theatre*, 4:1, 75–87. doi: 10.1386/smt.4.1.75_1

Bourdieu, Pierre et al. (2002). *The Weight of the World: Social Suffering in Contemporary Society*, Cambridge: Polity Press.

Bourriaud, Nicolas (1998/2002). *Relational Aesthetics*, Dijon: Les presses du reel.

Bradby, David, and Williams, David (1988). *Directors' Theatre*, London: Macmillan.

Bradley, Arthur (2011). *Originary Technicity: The Theory of Technology from Marx to Derrida*, Houndmills: Palgrave Macmillan.

Broadhurst, Sue, and Machon, Josephine (eds) (2012). *Identity, Performance and Technology: Practices of Empowerment, Embodiment and Technicity*, Basingstoke: Palgrave.

Brooks, Daphne (2021). *Liner Notes for the Revolution: The Intellectual Life of Black Feminist Sound*, Cambridge, Massachusetts, London, England: The Belknap Press of Harvard University Press.
Brown, Ross (2005). 'The theatre soundscape and the end of noise', *Performance Research*, 10:4, 105–119.
Brown, Ross (2020a). *Sound Effect: The Theatre We Hear*, London: Bloomsbury Methuen.
Brown, Ross (2020b). *The Sound Effect*, manuscript version.
Buchmann, Sabeth, Lafer, Ilse, and Ruhm, Constanze (eds) (2016). *Putting Rehearsals to the Test: Practices of Rehearsal in Fine Arts, Film, Theater, Theory, and Politics*, Berlin: Sternberg Press.
Butler, Judith (1990). *Gender Trouble: Feminism and the Subversion of Identity*, New York/London: Routledge.
Butler, Judith (2015). *Notes toward a Performative Theory of Assembly*, Cambridge MA: Harvard University Press.
Butt, Gavin (2005). *After Criticism: New Responses to Art and Performance*, Oxford: Wiley Blackwell.
Carlson, Marvin (1996). *Performance: A Critical Introduction*, London and New York: Routledge.
Cavarero, Adriana (2005). *For More than One Voice: Toward a Philosophy of Vocal Expression*, Stanford: Stanford University Press.
Chapple, Freda (2006). 'Digital opera: Intermediality, remediation and education', in Chapple, Freda and Kattenbelt, Chiel (eds), *Intermediality in Theatre and Performance*, Amsterdam/New York: Rodopi.
Chapple, Freda and Kattenbelt, Chiel (eds) (2006), *Intermediality in Theatre and Performance*, Amsterdam/New York: Rodopi.
Chatzichristodoulou, Maria, Lavender, Andy, and Nedelkopoulou, Eirini (2017). 'Encountering the digital in performance: Deployment | engagement | trace', *Contemporary Theatre Review*, 27:3.
Conquergood, Dwight (2002). 'Performance studies: Interventions and radical research', *The Drama Review*, 46:2, 151–52.
Conquergood, Dwight (2013). *Cultural Struggles: Performance, Ethnography, Praxis*, edited and introduced by Patrick E. Johnson, Ann Arbor: University of Michigan Press.
Costley, Carol, and Fulton, John (eds) (2018). *Methodologies for Practice Research: Approaches for Professional Doctorates*, London: Sage.
Curtin, Adrian (2014). *Avant-Garde Theatre Sound: Staging Sonic Modernity*, New York: Palgrave.
De Spain, K. (2003). 'The cutting edge of awareness: Reports from the inside of improvisation', in Albright, A.C. and Gere, D. (eds), *Taken by surprise: A dance improvisation reader*, Middletown, CT: Wesleyan University Press.
Demailly, Lise, and de la Broise, Patrice (2009). 'The implications of deprofessionalisation', *OpenEdition Journal*. http://journals.openedition.org/socio-logos/2307; doi: https://doi.org/10.4000/socio-logos.2307
Denzin, Norman (2003). *Performance Ethnography: Critical Pedagogy and the Politics of Culture*, Thousand Oaks: SagePrint.
Derrida, Jacques (1988/1972). 'Signature event context', in Weber, Samuel and Mehlman, Jeffrey (eds), *Limited Inc*, Evanston: Northwestern University Press, pp. 1–23.
Desmond, Matthew (2014). 'Relational ethnography', *Theory and Society*, 43:5, 547–79.
Dobson, James E. (2019). *Critical Digital Humanities: The Search for a Methodology*, Champaign: University of Illinois System.
Eckersall, Peter, Grehan, Helena, and Scheer, Edward (eds) (2017). *New Media Dramaturgy: Performance, Media and New-Materialism*, London: Palgrave Macmillan.

Feld, Steven (2015). 'Acoustemology' in Novak, David and Sakakeeny, Matt (eds), *Keywords in Sound*, Durham, NC: Duke University Press.

Felski, Rita (2015). *The Limits of Critique*, Chicago: University of Chicago Press.

Fisher, Tony, and Gotman, Kélina (eds) (2020). *Foucault's Theatres*, Manchester: Manchester University Press.

Fleming, Peter (2021). *Dark Academia: How Universities Die*, London: Pluto Press.

Flynn, Alex, and Tinius, Jonas (2015). *Anthropology, Theatre, and Development: The Transformative Potential of Performance*, London: Palgrave Macmillan.

Fowlkes, Diane L. (1997). 'Moving from feminist identity politics to coalition politics through a feminist materialist standpoint of intersubjectivity in Gloria Anzaldúa's Borderlands/La Frontera: The new mestiza', *Hypatia*, 12(2), 105–24. http://www.jstor.org/stable/3810472

Frayling, Christopher (1993). 'Research in art and design', Royal College of Arts. http://researchonline.rca.ac.uk/384/3/frayling_research_in_art_and_design_1993.pdf

Friedner, Michele, and Helmreich, Stefan (2012). 'Sound studies meets deaf studies', *The Senses & Society*, 7(1): 72–86. doi: 10.2752/174589312X13173255802120

Foucault, Michel (1961/1965). *Madness and Civilization: A History of Insanity in the Age of Reason*, translated by Richard Howards, New York: Vintage Books, Random House.

Foucault, Michel (1963/1973). *The Birth of the Clinic: An Archaeology of Medical Perception*, translated by Alan Sheridan, London and New York: Routledge.

Foucault, Michel (1966/1970). *The Order of Things: An Archaeology of the Human Sciences*, New York: Pantheon Books.

Foucault, Michel (1969/1998). 'What is an author' in *Aesthetics, Method and Epistemology*, The New Press, New York.

Foucault, Michel (1972). *The Archaeology of Knowledge and the Discourse on Language*, translated by A.M. Sheridan Smith, New York: Pantheon Books.

Galloway, Alexander R. (2014). 'The cybernetic hypothesis', *Differences*, 25:1, 107–31.

Goh, Annie (2016) 'The dimension of sound in Flusser: Implications for a sonic media archaeology' MAP 7 (April), http://www.perfomap.de/map7/media-performance-on-gestures/the-dimension-of-sound-in-flusser-implications-for-a-sonic-media-archaeology/annie-goh-the-dimension-of-sound-in-flusser.pdf

Graff, Gerald (1987). *Professing Literature: An Institutional History*, Chicago and London: The University of Chicago Press.

Grehan, Helena (2019). 'Slow listening', *Performance Research*, 24:8, 53–58. doi: 10.1080/13528165.2019.1718431

Harvie, Jen, and Lavender, Andy (eds) (2010). *Making Contemporary Theatre: International Rehearsal Processes*, Manchester and New York: Manchester University Press.

Heddon, Deirdre (2017). 'The cultivation of entangled listening: An ensemble of more-than-human participants', in Harpin, Anna and Nicholson, Helen (eds), *Performance and Participation: Practices, Audiences, Politics*, Palgrave: Basingstoke, pp. 19–40.

Henriques, Julian (2011). *Sonic Bodies: Reggae Sound Systems, Performance Techniques, and Ways of Knowing*, London and New York: Continuum.

Hessler, Stefanie (2018). *Tidalectics: Imagining an Oceanic Worldview through Art and Science*, Cambridge: Massachusetts Institute of Technology Press.

Home-Cook, George (2015). *Theatre and Aural Attention*, Basingstoke: Palgrave Macmillan.

Hoyle, Eric (2008). 'Changing conceptions of teaching as a profession: Personal reflections' in Johnson, D. and Maclean, R. (eds), *Teaching: Professionalization, Development and Leadership*, Springer, Dordrecht. doi: https://doi.org/10.1007/978-1-4020-8186-6_19

Hunter, Lynnette (2019). *Politics of Practice: A Rhetoric of Performativity*, Cham: Palgrave Macmillan.

Ingold, Tim (2000). *The Perception of the Environment Essays on Livelihood, Dwelling and Skill*, London and New York: Routledge.
Jackson, Shannon (2004). *Professing Performance: Theatre in the Academy from Philology to Performativity*, Cambridge: Cambridge University Press.
Jackson, Shanon (2011). *Social Works: Performing Art, Supporting Publics*, New York and London: Routledge.
Keita, Maghan (2005). 'Africans and Asians: Historiography and the long view of global interaction', *Journal of World History*, 16(1), 1–30. http://www.jstor.org/stable/20079302
Kelly, Mark G.E. (2021). 'Must we cancel Foucault?', *TELOS*. http://www.telospress.com/must-we-cancel-foucault/
Kendrick, Lynne (2017). *Theatre Aurality*, London: Palgrave Macmillan.
Kershaw, Baz, and Nicholson, Helen (2011). *Research Methods in Theatre and Performance*, Edinburgh: Edinburgh University Press.
Klich, Rosemary (2017). 'Amplifying sensory spaces: The in- and out-puts of headphone theatre', *Contemporary Theatre Review*, 27: 3, 366–78. doi: https://doi.org/10.1080/10486801.2017.1343247
Kondo, Dorinne (2018). *Worldmaking: Race, Performance, and the Work of Creativity*, Duke University Press.
Kunst, Bojana (2015). *Artist at Work: Proximity of Art and Capitalism*, Alresford: Zero Books.
Latour, Bruno (2004). 'Why has critique run out of steam? From matters of fact to matters of concern', *Critical Inquiry*, 30:2, 225–48.
Latour, Bruno (2005). *Reassembling the Social: An Introduction to Actor-Network-Theory*, Oxford: Oxford University Press.
Lehmann, Hans-Thies (1999/2006). *Postdramatic Theatre*, translated and introduced by Karen Jürs-Munby, London and New York: Routledge.
Lord, Albert (2000). *The Singer of Tales*, Cambridge MA, London: Harvard University Press.
Machon, Josephine (2009). *(Syn)aesthetics: Redefining Visceral Performance*, London: Palgrave.
Machon, Josephine (2013). *Immersive Theatres*, London: Bloomsbury Red Globe Press.
Mackey, Sally (2016). 'Applied theatre and practice as research: polyphonic conversations', *Research in Drama Education: The Journal of Applied Theatre and Performance*, 21:4, 478–91, doi: 10.1080/13569783.2016.1220250
Maisuria, Alpesh, and Helmes, Svenja (2020). *Life for the Academic in the Neoliberal University*, London: Routledge.
Martin, Carol (ed) (2010). *Dramaturgy of the Real on the World Stage*, Basingstoke and New York: Palgrave Macmillan.
Masura, Nadja (2020). *Digital Theatre: The Making and Meaning of Live Mediated Performance, US & UK 1990-2020*, Cham: Palgrave Macmillan.
McAuley, Gay (1998). 'Towards an ethnography of rehearsal', *New Theatre Quarterly*, 14:1, 75–85.
McAuley, Gay (2006). 'The emerging field of rehearsal studies', *About Performance* 6, 7–13.
McAuley, Gay (2012). *Not Magic but Work: An Ethnographic Account of a Rehearsal Process*, Manchester: Manchester University Press.
Merrill, Lisa (2013). '"Soundscapes of power": Attending to orality, communicating class, and hearing the humor in Dwight Conquergood's "Voice"' in Dwight, Conquergood, *Cultural Struggles: Performance, Ethnography, Praxis*, Ann Arbor, MI: University of Michigan.
Mermikides, Alex, and Smart, Jackie (2010). *Devising in Process*, Basingstoke and New York: Palgrave.
McEachern Yoon, Duncan (no date) 'World literature and the postcolonial: Ngugi's globalectics and Glissand's poetics'. http://www.globalsouthproject.cornell.edu/world-literature-and-the-postcolonial-ngugirsquos-globalectics-and-glissantrsquos-poetics.html

McLuhan, Marshall (1962). *The Gutenberg Galaxy: The Making of Typographic Man*, Toronto: University of Toronto Press.

Midgelow, Vida L. (2020). *Doing Arts Research in a Pandemic*. https://www.theculturecapital exchange.co.uk/wp-content/uploads/2020/06/Doing-Arts-Research-in-a-Pandemic-final-edit.pdf

Moy, Ron (2015). *Authorship Roles in Popular Music: Issues and Debates*, London: Routledge.

Moosavi, Leon (2020). 'The decolonial bandwagon and the dangers of intellectual decolonisation', *International Review of Sociology*, 30:2, 332–54. doi: 10.1080/03906701.2020.1776919

Nancy, Jean-Luc (1991). *The Inoperative Community*, edited by Peter Connor, Minneapolis: University of Minnesota Press.

Nelson, Robin (2013). *Practice as Research in the Arts: Principles, Protocols, Pedagogies, Resistances*, Basingstoke: Palgrave Macmillan.

Ngũgĩ wa Thiong'o (2007). 'Notes towards a performance theory of orature', *Performance Research*, 12:3, 4–7.

Ngũgĩ wa Thiong'o (2012). *Globalectics: Theory and Politics of Knowing*, New York: Columbia University Press.

Ong, Walter (1982/2002). *Orality and Literacy: The Technologizing of the World*, London and New York: Routledge.

Ovadija, Mladen (2013). *Dramaturgy of Sound in the Avant-Garde and Postdramatic Theatre*, Montreal & Kingston, London, Chicago: McGill-Queen's University Press.

Parker-Starbuck, Jennifer (2017). 'Karaoke theatre: Channelling mediated lives', *Contemporary Theatre Review*, 27:3, 379–90. doi: https://doi.org/10.1080/10486801.2017.1343243

Pettitt, Thomas (2010) 'Opening the Gutenberg parenthesis: Media in transition in Shakespeare's England', paper written for Media in Transition 5: *Creativity, Ownership and Collaboration in the Digital Age Conference* at MIT, 27–29 April 2010. http://www.learning ace.com/doc/2629844/ce0901442755af1b46439e4ee6cd269d/pettitt-gutenberg-parenthesis-paper

Porcello, Thomas (2004). 'Afterword', in Porcello, Thomas and Greene, Paul D. (eds), *Wired for Sound: Engineering and Technologies in Sonic Cultures*, Middletown, Connecticut: Wesleyan University Press, pp. 269–81.

Radosavljević, Duška (2009). 'The need to keep moving: Remarks on the place of a dramaturg in 21st century England', *Performance Research: On Dramaturgy*, 14: (3), 45–51. doi: https://doi.org/10.1080/13528160903519500

Radosavljević, Duška (2012). 'Sarah Kane's Illyria as the land of violent love: A Balkan reading of blasted', *Contemporary Theatre Review*, 22:4, 499–511. doi: 10.1080/10486801.2012.718270

Radosavljević, Duška (2013a). *Theatre-Making: Interplay Between Text and Performance in the 21st Century*, Basingstoke: Palgrave Macmillan.

Radosavljević, Duška (2013b). *The Contemporary Ensemble: Interviews with Theatre-Makers*, Abingdon: Routledge.

Radosavljević, Duška (2019). 'The heterarchical director: A model of authorship for the twenty-first century' in Boenisch, Peter, Bradby, David, and Williams, David (eds), *Directors' Theatre*, second edition, London: Palgrave Macmillan Red Globe Press.

Radosavljević, Duška (2020). 'Biljana Srbljanović and Ivana Sajko: Voice in the place of silence', in Delgado, Maria, Lease, Bryce, and Rebellato, Dan (eds), *Contemporary European Playwrights*, London: Routledge.

Rancière, Jacques (2007). *The Emancipated Spectator*, New York: Verso Books.

Rice, Tom (2018). 'Acoustemology' in Hilary Callan (ed.) *The International Encyclopedia of Anthropology*, London: Wiley. (manuscript version on https://exeter.rl.talis.com/items/9FB90856-FF69-3DED-12BB-6CD2DB7A75BF.html)

Ricoeur, Paul (1965/1970). *Freud and Philosophy: An Essay on Interpretation*, translated by Denis Savage (New Haven – London: Yale University Press).

Risam, Roopika (2018). *New Digital Worlds: Postcolonial Digital Humanities in Theory, Praxis, and Pedagogy*, Evanston: Northwestern University Press.

Robinson, Dylan (2020). *Hungry Listening: Resonant Theory for Indigenous Sound Studies*, Minneapolis: University of Minnesota Press.

Roesner, David (2014). *Method and Metaphor in Theatre-Making*, Farnham/Burlington: Ashgate.

Romanska, Magda (2015). *The Routledge Companion to Dramaturgy*, London and New York: Routledge.

Saltz, David Z. (2004). 'Performing arts' in Susan Schreibman, Ray Siemens, and John Unsworth (eds), *A Companion to Digital Humanities*. Oxford: Blackwell. http://www.digitalhumanities.org/companion/

Samuels, David W., Meintjes, Louise, Ochoa, Ana Maria, and Porcello, Thomas (2010). 'Soundscapes: Toward a sounded anthropology', *Annual Review of Anthropology*, 39:1, 329–45.

Sandywell, Barry (2015). 'The medium is the massage', *Information, Communication & Society*, 18:12, 1408–12. doi: 10.1080/1369118X.2013.868021

Savage, Karen, and Symonds, Dominic (2018). *Economies of Collaboration in Performance: More than the Sum of the Parts*, Cham: Palgrave Macmillan.

Schininà, Guglielmo (2004). 'Here we are – Social theatre and some open questions about its developments', *The Drama Review*, 48:3, (T183), 17–31.

Seal, Andrew (2018). 'How the University Became Neoliberal'. https://www.chronicle.com/article/how-the-university-became-neoliberal/

Sedgwick, Eve Kosofsky (2003). *Touching Feeling: Affect, Pedagogy, Performativity*, Durham: Duke University Press.

Shah, Rajni (2021). *Experiments in Listening*, Lanham: Rowman & Littlefield Publishers.

Shepherd, Simon (2012). *Direction*, Basingstoke: Palgrave Macmillan.

Solakidi, Sylvia (2021) 'The Hearing Body in Robert Wilson's and Mikhail Baryshnikov's Letter to a Man' in Pitrolo, Flora, and Radosavljević, Duška (eds) 'Aural/Oral Dramaturgies' (Special Topic), Critical Stages, 24. https://www.critical-stages.org/24/the-hearing-body-in-robert-wilsons-and-mikhail-baryshnikovs-letter-to-a-man/

Sontag, Susan (1966). *Against Interpretation and Other Essays*, New York: Farrar, Straus and Giroux.

Steintrager, James A., and Chow, Rey (2019). *Sound Objects*, London and Durham: Duke University Press.

Stern, Tiffany (2000). *Rehearsal from Shakespeare to Sheridan*, Oxford: OUP.

Sterne, Jonathan (2011). 'The Theology of Sound: A Critique of Orality', *Canadian Journal of Communication*, 36, 207–25.

Stiegler, Bernard (1998). *Technics and Time, 1: The Fault of Epimetheus*, Translated by Richard Beardsworth and George Collins, Stanford: Stanford University Press.

Szatkowski, Janek (2019). *A Theory of Dramaturgy*, London: Routledge.

Thomaidis, Konstantinos (2017). *Theatre and Voice*, London: Palgrave.

Tinius, Jonas (2020). 'Die Ethnografie as methode der theaterwissenschaften?', in Balme, Christopher and Szymanski-Düll, Berenika (eds), *Methoden der Theaterwissenschaft*, Tübingen: Narr Forum Modernes Theater Schriftenreihe, pp. 313–34.

Trencsényi, Katalin, and Cochrane, Bernadette (2014). *New Dramaturgy: International Perspectives on Theory and Practice*, London: Bloomsbury.

Trimingham, Melissa (2002). 'A methodology for practice as research', *Studies in Theatre & Performance*, 22:1, 54–60.

Turner, Cathy, and Synne, Behrndt (2007). *Dramaturgy and Performance*, Basingstoke: Palgrave.

Turner, Cathy (2015). *Dramaturgy and Architecture: Theatre, Utopia and the Built Environment*, Basingstoke: Palgrave Macmillan.

Tynan, Lauren (2021).'What is relationality? Indigenous knowledges, practices and responsibilities with kin', *Cultural Geographies*, 28:4, 597–610. https://doi.org/10.1177/14744740211029287

Verstraete, Pieter (2011). 'Radical Vocality, Auditory Distress and Disembodied Voice: The Resolution of the Voice-Body in The Wooster Group's La Didone', in Kendrick, Lynne and Roesner, David (eds) *Theatre Noise: The Sound of Performance*. Newcastle: Cambridge Scholars Publishing.

Voegelin, Salomé (2014). *Sonic Possible Worlds: Hearing the Continuum of Sound*, London: Bloomsbury.

Wenger, Etienne (1998). *Communities of Practice: Learning, Meaning, and Identity*, Cambridge: CUP.

White, Gareth (2012). 'On immersive theatre', *Theatre Research International*, 37, 221–35.

White, Gareth (2013). *Audience Participation in Theatre: Aesthetics of the Invitation*, Basingstoke: Palgrave.

Woodmansee, Martha (1992).'On the author effect: Recovering collectivity', *Cardozo Arts & Entertainment Law Journal*, 10, 279–92.

Worthen, W.B. (1997). *Shakespeare and the Authority of Performance*, Cambridge: CUP.

Worthen, W.B. (2012) 'The written troubles of the brain: *Sleep no more* and the space for character', *Theatre Journal*, 64, 1, 79–97. doi: 10.1353/tj.2012.0017

Worthen, W.B. (2020). *Shakespeare, Technicity, Performance*, Cambridge: CUP.

Woynarski, Lisa (2020). *Ecodramaturgies: Theatre, Performance and Climate Change*, Cham: Palgrave Macmillan.

2
POST-VERBATIM

'If I had my way', wrote Matt Trueman, the then theatre critic of London's portal *What's On Stage,* 'verbatim would be "verboten"' (Trueman 2018). This injunctionary play on words[1] indicated a saturation with the form which in the preceding 20 years became so ubiquitous in British theatre that, as Trueman put it, 'too often, verbatim theatre for[got] to be theatre'. Trueman complained of often conspicuous editorial interventions, the interviewer-interviewee power imbalance, the 'violence of appropriating the voices of others', and of the ways in which the use of collected testimonies from various demographics for purposes of theatre production was increasingly leading to superficial and lazy outcomes:

> Verbatim theatre has to be more than journalism. It must do more than a documentary. Otherwise, why not let people speak for themselves? Give them space instead of taking their words.
>
> (Trueman 2018)

Though much has been written about verbatim theatre in recent scholarship (Hammond and Steward 2008, Radosavljević 2013, Martin 2010, 2013, Wake 2014, Inchley 2015, McCormack 2018, Stuart Fisher 2020, Garson 2021), it is worth briefly revisiting some of the most relevant aspects of this form before proceeding to focus on ways in which the boundaries of the term 'verbatim theatre' and its denotations are being redefined and/or left behind by theatre- and performance-makers in pursuit of conceptual and formal alternatives. Interestingly, 'post-verbatim', as I will argue in this chapter, also inadvertently engages in 'giving space' though maybe not in the way that Trueman asks for above.

I previously analysed verbatim theatre as a mode of authorship whose dynamic reconfiguring of the pre-existing text/performance relationships enhances the engagement of the audience and the political and social significance of theatre

DOI: 10.4324/9781003096337-2

(Radosavljević 2013). Picking up on some underexplored strands of this previous enquiry, here I will investigate more closely the ethnographic provenance of Anna Deavere Smith's method of working in an attempt to pinpoint some key reasons behind its enduring effectiveness. Having previously only read about Smith's work, my thinking is now informed by a first-hand experience of seeing *Notes from the Field* (2018) which gave me an insight into the specific mode of authority contained in Smith's 'distinctive virtuosity' (Worthen 1997: 86).

> Anna Deavere Smith literally steps into another pair of shoes to channel one of her many real-life characters onto the stage. Sometimes she remains barefoot, and sometimes she surreptitiously adds small garments to suggest archetypes – such as a cloak for a pastor or a hoodie for a street protester. Throughout most of the first half of this show, she also wears brocade trousers with sewn- on patches down the front of her legs. The patches, made of the same material as the trousers, are quite conspicuous, almost ornamental. This approach to costuming choices (designed by Ann Hould-Ward) acts as a kind of metaphor for the author's methodological approach too – dynamic, versatile, exact, raw, and stylistically detailed.
>
> (Radosavljević, see Appendix 2.1 for full text)

My first impressions quoted here are in sync with Trueman's whose article above juxtaposes his disillusionment with verbatim theatre more generally with unreserved admiration for the specific way Smith makes the form 'count': by showing how 'to embody' is 'to empathise' (op.cit.). The way in which the visual design of the performance metaphorises and manifests the work's creative methodology which I found striking (Figure 2.1) is not dissimilar from the way in which Trueman perceives Smith's acting as making both the actor and the character visible at the same time.

Operating under the assumption that innovation presupposes an element of continuity as well as change, I consider 'post-verbatim' genealogically connected to verbatim theatre itself.[2] The main intention here is to recognise the epistemological significance of the artist-led transformation of practice rather than to engage in taxonomy, or coinage of terms.

Following a brief recap on the genealogies of verbatim theatre, this chapter derives a workable definition of 'post-verbatim' in three inter-related ways: (1) by distilling the underlying features of Anna Deavere Smith's continuously poetically[3] effective performative ethnography via social scientist Norman Denzin, (2) by isolating the notion of counterpoint as a necessary dramaturgical principle in engendering intersubjective audience engagement within the use of multi-voiced material, and (3) by teasing out key themes emerging compositely from the testimonies and conversations collected in LMYE #2 Post-Verbatim sample as part of the A/OD project. According to the key overarching questions of this project, my analytical focus is on compositional strategies, interdisciplinary connections, and the role of technology in the dramaturgies of speech and sound.

FIGURE 2.1 *Notes from The Field* (2018) by Anna Deavere Smith
Photo: Joan Marcus

By extension, the focus is also on the anthropological 'technicity of theatre' (Worthen 2020) and its socio-political potential for collective critique.

Genealogies of Verbatim Theatre: A Brief Recap and an Ethnographic Addendum

Although varieties of documentary theatre exist in many theatre-making cultures, including most prominently the United States and Germany,[4] 'verbatim theatre' as a specific form of documentary theatre evolved in the United Kingdom between the 1960s and the early 2000s when it actually permeated the mainstream and began to gain international influence. This exertion of influence occurred partly thanks to the enterprising workshop programmes of the International Department of London's Royal Court theatre and partly thanks to direct adoption of anglophone theatre vocabulary and practices in other English-speaking parts of the world, such as Australia, the United States, and South Africa.

The term was first used by the British scholar Derek Paget in 1987 to describe the practices of collective authorship by means of real-life testimonies at the Victoria Theatre in Stoke-on-Trent in the mid-to-late 1960s, led by director Peter Cheeseman. According to Paget, the form was in turn inspired by specific BBC radio documentary practices of the late 1950s and early 1960s, whose crowning example was Joan Littlewood's documentary musical *Oh, What a*

Lovely War, initiated as a radio project (1961) and later evolving into a stage play (1963) and film (1969). This frequently recounted aspect of verbatim theatre's origin story via radio (see also Stuart Fisher 2020: 69) acquires additional relevance in the present context, particularly the ways in which its development has been aided by the sound recording and broadcasting technologies that also gave birth to the field of Sound Studies.

Increased mediatisation of the society has already been established as a factor in the emergence of verbatim theatre (Forsyth and Megson 2009). This includes the postmodern technologisation of knowledge (Martin 2010) and the gaps in the coverage of current affairs caused by the limitations of libel laws (Luckhurst in Holdsworth and Luckhurst 2008). Significantly for this study's concern with technology, Australian scholar Caroline Wake has developed new relevant ideas around the 'imbrication of life, media and performance' by observing and naming the mode of 'mediatized listening' (2014: 95) within verbatim theatre, which ultimately 'enables the audience to listen to how the media listen' (2014: 82). In other words, theatre's meta-perspective on society is deployed to show 'how media industries, media technologies and media practices intersect and diverge' rather than simply just filling the gap left out by the litigation-averse media coverage (2014: 95). By extension, Wake sees the specific form of 'headphone verbatim' (associated in Australia with Roslyn Oades and similar to UK-based Alecky Blythe's 'recorded delivery' method)[5] as a way of not just giving 'the voice to the voiceless' but as giving a 'reflexivity to the proceedings that encourages the audience to contemplate how our culture of communication(s) is produced in the first place' (2014: 83). Thus Wake significantly moves the focus of our understanding of verbatim theatre away from its perceived concern with speech, or processes of production, and towards a theoretical and practical concern with listening itself, or the processes of reception.

The term 'verbatim theatre' did not immediately catch on when it was proposed by Paget in 1987, possibly also because of a temporary discontinuation of the trend. Thus in a more recent article, Paget placed verbatim theatre within the 'rhizomatic', perpetually 'interrupted' and 'broken tradition' of left wing, alternative theatre (in Forsyth and Megson 2009). Reflecting on its more current manifestations in the early 2000s, Paget is strict in distinguishing the form of verbatim theatre from the other documentary theatre genre in the United Kingdom – tribunal play, more closely characterised by the use of written records, character acting, and realist mise-en-scene of a Stanislavskian/representational affiliation. By contrast, according to Paget, verbatim uses the presentational, Brechtian/Piscatorian theatrical rhetoric consisting of appropriate visual signifiers (placards, slides, film or computer-based visuals), aural content (pre-recorded speech and song transmitted on the stage), and 'emblematic', 'deliberately 2-D' acting techniques required by documentary theatre (2009: 229).[6] Paget focuses on Out of Joint's production of David Hare's *The Permanent Way* (2003) as an example to discuss in more detail, even though he qualifies the company's research-led script-development methodology as 'quasi-verbatim' because the words of the interviewees are not mechanically recorded but relayed via the actors' embodied recounting of the interviews. It is worth noting that Paget's taxonomisation does not play out so neatly in practice which continues to generate new variations of documentary theatre.

My interest in revisiting this article in some detail here connects to the problem of historiographic blanks and the lack of documentation of artistic methodology perceived by Paget,[7] which, in my view, enhances the need for an artist-centred research methodology as outlined in the Introduction(s) – capable of informing academic research and at the same time promoting and normalising the processes of reflection, documented transmission, and articulation of artistic methodologies as part of artistic practice. Additionally, as I have outlined in *Theatre-Making* (2013), I am interested in how we can historicise the development of methodological processes not so much along the pre-existing binary lines of the mainstream vs the alternative reinforced by Paget, but by perceiving this process as more nuanced, dynamically enmeshed, and dialectical in its course. Precisely in order not to devalue the efforts of those who confronted difficulties and limitations to forge the alternative theatre scene in the United Kingdom from the 1960s onwards, it is necessary to recognise the ways in which the alternative, counter-cultural, and marginalised artistic trends are capable of permeating and influencing the mainstream and rendering the established binaries obsolete.[8]

A parallel documentary theatre tradition evolving in the United States at the cross-section with ethnography, to which Anna Deavere Smith's work belongs, can also be seen to have contributed towards the revival of verbatim theatre in the United Kingdom in the early 2000s. In his book *Ethnotheatre* (2011), American theatre scholar Johnny Saldaña designates Smith as the 'superstar' of the genre who crystallised its form and 'demonstrated its artistic possibilities and social impact for both the academic and commercial worlds' (2011: 17). Saldaña credits Smith's training as a classical actor for her attunement to the intricacies of language and her social consciousness for her choice of subject matter. Her highly acclaimed early works using the ethnographic research method of interview in the process of making solo performance – *Fires in the Mirror* (1993) and *Twilight: Los Angeles, 1992* (1994) – were about the race riots in Brooklyn and LA, respectively. Literature scholar, Naomi Matsuoka (2002), notes that Smith's method was influenced by her admiration for the oral histories of Studs Terkel, the 1985 Pulitzer Prize winner for his book of interviews *The Good War*. Smith's body of work is frequently summarised by commentators, in an echo of her own stated intentions perhaps, as an attempt at capturing the 'American character' through language. It is important to note that Smith's chosen methodology for this task of capturing the composite American character – envisaged as an emergent entity – entails a process of aggregation and juxtaposition of material. Additionally, according to Dorinne Kondo, one of Smith's four dramaturgs on *Twilight* (1994), this is not a process that presupposes 'harmony', power-free relations, or unity of interpretation, but work that crucially contests existing models of liberal pluralism and multiculturalism, thus breaking new ground in the processes of consensus negotiation:

> In *Twilight*, we exceeded the representation of marginalized 'communities', performing an agonistics that upended the fundamental assumptions of liberal pluralist theater, its 'distribution of the sensible'
> (Kondo 2018: 131)

Unlike the work of ethnographic scholars explored in the Introduction(s), Smith's ethnographic practice is rooted within a primarily poetic rather than a scientific paradigm. My use of the term poetic here indicates both a concern with 'making' (cf. 'poeisis') and 'poetry'. Saldaña highlights Smith's belief that her interviewees speak in 'organic poems' and her texts are arranged on the page, when printed, in the form of poetry.[9] In an interview Smith gave to Richard Schechner in 2018, she explained that having conducted over 250 interviews around a specific topic, she may choose only a fraction of the testimonies to work with in the final version, based on 'care' for specific subjects or a desire to 'pay attention' to a specific point of view (2018: 47). It is a process which Wake perceives in her analysis of Smith's work as a particularly rigorous 'style of listening' – 'exacting to the point of being exhausting' (2013: 326).[10] However, Smith adamantly describes her editorial approach as based on feeling rather than opinion,[11] and the underlying intention is to 'help people in the audience ponder how they are connected' (Smith in Schechner 2018: 43). Like many other artists using verbatim testimony in theatre-making, Smith focuses on the failures of language (hesitations, repetitions, convolutions, errors, self-corrections) in her interviews as valuable portals to points of significance, poetry, or the final outcome.[12] This is rooted in Smith's belief that 'story is more than words: the story is its rhythms and its breaths' (Smith quoted in Saldaña 2011: 72). In the context of the A/OD project, this aspect of prosody, or the musicality of speech, requires underlining as a key generative aspect of Smith's methodology which holds particular significance for (post)verbatim theatre and for knowledge creation more broadly.

In the Introduction(s), I noted the potential relevance of ethnographic research methods to theatre and performance research. Despite the customary overreliance of this epistemic discipline on the research frameworks and methods of others, social scientist Norman Denzin has conversely taken inspiration from theatre and performance, and specifically Anne Deavere Smith, in his reconfiguration of ethnographic methodology which leans towards performative critique. For this reason, and because he is surprisingly rarely studied in the context of verbatim theatre,[13] it is worth dedicating a section to his pursuit.

Reconfiguring Critique through Performative Ethnography

In his 1997 book *Interpretive Ethnography*, Norman Denzin testifies to being influenced by Johannes Birringer's understanding of performance as a social practice that grapples with the influence of postmodern technologies on the embodied engagement with reality. Denzin perceives the epistemic field of ethnography as constantly changing and situates his enquiry always already on the verge of the future. Inspired by poststructuralism as well as the ideas of dialogic imagination and multiplicity of perspectives derived from Mikhail Bakhtin (1895–1975), Denzin's consequent propositions of 'messy ethnographic texts' – 'many sited', 'open ended', 'multivoiced' – are intended to problematise the predominating notions of realism and authority in existing ethnographic practices (1997: xvii). More specifically, in a way reminiscent of Cavarero, Denzin is sceptical about the ocular-centric authority of the 'voyeuristic cultural critic' and 'the politics of resistance that they attempt to write' (1997: xix). Instead, he seeks to establish an ethnographic epistemology going beyond vision and mimesis – 'an evocative epistemology that performs, rather than represents, the world' (1997: xvii). This new epistemology 'goes beyond the ocular based systems of knowing' and emphasises the other senses, 'especially hearing (the acoustical eye)' (1997: xix).

In this respect, he is particularly interested in oral performance of ethnographic records and their potential for 'overcoming the biases of an ocular, visual epistemology' because they destabilise the voyeuristic eye and bring the audience and performers into a 'shared field of experience' (1997: 94). Like Derek Paget (2009), Denzin also distinguishes between two 'generic performance aesthetics' – representational and presentational theatre-, and he favours the latter where 'the emphasis is on stylization, not realism' and 'there is no attempt to dissolve the performer into the role' (1997: 98). The less text-centric, more audience-centric, improvisational presentational mode, is also, according to Denzin, more capable of critique by virtue of offering a more participatory role to the audience: '[a]udiences complete performances by being there for the performance, they participate in mute dialogue' (1997: 101). This dialogic relationship remains central to Denzin's later work, where he more explicitly engages with 'co-performance' between audience and performer in the context of performative social science (2003: ix).[14] Denzin's dialogic, collaborative, performative, experiential idea of critique provides a crucial alternative to the heritage of critique highlighted as increasingly problematic in the 21st century by Latour (2004), Felski (2015), and others. Denzin's model implies that the more valuable agent of critique is the collective, heterogeneous, non-unanimous body of the audience rather than the singular appointed voyeuristic figure of a critic.

Crucially, Denzin uses the work of Anna Deavere Smith – specifically *Fires in the Mirror* (1993) and *Twilight: Los Angeles, 1992* (1994) – to refine his idea of 'performance ethnography'. Inspired by Smith, he expands the existing repertoire of qualitative methods by proposing the form of 'postmodern interview', based on the methodology of collage, montage, and fracture of linearity or causality. In the postmodern interview '[p]oints of view and style collide, switch back and forth, commingle' to produce 'an emotional, gestalt effect', likened to cubism, pentimento, and jazz for their shared ability to create a new composite effect from individual effects by various means (2003: 87). This principle is illustrated through the work of Anna Deavere Smith in a two-fold way. On the one hand, there is Smith's own technique of writing performance texts by collaging together testimonies which represent diverse points of view on a specific dramatic event and thus creating a space to bring together 'people who would not normally be together' (2003: 92). On the other hand, there is also an attempted account of Smith's specific methodology which is motivated by a number of interrelated intentions: (1) to capture 'American character' (2003: 87),[15] (2) to create theatre that includes previously excluded characters, (3) to create mirrors and criticise the society (2003: 90), (4) to listen, capture, and reperform the manner of speech as a way of evoking the character of the person speaking (2003: 90),[16] (5) to create 'an atmosphere in which the interviewee would experience his/her own authorship' (Smith in Denzin 2003: 91), (6) to address the difficult questions of politics of representation 'Who can speak for whom?', and – by cumulative composite effect of all of these means – (7) to expand further the ideas of creating a vocabulary for racial politics and the means for emancipation and social justice.

While Smith's use of collage, fracture of linear logic, and jazz to create an emotional gestalt effect are already noted by theatre scholars, Denzin additionally highlights the political significance of the encounter between those whose lives co-author and co-authorise the work. As articulated in a more recent contribution to the *Handbook of Arts-Based Research*, the poetic-performative aspect derived from documentary evidence is, according to Denzin, ultimately far more potent than the purely scientific one in 'chang[ing] the way we think about people and their lives': 'The poet makes the world visible in new and different ways, in ways ordinary social science writing does not allow' (Denzin in Leavy 2018: 682).

Additionally, the composite effect of Denzin's own writing, I argue, is a reconfiguring of the notion of social critique itself. The positioning of a performative, experiential, acoustical, and dialogic epistemology in opposition to the written, voyeuristic, ocular-centric, monologic one also reveals associations of the latter with the problematic aspects of the heritage of critique. The German Enlightenment method, associated with Immanuel Kant and his critics and followers, was primarily aimed at using autonomous analytical reasoning skills to question and resist the perpetuation of hegemonic assumptions of the religious and political authorities of the day. This model of critique is also tied in with the model of authority and authorship predominating at the time, which, as noted in the discussion that follows, is characterised by a monologic authorial consciousness, rather than the dialogic one that Denzin promotes in the aftermath of postmodernism. Ultimately, Denzin perceives performance as a generative form of cultural critique because dialogue or 'co-performance' – between the performer and the audience – is intrinsic to it.[17]

Here an important insight arises for the A/OD project: the problem is not critique itself, but the so-far predominating voyeuristic, texto-centric, hierarchical, and ocular-centric tools of the critic.

Consequently, it is necessary to ask: what are the potential alternative workings of the performative, experiential, collective, acoustical critique in contemporary theatre?

Counterpoint: A Performative Intervention

This section is titled 'counterpoint' both for reasons of form and content as the discussion now moves towards examples of post-verbatim theatre, which similarly to Smith's work emphasise the musicality of speech as a source of content capable of critique. The choice of the term counterpoint is deliberate and significant on a number of levels – in addition to its continued invocation of musicality as an inherent feature of contemporary theatre-making (Radosavljević 2013: 105–17), it also conceptually enacts the related notions of dialectics and polyphony without being limited to either of them.

Encyclopaedia Britannica defines counterpoint as juxtaposition of two or more different melodic lines in a necessarily harmonious way. Britannica notes that counterpoint is sometimes mistakenly used interchangeably with 'polyphony', while the Grove Dictionary of Music further clarifies that counterpoint is actually a 'means' to achieving the 'end' of polyphony, thus implying its status of technicity.[18]

Although counterpoint and polyphony are explored here in relation to post-dramatic theatre, their relevance is not restricted to contemporary performance practice.[19] Mikhail Bakhtin used the musicological term 'polyphony' as a means of advancing his groundbreaking idea of 'dialogic imagination' on the example of Fyodor Dostoyevsky's novels in two versions of his essay 'Problems of Dostoyevsky's Poetics' (1929 and 1963). Importantly in this work, Bakhtin uses the term polyphony to illustrate the way in which, for the first time in the history of the novel, and in contrast to a previously monologic authorial consciousness, Dostoyevsky's characters appear as autonomous ethical, freely acting subjects rather than being subjected to authorial control. As summarised by Liisa Steinby:

> The polyphonic or polysubjective novel is thus defined by the manner in which the characters, or 'heroes', appear in the novel: the ethically acting individuals do not have any 'finalized form' given to them by another subject (the author), but they appear only through their action and their consciousness, as expressed in their speech.
>
> (Steinby 2013: 39)

In terms of the author's relation to the characters, Steinby reports that a process of 'co-experiencing' the world is at work (2013: 38). This notion of polyphony, according to Steinby, refers to an equality of voices and is 'person-related' (2013: 40) rather than speech-related, in contrast to Bakhtin's later term 'heteroglossia'. This important distinction implies that, unlike heteroglossia which denotes different registers of speech in fiction, polyphony carries the potential to convey polysubjectivity and intersubjectivity – notions useful in the context of theatre-making too. Steinby further notes that this analogy to musical composition was deployed by Bakhtin as a metaphorical designation of a compositional approach in literature but, significantly, also functioned as an expression of an internalised formative influence of the German Romanticism on his intellectual outlook and training. This is an important aspect of Liisa Steinby and Tintti Klapuri's project which re-reads and re-contextualises Bakhtin's work in the 21st century with a view to its genealogies rather than its association with formalism and poststructuralism with which its initial reception in the West coincided. In reading Bakhtin's idea of polyphony by reference to Friedrich Schlegel (1772–1829), Steinby further clarifies significant differences between the two conceptions of analogy concerning music and literature. On the one hand, while in music it is the Romantic composer that always determines the structure of the work, in Bakhtin's polyphonic novel the characters do so, because the author's role is reduced. On the other hand, there is a crucial difference in what forms the basic unit of an artwork: 'for Bakhtin, the basic unit in a polyphonic novel is a human voice', and 'in Schlegel's view the basic units of the musical composition of a literary work of art are themes' (Steinby 2013: 44). Several scholars have recently resorted to 'heteroglossia' as an important means of discussing authorship in theatre and performance (McCormack 2018, Jestrovic 2020, Lech 2021), inspired in turn by Marvin Carlson (2006), Helena Buffery (2013), and Cristina Marinetti (2018) thinking about heteroglossia in relation to translation. However, despite the term's capacity to convey pluralism within speech and language, as highlighted by many of these authors, heteroglossia retains a certain linguistic bias. I focus here instead on the potential of polyphony and its constitutive tool, counterpoint, to encapsulate the dialectics contained in the multi-modal semantics of theatre.[20]

As part of his interest in the musicalisation of theatre-making, David Roesner has considered polyphony as a strategy of 'de-hierarchisation' of theatrical means (2008). He is particularly interested in how German-speaking directors such as Heiner Goebbels and Christoph Marthaler deploy musicalisation and their use of polyphony not as a structuring device but as a means of freeing the work from logocentrism, the hegemony of text and character, and the 'semiotic compulsion'. This ultimately bestows greater autonomy on various meaning-making tools and personnel of theatre and allows the audience to 'widen and reflect on their own modes of perception and observation' (2008: 44) by engaging with a 'playful multiplicity of conjunctions and confrontations' (2008: 51) and without the obligation to work out 'what it means'. More recently, Roesner has developed his thinking in relation specifically to 'simultaneity' as an aspect of polyphony and how his previously proposed notion of musicality functions as a dispositif in theatre-making (2014: 36).[21] I adopt these contextual aspects of polyphony in theatre-making as I proceed to focus more specifically on the semantic significance of counterpoint in relation to audience reception or 'co-performance' in watching verbatim theatre.

The metaphor of theatre appears attractive in theoretical considerations of the processes of reception, of music and literature alike. Adorno's Hegelian idea of music as a 'dynamic totality' engages the listener in an 'internal world theatre' (1998: 101). Similarly, Bakhtin writes of a participatory equality between the author, the 'performers of the text (if they exist)', and the readers or listeners who 'recreate and in so doing renew the text' (1981: 253). Though these conceptions imply different levels of the listener/reader's agency, both of the described processes are metaphorical or hypothetical. The actual corporeal co-presence of the artist and the audience in a theatre opens up a different potential for dialogue, even when this dialogue is incommensurable, non-verbal, or merely consisting of an affective exchange. Following Schlegel's thinking about the basic units of music and literature, the question arises: what might be considered a basic unit of live performance? Aristotle offered 'action', but this might be up for discussion in the context of postdramatic theatre of speech and sound. Perhaps one potential answer is 'call and response' – an unanticipated antiphonic example of Denzinian 'co-performance' – proposed by Mirčev and Henriques (LMYE Salon#1)?

Needless to say, polyphony is not just a random layering of individual voices or melodic lines. An interesting perspective on the juxtaposition of documentary material and music is provided by Fred Moten in his essay 'Quasi una fantasia' where he discusses François Girard's *Thirty Two Short Films about Glenn Gould*. Moten reminds that an element 'understood to be essential to documentation' (2017: 41) is linear temporality, and yet, music itself, in the sense of Adorno's 'dynamic totality', 'is understood to move and work in excess of linear sequence' (2017: 40). Additionally, Moten explains via Adorno that music contains a temporal seriality that offers scope for restructuring by contrapuntal means, the key example being Beethoven's op. 27 – 'quasi una fantasia' – whereby 'fantasy refers to a mode of polyphonic composition that is at once improvisatory, transportive (of composer, performer, and listener), and montagic (not only in its sequencing of musical sections that are not thematically connected but in its yoking together of seemingly disparate emotional contents)' (2017: 40). Moten's analysis of the counterpoint in music and documentary material is directly relevant to understanding the musicality of spoken documentary text, working in 'excess of linear sequence'.

For the needs of the present study concerned with embodied performance rather than strictly musical, literary, or cinematic experience, I think of polyphony's constituent counterpoint as a means of constructing a multi-faceted process of call and response with (the multiple subjectivities of) the audience. On the affective level, it is possible to think of this dialogue by reference to the notion of entrainment – our innate ability as a species to biologically respond to rhythm. In this, I take specifically the social aspect of entrainment[22] described by Gary Tomlinson (2015) as 'the loose structuring of human interactions according to broad rhythms of turn taking, where breaks in the pattern constitute disruptions in expectation with affective and communicative consequences' (2015: 79). George Home-Cook has similarly outlined the phenomenological intricacies of the processes of audience attention in theatre noting its 'embodied, enactive and intersensorial' aspects in 'shaping' meaning (2015: 170). On a meaning-making level, I am interested in how a structural counterpoint within a piece of performance configures the audience's attention in a way analogous to experiencing music but simultaneously accounting for non-musical content too. Unlike in music where the response can be primarily affective, theatre can generate its own counterpoint between the affective and the rational experience. By this I mean the opportunity for an individual audience member to simultaneously experience affective displeasure and the intellectual closure predicated on it.[23] I propose that in order for this dialogic process between a work of theatre and the audience to occur, the work must offer opportunities for 'turn taking', 'breaks in the pattern', and 'disruptions in expectation with affective and communicative consequences' (Tomlinson ibid.).[24] In other words, the work must create space for the audience's co-creation of meaning to occur. As hinted by Bakhtin, polyphony and, I would say, specifically counterpoint, has the potential to create this space, as will be shown in the example of Nic Green's *Cock and Bull* (2017).

For illustration drawn from theatre-making practice, Bella Merlin (2007) refers to counterpoint as a means of accessing meaning as an actor in working on the verbatim production of *The Permanent Way* (2003). She uses the term to describe how she approaches 'embodying the spirit' of her interviewee through a counterpoint between her subject's physicality and their emotional state (2007: 43). The same principle is at work when she later describes a particularly productive moment in the process of actioning, whereby her replacing the action 'to appal' with 'to amuse' delivered a more effective result because it 'ensured that [the] tension between "action" and "intention" was maintained' (2007: 46). Merlin's use of the term 'counterpoint' implies a certain degree of intuitive interpretation; however, it is this measured juxtaposition that in my mind creates a semantic gap or a space to engage the audience in the process of co-creation of meaning. The counterpoint represents a necessary cognitive dissonance or disruption that will engage the audience to make sense of it. Merlin calls her approach 'responsive listening' which is a process she deploys in interviewing her subjects but also, crucially, which she seeks to engender in her audience. In line with Home-Cook (2015), Wake (2014), and Jean-Luc Nancy (2007),[25] ideas on embodied listening become important here and they evoke the theatrical potential of Feld's 'acoustemology'. In all of these cases a form of intersubjective dialogue is at work between the content being presented and the audience's act of attending.

Bella Merlin and David Roesner have explored together their shared interest in the musicality of verbatim theatre. Their 2018 'meta-musical experiment' was a practice-research investigation of musicalisation strategies in working with verbatim material. Perhaps the most important aspect to take forward from this work is the question of 'loyalty' to the 'original' that emerged in attending to the compositional potential of gathered testimonies and confronting the inevitability of the constructed nature of any documentary artform. Roesner and Merlin resolve the question of loyalty through the idea that the only accurate account of something exists within the workings of a 'multilayered and multivocal' approach (2018). This is certainly an idea that evokes Smith and Denzin again.

In understanding verbatim theatre's potential to deploy the use of documentary material in a way that affirms and expands its complex efficiencies as primarily theatre, it is paramount to observe the inherently dialectic nature of this form (which can contain document and fabrication, listening and speaking, reporting and imagination), and a simultaneous contrapuntal interest in both the semantic status of the spoken word and its musical, intuitive, and poetic rendering in performance-making. I use the term 'dialectic' as a reiteration of my stated commitment towards embracing contradictions, and the term 'counterpoint' as an expression of interest in the generative spaces found in between the contradictions that the layering of the simultaneous polyphonies offers. Bakhtinian notions of the 'dialogism' and 'heteroglossia' might be similarly relevant in the way that they contain notions of plurality and tension. As will be shown later, key terms for the dramaturgies of speech and sound also include 'collage' and 'montage' and at this point of transition towards analysis of the data, it is appropriate to end on a performance-specific idea of the 'vocal assemblage' proposed by Konstantinos Thomaidis in a dialogue with Brandon LaBelle in LMYE Salon #2:

> **KT:** I have been toying with this idea – and that's a dramaturgical device as well as perhaps a theoretical device – of the 'vocal assemblage'. That as you voice you might be thinking about your voice because you do a kind of reduction: 'Okay, here is Konstantinos' voice', but at the same time you hear Brandon's silence or the way he will respond, and you hear the technology and you hear the devices. So it's always co-constituted, it's co-devised. […] it's internal/external, if that makes sense?
> **BL:** Yes. [T]hat's wonderful. I really love this idea of the 'vocal assemblage' […] This co-constitution and maybe this takes us back a bit to the earlier reflection about the performance of the voice being 'me and not me', being 'I and not I'. The way in which the voice authenticates us. And it makes me think about Adriana Cavarero [2005] and her insistence on the voice giving a certain articulation to the uniqueness of oneself (2021: 7–8).

Towards Post-Verbatim Theatre: Holding onto Contradictions

The idea of 'post-verbatim' theatre occurred to me in the process of watching Nic Green's *Cock and Bull* at the South Bank Centre in London in April 2017. Like some of the pre-existing body of work designated as verbatim, *Cock and Bull* (2017) took as its departure point the documentation of spoken words. In this case, specifically, the source of verbal material were the political speeches delivered at the 2014 Conservative Party conference in Birmingham. However, *Cock and Bull* combines vocal and dance performance and its main means of expression is an embodied rather than a primarily verbal rendition of the found material. *Cock and Bull* unequivocally commits to the performance aesthetic defined by both Paget (2009) and Denzin (1997, 2003), respectively, as 'presentational', highly 'stylised' and 'emblematic', and as conveying the musicality as well as the semantics of the verbal content of its source texts. The musicalisation of the material serves the creation of an affective engagement, and the source text is still integral to the semantic content of the piece, only the main intention of the artist in processing the text for performance here is critique, rather than 'loyalty'.

I have previously noted that the issue of performance-to-text fidelity (the term I chose instead of loyalty following the adaptation studies vocabulary) is most easily resolved in the medium of non-verbal performance (2013: 70–1), as illustrated by the dance adaptations of novels which draw attention to the non-verbal renderings of the text rather than the depiction of story, character or dialogue. Complementary to this is André Gerber's argument that, by resorting specifically to Denzin's idea of non-mimetic, presentational, postmodern performance aesthetic, theatre has the unique potential to deploy 'visual metaphor' as a means of communicating the 'unsayable'[26] in the verbatim data 'without ethically undermining the intent of the original utterances themselves' (2019: 5). It is interesting therefore that in a series of attempts at verbatim theatre – *To Be Straight with You* (2007–2009), *Can We Talk about This?* (2011–12), *John* (2014–15) – the acclaimed dance company DV8, led by Lloyd Newson, opted for a substantial use of spoken testimonies in conjunction with a movement choreography and other stage effects. Jess McCormack (2018), conducts a thorough analysis of the use of verbatim testimonies in these works, and significantly, she deploys a Bakhtinian, heteroglossic understanding of the processes of translation involved in such performance-making. In an initial contextualising analysis of a brief section from *To Be Straight with You*, McCormack illustrates how the simultaneous performance of the verbatim speech and its movement translation on stage – consisting of deliberate choices in relation to the rhythm of movement and specific uses of different aspects of physicality of the dancer(s) in the space – invokes several simultaneous 'voices' or several layers of core meaning-making, and thus creates a positive example of heteroglossic performance which, as per Bakhtin's ideals, challenges the existence of a monologic authoritative voice (2018:20–2). In a following chapter, McCormack further cites a polemic between choreographer Lloyd Newson and broadcaster Kenan Malik, who had provided a testimony for the making of DV8's *Can We Talk about This?*. The polemic concerns the relationship between the words and the movement – specifically involving Malik's objection that a lack of 'physical equivalence' to the words (2018: 39) was an obstacle in the audience's understanding of the intended meaning, which Newson strongly disputed. In fact, as McCormack later shows in greater detail, DV8's choreography 'moves between existing in an obvious relationship [to the words], an opposite relationship[,] or somewhere in the vast space in-between' and that Newson's methodology 'aims to expose the polysemous makeup of meaning' (2018: 73).

My perception of these works by DV8, by comparison to some of their earlier non-verbatim pieces and by comparison to Nic Green's use of verbatim testimony, was that they were less effective in creating a clear communication with the audience, as alluded by Malik but not necessarily for reasons spelled out by him. The layering of the verbatim text on top of a choreography created a complex and dense score which, as Newson himself confessed, required multiple viewings for fuller appreciation of nuance (Newson in McCormack 2018: 42). Rather than centring audience engagement, or a process of transformation of the text material into movement (as dance adaptations of novels may have done before), this heteroglossic content potentially resulted in a cacophonous oversaturation of meaning. While it may have served to create impressive performative display, as testified by Malik,[27] the performance also created semantic obstacles to the audience engagement. It follows that heteroglossic layering of text and performance vocabularies alone may not be enough to open up a space for the audience to participate in the co-creation of meaning. What is needed is a commitment to and the means for creating that space, as I argued earlier.

By contrast, drawing on their found verbal material, Nic Green and her collaborators, Rosana Cade and Laura Bradshaw, did set out to create an immersive sonic space and an intersubjective experience for the audience to engage in. Furthermore, the work engaged the audience in a process of critique that is, contrary to convention, multi-faceted (rather than linear), collective (rather than being reserved for an appointed individual authority), and affective (rather than strictly analytical and intellectual). It is therefore worth exploring in more detail how this piece achieved its 'emotional gestalt effect'.

An image that remains etched in my memory years after seeing this piece is one in which, following trance-inducing repetition of empty male rhetoric and posturing, three naked female bodies stand in a pool of light, dripping with sweat, singing together in most perfect unison (Figure 2.2.) – a powerful wordless counterpoint to the established object of their critique (the masculine, jagged, party-political empty rhetoric). Other important distinctive features include its in-the-round staging, minimalism and repetition, and a very sparse, rhythmic, musicalised use of verbal text, layered with dynamic movement sequences. This work too might have needed to be seen multiple times for full appreciation but less so because of its density and more for a strangely rewarding experience its sharp satire offered and whose affective content held the potential to be received differently in different collective configurations. I did not write a personal response at the time of watching the piece; however, numerous other accounts are available. In the LMYE Laboratory #2 'making of' documentary, Nic Green discusses the text by blogger and critic Meghan Vaughan '5 Times I tried to write about Cock and Bull', largely focusing on the impossibility of articulating a response that holds true for all repeated viewings of the piece. This task is made more difficult by the fact that *Cock and Bull* also exists in two versions, the shorter 1-hour version that I saw, and a longer durational version that lasts 7 hours and 41 minutes 'the average length of a sitting in the House of Commons' (Green in LMYE Lab#2, 2021: 2). I would argue that the difficulty contained in articulating a single representative critical response does not indicate any deficiency on the part of the piece. On the contrary, it highlights that the work of critique is also potentially a layered process dependant on a polyphonic, polyvalent convergence of intersubjective, and potentially incommensurable, perspectives. Vaughan's text thus brings into question the conventional entitlement to critique bestowed on a single authority to produce a response on behalf of the audience. Further, it follows that the sheer affective power of Green's piece makes the hermeneutic or analytical focus on its reception less useful than the potential focus on its construction. Therefore, the process of critique can be perceived to be integral to the dramaturgical dialogic encounter the piece convenes with the audience as a collective.

In commissioning the 'making of' presentation from Green, in keeping with the methodological principles I outlined earlier, I asked her to focus on her formative influences, inspirations, the process of making the piece, and any dramaturgical strategies deployed. Green prefaced her presentation by noting that it was neither definitive nor all-encompassing and that many possible 'ways in' were left out in the selection of material presented on this occasion. Similarly, it is important for me to say that Green's presentation alone is not comprehensively definitive of what I mean by 'post-verbatim' as the definition will be derived, analogously to Anna Deavere Smith's composite method, by placing insights from Green's presentation alongside others gained from the remaining interviews and conversations under this remit. Therefore, what I highlight from Green's presentation here is also related to how it can be perceived as resonating with the insights emerging from the rest of the sample. I invite the reader to enter the polyphonic space of this analysis as a co-creator of meaning and pursue this process further by reference to other similar works.

FIGURE 2.2 *Cock and Bull* (2017) by Nic Green, Rosana Cade, and Laura Bradshaw
Photo: Jemima Yong

Green foregrounds an interest in rhythm and sound and the 'use of language [...] as sonic material' (LMYE Lab#2 2021: 2) as part of her performance idiom. The privileging of the musicality of language is explicit and certainly evident in how she deploys found text to form part of the aural texture of the work. However, this is not a matter of mere stylisation. Green's engagement with it is prompted by a spirit of critical resistance to the found material (as opposed to the more customary spirit of loyalty in presenting the original text in verbatim theatre). This evokes an idea of Mladen Dolar who proposes that the conventional sense of 'listening' which presupposes 'obeying' (in many languages) is complicated by one's perception of the visual embodied element of voice/listening (2006: 75–6), whereby the visual aspect of the listening process opens up additional scope for meaning-making.[28] This is precisely the configuration that Green makes use of in her process of embodied listening to the original material and in the embodied listening process she engenders in her audience. In 2017, Green wrote an article about *Cock and Bull* for *The Guardian* in which she reflected on how she was provoked by the political sound-bite rhetoric producing the effect of the words becoming 'cleverly disengaged from their meaning to prevent reaction or counterpoint' or any collective engagement with the policies of political administration (LMYE Lab#2 2021: 3). She reveals that a significant influence in the conception of this piece were the strategies of deconstruction of political speeches found in the works of Lenka Clayton (specifically *Quaeda Quality Question Quickly Quickly Quiet* 2002) and Graham Fitkin and Joby Burgess (*Chain of Command* 2018), which helped to uncover the subliminal workings of these speeches on an affective level. Equally important and influential were performative strategies of creating a space with an energy of unison where the audience could 'reflect on how they feel about [the abstraction of the content they are presented with]' (LMYE Lab#2 2021: 6–7). Further she lists specific choreographic and compositional techniques drawn from contemporary music, such as 'phasing', 'augmentation', 'addition and subtraction' that help the dancers form a 'rhythmic backbone' of the piece. The piece is highly intertextual in the way in which it cites other musical, dance, and performance art works but it is also structured on the principle of repetition or looping where each loop provides opportunities for nuanced change. Ultimately the piece is also a satire of the political elites, the way they hold power and the 'wounded masculinity' they represent. Nonetheless, *Cock and Bull* 'does not want to tell people what to think'. It is not an 'effectively political piece' but a piece 'trying to turn the effects of this political world into affect in this space'. Thereby, within the structure of repetition, 'the only thing that changes is you' (2021: 12).

Cock and Bull is, in my view, an exceptionally successful example of how strategies of verbatim theatre such as montage, fracture, aggregation, polyphony, and embodiment can expand beyond the existing limitations of the form concerned with loyalty, verisimilitude, and 'truth-telling' (Stuart Fisher 2020) into new territories of political performance that uses the counterpoint between form and content to engage the audience in its critical, discursive, and emotional gestalt.²⁹ Not all experimentations with the form of verbatim theatre culminate in such a way, although that doesn't mean that they are less notable or worthy of analysis. It might be useful to turn now to a few other examples of artists taking their interest in speech and sound beyond the existing conventions of verbatim theatre.

By thematic association, another example of an artist who has used political speeches as a source for performance-making,³⁰ featured in Auralia.Space LMYE Gallery#2 Post-Verbatim, is the Belgian performer Valentijn Dhaenens. Dhaenens' first solo piece *BigmoutH* (2011) was a virtuosic lecture performance consisting of a collage of significant speeches from the history of public speaking ranging from the ancient Greece to the present day, forensically explored in relation to each other, and delivered with the help of a loop pedal. Thematically, Dhaenens was interested in the power of public speaking to influence crowds and change the course of history; however, he was left dissatisfied by the 'pop concert' effect of this piece in that the proven ability of his performance to exhilarate the crowd overshadowed his deeper thematic concerns. He attempted to resolve this problem 'contrapuntally'³¹ by subsequently creating *SmallWaR* (2013), a piece which was conceived by opposition to *BigmoutH* in every way: where *BigmoutH* was about politicians, *SmallWaR* was about the people manipulated by them; where *BigmoutH* was dynamic, *SmallWaR* was focusing on the monotony of the First World War as documented in soldiers' letters from the trenches; the predominantly male energy of *BigmoutH* was contrasted by the strong female energy of nurses in *SmallWaR*; where *BigmoutH* was all about sound, *SmallWaR* was applying the sound looping methodology to visual footage in order to create frequently needed crowd scenes. Finally, where *BigmoutH* was exhilarating, *SmallWaR* often left the audience disappointed. However, the value of this work is heightened by methodically considering Dhaenens' simultaneous creative trajectory as part of the collective SKaGeN that he had been a member of since graduating from drama school. Here the element of cultural context becomes relevant too. Dhaenens lists a number of factors of foundational significance in his collective's work including the absence of a classical tradition in the Flemish theatre which had paved the way for the Flemish wave of the 1980s characterised by the work of dance and interdisciplinary performance collectives using documentary and autobiographical materials in performance-making. Collage was the favoured dramaturgical method in devising work, and the intertextual approach – in the case of SkaGeN in particular – extended also to frequent referencing of the popular culture, TV, and film in their performances. An important insight regarding Post-Verbatim theatre can be drawn from Dhaenens and SKaGeN's notion of 'necessary theatricalisation' of the documentary material which is simply integral to the process: a concern with form is explicit in the company's work; they seek to create a distance from the character by making the actor always more visible than the character; and they 'look for dreamlike tactics to show a different perspective on realistic material' (Dhaenens in LMYE Gallery#2, 2021: 8). In my review of *Pardon/In Cuffs*, a piece by SKaGeN based on a documentary film by Raymond Depardon about petty criminals, I observed the company's aesthetic approach as follows:

> The crucial aspect of this production is the acute and explicit severance of the style of the text from the style of its theatrical representation. In the initial scene the public prosecutor played by van den Broek is wearing an elegant satin gown. Incrementally throughout the show the actions accompanying the naturalistic dialogues are purposeful and surreal exaggerations of the potential subliminal content – a con artist is doing a three-point shuffle as he delivers his testimony, a prosecutor tenderly kisses a criminal to whom she has taken a liking – to the extent where they become pure metaphor. Complex dances, wrestling matches, and illusionist acts emerge from these seemingly prosaic exchanges with such appeal and lyrical finesse that they certainly make the audience more elated than they could have hoped given the subject matter of the piece.
>
> (Appendix 2.2)

The counterpoint of form and fact which could be perceived as foundational to post-verbatim theatre therefore does not have to occur entirely through musicalisation in performance-making. Theatre is not an exclusively aural medium and there is much to be said about the power and significance of the stage metaphor that accompanies speech and sound in theatre (this is also present in Nic Green's work, for example, in the way the dancers use the golden paint on their mouths and hands which gradually rubs off on everything they touch and turns to grime; Figure 2.3).[32]

The Irish-British company Dead Centre additionally expands the boundaries of post-verbatim as a technical designation in a number of interesting ways including their Beckettian concern with the stage metaphor, and their explicit performative grappling with the Lacanian 'Real' – or the 'kernel of unrepresentability' of real life (Moukarzel in LMYE Gallery#2, 2021: 5). Rooted in the studies of Philosophy as well as classical and experimental theatre training, Dead Centre's work is characterised by understated conceptual and metaphysical considerations which filter through into stage works that frequently engage the audience in metatheatrical frameworks. Their body of work does not in fact feature any conventional verbatim theatre at all; however, several insights gained from their interview are relevant here and they foreshadow and provide the link to the following chapters too. The first aspect is once again a concern with form – a consideration of the technicity of theatre, which as shown by Worthen (2020) is also especially characteristic of Samuel Beckett. Dead Centre explicitly acknowledge Beckett among their influences for the way in which his work integrates an interest in language, scenography, and innovation, and the way in which this approach asserts its relevance further as we move deeper into the digital age. Their 2013 work *Lippy* is a play within the play that confronts the ethical impossibility of telling someone else's story (Appendix 2.3). The piece tackles the factual

FIGURE 2.3 *Cock and Bull* (2017) by Nic Green, Rosana Cade, and Laura Bradshaw
Photo: Jemima Yong

event of a suicide pact by four women in the Irish village of Leixlip in the early 2000s, and it does so by treating this event as an example of the Lacanian Real that 'refuse[s] to be shown, refuse[s] to be appropriated into narrative and meaning' (Moukarzel in LMYE Gallery#2 2021: 5). This further evokes Beckettian concerns with the capacity of theatre to contemplate meaning and meaninglessness. Directors Ben Kidd and Bush Moukarzel clarify that even though this work was perceived within the lineage of works dealing with re-staging the real, their interest was rather in how it exists within the lineage of playwriting more broadly, and specifically in relation to the ethics of the 'putting of words in somebody's mouth' (2021: 5). In a way that evokes Anna Deavere Smith's focus on the generative failures of spoken language, Moukarzel too, with the help of Adorno's lectures on Kant, underlines the importance of holding on to contradictions rather than yielding to the temptation to cut them out. This was the principle that led the company towards Chekhov's *Platonov*, a play often perceived as flawed and as requiring cuts for clarity. Dead Centre's approach instead was to keep and confront the flaws as cues for creative intervention. A final aspect of their work as a company that resonates with the other works within the Post-Verbatim category in Lend Me Your Ears is the way in which they treat technology as an important dramaturgical component of their work. Specifically, they discuss not just their interest in the various technical aspects of theatre-making but also how they treat their technician as an artist – 'sound operator as a concert pianist' (ibid.: 9) – and an important co-performer in the live event.

Polyphonic Insights

This might be a useful point to recapitulate on what constitutes 'post-verbatim' theatre. First, is it a form or a technique? I have consistently referred to both verbatim and post-verbatim theatre as a form. The diversity of variations and problems around the representations of real in theatre in different cultures have been covered in greater detail by Martin (2010, 2013), Tomlin (2013), and Mumford and Garde (2016). The focus of this study is to document artistic innovation by reference to the artist's own agency as well as in relation to the socio-political contexts they operate in and are shaped by. This results in polyphonic insights which cannot be deemed comprehensive or representative, but the resonances they generate and the composite effects they form help to highlight relevant themes. The central question is: how the tools of making theatre that the artists deploy effect dramaturgical innovation? Sometimes those tools are ideological, sometimes technological, sometimes they are aesthetic, and sometimes, as in the case of much verbatim and post-verbatim theatre, they are sociological too. Here I am reminded of the work of Swiss/Belgian-based director Milo Rau, whose *Ghent Manifesto* (2018), called in amongst other things for at least one production per season to be 'rehearsed or performed in a conflict or war zone without any cultural infrastructure' (Hendrickx 2018). In his work too, a strongly perceivable feature is the creation of a space for a dialectical – both affective and intellectual – engagement of the audience (see Appendix 2.4). Post-verbatim theatre's use of counterpoint between theatrical presentation and real-life functions as both a technique and a form, thus privileging theatre's technicity as a critical tool for social and political engagement.

In their edited volume *Postdramatic Theatre and Form*, Boyle et al. (2019) have successfully urged that 'we shake off common conceptions of form as mere ornamentation or as something that seals an artwork off from society' (2019: 1) and that form is 'integral rather than incidental to theatre' (2019: 15). Kasia Lech advances a similar argument in *Dramaturgy of Form* (2021), specifically in relation to verse. I take this as a cue to add to their projects of rehabilitating the considerations of form at the core of 21st-century theatre without this implying an elision of the matters of political and social significance (see also Grochala 2017).

This chapter so far has shown how the definitive aspects of (post-)verbatim theatre that ensure its survival are contained in a cultivation of multiple dialectical processes that entail the inextricable, explicitly contrapuntal workings of form and content, fact and fabrication, science and music, document and poetry, speaking and listening, critique and affect, mundanity and metaphor, and (re)presentation and unrepresentability. In this respect, the more generative aspect of post-verbatim theatre is its potential for polyphony/counterpoint/dialogism rather than the channelling[33] of real voices per se. This also allows 'verbatim' theatre to evolve and outgrow its literal association with 'exactly the same words as were originally used' (Cambridge Dictionary, https://dictionary.cambridge.org/dictionary/english/verbatim) and accommodate processes of transformation, as theatre is not merely a vehicle for words. Post-verbatim has additionally shown how the dramaturgies of speech and sound, through their ontological capacity to immerse, also possess the capacity to conduct critique as a collective, heterarchical, and embodied process.

In selecting the artists to be interviewed about this topic for the A/OD project, I was interested in the makers of works that could be seen as pushing the boundaries of the form of verbatim and the works that were departing from the representational and mimetic mode of theatrical realism towards more conceptual and problematised uses of the found speech material. Retrospectively, I also realise that in gathering and processing my material I have unconsciously applied Norman Denzin and Anna Deavere Smith's methodologies of amassing dialogic, multivoiced data to be processed partly intuitively, and in pursuit of a discursive gestalt that investigates a specific question (in this case 'what constitutes post-verbatim theatre?'). Because the outcome here is academic work rather than ethnodrama, my field research remains in conversation with other theoretical and/or empirical sources generated through conventional literature review. This intuitive approach has resulted in occasionally privileging the case studies (such as Smith's work) that offer fundamentally relevant insights, even if these insights are drawn from sources outside the field research.

In anticipation of the forthcoming chapters, and in conclusion to this one, it is useful to briefly extrapolate from the rest of the evidence collected under the remit of post-verbatim, three other interrelated themes: dramaturgical value of technology, politicity of form, and (trans-)cultural contingency of post-verbatim theatre.

Valorisation of technology in working with speech and sound dramaturgically, signalled in the work of Valentijn Dhaenens and Dead Centre, is echoed by the Australian theatre-maker Kate Hunter. In her case, a Zoom sound recorder becomes a collaborator as '[audio recorded] instructions [to self] become another partner' in the process of devising (Hunter in LMYE Gallery#2 2021: 4). This working principle also evokes a testimony offered by the Indian performance-maker Maya Krishna Rao in LMYE Gallery#1 about how she works with camera as a 'co-actor' in devising work. It is perhaps also symptomatic that Kate Hunter's practice is rooted in embodied training methodologies of Tadashi Suzuki and Viewpoints. In a way furthermore evocative of both Green and Nancy (2007), she privileges the notion of 'listening with all our body' (ibid.: 6) as well as thinking musically when putting together material – using repetition, coda, rhythm, and counterpoint. Hunter's piece *Earshot* (2017) was a collage of speech and sound thematising 'accidental poetry' of daily life.[34] In her compositional process, Hunter used eavesdropping – which Caroline Wake (2014) has problematised in ethical terms. However, while upholding the ethical questions, Hunter also believes that the processes of remediation, reshaping, and dramaturgical processing of the material which no longer constitutes testimonies of participants 'explodes the traditional relationship [...] with verbatim' (ibid.: 8). Additionally, it is interesting to consider in this context an aspect of mediatisation in everyday life, whereby an increased use of mobile phones in public places actually imposes a process of involuntary eavesdropping on the members of the public, which may sanction further reflexivity or satire. The suggested focus on compositional processes and the form of the composition rather than the content of such post-verbatim work opens up other possibilities for dramaturgical understanding as illustrated by Fred Moten's already mentioned triangulation between documentary linearity, fantasy, and counterpoint:

> Perhaps dramatic documentary emerges from a sort of obsessive and compositional overhearing—a discomposing loss or lack of normative composure that happens to or is imposed upon the composer in diners, at the telephone, in sites where interview and inner view converge, where simultaneity works through and over sequence, marking the motivation behind the valorization of fantasy.
>
> (2017: 47)

The A/OD resident dance company, Gracefool Collective (Figure 2.4), bring to the topic of Post-Verbatim additional formal interests in ceremonial public speaking, lip-syncing, and verbal mimicry which they explore in their work on the level of technicity rather than reperformance of found text, as well as for the capacity of these techniques to generate modes of interaction with the audience. Ultimately this is related to one of the foundational principles of their performance idiom as a company concerned with the terms of audience engagement. Potentially influential in this respect might have been their student experience at the Northern School of Contemporary Dance in Leeds when the change of artistic leadership created a radical transformation in their training practice away from technique-intensive towards DIY, politicised practices of physical performance-making. In this way, they were able to add to the rigour of their initial technical training crucial dramaturgical considerations of how they would communicate with their audience using direct address, comedy, site specificity, and political engagement. In *This is Not a Wedding* (2017), which began with a decision to create performance that has the recognisable structure of ceremony, they engage an audience member in delivering a wedding speech by feeding them lines to say – an invitation that makes dramaturgical sense within the participatory framework they have established in their piece. This is a particularly effective choice because a wedding speech can be assumed to be a familiar formula of public discourse that anyone can appropriate and at the same time provides a mode of playful participation. Furthermore, in this way they display and experientially share with the audience the technicity of verbatim itself – the remediation of someone else's words – by turning the relationship around and putting the audience member in the shoes of a verbatim performer. The purpose is a satirisation of weddings as outdated forms of social contract, which the audience is playfully co-opted into rather than simply presented with. In this respect, we are reminded that politicity of form – as satire has always shown us – can act on the level of humorous affective engagement too and not exclusively on the level of analytical discursive critique.

At the other end of the scale, Argentinian Lola Arias featured in LMYE Gallery #2 works not just with real people's testimonies, but actually with the owners of those testimonies by putting them on stage and building a dramaturgical scaffolding within which to tell their stories. She works with members of the public, the owners of the stories she is interested in, and other artistic collaborators, over extended periods of time, leading a process of substantial improvisations and relevant research to find the shape and the nuance of the piece. However, her work too can also begin with form- rather than content-related decisions. Her most famous creation *Minefield* (2017), featuring the British and Argentinian veterans of the Falklands war (Appendix 2.5), began with a powerful dramaturgical choice to create a British-Argentinian music band on the stage, and this also determined her casting process – looking primarily for the veterans who could play musical instruments. Similarly *What They Want to Hear* (2018), a piece with and about the Syrian migrant Raaed Al Kour she made at the Munich Kammerspiele, which can be seen as belonging to the German trend of postmigrant theatre (see Cornish in Boyle et al. 2019: 179–95), began with the interest in the capacity of storytelling to save one's life by convincing the authorities it is a story worthy of being granted political asylum. Raaed Al Kour's story was unfortunately not convincing enough for the authorities even if it was for theatre audiences. What role does culture and cultural contingency play in these authorial processes? In *Minefield*, Arias deals with her own cultural heritage; however, in her work in Germany, with Al Kour, other migrants and other communities, she is using her expertise and her cultural capital as a migrant theatre director to amplify the voices of the marginalised. The relations between Arias, her

FIGURE 2.4 *This is Not a Wedding* (2017) by Gracefool Collective

Photo: Drazen Priganica

collaborators, and the audience are not built on the familiar models of cultural contingency, social empowerment, or ethnographic research, but on the counterpointed experiences of life and theatre, inside and outside, expertise and non-expertise, legal migration and illegal immigration, a story that works and a story that doesn't.

By contrast, *The Fall* (2016), the work of the Fall Collective from South Africa, is rooted in collective chronicling and processing of the deeply traumatic memories of the decolonisation work surrounding the Rhodes Must Fall events in Cape Town in 2015. In LMYE Lab #2, the collective members Thando Mangcu and Tankiso Mamabolo designate this work as 'protest theatre', a form which carries the provenance of Western political theatre heritage passed down to them through still colonially inflected systems of training. However, using the power of personal experience and the vernacular oral and musical traditions of South Africa as their departure point, they find their voice as a company and proceed to exert a considerable impact through international touring, prompting and adding to the decolonisation movements throughout the anglophone world.

Similarly, Emma Frankland in making *Hearty* (2018–20) (LMYE Lab# 2), the fifth part of her cycle about gender transition *None of Us is Yet a Robot*, also bases her work on personal experience, however not without a desire to relate Western concepts of gender essentialism/fluidity to those of other cultures. Hence in her process, she visits Canada, Brazil, and Indonesia to talk to the indigenous communities in these disparate parts of the world about their conceptions of gender and their personal and historic experiences of Western oppression against transgender and gender fluidity. Frankland's aim is not to represent or speak on behalf of any of the cultures she encounters in her ethnographic work, she is primarily telling her own story, but this story is placed at an intersection of a network of influences, resonant verbatim statements shared for purposes of amplification ('We Are a Hearty Sisterhood'), repurposing ('Lop the Dick Off'), or counterpoint ('She Refuses to Endure'). Regardless of their personal cultural designation, all of these artists align themselves with networks of international communities in their desire to speak to power. Similar to Green, they could be seen to convene the space in which the energy of unison contrapuntally holds the space for collective critique. These are not the works that aim to merely uncover the workings of the hegemonic order within their own specific cultural contexts but the works whose non-culture-specific relational emphasis on form allows for trans-cultural significance.

Thus, post-verbatim is not merely a term to designate practices and works that expand the boundaries of verbatim theatre. I perceive it also as a form of permission to ethically dissolve those boundaries: to engage in verbatim theatre-making without the obligation of unquestioned loyalty, to deconstruct pre-existing notions of authority, to transform, to refract, to contrapuntally align and compare, to theatricalise, to confront the unrepresentability of the real, and to consistently co-opt the audience into processes of affective critique. This freedom mobilises the apparatus of theatre to communicate with the audience not only by transmission or channelling of found materials but through an embodied, affective and intellectual reckoning. This is what ultimately enables the legacy of verbatim theatre to be continued.

Notes

1 Trueman uses the visual similarity to 'verbatim' of the German word 'verboten' ('forbidden') to produce the pun, as well as possibly ironising his prerogatives as a theatre critic.
2 Here, I conceptually take inspiration from the term 'postdramatic' which, as shown by Lehmann (1999/2006), is predicated on the dramatic but no longer bound by its conventional limitations. In my view, the same applies to the notion of 'post-critique' in its relationship to 'critique'.
3 I use this term to evoke both the Greek 'poeisis' ('making') and contemporary English 'poetry'.
4 A relevant book-length study of the genealogies and contemporary manifestations of German documentary theatre is available in Ulrike Garde and Meg Mumford's 2016 title *Theatre of Real People*.
5 Both Blythe and Oades use the technique of the live in-ear audio feed that cues the actors' lines which they have explicitly borrowed from the British-American actor and director Mark Wing-Davey and which he in turn developed after working with Anna Deavere Smith. See also Wake (2013) for a more detailed analysis of the genealogy of 'headphone verbatim'.
6 These acting techniques are contrasted to the '3-D individualisation of naturalistic theatre that seeks to make the actor psychologically credible as an historical figure' (2009: 229).
7 Paget goes on to note how metropolitan newspaper critics in London received this work without any awareness of the political or methodological histories of the form, or even that the term 'verbatim theatre' had already existed for 15 years in the academic realm, thus illustrating the ways in which the alternative theatre traditions remain perennially undocumented, invisible, and broken, by either the makers themselves or the journalists. In this respect too, Paget's conclusionary hope is placed in the figure of the 'witness' that documentary theatre produces and endorses in a number of ways, made even more crucial by the endemic loss of trust in mediatised societies, the rise of postmodern doubt in documents, and 'information-management (aka "spin")' (2009: 235).
8 This is noted by Maggie Inchley too when she opts not to refer to the realities of the marginalised communities as 'alternative' but rather 'negotiated and permeable by structures associated with mainstream practice and response' (2015: 3).
9 Interestingly Kondo notes a corporeal, non-literary nature of script development in Smith's rehearsal process, testifying that the 'dramaturgs hardly ever saw a script' and 'reacted to Smith's *performances*' in the initial stages of working on the piece (2018: 103, original emphasis).
10 Similarly, within the creative process, Kondo notes that Smith's 'willingness to listen, every night, even in the face of harsh criticism, continues to elicit my fierce loyalty to her work' (2018: 135).
11 In the interview with Schechner, Smith explicitly devalues 'opinion' in relation to her creative work.
12 Mikhail Ugarov similarly qualifies these failures of language as 'the score of the mental life' of the speaker (in Radosavljević 2013: 133).
13 Gerber (2019), cited later in this chapter, is a notable exception to this.
14 'I seek a critical postmodern, performance aesthetic for a performative cultural studies' is a mantra repeated throughout both of Denzin's books (1997, 2003).
15 'American character lives not in one place or the other but in the gaps between the places, and in our struggle to be together in our differences' (Smith 1993: xii).
16 She sees that a person can be completely present in his or her speech and this is a 'gift' (Smith 1993: xxvii, xxxi).
17 Although perhaps lacking the racial justice nuance of Kondo's dramaturgical critique, Denzin's model, developed some 15 years earlier, is fundamentally in sync with it.
18 The Britannica article is here: https://www.britannica.com/art/counterpoint-music and the Grove article is here: https://www.oxfordmusiconline.com/grovemusic/view/10.1093/gmo/9781561592630.001.0001/omo-9781561592630-e-0000006690?rskey=d65zSf&result=1. Similarly, Hammond and Steward have empirically established that

'verbatim is not a form, it is a technique; it is a means rather than an end' (2008: 9).

19 Sven Bjerstedt informs me in personal correspondence that August Strindberg wrote about his dramaturgical aims with his play *Master Olof* as follows: 'instead of the opera-like iambic drama with soli and numbers, I composed it polyphonically, a symphony where all parts were plaited together, main and secondary characters were tarred with the same brush, and nobody was accompanying the soloist' (August Strindberg, *Teater och Intima teatern*, Stockholm: Norstedt [1908] 1999: 12, translation by Bjerstedt). Reference received with thanks.

20 Edward Said has also famously used 'counterpoint' in his writings on colonial history – specifically in *Culture and Imperialism* (1993) – as a framework for narrating the multiplicity of conflicting Arab-Israeli histories and particularly from his personal position of an American Palestinian academic.

21 'I refer to the constant simultaneity of events on the theatre stage, its potential polyphony and the many possibilities of interplays and relations, order and disorder, resonances or dissonances between all these events and the crucial role the director plays in shaping these relationships. The musicality dispositif focused amongst other things on the "harmony" of theatrical media (harmony understood here in a musical, not psychological or atmospheric sense), i.e. exploring the full range of formal and semantic relations, which go beyond a simple dichotomy of consonance and dissonance.' (Roesner 2014: 36)

22 Entrainment has also been studied in relation to watching performance in terms of measuring collective cardiac synchronicty in an audience (Ardizzi et al. 2020) or in relation to the specificities of a particular venue architecture (Shaughnessy on the Globe Theatre, London, 2015).

23 An example of a piece of performance predicated on the simultaneous experience of affective displeasure and intellectual closure is Tim Crouch's *The Author*, which I analysed in these terms in *Theatre-Making* (2013: 151–4).

24 This is not dissimilar to Brecht's claim that '[t]he episodes must not succeed each other indistinguishably but must give us a chance to interpose our judgment' (Brecht in Willett 1964: 201), the main adjustment being that the audience response is not solely restricted to 'judgment' but accommodates a full range of possibilities.

25 Rebecca Collins (2017) too makes a fascinating contribution on the subject of aural spatiality and sonic materiality using Nancy's idea of the 'sonorous body' 'to consider how sound might operate in the depths of presentation, rather than on the surface as representation' (2017: 167).

26 For example, according to Gerber, the 'unsayable' might refer to sensitive material, ethical requirement to protect the source, or to cases of censorship.

27 'Their ability to dance and talk at the same time still leaves me breathless and bewildered.' (https://kenanmalik.com/2012/03/18/we-should-talk-about-this/).

28 Dolar goes on to illustrate his point by analysing the visual montagic representation of 'voice' in Francis Barraud's 1898 painting 'His Master's Voice' made famous as the logo of the HMV record label: 'It leaves out the level of using the voice for "intersubjective communication"; it makes the voice appear in its object-like quality by assembling together the animal and the machine, short-circuiting humanity. […] The object emerges in the very disparity of technology and animality.' (2006: 76).

29 In his analysis of *London Road* (2011), Demetris Zavros also delves into analysis of form and content in Alecky Blythe's musical hybrid going beyond notions of fidelity/authenticity/verisimilitude and truth. While he doesn't explicitly suggest this work is post-dramatic or post-verbatim in the context of the article, he does borrow from Lehmann's 'politics of perception' to propose that it creates a new space of ethico-political engagement for the audience (beyond the politics of 'authenticity' and verisimilitude that Blythe was aiming for). (See Zavros 2021).

30 Contemporary performance practice offers a multitude of examples of performances based on political speeches including Tim Crouch's *John, Antonio and Nancy* (2010), Guillermo Calderon's *Discurso* (2011), Tim Etchells' *Although We Fell Short* (2011), Hannah Silva's *Opposition* (2011), Lisbeth Gruwez's *It's going to get worse and worse and worse, my friend* (2012), Oliver Bray and Mark Flisher's *The Speech Maker* (2011), Annie Dorsen's

Spoken Karaoke (2012), Lucy Ellinson, Chris Thorpe and Steve Lawson's *Torycore* (2013), and Spordikirik Rekvere's *Suite No 2* (2016). With thanks to Alex Chisholm, Alexander Devriendt, Richard Gregory, Andrew Haydon, Vlatka Horvat, Alexander Kelly, Andrzej Łukowski, Maria Mytilinaki Kennedy, and Steve Scott-Bottoms for crowdsourcing these titles on my Facebook page on 30 April 2017.

31 This is not counterpoint as understood in music or within the duration of a single performance, which requires simultaneity. Here the term is used figuratively to emphasise the intended contrasts between the two pieces of work created in succession. Nonetheless the use of this term by Dhaenens is striking in that it resonates with Green and the rest of the sample, and additionally this form of counterpoint is relevant for the methodological considerations of the development of this artist's 'performance idiom'.

32 This 'gold to grime' moment is highlighted in Matt Trueman's review of the piece (2016) and also mentioned by Green in her LMYE interview.

33 Jennifer Parker-Starbuck, however, rightly points out another formally significant manifestation of the transmission or channelling of 'ideas about the contemporary moment through a performer's body' in karaoke theatre (2017: 379–80) – a topic concerning the influence of technology that will be explored further in the next chapter.

34 Recorded by Hunter surreptitiously in public places, the material is performed using the in-ear live feed technique of 'headphone verbatim' as it is known in Australia. The piece deploys both analogue and digital means of spatialising the sound as well as the live transcription of speech through dictation software for visual effect.

Bibliography

Adorno, Theodore (1998). *Beethoven: The Philosophy of Music*, Rolf Tiedemann (ed.), translated by Edmund Jephcott, Cambridge, Maiden: Polity Press.

Ardizzi, M., Calbi, M., and Tavaglione, S. et al. (2020). 'Audience spontaneous entrainment during the collective enjoyment of live performances: Physiological and behavioral measurements', *Scientific Reports* 10, 3813. doi: https://doi.org/10.1038/s41598-020-60832-7

Bakhtin, Mikhail (1981). *The Dialogic Imagination: Four Essays*, Michael Holquist (ed.), translated by Caryl Emerson and Michael Holquist, Austin: University of Texas Press.

Boyle, Michael Shane, Cornish, Matt, and Woolf, Brandon (eds) (2019). *Postdramatic Theatre and Form*, London: Methuen Bloomsbury.

Buffery, Helena (2013). 'Negotiating the translation zone: Invisible borders and other landscapes on the contemporary 'heteroglossic' stage', *Translation Studies*, 6:2, 150–65. doi: https://doi.org/10.1080/14781700.2013.774993

Carlson, Marvin (2006). *Speaking in Tongues*, Ann Arbor: University of Michigan Press.

Collins, Rebecca (2017). 'Aural spatiality and sonic materiality: Attending to the space of sound in performances by Ivo Dimchev and Alma Söderberg', *Contemporary Theatre Review*, 27:3, 379–90. doi: https://doi.org/10.1080/10486801.2017.1343243

Denzin, Norman K. (1997). *Interpretive Ethnography: Ethnographic Practices for the 21st Century*, Thousand Oaks, London, New Delhi: Sage Publications.

Denzin, Norman K. (2003). *Performance Ethnography: Critical Pedagogy and the Politics of Culture*, Thousand Oaks, London, New Delhi: Sage Publications.

Denzin, Norman K. (2018). 'The pragmatics of publishing the experimental text', in Leavy, Patricia (ed.), *Handbook of Arts-Based Research*, New York: Guilford Press.

Dolar, Mladen (2006). *A Voice and Nothing More*, Cambridge: MIT.

Felski, Rita (2015). *The Limits of Critique*, Chicago: University of Chicago Press.

Forsyth, Alison, and Megson, Chris (eds) (2009). *Get Real: Documentary Theatre Past and Present*, Basingstoke: Palgrave Macmillan.

Garson, Cyrielle (2021). *Beyond Documentary Realism: Aesthetic Transgressions in British Verbatim Theatre*, Berlin/Boston: De Gruyter.

Gerber, André Kruger (2019). 'Visual metaphor as tool to stage the "unsayable" in the verbatim, youth theatre production Wag, ek kry gou my foon [en soos sulke goed]', *South African Theatre Journal*, 32: 158–77. doi: 10.1080/10137548.2019.1624604

Grochala, Sarah (2017). The Contemporary Political Play: Rethinking Dramaturgical Structure, London: Methuen Bloomsbury.

Hammond, Will and Steward, Dan (eds) (2008). *Verbatim Verbatim: Contemporary Documentary Theatre*, London: Oberon Books.

Hendrickx, Sébastien (2018). 'Playful dogmatism: Milo Rau and Joachim Ben Yakoub in conversation', *The Theatre Times*, 7 October, https://thetheatretimes.com/playful-dogmatism-milo-rau-and-joachim-ben-yakoub-in-conversation

Holdsworth, Nadine, and Luckhurst, Mary (eds) (2008). *A Concise Companion to Contemporary British and Irish Drama*, Malden, MA, Oxford and Carlton: Blackwell.

Home-Cook, George (2015). *Theatre and Aural Attention*, Basingstoke: Palgrave Macmillan.

Inchley, Maggie (2015). *Voice and New Writing 1997–2007: Articulating the Demos*, Basingstoke: Palgrave Macmillan.

Jestrovic, Silvija (2020). *Performances of Authorial Presence and Absence: The Author Dies Hard*, Cham: Palgrave Macmillan.

Josselson, Ruthellen (2011). '"Bet you think this song is about you": Whose narrative is it in narrative research?', *Narrative Works*, 1:1, 33–51, https://journals.lib.unb.ca/index.php/nw/article/view/18472

Kondo, Dorinne (2018). Worldmaking: Race, Performance, and the Work of Creativity, Duke University Press.

Latour, Bruno (2004). 'Why has critique run out of steam? From matters of fact to matters of concern', *Critical Inquiry*, 30:2, 225–48. http://www.bruno-latour.fr/sites/default/files/89-CRITICAL-INQUIRY-GB.pdf

Lech, Kasia (2021). *Dramaturgy of Form: Performing Verse in Contemporary Theatre*, London: Routledge.

Lehmann, Hans-Thies (1999/2006). Postdramatic Theatre, translated and introduced by Karen Jürs-Munby, London and New York: Routledge.

Marinetti, Cristina (2018). 'Theatre as a 'translation zone': Multilingualism, identity and the performing body in the work of Teatro Delle Albe.' *The Translator*, 24:2, 128–46. doi: https://doi.org/10.1080/13556509.2017.1393122

Martin, Carol (ed.) (2010). *Dramaturgy of the Real on the World Stage*, Basingstoke, New York: Palgrave Macmillan.

Martin, Carol (2013). *Theatre of the Real*, Basingstoke: Palgrave.

Matsuoka, Naomi (2002). 'Murakami Haruki and Anna Deavere Smith: Truth by interview', *Comparative Literature Studies*, 39:4, 305–313.

McCormack, Jess (2018). *Choreography and Verbatim Theatre: Dancing Words*, Cham: Palgrave Pivot.

Merlin, Bella (2007) 'The Permanent Way and the impermanent muse', *Contemporary Theatre Review* 17(1): 41–9. doi: https://doi.org/10.1080/10486800601096030

Moten, Fred (2017). *Black or Blur: Consent Not to Be a Single Being*, Durham: Duke University Press.

Mumford, Meg, and Garde, Ulrike (2016). *Theatre of Real People: Diverse Encounters at Berlin's Hebbel am Ufer and Beyond*, London: Bloomsbury Methuen.

Nancy, Jean-Luc (2007). *On Listening*, translated by Charlotte Mandell, New York: Fordham University Press.

Paget, Derek (1987). '"Verbatim theatre": Oral history and documentary techniques', *New Theatre Quarterly*, 3:12, 317–36.

Paget, Derek (2009). 'The "broken tradition" of documentary theatre and its continued powers of endurance', in Forsyth, Alison and Megson, Chris (eds), *Get Real: Documentary Theatre Past and Present*, Basingstoke: Palgrave Macmillan.

Parker-Starbuck, Jennifer (2017). 'Karaoke theatre: Channelling mediated lives', *Contemporary Theatre Review*, 27:3, 379–90. doi: https://doi.org/10.1080/10486801.2017.1343243

Radosavljević, Duška (2013). *Theatre-Making: Interplay Between Text and Performance in the 21st Century*, Basingstoke: Palgrave.

Roesner, David (2008). 'The politics of the polyphony of performance: Musicalization in contemporary German theatre', *Contemporary Theatre Review*, 18:1, 44–55. doi: https://doi.org/10.1080/10486800701749587

Roesner, David (2014). *Method and Metaphor in Theatre-Making*, Farnham/Burlington: Ashgate.

Roesner, David, and Merlin, Bella (2018). 'The document as music. Exploring the musicality of verbatim material in performance', *Journal for Artistic Research*, 15. https://www.researchcatalogue.net/view/353508/353509/0/0

Said, Edward (1993). *Culture and Imperialism*, New York: Vintage.

Saldaña, Johnny (2011). *Ethnotheatre: Research from Page to Stage*, Walnut Creek, CA: Left Coast Press.

Schechner, Richard (2018). 'There's a lot of work to do to turn this thing around: An interview with Anna Deavere Smith', *The Drama Review*, 62:3, 35–50. doi: https://doi.org/10.1162/dram_a_00771

Shaughnessy, Robert (2015). *Connecting the Globe: Actors, Audience and Entrainment*, Cambridge: Cambridge University Press, 294–305. doi: https://doi.org/10.1017/CBO9781316258736.023

Smith, Anna Deavere (1993). *Fires in the Mirror: Crown Heights, Brooklyn, and Other Identities*, New York: Anchor Books/ Doubleday.

Steinby, Liisa (2013). 'Concepts of Novelistic Polyphony: Person-Related and Compositional-Thematic' in Steinby, Liisa, and Klapuri, Tintti (eds) *Bakhtin and His Others: (Inter)subjectivity, Chronotope, Dialogism*, London, New York, Delhi: Anthem Press.

Stuart Fisher, Amanda (2020). *Performing the Testimonial: Rethinking Verbatim Dramaturgies*, Manchester: Manchester University Press.

Tomlin, Liz (2013). *Acts and Apparitions: Discourses of the Real in Performance Practice and Theory, 1990-2010*, Manchester: Manchester University Press.

Tomlinson, Gary (2015). *A Million Years of Music: The Emergence of Human Modernity*, New York: Zone Books.

Trueman, Matt (2016). 'Edinburgh review: Cock and Bull (Forest Fringe)', *What's on Stage*, 13.08, https://www.whatsonstage.com/edinburgh-theatre/reviews/cock-and-bull-forest-fringe-festival-nic-green_41533.html

Trueman, Matt (2018). 'Too often, verbatim theatre forgets to be theatre', *What's on Stage*, 21.06., https://www.whatsonstage.com/london-theatre/news/verbatim-theatre-blog-notes-from-the-field_46903.html

Wake, Caroline (2013). 'Headphone verbatim theatre: Methods, histories, genres, theories'. *New Theatre Quarterly*, 29, 321–35. doi: 10.1017/S0266464X13000651

Wake, Caroline (2014). 'The politics and poetics of listening: Attending headphone verbatim theatre in Post-Cronulla Australia'. *Theatre Research International*, 39, 82–100. doi: 10.1017/S0307883314000029

Willett, John (1964). *Brecht on Theatre: The Development of an Aesthetic*, London: Methuen.

Worthen, W.B. (1997). *Shakespeare and the Authority of Performance*, Cambridge: Cambridge University Press.

Worthen, W.B. (2020). *Shakespeare, Technicity, Performance*, Cambridge: CUP.

Zavros, Demetris (2021). 'Encounters with "the same" (but different): London Road and the politics of territories and repetitions in verbatim musical theatre', *Studies in Musical Theatre*, 15:3, 215–31. doi: https://doi.org/10.1386/smt_00076_1

3
AMPLIFIED STORYTELLING

Exposition

Kate Caryer's The Unspoken Project is a London-based professional theatre company that specialises in working with people with communication difficulties. As Caryer explains in the LMYE Laboratory #3, the focus of her work is not exclusively on disabled or non-disabled people, but complexities around designation and representation inevitably enter the considerations. Moreover, the implied binary itself is false. Caryer uses augmentative and alternative communication (AAC), the technology that supplements or replaces speech for people with communication impairment or lack of biological speech. However, as explained by Caryer and her collaborator Ky Hall, there is a significant difference between biological speech and voice: 'for AAC users, their communication aids, eye gaze, picture boards and sign languages become their voice in a far more meaningful way than their own biological speech ever could' (Hall in LMYE Lab#3 2021: 3). Hall rightly highlights that people with biological speech 'may still feel "voiceless" because they do not feel represented in society' (Hall in LMYE Lab#3 2021: 4). Similarly, Caryer notes that one of the professional actors in her production at Soho Theatre *The Voice Monologues* (2018) did not have a speech impairment but was neuro-divergent so 'disabled in a different way' (Caryer in LMYE Lab#3 2021: 6). For the purposes of the theatre project focused on communication, this actor was considered non-disabled. In *The Voice Monologues* (2018), billed on Unspoken's website as a 'celebration of communication', Caryer worked with a selection of AAC-users as authors of texts and an ensemble of ten actors half of which were AAC users and the other half of which did not have speech impairments. Non-AAC-using actors performed the texts written by AAC-using authors and the AAC-actors performed famous speeches from history such as Martin Luther King Jr's 'I have a dream'. It follows that the fundamental structural principle which made the 'celebration of communication' in its fullest sense possible was the polyphonic layering of the different means of expression.

Scholars writing about disability and theatre such as Petra Kuppers and Matt Hargrave have long argued that, rather than being a separate aesthetic paradigm, disability adds a further layer to the contemporary mainstream performance aesthetics. Matt Hargrave (2015) even declares 'the end of disability arts' on page 1 of his book, noting however that this paradigm shift has occurred in practice more so than in relevant critical literature (2015: 21). I agree with this view. Arguably, disability has only become visible as such on the 19th- and 20th-century stages in the context of the realist, mimetic paradigm of socio-political and psychological representation in drama, whereas postmodern, postdramatic, and postmimetic conceptions of performance have opened up other possibilities.

In opening the chapter on storytelling with a story about a theatre project which places AAC at the centre of its dramaturgical apparatus, rather than, say, Homer, or the Arabian Nights, or any other more conventional way into the subject of 'storytelling', I wish to signal the crucial role of technology in enabling personal and artistic expression. In the Introduction(s) to this book, I have touched on the problem of technological determinism, the critical view dominant in the late 20th century that the overemphasis on the role of technology in human behaviour may occlude the role of socio-political agency and social justice in contemporary life. Much contemporary critical literature – specifically in the fields of new media theory and trans- and post-humanism – has moved beyond this concern into exploring the multifaceted, entangled significance of new technologies in contemporary life and culture. In the case of the Unspoken Project, it is clear that the technology serves to enhance agency when it is available to the users, which, as Hall and Caryer point out, is not always the case due to financial, political, and class privilege. Performance frames and makes ponderable the relations between the story, the storyteller(s), and the possible means of communication. This is most effectively highlighted by the Unspoken Project's contrapuntal example but also, further back in the Western tradition at least, by frequent mythologising of blindness (Homer, Tiresias, Oedipus) in relation to narrative insight. Ultimately, if according to Worthen (via Stiegler) theatre represents a constitutive prosthetic for our species, then it must include the full spectrum of physical ability.

In Chapter 2, I explored the contemporary theatre-making processes that foreground the use of speech – specifically found speech material – using the musicalisation tools of polyphony and counterpoint (as opposed to loyal transmission) in order to engender an intersubjective relationship with the audience. This chapter will take a different approach to oral composition, taking a long historical perspective which might serve to juxtapose or reframe the findings of the preceding discussion. Because of the thematic focus of the previous chapter on documentary, in mentioning Lola Arias's piece *What They Want to Hear* about a Syrian archaeologist struggling to tell his life story so as to be granted political asylum in Germany, I omitted to note the obvious trope in this work that evokes Scheherazade's own famous storytelling for survival. This trope highlights a more vital aspect of technicity of the expressive arts – its life-saving power. In this chapter, I wish to build scope for considerations of the role of technology in dramaturgical innovation not only as a technical aid but as a means of reconceptualising processes of theatre-making: how the linearity inherent to writing might be problematised and augmented by the notions of montage or sampling, looping, and layering, which are brought into the creative process by the sound technologies.

I take the notion of storytelling in its broadest sense that accommodates both theatre and oral traditions in focusing on emergent forms within the intersection between the two in the 21st century. After an initial historicisation of the topic of storytelling and authorship, and a grappling with the specific example of the Serbian orature to highlight the potential interplay of storytelling, music, technology, and politics in engendering the audience's intersubjective engagement, I will eventually highlight some insights from the A/OD project into how technologies that have become more ubiquitously available in the 21st century, such as microphones, headphones, editing software, and mobile phones, facilitate new dramaturgical opportunities: sometimes succeeding or expanding the artists' pre-existing interests in corporeal expression (as in the case of ZU-UK, Quote Unquote, Melanie Wilson); sometimes reinventing storytelling by arriving at it from disparate directions of contemporary performance and popular culture (Kieran Hurley and SK Shlomo); sometimes just using technology in theatre to narrate non-verbally for the sake of personal, aesthetic, and political freedom (Eszter Kálmán).

As warned by Michael Wilson, in relation to the long historical perspective on oral traditions in particular, it is first important to account for dangers of 'uncritical reverence' and adulation of the past (2006: 24). These uncritical tendencies that valorise fixed meanings, myths, archetypes, and the virtuosity of the storyteller, are contrasted by the ideas of folk cultures and storytelling as ultimately subversive and progressive, as exemplified by the writings of by Mikhail Bakhtin and Waiter Benjamin, respectively.[1] In his historicisation of storytelling and theatre, Wilson notes important distinctions between the pre-industrial storytelling tradition and the 'storytelling revival' whose origins he dates to the counter-cultural movement of the late 1960s and the alternative theatre's disassociation from bourgeois conceptions in favour of community-building. For another perspective on the time Wilson associates with the 'storytelling revival', education scholars Catherine Heinemeyer and Sally Durham (2017) observe that storytelling as a form of pedagogy fell out of favour in the second half of the 20th century as it was perceived as a monolithic narrative mode that was in opposition to the pluralist, anti-authoritarian, relativist values of postmodernism. Thus, Heinemeyer and Durham (2017) note, the British education system in the period between 1960s and 1980s underwent a move towards experiential learning, child-led learning, and development of democratic values, which 'discouraged many teachers from embracing the apparently authoritarian role of storyteller' (2017: 38). In addition, an increased emphasis on measuring effectiveness in relation to educational goals and outcomes meant that the prevailing mood was 'suspicious of storytelling, with its unpredictable and intersubjective knowledge outcomes, and favoured more obviously active [...] forms of communication, in which pupils could demonstrate their conceptual understanding' (2017: 38). Additionally evident here is the distinction between narrative and abstract knowledge that Adriana Cavarero also explores with the aim of revalorising the former for its ability to 'reveal the finite in its fragile uniqueness', rather than 'capturing the universal in the trap of definition' (1997: 3).

Thus, storytelling contains relational epistemological potential (Tuhiwai Smith 1999) which has been rendered obsolete in the late 20th century by the crude Western epistemological associations of the form with the authoritarian and the anti-democratic, or with civilisational delay.

Wilson has highlighted the problem of Cultural Darwinism characteristic of the 19th-century ethnographic practices which, in the process of anthologising various bodies of ethnic oral traditions, assumed a linear idea of cultural progress. This enabled the Western industrialised societies to view the pre-industrial, non-Western cultures with a sense of cultural supremacy, exoticism, and nostalgia, which tacitly served to sanction and justify Western colonialism. Thus a revisiting of the topic of storytelling in the 21st century also opens up the potential to tackle this epistemological violence and consciously contribute to the decolonisation agendas. Though the discussion below is concerned primarily with dramaturgy rather than decolonisation per se, I will use my positionality as a native of a culture subjected to a type of Western 'imperialism of the imagination' (Goldsworthy 1998) known as 'Balkanism' (Todorova 1997), in order to derive new insights into the dramaturgical potential of contemporary storytelling.

In the context of this chapter, storytelling will be understood in an expanded sense to encompass an intersubjective narrative mode, delivered in verse or in prose, frequently (but not exclusively) performed by a single narrator for an audience, live and/or with the aid of technology (where technology may include a traditional musical instrument as well as digital software). Ultimately, the notion of 'amplification' will in this context be deployed in both of its present-day senses as either technological (electronic process of making sounds louder) and/or the political (processes of making marginalised voices heard).

Emplotment: From Gusle to Gestalt

Here I return to my native culture that I am experientially more entangled with than other marginalised cultures, and to the work of my friend Vuk introduced in the Preface. Serbia's perceived contribution to the European canon and epistemology has been negligible but Vuk's 19th-century ethnographic focus on recording Serbian oral literature could be seen to have contributed to Romantic fervour in Europe and, later on, to the transformative postulation of Milman Parry and Albert Lord's that the compositional practices they observed in their fieldwork in the Balkans revealed the nature of composition of Homeric verse: that performance preceded and preconditioned the text. This finding of potential interest to performance studies has hitherto remained relatively unexplored both in Serbia and elsewhere, partly due to the persisting Western European methodologies of studying oral heritage as text and partly due to the ontology of performance as an immaterial object of study. Given the performance studies focus of this book, I will therefore replace the traditionally used term 'oral literature' with Ngũgĩ wa Thiong'o's more accurate 'orature' (2007). This will also allow the current discussion to eventually connect to Ngũgĩ's optimistic notion of 'cyborality'/'cyberture' (2012) as a decolonising epistemology that prioritises network over hierarchy.

In seeking to record the ephemeral culture of the illiterate South Slavs, Vuk collected their epic, lyric and erotic songs/poetry,[2] fairytales, spells, incantations, and proverbs. Epic songs in particular, like much of Homer, also functioned as a form of historiography, and Vuk's Enlightenment bias therefore explicitly favoured the singers more mindful of the narrative logic in performing the epics than those exhibiting the performative or improvisational flair:

> Although there are plenty of people who know many songs, it is hard to find a person who knows the songs well and clearly. The late Tešan Podrugović was the one and only among all I met and listened to over the last ten years. [...] He knew how to play the gusle well, but he didn't know how to sing (or didn't ever want to), but instead he spoke the songs as if reading from a book; and for the collection of songs, those people are the best, because they are really mindful of the order and the thoughts, while the singers (especially those that are just the singers) often sing without thinking about what they are singing; they only know how to sing, and they can't speak (I had much trouble with such singers).
> (Karadžić 1824: xxxiii, my translation)

However, there is evidence that the performance aspect of the orature was just as important. I'm reminded, for example, that Vuk's division of the songs into 'male' and 'female' was determined by the style of their performance whereby the female songs are dialogic, collectively sung, and participatory (with the performance aspect more important than the song), while the epic songs are performed to an audience by a solo performer, accompanied by the one-stringed instrument gusle (Figure 3.1), and the transmission of the content is of key importance. This already implies a distinction that is of direct relevance to my concerns with polyphony vs transmission explored in the previous chapter; however, the stated emphasis on storytelling and its technicities necessitates further investigation of epic orature here. In 1827, the English author and politician Sir

John Bowring published his own collection of Serbian oral poetry in translation and in his Introduction reported a rare account of the audience reception of oral epic performance:

> At the end of every verse, the singer drops his voice, and mutters a short cadence. The emphatic passages are chanted in a louder tone. "I cannot describe," says Wessely,[3] "the pathos with which these songs are sometimes sung. I have witnessed crowds surrounding a blind old singer, and every cheek was wet with tears—it was not the music, it was the words which affected them." As this simple instrument, the Gusle, is never used but to accompany the poetry of the Servians, and as it is difficult to find a Servian who does not play upon it, the universality of their popular ballads may be well imagined.
>
> (Bowring 1827: xiv)

FIGURE 3.1 Gusle (2014)

Photo: Michael John Bowring[4]

There is much to unpack here regarding the audience reception and the significance of the instrument, and I will return to the various aspects of this historiographic preamble to the current chapter's focus. However, it is helpful – and relevant to the preceding discussion in Chapter 2 – to first of all take into account the key changes in the development of thinking around storytelling from the oral epic via the Bakhtinian dialogic/polyphonic narrative to the present day with a view to its changing cultural status and potential 21st-century manifestations.

In her long-historical study of the performativity of authorship, Silvija Jestrovic (2020) discusses the retroactive attribution of 'authorship' (or 'retrojection') in classical tradition to Homer as a composite figure based on a long line of performative repetition, transmission, and gradual transformation of the verbal content through performance by the *poietes* (singer/maker) and *rhapsodes* (weaver of songs). Classicists are not entirely clear on the changing uses over time of these two terms and the related *aoidos* (singer), but according to Jestrovic, *rhapsodes* are particularly important for the transmission of epics and are collectively referred to as the 'tribe of Homer' – *Homeridai* (2020: 40–1). Combining the claims of inherent dialogism and co-authorship evident in the oral epic composition by literary critic Andrew Bennett and classicist Gregory Nagy, Jestrovic, who is interested primarily in the performativity of authorship, ascribes the Bakhtinian notion of 'heteroglossia' to this type of author to reflect the authorial figure's inherently composite nature (a kind of performative palimpsest), constituted through live performance:

> The author, thus, comes into being from a performative situation where the distance between the performer/author and the audience is also fluid. Homer, the author, emerges in a collective body sustained and renewed through performance over a long period of time. Here, the author is both conceptually and literally a heteroglossic figure.
>
> (Jestrovic 2020: 42)

Thus in Jestrovic's designation, heteroglossia does not refer to the dialogic nature of the text itself but to the polyphonically layered nature of the authoring process through multiple re-performances and repetitions. Whether or not the epic text itself can be perceived as heteroglossic is open to debate – and according to Kasia Lech (2021) heteroglossia can be asserted to apply to all verse even if Bakhtin himself disqualified poetry from such categorisation – however, this is a less crucial question here.

In Bakhtinian terms, the text of the oral epic is not polyphonic as the only voice available in transmission is that of the singer, confined by a strict meter, even if and when dialogue is featured within the narrative. The voice is accompanied by the musical accompaniment and this combination of voice and music is the sole source of potential polyphony in performance. Though the singer uses the musical instrument mostly as a mnemonic and compositional tool, this type of polyphony may well create scope for counterpoint and space for the affective engagement of the audience as documented by Wesely (quoted in Bowring above). However, the text itself is not yet polyphonic in a Bakhtinian sense as, according to Bakhtin, the 'plurality of consciousnesses' (1989: 6) within the novel was the innovation of Dostoyevsky's. Liisa Steinby explains this further by retracing the way in which the Romantic quintessential genre of the novel emerged in practice and in theory by opposition to its predecessor the heroic epic, and became part of the metaphysical endeavour of the period:

> Where the epic presents the world as it is objectively given for the whole of the community, the novel, which is the most modern and most Romantic of literary genres, is the most subjective, expressing the world view of the creative subject, the poet.
>
> (Steinby 2013: 7)

The function of the arts, including the novel, in this German Romantic paradigm is cognitive and epistemological as it, according to Hegel, 'strives to grasp the existence in its entirety of the Absolute' (ibid.). Building on this, Hegel's aesthetic also views the arts as a means of representing the absolute in a perceivable form, but with modernity, the civilisation has reached a point where 'the complexity of the modern world can no longer be captured in the signifying form or *Gestalt* of a work of art' (in Steinby 2013: 7, original emphasis), and therefore philosophical thinking is needed to complete the comprehension of the totality of existence that evades the hero (of the novel). It is here, according to Steinby, that Bakhtinian understanding of the novel, foundationally informed by the German philosophy, makes an alternative contribution in that it proposes a model whereby the experience of the world becomes an intersubjective encounter between individual subjectivities and discrete perspectives of the ethically responsible subjects. Steinby further notes:

> The Dostoevskyan novel represents a subject-philosophical turn from the lonely 'I': not back to the collective 'us' of epic, but to the necessity of genuine encounter with other subjects, just as autonomous and individual as oneself. In the polyphonic novel, co-subjectivity is assigned to other persons outside oneself.
>
> (2013: 11)

And therefore she requalifies this 'polyphonic novel' more accurately as a 'polysubjective novel' – 'definitely a modern genre' (2013: 12). Though it is possible to envisage how this process more easily plays out in the theatre, a question arises as follows: how does the work of storytelling engender polysubjectivity and intersubjective engagement of the audience in the 21st century?

Interestingly, Adriana Cavarero claims that the epic poetry too 'anticipat[es] post-modernity in its narrative model' (1997: 26), characterised by impartiality which is shared by both the poet (Homer) and the historiographer (Herodotus) in their tendency to depict the heroic deeds of Greeks and Trojans in equal measure, leading to a multi-perspectival narration and richness of plot, driven by action. What this account, alongside Steinby's, suggests is a sense of continuity regarding basic features of authorship as multi-perspectival that connects the epic poetry and the dialogic 'polysubjective novel' as well as modernity and postmodernity. It follows that the implied sense of discrepancy in this historical continuum belongs to the eponymous individualist figure of the Romantic 'author', created in this historic period for the first time.[5]

The Romantic author also brings about the notion that the writers should break from tradition to create something 'original'. Both Jestrovic and book historian Martha Woodmansee (1992)[6] trace this impulse back to the 1759 essay 'Conjectures on Original Composition' by Edward Young, but the modern conception of the author, gradually developed in the latter half of the 18th century through the efforts of writers such as Goethe and Coleridge, 'come[s] to fruition' in 1815 with William Wordsworth's definition of 'genius' as a 'new element in the intellectual universe' (1992: 180). This was the moment when a shift occurred away from the norm of imitation as a means of aesthetic accomplishment (characteristic of the authorship of orature) towards 'originality'. Another important moment which contributed towards the Romantic concept of authorship was the formation of copyright laws, such as the 1710 British Copyright Act, whose implication of 'intellectual property', according to Ron Moy encouraged the development of consumer societies (2015: xxi).[7]

The long historical perspective makes it possible to see the 18th century as a relatively brief moment in the history of creative authorship, which the proximity bias perhaps makes seem definitive and continuously influential up to the present day. The Romantic author has verbally defined, publically established, and legally protected the latter-day figure of the author, and, additionally, ideas of celebrity, talent, ego, genius, originality, and subjectivity have been attributed not only to the figure of the author but also to the processes of creative authorship, as its constitutive aspects.

On the other hand, the long historical perspective also runs the risk of totalising perceptions of the processes that might have played out differently within specific realms. For example, the late 19th century which according to Bakhtin promoted a 'plurality of consciousnesses' in a dialogic novel coincided with a series of trends that led to the reduction of intersubjectivity within the theatre auditorium. On the one hand, Worthen (1997) and Puchner (2011) have shown how the professionalisation of the author (and the critic), prompted by the popularisation of the printing press, affected the division of labour and elevated the status of text in theatre. The emergence of the legally, publicly, and canonically circumscribed figure of the 'author' – retroactively applied to theatre artists such as Shakespeare who had been primarily a 'theatre man' rather than 'author' in his day and age – established a vertical hierarchy between the authorial genius and the general public. This hierarchy was compounded further by the late 19th-century emergence of naturalism and stage realism (significantly the foundation of Theatre Libre in Paris in 1887 by André Antoine and the foundation of Moscow Art Theatre in 1898 by Konstantin Stanislavsky and Vladimir Nemirovich-Danchenko), whereby its introduction of the largely prevailing stage convention of the 'fourth wall' further limited the visibility, and thus the agency, of the theatre audience. This shift, amply explored and challenged by much theatre scholarship of the 20th century, strictly renounced conventions such as asides and direct address, and arguably also reduced the scope for intersubjectivity, co-subjectivity, and polysubjectivity within the live encounter, leading to a largely unidirectional transmission of the fictionally hermetic stage content to the auditorium. To be clear, this did not of course preclude the possibility of Rancièrian (2007) emancipated spectating within the auditorium, or of Bakhtinian/Dostoyevskian polysubjectivity within the fictional world of the play itself – a quality that theatre is certainly even more capable of than the novel. However, while the 19th-century prose authorship gained a polysubjective dimension, the simultaneous introduction of the fourth wall in theatre did disrupt or diminish the audience's participation in the polysubjectivity of the live public encounter that had been a constitutive feature of this artform historically.

By relating Bakhtin's idea of the polyphonic novel to Hegelian perception of modernity as requiring a new intersubjective impulse that goes beyond the collective consciousness of the epic, Steinby implies a linear structure of progress that raises the question 'what next?'. It is not the task of this work to engage in this quest. By taking a long historical perspective and seeking resonances between the pre-Romantic and the postmodern/postdramatic ideas of authorship, I do not subscribe to the totalising Western idea of linear progress. Rather I wonder what insights a polyphonic conception of historiography of authorship might reveal? To this end, I open up the field to examples of authorship that provide a contrapuntal perspective and invite further reflection.

Culmination: Form vs Content

At this point, I am obliged to address another crucial problem that pertains to my focus on Serbian orature. The real reason I keep referring to Vuk Stefanović Karadžić by his first name rather than his full or last name is the unease I feel about the patronymic Karadžić that also now belongs to the convicted war criminal and Bosnian Serb leader, Radovan Karadžić. What is more, Radovan Karadžić, a former published poet and medical doctor, also popularised gusle-playing during the Bosnian war (1992–95). On his arrest in 2008, he was discovered to be living in disguise, under a false identity, working as an alternative health practitioner and frequenting Belgrade's ultranationalist bar The Madhouse, where he was often seen playing the gusle for gathered audiences (Borger 2008). The practice of oral composition had indeed continued throughout the 19th and 20th centuries in various everyday contexts in South East Europe,[8] although as noted by ethnomusicologist Jasmina Milojević this practice ceased and deteriorated in quality after the Second World War (2007: 124).

Although never restricted to the Serbs exclusively – Vuk did his ethnographic work throughout the region and Milojević indeed notes that the practice was present among Croats,[9] Bosniaks, Montenegrins, Macedonians, and Albanians as well as Serbs – the epic orature did acquire an association with nationalism due to its historiographic content and its association with the Romantic nation-building fervour. In the 19th century, this shared heritage served as a tool of national awakening among the South Slavs and fuelled their united efforts towards eventual liberation from the Ottoman and Austro-Hungarian colonialism. It was subsequently included into the local literary canon during the Yugoslav years where it was studied by reference to the theory and history of Western literature. In these classes, we learnt, probably via the influence of Gustav Freitag's *Die Technik des Dramas* (1863), inspired in turn by Aristotle's *Poetics*, that the Serbian oral poems had a five-part structure, consisting of: exposition ('ekspozicija'), emplotment ('zaplet'), culmination ('kulminacija'), peripeteia ('peripetija'), and resolution ('rasplet').[10] Other important formal considerations included the decasyllabic meter of the verse and the analysis of certain stylistic figures and oral formulas (the 'Slavic antithesis', for example).[11] The actual improvisatory techniques involved in composing the works or their relationship to music (which sounded 'boring' and primitive to the Yugoslav intelligentsia (Milojević 2007: 126)) were not deemed important.[12]

Wesely (quoted by Bowring above) claims that it is the power of the words that has the emotional effect on the audience in this context, and Cavarero indeed lends credibility to this thesis when she discusses the immortalising power of narration to give meaning to one's life story, as exemplified by Odysseus's tears when he listens to the rendering of his story in disguise (1997: 18) or by an ordinary Italian woman Emilia similarly moved by her friend's capture of her life story in words (1997: 55). On the other hand, Jestrovic provides an account of Jean-Jacques Rousseau shedding tears at his visit to the Drury Lane in London despite not understanding the language because, according to Rousseau 'the expression of pure emotion can be reached only when semantic meaning gives way to melodic meaning' (2020: 89) and more likely, according to Jestrovic, because of the nature of the collective experience in which the pubic gaze directed at the Romantic author elicited a performance from him. Rousseau's claim chimes with the contemporary biomusicological perspective which seeks to explain the complex nature of the affective response via the theory of entrainment which places the power of rhythm (or prosody) at the core of the potential of live performance to unify the audience response. My view is that the key is in the composite effect of the layering of the words, the music and the performance context. Ngũgĩ insists on a holistic approach to understanding orature as not only a multi-art form, but in fact a weltanschauung 'that assumes the normality of the connection between nature, nurture, supernatural and supernurtural' (2012:75). Though this would be an intriguing prospect in relation to Serbian orature for future study, the task at hand here is to determine the workings of the potential dialogue between form and content, or storytelling and its technicities.

Milojević further highlights that since its discovery by the enlightened West in the 19th century, the epic orature of the South Slav peasants carries a sense of anachronism and cultural delay. As an epistemological tool of the illiterate people, it has served to conserve, transmit, and perpetuate their outdated and patriarchal values, which, as Milojević compellingly claims, still survived well into the 20th and 21st centuries under various masks of contemporaneity due to the depth of their entrenchment. In this narrative, it then follows that the epic orature that continues to be created in the present day about the more recent history reasserts itself after 50 years of communist repression[13] in its most conservative, most radically nationalist, most explicitly warmongering form in the respective localities of the various South Slav nations. Milojević calls this practice 'novo guslarstvo'/'new gusle-playing'.[14] She links this to a retraditionalisation of the local societies in the early 1990s, the political manipulation of culture, and also to a commercialisation of the archaic form aided by recording technologies (noting DIY audio recordings of the live performances which became available on street markets at the time). Though much of this rings painfully true, the final upshot of Milojević's discussion, underpinned by the observation that the performative aspect of the form depends on the audience whose enthusiasm continues to keep it going, seems to imply a sense of desolate resignation about a complete degradation of the society and its culture.

Milojević's cultural pessimism is contrasted in an interesting way by the case study of 'Smrt popa Mila Jovovića' by the contemporary Serbian/Montenegrin/Yugoslav rock music artist Rambo Amadeus (real name Antonije Pušić). 'Smrt popa Mila Jovovića' ('The Death of Priest Milo Jovović'), which is included on Rambo Amadeus's 1991 album *M-91*, is a contemporary reworking of a 'new gusle' number of the same name, written in 1977 by Montenegrin poet/gusle-player Božo Djuranović. Atypically of the traditional epic poetry, this text uses eight rather than ten syllables; however, it has many of the recognisable oral-formulaic and archaic vocabulary features.[15] Contrary to Milojević's observation that the gusle-playing instrumentation and form of singing did not easily lend itself to pop culture adaptation (2007: 127), Rambo Amadeus proved the opposite and his version actually propelled the original to a much greater popular attention than it had previously had within the narrow confines of its own audience of 'new gusle' fans.

Rambo Amadeus's version capitalises on the analogy I mentioned in the Preface concerning the orature and hip hop.[16] Hip hop must be properly understood as a Black American cultural form to account for its struggles in gaining cultural significance (Tate 2003), and this lineage also pertains to rock music more widely as the next chapter will show. Additionally, hip hop generates its own multifaceted histories of contemporary performance practice including b-boying, graffiti writing, MCing, and DJing as well as a specific form of theatre-making, defined by Katie Beswick and Conrad Murray (2022).[17] Notwithstanding this larger context, to which I will return, the case study of the music video of Rambo Amadeus's 'Smrt popa Mila Jovovića' (Figure 3.2) will have to be analysed here within its specific cultural context of former Yugoslavia (whose relationship with

Amplified Storytelling 103

FIGURE 3.2 'Smrt popa Mila Jovovića' (1991) by Rambo Amadeus
Photo: Screenshot from the YouTube video

rock music, incidentally, carries its own political significance to be explored elsewhere). Although the choice of this case study is largely atypical of the rest of the A/OD project, it was crucial in its conceptualisation.[18] Its analysis here will therefore serve to illuminate some key insights about the polyphonic workings of multimodality in aural/oral dramaturgies.

The most immediately obvious feature of Rambo Amadeus's 'Smrt popa Mila Jovovića', both in its audio and video form (https://www.youtube.com/watch?v=s6X3aD3ki3s) is its use of sampling, which is frequently highlighted as definitive of hip hop (see JQ in LMYE Gallery#1 2020: 6).

The polyphonic nature of sampling, which juxtaposes extracts from well-known pre-existing works within the context of a new original work, can also be understood to contain the capacity for juxtaposition and, following on from the discussion in the previous chapter, for creating semantic gaps that engage the audience's attention. But there is more to the use of sampling in this case. The original song concerns a historical figure from the 19th century, a Montenegrin priest and rebel, 'pop Milo', who died in combat with the Ottomans. Although there are different narrative accounts of his death, the one given in the song is described as heroic but unnecessary as it is driven by hubris rather than acts of heroism (contrary to protocol, the hero is fatally shot when he challenges a Turkish leader to a duel). Rambo Amadeus made his version at the time when the interethnic wars in Yugoslavia were starting and the song can be interpreted as a satirical comment on these events, manifesting anachronistic and ill-conceived ideas of heroism, nationalism, and violent impulses. Additionally, the music video features dynamically filmed footage of the artist on a street singing to camera, combined with samples from Sergei Eisenstein's 1938 film *Alexander Nevsky* about the invasion of the Russian territory by the German Teutonic Order in the 13th century and featuring battle scenes in particular. Ivana Vuksanović provides a detailed reading of 'Smrt popa Mila Jovovića' (2015: 267–8) both on the musicological[19] and the visual level.[20] Because the subject of Vuksanović's research is humour in contemporary Serbian music, a particularly interesting aspect of the analysis highlights the incongruence 'created through the conjunction of the archaic epic verse with the modern, urban sound pattern of the rock drums and synthesiser' (2015: 267). According to the theory of humour, this incongruence is constitutive of the sense of irony created by the artist; however, it also highlights 'the leap that our consciousness performs from one associative context to another' – or, following the conclusions of the last chapter, we could say: from one modality to another – in order to process the 'intertextual collision of codes' (2015: 267). Thus, contrary to the 'new gusle' movement which conserves the form and the formula to produce new nationalist content, the audio-visual creation of Rambo Amadeus does the opposite. The artist does not merely narrate a story or even seek to make an explicit political comment; instead, he foregrounds formal innovation to engage the viewer/listener in a process of semantic decoding and interpretation of its complex 'collision' of narrative, sonic, and visual materials, so to engender a critique of populism, pseudohistoricism, and the war propaganda rhetoric of the current moment.

This strategy can be further understood in the context of the artist's performance idiom. *Psihološko-propagandni komplet M-91 (Psychological propaganda set M-91)* (1991) was Rambo Amadeus's third studio album and by this time he had established a distinct stylistic profile and conceptual approach already evident in his highly evocative, oxymoronic pseudonym, which had been coined in 1987. Kristian Džido, in his MA dissertation on Rambo Amadeus's music videos, notes that in his early career Rambo Amadeus was often described as an 'artist and media manipulator' (2020: 31), although Džido characterises all of the artist's media activity as ultimately a form of political activism which has taken a range of manifestations including anti-war public interventions in live music events, public speaking, documented environmentalist activity, and acting as an ambassador of good will on behalf of his native country Montenegro. Two other crucially important ingredients of Rambo Amadeus's performance idiom are also, as noted by Vuksanović (2015), humour and musical virtuosity, evident in his live concerts which often feature extensive improvisations and provide another platform for musical intertextuality. Vuksanović qualifies Rambo Amadeus's deliberate presentational ambiguity as a form of camp, specifically evident in his first album *O tugo jesenja (Oh, you sadness of autumn)* (1988), where he appears on one side of the sleeve dressed up as Milos Forman's film character Amadeus and on the other, dressed as Sylvester Stallone in the role of John Rambo – a juxtaposition usually perceived as an example of postmodern eclecticism. Perhaps it's interesting to note that Rambo Amadeus participated in the 2012 Eurovision contest on behalf of Montenegro, but his song 'Euro Neuro' has been repeatedly voted one of the competition's worst, as the author himself is proud to note.[21] Rambo Amadeus's major contribution to the local cultural scene is the coinage of the term 'turbofolk' which he ironically used as a designation for his second album *Hoćemo gusle* (*We want gusle*) (1989). As the artist has explained in multiple interviews, his own musical style and the term 'turbofolk' were intended to parody and comment on the social phenomenon of neo-folk music which swept the local popular music scene in the 1970s and 1980s, whereby music that sounded like folk music was composed using synthesisers and more contemporary technologies causing aesthetic dissonance and raising sociological and cultural questions about taste and consumerism. The greater irony was that Rambo Amadeus's term 'turbofolk' was hijacked by the popular music industry in the 1990s and now serves as a legitimate generic designation for the kind of pop/neo-folk music genre that became even more commercialised as an ideological tool in supporting the warmongering exploits of the Yugoslav/Serbian state under Slobodan Milošević (see Gordy 1999, Kronja 2004, LMYE Laboratory #4 Oliver Frljić 2021). This is where we arrive at the crucial questions of the instrumentalisation of technology and the technology of instrumentation.

In epic orature performance, the instrumental accompaniment of the gusle is seemingly invisible/inaudible to critical perception, partly because it serves predominantly as a rhythmic/mnemonic tool for the singer rather than a source of musical virtuosity, partly because of the traditional textual bias of the Western folkloric scholarship, and partly because of local academic elitism (Milojević op.cit.). The new gusle practice retains the original instrumentation and form, generating new content within the existing formal and thematic constraints in order to retain the fan base whose expectations of formal authenticity perpetuate this. The neo-folk music and turbofolk of the Serbian mainstream target the same popular sentiment of nostalgia for the past, replacing the old technologies of musical instrumentation with synthesisers. However, a significant difference between these forms and the work of Rambo Amadeus is contained in the artist's approach to his tools. Contrary to the reactionary cultural practices described by Milojević, the crucial element in the case of Rambo Amadeus's rendition is the evidence of a critical distance: a space created for the audience's reflection, and an ironic intervention of the author in the epic tradition. The appeal to the author status is also significant, not so much in terms of the performativity of Romantic exuberance (which Rambo Amadeus does possess) but because of the all-important interest in the metaphysical dimension of art, or at least the evidence of a dialogic imagination which follows such intervention. Rambo Amadeus engages his assumed audience's polysubjectivity on a number of levels (not excluding his appeal to a broad range of musical and cultural taste), and also uses the camera in the music video as a means of a direct address (Figure 3.3).

A profoundly influential aspect of the German Romantic metaphysical heritage is exemplified by the triadic dialectical method of thesis-antithesis-synthesis.

FIGURE 3.3 'Smrt popa Mila Jovovića' (1991) by Rambo Amadeus
Photo: Screenshot from the YouTube video

The method, attributed to Hegel but derived from the work of Kant and Fichte, when applied to logic, means that:

> one concept is introduced as a "thesis" or positive concept, which then develops into a second concept that negates or is opposed to the first or is its "antithesis", which in turn leads to a third concept, the "synthesis", that unifies the first two'
>
> (Maybee 2020)

In the essay on fiction and biography mentioned in Chapter 2, Fred Moten uses the insights gained from Sergei Eisenstein's writing on the dialectic method in film to resolve the workings of counterpoint at the centre of his enquiry. Specifically, Moten focuses on a quote from Eisenstein which conceives of conflict between the abstract idea of the thesis 'forming itself spatially [...] within the shot' before it 'explodes with increasing intensity in montage-conflict among the separate shots' in a way that is 'fully analogous to human psychological expression' (Eisenstein in Moten 2017: 64). On the basis of this, Moten concludes:

> Eisenstein [...] helps us to think montagic sequencing as counterpoint, dynamic totality as fantastic-documentary drive. Out of nothing, out of the mere insignificance of irreducible, conflictual seriality, comes everything.
>
> (Moten 2017: 65)

FIGURE 3.4 Scene from Eisenstein's *Alexander Nevsky* (1938) quoted in 'Smrt popa Mila Jovovića' (1991) by Rambo Amadeus

Photo: Screenshot from the YouTube video

This sort of amplificatory montagic counterpoint, out of which emerges 'everything' – or if not 'everything' then at least, once again, a critical space for reflection – is most clearly illustrated by the case study of Rambo Amadeus's music video version of 'Smrt popa Mila Jovovića' (Figure 3.4).

Peripeteia: Exploding the Narrative

According to Aristotle, peripeteia represents the second reversal in the plot leading towards the eventual resolution. Because in my childhood Serbian school education was mostly based on oral transmission, I cannot quote the exact words from a book that formed my understanding of 'peripeteia' in relation to Serbian oral poetry but I recall that peripeteia also represented the moment in the plot when a multitude of outcomes became possible, thus also causing a sense of suspense or uncertainty about which way the action will go next. At this point in the chapter, I will focus on a multiplicity of perspectives that our field research in A/OD highlighted about the technology of amplification and storytelling, before drawing conclusions about the technicity of amplified storytelling itself.

Contrary to the Aristotelian and Hegelian heritage, an important theme emerging from the artists' testimonies in Lend Me Your Ears collection about their ways of working is the idea of non-linearity. On the one hand, Valentijn Dhaenens (LMYE Gallery#2) and Kieran Hurley (LMYE Gallery#3) both challenged the implicit structure of my questioning to point out that, despite the fact that their output is inevitably perceived in a linear way, the work is never developed sequentially but in various parallel timelines. In their testimonies, this concerns the situation of the artist gestating and developing more than one work simultaneously, but the principle of non-linearity or resistance to predetermined form can also be contained in the way in which the artists think about the composition of performance material. Even when the actual process entails a series of conventionally linear developmental stages from conception to realisation, such as, Melanie Wilson's process (LMYE Gallery#3, 2021: 6), this does not mean that the content itself has a necessarily linear narrative line. Canadian duo Quote Unquote 'don't trouble [themselves] with linear narrative' and instead create 'pools of content' that they match later (Nostbakken in LMYE Gallery#3 2021: 5). In the work prioritising sound, narrative can be altogether non-verbal (as in the work of Eszter Kálmán LMYE Gallery#3), or sound can become a 'narrative property' (Wilson in LMYE Gallery#3 2021: 3) conducive to creating an atmosphere, a three-dimensional sense of space, or even an experiential encapsulation of psychological conditions such as dementia in Wilson's *Autobiographer* (2011) (Wilson in LMYE Gallery#3 2021: 4) and coma as in Shannon Yee's *Assembled, Slightly Askew* (2015) (LMYE #5). Additionally, many artists including SK Shlomo, Gracefool Collective, ZU-UK, Quote Unquote, and, more explicitly, She Goat in LMYE Gallery#5, talk about 'layering' in their work as a primary organisational dramaturgical principle. Dramaturgical focus on sound has generated other dramaturgical terms drawn from electronic sound processing practices such as 'sampling' (JQ in LMYE Gallery#1, Wilson in LMYE #3) and 'looping' (Sammy Metcalfe in LMYE Gallery#1, Nic Green in LMYE Lab#2, SK Shlomo in LMYE Gallery#3), which help to envisage new ways of handling dramaturgical material and supersede the narrative-based ways of thinking about dramaturgy. However, I will briefly dwell on 'layering' here as it provides a more capacious semantic remit (by invoking three-dimensional material entities such as cakes and dresses, as well as musical composition).[22]

Artists think about 'layers' directly by reference to the technological tools they may be using or, by analogy, more metaphorically, as elements of the dramaturgical texture of the work. Thus Quote Unquote describe their process of music composition, using software such as Garage Band or MultiTracks, as entailing visual layering of sound content (Quote Unquote in LMYE Gallery#3 2021: 10). Gracefool Collective (LMYE Lab#3, 2021: 2–13) talk about the process of layering through their use of movement, music, text, speech, singing, all potentially representing different levels of meaning to place into a simultaneous polyphonic relationship with each other on stage. ZU-UK similarly refer to different dramaturgical layers, whereby sound technology itself might be treated as a layer in its own right (Jorge Lopes Ramos in LMYE Gallery#3 2021: 8). By extension, my own process of writing this makes me think about how word-processing software enables reiterative editorial procedures, making layering more viable in textual composition than it might have appeared in the age of handwriting or even typewriting.

While Lech (2021) resorts to heteroglossia, to account for the semantic juxtaposition of form and content in verse, many of the artists interviewed here opt for 'modality' as a term that facilitates discussion of the multi-faceted nature of meaning-making in live performance. Specifically, ZU-UK discuss 'multimodality' in their work, and Kanta Kochhar-Lindgren deploys 'cross-sensory modality' as a means of enhancing accessibility (LMYE Library#3 2021: 1). The dictionary definition of 'modality' denotes 'a particular way of doing or experiencing something' (Cambridge Dictionary),[23] and this can imply particular uses of senses, or alternatively moods, and by extension tools. We have diagnostic modalities in medicine, modal verbs in linguistics (as verbs indicating potential such as 'could', 'should', 'would'), and modal jazz, characteristic of the 1950s and 1960s, and involving modulation between musical modes as, for example, in the improvised performances of John Coltrane (see Wallmark in Siddall and Waterman 2016: 234). Additionally, multimodality has, since 2009, become a central concern of the communication and writing composition studies in US academia, and this move has been promoted by calls to recognise the 'prevalence of sound as a modality of communicating experience' (Alexander and Rhodes 2014: 1).[24] Multimodality in this context refers to fostering diverse types of literacy which include not just the written text but also sound, images, signs, video, and digital data.

It can be posited that one aspect of adding technology to the practice of verbal narration leads to multimodality. Multimodality as a concept therefore seems to me slightly more useful and all-encompassing within a theatre context than heteroglossia or even polyphony. The acumen of multimodality is not focused exclusively on the words/language/voices/sound; and it is implicitly concerned with reception just as much as actual authorship. Nonetheless, heteroglossia and polyphony remain useful in this discussion in that these terms still contain inherents and discursively advanced notions of dialectic or counterpoint as key ingredient of fostering criticality in the process of reception.

The Homeric lyre and the South East European gusle are a form of technology that the singer uses to aid their extemporaneous performance. I have discussed above how the treatment of orature as a (civilisationally more valorised) form of literature within the Western canon and epistemology has occluded important aspects of its performance. The gusle-playing that has continued into the late 20th century in Serbia represents a stultified, politically reactionary mechanism for perpetuating nationalist feeling in the audience without generating artistically valuable content. Rambo Amadeus's version of the new gusle number 'Smrt popa Mila Jovovića' shows, on the other hand, how new audio-visual technologies can be deployed multimodally in the performance of this text to engender an intersubjective critical relationship with the audience. Thus what emerges as particularly significant about the performance of orature is not just the notion of speech per se but the fact that the act of speaking is addressed to an audience which is co-present, especially in live performance (Rambo Amadeus's direct address to camera emblematically emphasises this principle). Speaking to an audience, especially in live performance, as opposed to speech as dramatic dialogue which the audience listens in on, is a significant distinction.

However, what about the technologies of dramaturgical composition? How does the instrument help determine the dramaturgical form and content?

Here I would like to briefly return to the Black roots of popular music. In a groundbreaking academic article, Vijay Iyer (2004) uses jazz and specifically John Coltrane's style of improvisation as a means of challenging the Western notions of disembodied music-playing and narrative coherence in music and storytelling itself. Via musicologist George Lewis, Iyer approaches jazz and African American improvised music more broadly as primarily a dialogic practice, 'an encoded exchange of personal narratives' (2004: 393). Paying attention to both musical content and verbal banter in the outtakes on John Coltrane's *Giant Steps* album, Iyer extrapolates the idea of narrativity that is the outcome of 'a shift in emphasis from top-down notions of overarching coherence to bottom-up views of narrativity emerging from the minute laborious acts that make up musical activity' (2004: 395). The idea of musical improvisation as a holistic, embodied performance leads to the possibility that the idea of 'story' transcends the confines of coherence, antiphony and of relationships between the micro and the macro levels of musical performance. Instead, it 'dwells' in a single note as much as in an 'entire lifetime of improvisations': 'In short, the story is revealed not as a simple linear narrative, but as a fractured, exploded one' (2004: 395). In his fascinating discussion, Iyer, who is also a musician, proffers the view that an improviser is more concerned with making individual improvisations relate to each other and to the improviser's own personal 'sound' – their sound signature or 'performance idiom' as I call it – rather than with obeying standards of coherence. By extension, the notions of 'standards', 'structure', and 'coherence' belong to the analytical toolbox of the critical – presumably Western – listener, rather than the improviser.

Due to the close connection between sound and improvisation, the scope of the present study frequently encounters improvisation as a theme, which unfortunately cannot be fully and properly accommodated as a research object within this book. However, Iyer's study of jazz improvisation grants a helpful permission to consider narrativity as emergent rather than preordained and opens up new horizons for the A/OD project and for the dramaturgical research methodology at its core. Additionally, Iyer's distinction between the improviser and the listener in possession of specific 'critical tools' highlights the analytical critical tools of 'standards', 'structure', and 'coherence' as the biases of Western critical tradition which will require more fundamental reconsideration (as initiated in earlier chapters). Finally, Iyer's central analogy about the shift from top-down to bottom-up conceptions of creativity and narrative can be expanded to accommodate some otherwise overlooked aspects of the performance-making process.

In his account of making *Beats* (2011), a solo show about the criminalisation of rave culture in 1990s Britain, Scottish theatre-maker Kieran Hurley (LMYE Gallery#3 2021: 6) reveals that the innovative form of this piece performed at a desk with a live accompaniment from a DJ, largely emerged out of the material circumstances of its own making – the fact it was commissioned as a reading, by an experimental multi-artform space (Arches in Glasgow), and that he worked on it with an enterprising technical collaborator. Similarly, in working with director Alex Swift on *Heads Up* (2016), Hurley notes that the formal considerations concerning the physicality, style, attitude, and energy in rehearsal, determined and 'informed [the writing] of the text' (LMYE Gallery#3 2021: 8). *Heads Up* (Figure 3.5), as its name suggests, is a warning about the constant and worsening state of crisis experienced on a global level, a paraphrase, as Hurley notes (LMYE Gallery#3 2021: 8) of the variously attributed quote, made famous by the opening of Mark Fisher's *Capitalist Realism* (2009) that it is 'easier to imagine the end of the world than the end of capitalism' (2009: 1). Dramaturgically, the piece builds up to what I referred to as a moment of 'rupture' on seeing the piece at the Edinburgh Fringe (Appendix 3.1) – described by Hurley as a moment of 'turning the gun on myself'. This is a moment in the text where this 21st-century author, the storyteller, explicitly refers to himself in order to deliberately relinquish control of the narrative.[25] For Hurley as a theatre-maker, the attraction of this gesture was the momentary syncing up with the here and now of 'the shared space of the theatre' (LMYE #3 2021: 9), the procedure designated by Hans-Thies Lehmann as 'the irruption of the real': 'not the assertion of the real as such [...] but the unsettling that occurs through the *indecidability* whether one is dealing with reality or fiction' (1999/2006: 101, original emphasis).

FIGURE 3.5 *Heads Up* (2016) by Kieran Hurley
Photo: Niall Walker

This kind of ambiguity effect, created by a deliberate collision – or 'irruption' – of the real time and place of performance into the 'fictive cosmos', is a foundational feature of theatre as an artform. The irruption of the real could be seen as definitive of the modality of theatre itself, if there were such a thing, made even more significant by the temporary suspension of its use in the context of the 19th- and 20th-century realist dramatic theatre. Lehmann, for example, notices the 'disruptions of closure' of the fictive cosmos (1999/2006: 100) in various conventionalised forms such as direct address in Shakespeare's work. Except for its ontological considerations in performance theory, before Lehmann, the dramaturgical potential of the here and now of performance may have only come under academic scrutiny of metatheatricality, or more broadly auto-reflexivity. It is also possible to claim that the main constitutive element of the ambiguous interplay between the here and now of performance vis-à-vis the fictional world on stage is the co-presence of the audience. Hence, the dialogic, polysubjective engagement of the audience in the here and now becomes the sine qua non of the 'storytelling revival' within the amplified apparatus of postdramatic theatre.

In writing about the works that prioritise speech and sound such as Hurley's *Heads Up* and *Beats* (Appendices 3.1 and 3.2), I often posed the question about what distinguished them from radio plays. The answer always is: the potential created by the live co-presence of the audience. I qualify this potential as dialogic, even when the work does not explicitly convene a dialogue on stage or with the audience, and this is enabled by Iyer's discussion of 'the dialogical construction of multiplicities of meaning' inherent to jazz, whereby communication is considered a process, 'as a collective activity that harmonizes individuals rather than a telegraphic model of communication as mere transmission of literal, verbal meanings' (2004: 394). Different degrees of dramaturgically contingent audience involvement can be detected in the works of the 21st-century storytellers such as Kieran Hurley who, in my perception, invites 'poetic activism' (Appendix 3.2), Nassim Soleimanpour who 'lead[s] the audience to believe that the success of the show really depends on them' (Appendix 3.3), Rachel Mars whose own polyphonic storytelling is a cross between therapy, sermon, and exorcism (Appendix 3.4), Ontroerend Goed who convene a collective act of 'imaginative virtuosity' (Appendix 3.5), or Dead Centre who put the audience inside the head and potentially inside the body of the protagonist (Appendix 3.6). These works, even though they foreground speech and sound, are also at the same time 'embodied' in a way similar to Iyer's conception of jazz – and indeed the interviews with Quote Unquote, ZU-UK, Melanie Wilson, and Kieran Hurley in LMYE Gallery#3 testify to this sense of embodiment – as well as being spatial and immersive or relational.

Theatre is inherently multimodal; however, the increased deployment of technology as part of live performance also creates, according to the artists we interviewed, new opportunities for exploration of theatre form and deliberate interplay between the fictional and the real. Michael Wilson drew a strict distinction between the more intimate community-oriented variety of storytelling in the United Kingdom and the 'platform storytelling' in the United States characterised by bigger audiences, virtuosic display, and the use of the microphone (2006: 59). The theatre-makers we interviewed testify to more creatively inspired and dramataurgically contingent uses of the microphone for the purposes of storytelling. Microphones in a very obvious way allow for amplification of voices which can be an important political and aesthetic act. ZU-UK (Figure 3.6) frame the act of giving the audience a mic as a significant act of voice-giving (LMYE Gallery#3 2021: 15). However, very frequently the fusion and separation of live and pre-recorded voice are deployed for the purposes of intersubjectively engaging the audience in moments of playful ambiguity. This 'mic drop out' moment is featured in *Lippy* and described as a 'seductive and a joyful gag, [that] has this emotional resonance of a dislocation and a disembodying of the voice' (Moukarzel in LMYE Gallery#2 2021: 5). Sleepwalk Collective (LMYE Lab#1) and Ontroerend Goed (Appendix 3.5) have used it too, and ZU-UK are interested in it as a way of exploring the audience's 'slippages of perception' (ZU-UK in LMYE Gallery#3 2021: 12).

A similar process of using sound technology to playfully alter terms of engagement is facilitated by headphones, despite their tendency to 'exclude the exterior world of the here and now and enable mediated sound to enter into and resonate throughout the body' thus 'emphasis[ing] the mediatised synergy of

FIGURE 3.6 *East London Worker's Party* (2016) by ZU-UK
Photo: Ludovic des Cognets

body and world' (Klich 2017: 370–71). This technological potential is harnessed by the works of Silvia Mercuriali (LMYE #1), ZU-UK, and Melanie Wilson, all of whom have used the 'cloistered sanctuary' (Klich 2017: 366) bestowed by the headphones as a means of reframing the audience's perception of the here and now of the real world. Following Lehmann, one might call this process: irruption of the fictional into the real. Melanie Wilson refers to this sort of event of live listening, experienced by headphone-wearing audience without the co-presence of the performers as 'refracted liveness' (LMYE Gallery#3 2021: 4) whereas Silvia Mercuriali sees it as 'putting a different spin on reality' (LMYE Gallery#1). In such cases, technology therefore amplifies the audience's own imaginative and creative experience.

Resolution

The final point to make is that storytelling and especially the role of the storyteller, prioritises the marginalised – Vuk's singers were either outlaws, running away from the authorities (like Tešan Podrugović), or the disabled, singing to support themselves (like Blind Živana and Blind Jeca).[26] According to Cavarero, this has a cultural and philosophical rationale too. On the one hand, blindness is the trait of both archetypal singer/storytellers like Homer and mythical seers like Tiresias. According to Cavarero, Tiresias can even be considered the audience's counterpart on the stage in that both Tiresias and the audience know the whole story, but while the audience can watch and not participate, Tiresias can participate without being able to see the proceedings (1997: 25). In some ways, Tiresias as the audience's ambassador is a dramaturgical extension or encapsulation of our intellectual and affective agency on the stage which also facilitates a level of intersubjective dialogue between the fictional world and the real world of the auditorium. Additionally, the blindness – sometimes seen in romantic terms as a lack compensated for by the singing/musical/storytelling talent – can also be perceived as a proof of the storyteller's credentials. It is interesting that Oedipus too, as noted by Cavarero (1997: 14), goes blind once he learns his whole story. Cavarero's interest is in storytelling vis-à-vis philosophy and the way in which in the Western tradition, philosophy has only engaged in abstraction and 'definitory knowledge that regards the universality of Man' (1997: 13). As a result, what it means to be a woman – especially where women have also been traditionally excluded from public life – is most effectively expressed, according to Cavarero, in the intersubjective, relational endeavour of storytelling, or the exchange of the particular 'in-born self-exhibitive impulse of uniqueness' (1997: 62).[27]

In this respect, it is symptomatic that when the Canadian female duo Quote Unquote attempt to tell the story of their protagonist Cassandra in *Mouthpiece* (2015), they do so through a deliberately polyphonic modality both in terms of the writing and performance, whereby both actors play the same character simultaneously on stage:

A lot of the writing that we were doing at the time was allowing ourselves to write the many voices that are happening simultaneously. So in the same piece of writing, writing about how much you love being catcalled, and the other voice saying how offended you are being catcalled. The things that are happening at the same time with different voices in our heads. It just came out that there were multiple voices in a lot of the text that we were writing that felt congruent with our experience, which is: 'I'm not one thing, I'm so many. And they're all happening at the same time. And they're often contradicting each other. I'm not just this way or that way. I'm this way and that way at the same time, and they directly oppose each other.' And so once we began to articulate that through the writing, we realised that to put out there the truth that I do feel both ways, felt like the main thrust of how we were going to communicate the message, that we can't just paint a portrait of a woman, who's just one way, we have to show so many ways she is. And the play could be probably ten women playing the one woman. We decided very purposefully to flip back and forth, and mix up who's which personality and has what opinion, because we wanted to make it very clear that it wasn't the angel and the devil on your shoulder. It's not the virgin and the whore. It's the mess of things in between. And they often happen in a less binary way. So coming to the conclusion that it should just be one person, and we should both play her, felt like the clearest way to make that point.

(Sadava/Quote Unquote in LMYE Gallery#3 2021: 4)

It is not difficult to extend Cavarero's thesis to other members of the Western society that do not fit in with the 'universality of [Western] Man' – or those that are marginalised on the grounds of race, class, sexuality, disability, and other protected characteristics. The particularity of their stories – the 'in-born self-exhibitive impulse of uniqueness' – manifests as 'the desire for biography' (Cavarero 1997: 62) that drives them into an intersubjective relationship with the other. This is where The Unspoken Project's determination to work collectively and across the boundaries of ability is significant. Additionally, this storytelling practice, necessarily multimodal in its expression through instrumentalisation of contemporary technology, draws attention to the inherent multimodality of theatre itself and of the age we live in. AAC technology makes Kate Caryer's storytelling audible, but the act of storytelling, especially when effectively shared, is always already an act of amplification in its own right.

Notes

1 Wilson refers to Bakhtin's discussion of popular cultures in 'Rablais and His World' and to Benjamin's 1936 essay 'The Storyteller', also available here: https://arl.human.cornell.edu/linked%20docs/Walter%20Benjamin%20Storyteller.pdf.
2 The words for song and poem are the same in Serbo-Croatian – 'pesma'.
3 The quoted author is Eugen Wesely, a high school teacher from Vinkovci, (present day Croatia), who had published a volume on *Serbian Nuptial Songs* the year before, full

citation: Wesely, E. E. (1826) *Serbische Hochzeitslieder*. Pest. His name is misspelt in a potential attempt at anglicisation in Bowring.
4 Photographer Michael John Bowring, who lives in Serbia, is a descendent of Sir John Bowring (1792-1872), one of the first translators of the Serbian epic poetry into English.
5 In a chapter dedicated to the Romantic author, Jestrovic describes this figure as often male, and a 'charismatic free spirit, destined to become an author, troubled in one way or another; he/she was also a lover of nature and justice and often revolutionary in his/her socio-political worldviews' (2020: 80). Jestrovic describes the way in which the public persona of the author is facilitated in this period by the emergence of the public sphere, a process which also brings about expectations of heightened performativity of the authorial persona in the public domain as well as within the authors' work. Typical figures are the flamboyant personalities of Jean Jacques Rousseau, Lord Byron, Alexander Pushkin, whose lives (and deaths) are also marked by the kind of drama capable of igniting the public imagination.
6 Woodmansee was my original source in the exploration of the history of authorship for my David Bradby lecture 'Theatre after Gutenberg' (2016), which laid out the beginnings of this research.
7 In contextualising the notion of authorship in popular music, Ron Moy traces another relevant chronology of authorship: from the Hellenic tradition/collective author representing a vessel of god's voice, via the Dark Ages' author taking 'his' authority from a deity and in the 1390s Chaucer declaring himself a 'compiler', to Gutenberg's printing press in 1439 leading to individuation of the author and a linking of the terms author and authority, which further resulted in the 17th-century establishment of the canon and led to the 18th-century Romantic ideas of authorship. Moy concludes this timeline with the emergence of academic criticism at the end of 19th/beginning of 20th century, which he speculates could have been a reaction against romantic tenets of authorship particularly through its insistence on scientific rigour. Academic criticism further led to a fragmentation of stances in relation to authorship, including the poststructuralist stance.
8 A quote from the turn of the 20th century: 'Even the present member of the National Assembly not infrequently speaks in blank verse when his feelings are roused to an exalted pitch. During the winter of 1873-74, happening to be in Kragujevac during the meeting of the National Assembly, I had the opportunity of hearing a certain peasant, Anta Neshich, member of the Assembly, recite in blank verse to numerous audiences outside the Assembly Room the whole debate on the bill for introducing the new monetary system into Serbia, concluding with the final acceptation of the bill'. ([Elodie Lawton] Mijatovic quoted in Mügge, 1916: 18). Also in 2008, a 'Song about Novak Djoković' and specifically his victory over Roger Federer at the Australian Open, composed in the typical decasyllabic of the Serbian epic poetry was widely shared on social media, though this example was clearly more tongue-in-cheek. 'Pesma o Novaku Djokovicu' https://opusteno.rs/knjizevni-kutak-f21/pesma-o-novaku-djokovicu-nole-t1708.html.
9 'Certain Imota Dinaroid on his web page *Hrvatski guslar (Croatian gusle-payer)* (www.tblog.com), in the article titled 'Vratimo dostojanstvo hrvatskim guslama' ('Let's return dignity to the Croatian gusle'), criticises Croats for having so easily allowed Serbs to claim their instrument. The greatest grievance he holds against them is that Jozo Karamatić had made himself and the Serbs world-famous with his song 'Ubistvo u Dalasu' ('The Murder in Dallas'), about the death of John Kennedy, and he was in fact a Croat from Herzegovina'. (2007: 128, my translation)
10 A quick note to relate the technical terms 'zaplet' and 'rasplet' – derived from the verb 'plesti' 'to weave' – back to Homeric 'rhapsode' ('the weaver'), discussed by Jestrovic (2020).
11 The Slavic antithesis is a stylistic formula in Serbian epic poetry, a type of via negativa consisting of a question, followed by a negative answer, followed by a positive answer. A commonly cited example of this is the opening to 'Hasanaginica'.
12 The continued absence of sustained and rigorous scholarly attention to the performative and formal aspects of these ethnographic practices is caused by a combination of factors:

partly by an ongoing elitism noted by Milojević, partly by a systemic emphasis on dramatic theatre at the expense of other forms of performance, and partly by the more globally prevailing notion of the late 20th century that the study of form is less valuable because it is apolitical or reductive, as noted in the Introduction(s).

13 Milojević identifies an ideological dimension to the post-World War 2 decline of orature in that 'the war victories of the partisans in the Second World War have not been immortalised in song' and deduces 'some kind of more or less explicit ban against' the practice during the rule of Josip Broz Tito (Milojević 2007: 124, my translation).
14 As a musicologist, Milojević rightly focuses on the musical instrument as the defining aspect of the epic orature performer's composite identity.
15 For example: 'Planu Milo kao munja, poleće mu sablji ruka, a dva oka ko strijele, sijevnuše u hajduka'.
16 This is corroborated by one of the commenters on the YouTube link, branko1408 noting, probably with the 'expertise' stemming from hip hop fandom: 'the eight-syllable structure is particularly suitable for rap'.
17 Beswick and Conrad have both separately contributed to Lend Me Your Ears #1. Additional relevant contributions include JQ (LMYE #1), SK Shlomo (LMYE #3 and #4), Mtthew Xia (LMYE#4), Arinze Kene (LMYE #4), A.D. Carson (LMYE #4), Rokia Bamba in Auralia.Space Studio. Outside the remit of this project, examples of hip hop theatre and performance to be taken into consideration include the respective works of director Abd Al Malik, poet Kae Tempest's, Lin-Manuel Miranda's *Hamilton* (2015), Jonzi D's work, ZooNation – the Kate Prince Company, Companie Kafig, Victor Quijada's RUBBERBANDance group. With thanks to Caridad Svich for bringing some of these examples to my attention.
18 The significance of this case study in the initial conceptualisation of this research project is evidenced in my David Bradby TaPRA keynote 'Theatre after Gutenberg' (2016): https://www.academia.edu/28301382/Theatre_After_Gutenberg_TaPRA_2016_David_Bradby_Keynote_6_September_2016_University_of_Bristol.
19 'The sound of the gusle is replaced by a developed rhythmic section consisting of rock drums in the song. The sound of the drums, which is the only support for the voice in the opening verses simultaneously signifies tribalist-ritual social practices (for example, going to war!) and the alternative, rock culture (of the rebellious type). In the course of the song, the simplified musical matrix (the deep pedal tone on the synthesiser and the rhythmic sound of the drums) is layered with various other samples: the hum from an unknown source, the sound of gusle, the sound of the hunting horn, sampled voice singing meaningless syllables (nya-mon-nye-nye-nye-nya-nyon), a segment from a dirge… These samples are a compensation for the absence of the primary musical components of an active melody and harmony, but they also form the intertextual "knots". The comic fusions arise out of direct juxtapositions of the drums and the gusle, the serious content of the song and the flippant nya-nya sounds, while the simulation of the dirge, sung in a male voice ("Oh, dear brother, you are off to the army"), changes the usual joyful tone of the army send-off to a sorrowful one'. (Vuksanović 2015: 267, my translation).
20 'The video has been realised through interchange of two types of visual narrative. One type are the sequences where Rambo as a narrator communicates in various ways with the camera (or the TV audience) – stares into its face, looks at it from on high, motions its gaze towards the sky… - or he addresses some children gathered around the church (conveying the symbolic meaning of the oral tradition being passed down from generation to generation). The background details of these sequences (the children, the dome of the Russian church on Tašmajdan, the facades of old houses) function in harmony with the archetypes that epic poetry anyway activates: pride, children, God, traitors, territory, graves… On the other hand, Rambo's image (long hair, fur coat, jeans…), as well as the already mentioned [aggressive] gesticulation, undeniably originate from the rock culture. The second type of the visual narrative is provided by sequences from Eisenstein's film *Alexander Nevsky*. Even though there is a parallelism between the heroic-epic character of the poem and the film, the ironic distancing is achieved through a confusing

juxtaposition between the information provided by the images and the words (we see the Templars' attire, but the words speak of the Turks; we see the sword, axe and mace, and the words mention the sabre…) or between image and sound (we are looking at a horn but we hear the gusle…)…' (2015: 267–8, my translation).

21 See the following: 'The 7 worst songs of Eurovision 2012' (https://foreignpolicy.com/2012/05/24/the-7-worst-songs-of-eurovision-2012/), 'The worst songs?' (http://www.nulpoints.net/the-worst-songs/), 'Eurovision 2017: The worst lyrics in the song contest's history' (https://www.independent.co.uk/arts-entertainment/music/news/eurovision-worst-lyrics-song-contest-history-lordi-hard-rock-hallelujah-rambo-amadeus-10267483.html), 'Rambo Amadeus Euro Neuro is the worst song on Eurosong' (https://newsbeezer.com/serbiaeng/rambo-amadeus-euro-neuro-is-the-worst-song-on-eurosong/).

22 In more metaphysical terms, Ngũgĩ quotes Micere Mugo's conceptualisation of orature through the notion of layers to aesthetically reflect 'interconnectedness of reality'. Specifically, Mugo uses an 'onion structure theory' for this purpose whereby the inner core is then surrounded by 'accumulating layers'. Ngũgĩ reports: 'Orature reflects a reality of connected circles from the inner being of the individual and social person to the outmost circle of "the sun, the moon, the stars, the sky and the rest of the elements"' (2012: 75).

23 Please see: https://dictionary.cambridge.org/dictionary/english/modality

24 Alexander and Rhodes' volume opens with the following contextually useful quote: 'In 2009, Cynthia L. Selfe published an essay in *College Composition and Communication* (*CCC*), "The Movement of Air, the Breath of Meaning," that both galvanized the move in our field to embrace multimodal and multimedia compositional practices and articulated the potential consequences for our disciplinarity in a way that provoked immediate attention and debate. Focusing specifically on the prevalence of sound as a modality of communicating experience, exploring insights, and representing identity, Selfe criticizes the lack of attention in composition courses to sound as a communicative domain.' (2014: 1)

25 'And you are a man, sat at a desk, telling a story about the end of the world. And you are sat in a room in this city, listening to a man tell a story which he has told you is about the end of the world. And he knows that you know that it's only the end of the world in this story because he's decided that it has to be, as he speaks and says that I am here. And you are here. And what we have is now.' (Hurley 2016: 46)

26 The aspect of disability possibly acquires a further layer of significance in noting that Vuk Stefanović Karadžić is popularly remembered for his prosthetic leg caused by juvenile rheumatism and which he personally credited with determining his academic career (https://www.iserbia.rs/novosti/anegdote-iz-zivota-vuka-karadzica-2-deo-2101).

27 This is why, Cavarero claims, female friendships are based on the narration of personal stories more so than male ones, which are more often concerned with the what rather than the who (1997: 62).

Bibliography

Alexander, Jonathan, and Jacqueline, Rhodes (2014). *On Multimodality: New Media in Composition Studies*, Champaign: Conference on College Composition and Communication, National Council of Teachers of English.

Bakhtin, Mikhail 1989 [1984]. *Problems of Dostoevsky's Poetics (Problemy poetiki Dostoevskogo*, 1963), edited and translated by Caryl Emerson. Minneapolis: University of Minnesota Press.

Benjamin, Walter (no date). 'The storyteller: Reflections on the works of Nikolai Leskov'. https://arl.human.cornell.edu/linked%20docs/Walter%20Benjamin%20Storyteller.pdf

Beswick, Katie, and Murray, Conrad (2022). *Making Hip Hop Theatre: Beatbox and Elements*, London: Bloomsbury Methuen.

Borger, Julian (2008). 'The night Karadzic rocked the Madhouse', *The Guardian*. https://www.theguardian.com/world/2008/jul/23/radovankaradzic.warcrimes5

Bowring, John (1827). *Servian Popular Poetry*, London: Thomas Davison, Whitefriars. https://www.gutenberg.org/files/39028/39028-h/39028-h.htm#footnote0m

Cavarero, Adriana (1997/2000). *Relating Narratives: Storytelling and Selfhood*, translated and with an introduction by Paul A. Kottman, London, New York: Routledge.

Džido, Kristian (2020). *Aktivizam u medijima na primeru muzičkih spotova Ramba Amadeusa*, Academy of the Arts, Novi Sad, MA thesis.

Fisher, Mark (2009). *Capitalist Realism: Is There No Alternative?*, London: Zero Books.

Goldsworthy, Vesna (1998). *Inventing Ruritania: The Imperialism of the Imagination*, New Haven/London: Yale University Press.

Gordy, Eric D. (1999). *The Culture of Power in Serbia: Nationalism and the Destruction of Alternatives*, University Park: Pennsylvania State University Press.

Hargrave, Matt (2015). *Theatres of Learning Disability: Good, Bad, or Plain Ugly?*, London: Palgrave Macmillan.

Heinemeyer, Catherine, and Durham, Sally (2017). 'Is narrative an endangered species in schools'? Secondary pupils' understanding of 'storyknowing', *Research in Education*, 99(1): 31–55. doi: 10.1177/0034523717740151

Hurley, Kieran (2016). *Heads Up*, London: Oberon Books.

Iyer, Vijay (2004). 'Exploding the narrative in jazz improvisation'. https://jazzstudiesonline.org/files/jso/resources/pdf/IYER–Exploding%20the%20Narrative.pdf

Jestrovic, Silvija (2020). *Performances of Authorial Presence and Absence: The Author Dies Hard*, Cham: Palgrave Macmillan.

Karadžić, Vuk Stefanović (1824). *Narodne srpske pjesme: Knjiga prva*, Lipisca: Brejtkopf i Eršl, https://books.google.co.uk/books?id=jccGAAAAQAAJ&printsec=frontcover&source=gbs_ge_summary_r&cad=0#v=onepage&q&f=false

Klich, Rosemary (2017). 'Amplifying sensory spaces: The in- and out-puts of headphone theatre', *Contemporary Theatre Review*, 27: 3, 366–78. doi: https://doi.org/10.1080/10486801.2017.1343247

Kress, Gunther (2010). *Multimodality: A Social Semiotic Approach to Contemporary Communication*, New York: Routledge.

Kronja, Ivana. (2004). 'Turbo folk and dance music in 1990s in Serbia: media, ideology and the production of spectacle', *The Anthropology of East Europe Review*, 22:1, 103–14.

Lech, Kasia (2021). *Dramaturgy of Form: Performing Verse in Contemporary Theatre*, London: Routledge.

Lehmann, Hans-Thies (1999/2006). *Postdramatic Theatre*, translated by Karen Jürs-Munby, Abingdon and New York: Routledge.

Maybee, Julie E. (2020). 'Hegel's Dialectics', in Edward N. Zalta (ed.) *The Stanford Encyclopedia of Philosophy* (Winter 2020 Edition). https://plato.stanford.edu/archives/win2020/entries/hegel-dialectics/.

Milojević, Jasmina (2007). 'Novo guslarstvo – Ogled o tradicionalnom muzičkom obliku u popularnoj kulturi', *Kultura*, 116/117, 123–40.

Moten, Fred (2017). *Black or Blur: Consent Not to Be a Single Being*, Durham: Duke University Press.

Moy, Ron (2015). *Authorship Roles in Popular Music: Issues and Debates*, London: Routledge.

Mügge, Maximilian A. (1916). *Serbian Folk Songs, Fairy Tales and Proverbs*, London: Drane's Danegeld House.

Ngũgĩ wa Thiong'o (2007). 'Notes towards a performance theory of orature', *Performance Research*, 12:3, 4–7.

Ngũgĩ wa Thiong'o (2012). *Globalectics: Theory and the Politics of Knowing*, New York and Chichester: Columbia University Press.

Pettitt, Thomas (2010). 'Opening the Gutenberg parenthesis: Media in transition in Shakespeare's England', paper written for *Media in Transition 5: Creativity, Ownership and Collaboration in the Digital Age Conference at MIT*, 27–29 April 2010. http://www.learningace.com/doc/2629844/ce0901442755af1b46439e4ee6cd269d/pettitt-gutenberg-parenthesis-paper

Puchner, Martin (2011). 'Drama and performance: Toward a theory of adaptation', *Common Knowledge*, 17:2, 292–305.

Rancière, Jacques (2007). *The Emancipated Spectator*, London: Verso Books.

Siddall, Gillian, and Waterman, Ellen (eds) (2016). *Negotiated Moments: Improvisation, Sound and Subjectivity*, Durham and London: Duke University Press.

Steinby, Liisa (2013). 'Bakhtin and Lukács: Subjectivity, Signifying Form and Temporality in the Novel' in Steinby, Liisa, and Klapuri, Tintti (eds) *Bakhtin and His Others: (Inter)subjectivity, Chronotope, Dialogism*, London, New York, Delhi: Anthem Press.

Tate, Greg (2003). *Everything but the Burden: What White People Are Taking from Black Culture*, New York: Broadway Books.

Todorova, Maria (1997). *Imagining the Balkans*, Oxford: OUP.

Tuhiwai Smith, Linda (1999). *Decolonizing Methodologies: Research and Indigenous Peoples*, London and New York: Zed Books Ltd.

Vuksanović, Ivana (2015). *Humor u srpskoj muzici 20. veka*, Beograd: Fakultet muzičke umetnosti, PhD thesis.

Wallmark, Zachary (2016). 'Theorizing the saxophonic scream in free jazz improvisation', in Siddall, Gillian and Waterman, Ellen (eds) *Negotiated Moments: Improvisation, Sound and Subjectivity*, Durham and London: Duke University Press.

Wilson, Michael (1997). *Performance and Practice: Oral Narrative Traditions among Teenagers in Britain and Ireland*, Aldershot: Ashgate.

Wilson, Michael (2006). *Storytelling and Theatre: Contemporary Storytellers and their Art*, Houndsmills: Palgrave Macmillan.

Wong, May (2019). *Multimodal Communication: A social semiotic approach to text and image in print and digital media*, Cham: Palgrave Macmillan.

Woodmansee, Martha (1992). 'On the author effect: Recovering collectivity', *Cardozo Arts & Entertainment Law Journal*, 10, 279–92.

Worthen, W.B. (1997). *Shakespeare and the Authority of Performance*, Cambridge: CUP.

4
GIG THEATRE

Most simply, the form of gig theatre can be described as the kind of theatre that assumes the stage aesthetic of a rock music gig. In terms of its mise-en-scene, gig theatre expands the process of theatricalisation of sound technology observable in amplified storytelling, whereby the technology is not only used for its auxiliary purpose but as an integral part of the dramaturgical apparatus, for artistic expression. In gig theatre, in addition to multiple microphones, the set often contains the drum kit, synthesisers, guitar amplifiers, and other electronic music-making tools associated with live performances of popular music. The performers in gig theatre simultaneously fulfil the roles of actors and musicians and engage in complex code-switching between the two registers of performance throughout the duration of the show. Although the term 'gig theatre' is sometimes used by artists to describe their own work, it has primarily gained currency through arts journalism coverage of this type of hybridisation emerging within the ecologies of British music and theatre festivals (Latitude, Glastonbury, Edinburgh Fringe, and others). However, the kind of theatricalisation of the rock iconography characteristic of gig theatre is not unique to the United Kingdom, as exemplified by Young Jean Lee's We're Gonna Die (2011), Lola Arias's *Minefield* (2017), Aris Biniaris's *Hill 731* (2019), or Christopher Rüping's *Dionysos Stadt* (2018).

This chapter is most directly linked to my previous work in *Theatre-Making* (2013a) and *The Contemporary Ensemble* (2013b) as gig theatre most obviously illustrates the ways in which collaborative ways of working, coupled with a deprofessionalised, multi-skilled creative approach, have led to dramaturgical innovation and a potential paradigm shift in performance-making. By this I mean, individuals involved in making gig theatre in the United Kingdom are often working in contexts where the 19th-century division of labour into acting, directing, playwriting, and design does not necessarily apply, involving instead DIY ensemble work, playing in a band or as a band, and – when they found their calling as a writer — writing, not as a profession but as an expression of these cumulative creative endeavours. Explicit examples of this in my previous research include Anton Adassinski of Derevo, Adriano Shaplin of the Riot Group,[1] Chris Thorpe of Unlimited Theatre, and playwright Simon Stephens, all of whom have either been in bands, compared their ensemble membership to being in a band, or credited specific bands as influential on their authorship model. My overarching interest in ensemble is focused on how ensemble challenges some of the persisting romantic ideas of authorship discussed in the previous chapter (divine inspiration, genius, individual ownership, and celebrity).

Here the work is necessarily circumscribed by specific cultural contexts in order to be properly understood. My research methodology, focused on illuminating the formative circumstances influencing the creative idioms of selected artists, demonstrates that theatre artists are not just the producers but also the products of their cultures. Individual theatre-makers are immersed within distinctive formative circumstances depending on their own specific networks of influence, but certain aspects of cultural immersion can be seen to be shared across cultures. One such element is the phenomenon generically referred to as 'popular music' or 'rock music'[2] which has since the second half of the 20th century, with the expansion of the recording industry, exerted global influence. Arguably, popular music has in this time fostered its own formal innovations, bottom-up divisions of labour contrary to the otherwise prevalent Taylorist model of workflow organisation,[3] and relationships with the audience that stand in contrast to mainstream bourgeois theatre production.

There has now been a long line of work in sociology of culture exploring rock music fandom as an expression of self- and community-belonging. Joseph Kotarba (2013) has summarised this effectively by claiming that rock music, which has marked the growth of so many generations since the baby boomers (those born in the period 1945–64), particularly in America, is no longer just a 'feature of youth culture', but 'a key feature of adult culture' (Joseph Kotarba 2013: 3). Similarly, technological advancement and mass production throughout the 20th century has given rise to the perennially problematised phenomenon of popular culture consumption starting with the Frankfurt School onwards. In the context of rock fandom, and in continuation of the themes explored in the previous chapter, Daniel Cavicchi makes an interesting point about the affective power of sound technology that 'the microphone, because it favored a relaxed and more personal style of singing, opened up new ways of understanding and interpreting old songs' (1998: 5) which in turn exacerbated stereotypical fan behaviours to the point of fantasy and hysteria. The use of the microphone on the stage, though perceived by Michael Wilson as an impediment to intimacy in storytelling (2006: 59) or as an indication of an actor's inability to vocally project into the auditorium, has by now become a more ubiquitous creative tool for performative display, dramaturgical effect, or for calibrating the audience's attention (Kate Hunter in LMYE Gallery#2, ZU:UK in LMYE Gallery#3, SK Shlomo in Gallery#3).

Kotarba further offers a useful definition of rock music – though he uses the term rock'n'roll as the generic hold-all to include 'heavy metal, pop, New Age, Christian pop, and even rap/hip hop' – as originally 'created for and marketed toward young people', 'primarily guitar driven and amplified', rooted in 'African American musical styles', 'usually danceable', and 'best when played or performed loudly' (2013: 3). In addition, he offers a useful periodisation of the American rock music by reference to four key moments: 1) its foundational association with the 'youth culture' in the 1950s, 2) its diversification through taking on 'broader political implications' of the civil rights and anti-war movements in the 1960s and 1970s (2013: 7), 3) its loss of critical appeal through entrenchment in and control by the entertainment industry in the 1970s and 1980s (accompanied in the United Kingdom by a revolt against the corporatism through punk and new wave as well as the theoretical work of the Birmingham School of Cultural Theory and specifically the emergence of the notion of 'subculture' defined by Dick Hebdige in 1979), and finally, 4) the understanding of rock music as 'simply culture' since the 1980s onwards, a pastiche of popular music, a 'postindustrial or postmodern culture undergoing radical transformation' (Kotarba 2013: 8). Similarly, Simon Reynolds's decade by decade, genre by genre 'surging-into-the-future' historiography of popular music[4] also dissolves into a final phase in the 2000s of 'rampant recycling', 'revivals' or, in one catchy word forming the title of his book: 'retromania' – the 'preserve of aesthetes, connoisseurs and collectors, people who possess a near-scholarly depth of knowledge combined with a sharp sense of irony' (2011: xi–xii). It would be tempting to simply subsume the emergence of gig theatre as a form into this pervasive trend; however, I suspect there is more insight of dramaturgical value available on closer inspection.

Certainly, there are generations of geographically diverse theatre-makers in their creative prime whose childhoods – like mine in socialist Yugoslavia – coincided with the emergence of the globally renowned MTV providing rock music videos 'around the clock' (Kaplan 1987). Whether or not they happened to be avid watchers/listeners or whether they had fan allegiances to specific musical genres, their work could be seen to be manifesting creative idioms influenced by popular music. I am thinking, for example, of the compositional or music video narrative strategies of sampling and montage resorted to by Valentijn Dhaenens, Lola Arias, the Q Brothers, Nic Green, SK Shlomo, Conrad Murray, Quote Unquote, Oliver Frljić, and Matthew Xia (all documented in LMYE interviews, and also exemplified in the previous chapter in the case of Rambo Amadeus). Dramaturgically speaking, these artists from different cultures have more in common with each other than they do with the earlier generations of theatre-makers such as Peter Brook, Peter Hall, Peter Stein or even the more adventurous Pina Bausch, Anne Teresa de Keersmaeker, and others.

This chapter examines some potential genealogies of gig theatre in order to also contextually understand the workings of its dramaturgy which integrates strategies of popular music and (post)dramatic theatre. Because of its hybrid nature, gig theatre requires a polyphonic historiography that accounts for its potential relations to the genealogies of rock music genres, political histories, and (sub)cultural contexts as well as to the histories of theatre and performance. This is impossible to accommodate within a single chapter but I will select some points of consonance and counterpoint in conjunction with some of the examples featured in LMYE#4 to illuminate key aspects of the form as potential points of departure for future work.

Alongside (post-)verbatim theatre and amplified storytelling, gig theatre is a manifestation of the aural/oral dramaturgies scoped by this book, but it also very easily aligns with the 'alternative theatre' provenance of verbatim as established by Paget (2009, via Craig 1980) and the 'storytelling revival' as established by Wilson (2006). Sara Freeman has identified that 'alternative theatre' in Britain has been notoriously difficult to historicise due to the 'contested' vocabularies applied to it. Even though she opts for the method of Foucauldian genealogy in order to map some of these 'names, histories, and valuations' of British theatre made outside of the West End, Freeman observes that what is at stake is a 'network of inference and interpretation that is ever-shifting and necessarily ideological' (2006: 364). As noted in the Introduction(s), Foucauldian principles also underpin my research, but as I move through this book, the multimodal nature of my object of research increasingly challenges the viability of clear unidirectional lines in tracing relations, in favour of divergences, disruptions, webbed intersections, and their inherent capacities to contain contradictions. I will allow for the possibility that my largely experimental DIY attempt at a polyphonic historiography of gig theatre here may ultimately need to leave the order implied by genealogies themselves behind and move towards other, knottier structures such as networks, the topic I leave for the final chapter.[5]

This chapter therefore begins by outlining the emergence of the term charting specifically its use and elaboration by theatre journalists vis-à-vis the stated intentions of the authors, where available. It then moves to trace some more intricate genealogies of this form in the United Kingdom, before attempting to draw some definitive features of the dramaturgy of gig theatre by closer examination of a selected case study. The conclusion returns to issues of cultural contingency to ask to what extent gig theatre is a British phenomenon. Threaded through this structure is also a charting of potential interrelations between gig theatre and musical genres (specifically rock music, punk, post-punk, and rave).

Gig Theatre: The Term

To avoid early sedimentation of suggested definitions that follow, it is worth foregrounding the ongoing instability of the term 'gig theatre' by reference to what selected artists interviewed as part of the A/OD project understand by the term. Here are extracts from four different conversations, offering a range of takes:

> **CB:** I guess with other things I see I'm like: 'Oh, yeah, that's clearly gig theatre', but I'm not very good at, maybe, working out when I would apply it to us. Even though I'm sure we – have we described our work as that before?
> **AS:** I don't think we ever have–
> **CB:** No, we haven't.
> (Clare Beresford and Alex Smith/Little Bulb
in LMYE Gallery#4 2021: 6)

> **CBB:** I guess I would like to take this opportunity to say that I don't think I really know entirely what you mean by gig theatre.
> (Christopher Brett-Bailey in LMYE Gallery#4 2021: 8).

> **DR:** I'm not sure that I actually got a clear sense of how you feel about your work being described as 'gig theatre'. How do you feel about that label?
> **HG:** I don't love it as a label actually–
> **AG:** Me neither–
> **HG:** I think it feels like […] a knowable thing. You know what you're going to get from a piece of gig theatre. […] Even though that's probably quite useful branding in some way – I wouldn't want anyone coming to our show and going: 'This is exactly what I'm going to get', because I think I want to be able to be a bit more surprising than that.
> […]
> **AG:** My problem with it is: it feels like a brand, and I don't really want to be making work that's in a brand. I want to be making – yeah, slippery work.
> (Helen Goalen and Abbi Greenland/RashDash in
LMYE Gallery#1, 2020: 13-4)

> **JM:** I also knew I really wanted to write a piece of gig theatre.
> (James Meteyard/*Electrolyte* in LMYE Gallery#4 2021: 5)

The British Newspaper Archive reveals that the first recorded – though quickly forgotten – use of the term 'gig theatre' appears in the Irish press and is attributed to actor/writer Donal O'Kelly as a description of his piece *The Hand* presented at the Dublin Festival 2002.[6] In anticipation of the Festival, Brian Lavery of the Irish *Independent* wrote:

> *The Hand* is a debut presentation of O'Kelly's idea of gig theatre, a concept that, if it works, will eliminate the boring parts of regular drama, will forge a more open, honest bond between the actors and the audience, and will do it through music. The play becomes a kind of album, with each scene as a track.
> (Lavery 2002: 10)

Lavery further quoted the author's intention to break down the reverent theatre silence, create an atmosphere of a pub, and engage the audience's imagination through eschewing representational theatre conventions: 'I just don't find it interesting to give representational images of what you want the audience to see. If you flick the right hint, they can put a much better picture in their minds' (ibid.: 11). Immediately discernible from this example is a set of traits that will go on to characterise more recent gig theatre, and the artist's quoted intention might also be understood in accordance with the preceding discussion in this book regarding the engagement of the audience's polysubjectivities.

The Hand however did not impress the critics at the time. The *Evening Herald* (Dublin) determined that: 'The mood of the evening lands – sometimes uncomfortably – between Under Milk Wood and Tom Waits in one of his fistfight-in-the-junkyard phases', and noted the incongruity of the piece's intended aesthetic and the black limousines outside its venue on the opening night of the festival. *The Irish Times* was equally resistant, complaining of the lack of acting in this show made by a famously visceral performer. The concert-like presentation was deemed disruptive, and the addition of jazzy score to O'Kelly's writing already characterised by musicality[7] seemed 'excessive' and 'almost formulaic' (O'Toole 2002).

Perhaps O'Kelly was ahead of his time, or the ceremonious opening night of the Dublin Festival was the wrong context for his innovation; however, this example, especially in the way it is documented, incidentally illustrates yet another symptomatic feature of gig theatre in its more contemporary manifestation – its contextual association with festival culture.

Following this early documented instance, the use of the term 'gig theatre' seems to have been discontinued for about a decade. Then in the run up to the Edinburgh Fringe 2016, both *The Stage* and *The Skinny* ran features on the newly emerged trend. Holly Williams in *The Stage* listed a number of previous Edinburgh hits as defining of 'gig theatre': Kieran Hurley's *Beats* (2012), Lucy Ellinson, Chris Thorpe and Steve Lawson's *Torycore* (2013), Brigitte Aphrodite's *My Beautiful Black Dog* (2015), and Middle Child's *Weekend Rockstars* (2015).[8] She also acknowledged the significance of Latitude Festival – a Suffolk relative of the Glastonbury Festival and Leeds and Reading Festivals – whose dedicated theatre stage became a 'major platform' for this form since the festival's foundation in 2006 (Williams 2016). This again points to a direct link between the emergence of the form of gig theatre and the material circumstances of cultural production, specifically the fertile ground of the music festival and the existence of a captive audience with pre-defined expectations.

Both Williams and Amy Taylor at *The Skinny* note the more 'relaxed' code of behaviour in a gig theatre show as its distinguishing characteristic. This intention is particularly well articulated as part of Middle Child's own mission on their website as follows:

Direct address features heavily and our audiences are welcome to photograph the show, or go to the bar or the toilet halfway through and catch-up with their friends when they return. We want our fans to feel relaxed, welcome and as much a part of the night as what they see on the stage.

(Middle Child website)

As well as the idea of accessibility, the desire to engage new, less elite demographics seems very important to the makers of gig theatre. Sabrina Mahfouz, the author of the gig theatre play *With a Little Bit of Luck*, produced by Paines Plough in 2016, is quoted as saying that the form was a 'natural by-product of employing writers interested in wider pop culture' and that 'tapping into a beloved genre or collaborating with a musician can massively widen your audience pool, but it can also help break down barriers to theatre among audiences who fear it's "not for them"' (Williams 2016).

Another theme that resonates across much journalism about the form is also the notion of collaboration and trans-disciplinarity, as indicated by Mahfouz above. Both *The Stage* and *The Skinny* articles mention *Wind Resistance* (2016) by folk musician Karine Polwart, described by Taylor as being about the principle of co-operation, as observed in the behaviour of birds. This piece was commissioned and dramaturged by David Greig under his tenure as Artistic Director at the Royal Lyceum, Edinburgh, and as observed by Williams, it echoes some of Greig's own interests explored in *The Strange Undoing of Prudencia Hart*, 'a raucous ceilidh show staged in pubs' (Williams 2016).[9] David Greig's thoughtful dramaturgical innovations using music have received academic attention elsewhere (Rodosthenous 2011, Wallace 2013, Rodríguez 2019), and he is certainly a significant figure contributing to the story of gig theatre in the United Kingdom.[10]

A year later, in 2017, Holly Williams wrote about gig theatre again, from the perspective of its potential contribution to the flagging music industry. For cross-referencing purposes, it is worth noting that according to official statistics 'the music industry generated a record $43 billion in 2017, but recording artists saw just 12% of that revenue, or $5.1 billion, and the "bulk" of their revenues came from touring' (Delfino 2018). Festivals were once again a focus of Williams's second article on the topic and specifically the programming of the Manchester International Festival (MIF), as well as a number of other contextualising examples of collaborations between musicians and theatre-makers. Former frontman of Noah and the Whale, Charlie Fink, who was at the time launching his new solo LP via a play at the Old Vic, provided a musician's perspective on the benefit of this collaboration (incidentally once again with playwright David Greig), noting that in the age when people were listening to individual songs and playlists the idea of an album was no longer a viable organising structure: 'How can you give the relevant necessity to ten songs being all together? Theatre seems like the place to do it.' (Williams 2017).[11]

Finally, it is worth noting Williams's conclusion that most of these collaborators identify a crucial shared commonality that distinguishes gig theatre from the forms of cultural consumption taking place via screens or mobile phones: liveness and the associated value of community.[12] Liveness in the context of rock music has of course been famously problematised by Philip Auslander (1999/2008) as an ontological aspect of performance that only emerges as a category vis-à-vis processes of mediatisation in the 20th century, and the author has updated his thinking by reference to the digital media (Auslander 2012), but his overarching thesis holds throughout different versions that the live/mediatised binary is not a matter of essential difference but subject to the system of value of cultural economy. My methodological commitment to the artist-centred approach, specifically in this chapter, requires that I consider Williams's finding as a relevant factor of gig theatre. Equally, for the sake of the discussion here, I will commit to the term 'community' as ear-marked by the theatre-makers, rather than, for example, the less totalising more theoretically capacious 'assembly' offered in different ways by both Bruno Latour (2005) and Judith Butler (2015).

In summary, key features of the significance of gig theatre as identified by theatre journalists' overview of artistic practice include: widening audience access, relaxing of theatre-going codes, transdisciplinarity/collaboration, celebrating liveness, and community-building.

It is useful to add to this a definition of 'gig theatre' coming, possibly for the first time, from an academic source. In her book *Theatre Aurality* (2017), Lynne Kendrick positions gig theatre, alongside music theatre, within the context of Hans-Thies Lehmann's 'concept of postdramatic theatre' and immersive performance (2017: 40). Chapter 2, endnote 20 in Kendrick's book attempts a rather all-encompassing critical take on gig theatre which accounts for three potential levels of analysis: the formal aspect of gig theatre and its hybridity facilitated by theatre's postdramatic embracing of the aesthetics and technologies of a music gig, the neoliberal economic context of precarity and gig economy promoting resource-light theatre-making, and the experimental ethos characterised by risk and radicalism (2017: 47–8). Much of this will resonate throughout the rest of this chapter, and it is certainly essential to acknowledge that the emergence of gig theatre is predicated on economic constraints as well as aesthetic idealism.

As illustrated by the selected artists' quotes above, James Meteyard, the writer of *Electrolyte* (2018) is one of the few contemporary theatre-makers fully embracing the label of gig theatre as a designation for his work. Another example of a company similarly subscribing to the promotion of 'gig theatre' is Hull-based Middle Child, mentioned above. Williams's early examples go back to Hurley's *Beats* (2012), but it is worth noting that the emergence of the form had certainly preceded the term's application.[13] I have a recollection that I first heard the term 'gig theatre' by word of mouth at the end of the Edinburgh Fringe 2010 in reference to a number of theatre pieces forming the zeitgeist by using live music on stage. The memory of David Greig and Gordon McIntire's high-profile *Midsummer*, at the Traverse the year before was still lingering, and in 2010, Fringe theatre in the form of gig included, in among others, Little Bulb's roof-raising rite of passage piece *Operation Greenfield*, Christopher Brett Bailey's 'punk rock musical' *The Inconsiderate Aberrations of Billy the Kid*,[14] and the quietly charming

Another Someone by RashDash (see Appendix 4.1). According to the testimonies above, these artists were oblivious to the 'branding' their formal innovations were generating, but by 2016–17, the term was available as a potential marketing tool, becoming ripe for analysis for its co-optation by neoliberal capitalism.

While Kendrick's threefold definition rightly perceives gig theatre as a manifestation of several synchronous aesthetic, political, and economic factors, my interest here, based on the empirical evidence collected as part of the A/OD project, is to understand how gig theatre is also a result of various long-term cultural and historical influences converging and distilling in it. In this endeavour, another concept offered by Kendrick is crucial in encapsulating many of the features described above including inclusivity, collaboration, liveness, and community-building (all equally characteristic of the festival settings too). In her book-length theorisation of theatre aurality, Kendrick identifies 'aural intersubjectivity' as one of seven key characteristics of contemporary theatre and performance 'that is formed through sound' (2017: 39) – i.e. performances elsewhere referred to as 'immersive' or 'participatory' (and in my previous work as 'relational').[15] Kendrick' notion of 'aural intersubjectivity' – which helpfully augments and amplifies the theme of intersubjectivity emerging in the previous chapters via Bakhtin and Bakhtinian scholars – is predicated on a very careful consideration of 'subjectivity' as 'the self which can be constructed by sound – particularly in performance' (2017: 20). Kendrick is specifically interested in processes by which in some contemporary performances sound can construct subjectivities that cast the audience into specific roles or even allow them to assume the role of the protagonist. This might suggest that gig theatre casts the audience in the dual role of rock music fans and theatre-goers, but in the context of this chapter, I am interested in the constructive potential of sound to create and convene temporary communities. This notion of subjectivity, and, by extension, aural intersubjectivity is meticulously defined by Kendrick in concert with several 20th-century thinkers such as Don Idhe, Jean-Luc Nancy, Veit Earlmann, Steve Connor, and Frances Dyson in order to challenge the inside-outside, Cartesian and sensory divisions characteristic of the endemic ocularcentricity of Western philosophy – making it an indispensable means by which to potentially understand the audience's theatre experience as a shared one. Though this does not presuppose a shared sense of identity, commensurability of interpretation, or that all individual audience members' experiences are identical, it recognises the inherently constitutive potential of sound in intentionally constructing audience subjectivities or a preordained temporary polysubjectity in aural theatre which allows us to assume the collective 'we'.[16] As the discussion below shows, this aural theatrical 'we' is understood as a sine qua non of the story of gig theatre both in terms of its dramaturgy and its historiography.

Historicising Gig Theatre 1: Storytelling, Punk, and Genre

The roots of gig theatre that hark back to the simple folkloric traditions are not unrelated to the model of the singer/storyteller explored in the previous chapter in its 21st century amplified incarnation. In reflecting on his Olivier-nominated,

FIGURE 4.1 *This Is How We Die* (2013) by Christopher Brett Bailey
Photo: Screenshot From The Production

fringe-to-West End gig theatre piece *Misty* (2018) in his LMYE Gallery interview, Arinzé Kene perceives it primarily as a way of 'pushing the boundaries of storytelling' (LMYE #4 2021). Here we might also place the solo works of Kieran Hurley's *Beats* (2012) and *Heads Up* (2016), and Christopher Brett Bailey's *This is How We Die* (2013) (Figure 4.1) – all three incidentally delivered in a fashion reminiscent of American artist Spalding Gray (1941–2004) with the author/performer seated at a desk, reading their script into the microphone.

Wilson places Gray and his British counterpart Ken Campbell (1941–2008) within the same category of autobiographical storytelling that had many shared features including an interest in improvisation and 'oral writing' (Gray quoted in Wilson 2006: 132), although neither, according to Wilson, was accepted by the storytelling community. Both Hurley's and Bailey's performances feature live musical accompaniment: in Hurley's case, this implies live mixing of pre-recorded music, and in Bailey's case, live music represents a dramaturgical sting in the tail. Despite these apparent similarities, the two artists do have starkly different artistic idioms and this side-by-side comparison also represents an opportunity to chart a significant divergence within the genealogies of gig theatre. As described before, Hurley's work is often rooted in its Scottish context, and *Beats* in particular is musically located within the British rave music scene of the early 1990s. From those early beginnings onwards, Hurley evolved his playwriting career in a more straightforward dramatic theatre direction exemplified by *Mouthpiece* (2018) at Edinburgh's Traverse theatre and the feature film adaptation of *Beats* (2019). American/Canadian-born Bailey, on the other hand, has a multi-faceted artistic practice working as a performer in other artists' projects as well as authoring solo and collaborative works of new music and theatre. In 2018, *This is How We Die* (2013) was presented as part of a triptych at Battersea Arts Centre with his two other works: an experimental musical performance with text, *Kissing the Shotgun Goodnight* (2016), and the music-only installation *This Machine Won't Kill Fascists but It Might Get You Laid* (2011). His formative influences are not determined by an immersion in the popular culture contemporary to his formative years but informed by a more connoisseur-like devotion to rock music culture as a whole, ranging from Jimi Hendrix to the German band Can, and combined with an enthusiasm for stand-up comedy, especially American artists of the older generation such as George Carlin, Richard Prior, Woody Allen, and Lenny Bruce. Hence Bailey's resistance towards labels such as 'gig theatre' may be linked to an unwillingness to simplify these complex networks of influence. Bailey perceives live music's presence in devised theatre as a historical phenomenon:

> What about the shows that were done by Andy Warhol in the '60s? You know, *Pork* by Andy Warhol is probably the grandparent show of gig theatre.
> (LMYE#4 2021: 9)

Additionally, he identifies Ken Campbell who he was taught by at East 15 as a major influence on his own work:

> A lot of his projects back in the '70s, the Ken Campbell Road Show – I mean they would be putting ferrets down their trousers, and all the stuff would be happening in a bar and everybody was drunk the whole time. The whole idea of it was: I guess you'd kind of call it 'punk', before and alongside punk, but it wasn't even a musical idea, it was an anarchy idea because it came out of humour really.
> (LMYE#4 2021: 9)

Bailey makes an important point here about the semantic convergence of ideological influences drawn from theatre, art, music, storytelling, and comedy which can be perceived synoptically or synaesthetically in theatre by reference to a term denoting musical genre ('punk'). Conversely, musical genre has, especially in relation to taxonomies of popular music, had the function of categorisation, delimitation, and separation. Despite the genre-blurring intervention of postmodernism elsewhere, the notion has, arguably, persisted in relation to music marketing and fandom longer than in other artforms. It might be equally tempting to consider potential varieties of gig theatre by reference to their generic allegiance (for example, Arinzé Kene and Kae Tempest's to hip hop, or Hurley's and Mahfouz's respective allegiance to electronic musics), but this would be misleading. The notion of musical genre soon gets blurred in theatre – as Pitrolo notes: 'music is sometimes so deeply tied into some artists' work that genre taxonomies don't seem to fit' (LMYE Guides: 'Genre', 2022). Possibly this is because theatre is more than just music.

In an interview Emma Rice (ex-Kneehigh theatre) gave me in 2009, she discussed how influential her training with the Polish Gardzienice theatre had been on her as a young theatre artist. However, Rice eventually came to a realisation that some aspects of Gardzienice's rigorous methodology, such as the fetishisation of folk music, had their cultural equivalent in her own formative experiences in the United Kingdom:

> [W]e did not sit around fires and sing songs, we listened to Bay City Rollers, but that is still folk culture. That is really where *Don John* is my letter of love to my childhood. It sounds like punk, it is punk, but it is still my folk culture, it is what I listened to with my mates in my bedroom.
> (Radosavljević and Rice 2010: 96)

Although Kneehigh Theatre is not commonly invoked in the story of gig theatre, I consider the frequent use of live music in their community-oriented productions an early precursor to this form. It is interesting and symptomatic that Rice above conflates folk and punk even though Bay City Rollers would not be considered by reference to either of those musical genres. What I think Rice means when she uses these terms is not to strictly qualify the genre of the music used in her work but the mode of audience engagement her theatre seeks (folk) and Kneehigh's iconoclastic positioning as a company on the margins of institutional theatre in the United Kingdom (punk).[17] It is also possible that Rice is pointing to the musical genre of punk as part of the 'British folklore' (especially the way it seems when perceived from the outside). However, what this example also emphasises is Kneehigh's and Rice's prevailing allegiance to theatre as a mode of storytelling that can use various tools to tell a story,[18] including music:

> I am a storyteller – and in the end you can tell a story with a cup of coffee or a film or a dance or a piece of music, [it] is one of the part of the armoury.
> (2010: 95)

It is in the multimodal nature of theatre to draw attention to and reveal the plurality of input (in)forming the semantic content of the musical performance. In addition to the aural intersubjectivity that is at work in gig theatre, an important aspect is the interpretive 'frame' between the performance and the audience which, even though it carries a visual bias, still pertains to live performance. In his latest book about the 'performing musical persona', *In Concert* (2021), Philip Auslander deploys genre as one of the three key concepts for his analysis and defines it as 'frame' at the interface between the performance and the audience. Although he recognises that genre is a 'contested concept' (2021: 7) which, he notes, does not reflect the generation Z's leaning towards fluidity, Auslander finds it necessary as a designation of a 'cognitive process' (2021: 8) and a social consensus around the 'performance of music as a social interaction' (2021: 9). The notion of a frame also resonates with David Roesner's deployment of Foucauldian 'dispositif' (the term sometimes translated in English as 'apparatus') as a means of defining 'musicality', a 'model, method and metaphor' inherent to both making theatre and watching theatre: a 'frame in which attention and emphasis is, for example, given to sonoric aspects of language, or rhythmic structures of movements' (2014: 13), but at the same time potentially carries the Foucauldian interests in the institutional and ideological content of the work. It is interesting that both thinkers are striving for a concept that can contain a combination of the musical, the visual, and the sociological/ideological as an organising principle and shorthand in their discussion of the complexities of musical performance.[19] This echoes the uses of the term 'punk' above that contain more than the narrow designation of musical genre. My aim here is not to seek a more effective solution for this terminological problem, other than to urge an expanded understanding of the terms 'frame' or 'punk' and/or possibly 'punk frame', but I do think that the intended counterpoint between the musical, the visual, and the ideological content of the terminology used thus far is relevant for the story of gig theatre. It could be added that the most effective attempts at terminological encapsulation of this do not necessarily withstand the test of time. In 1999, Auslander had offered a persuasive notion of 'rock ideology' via Susan Douglas' definition of rock'n'roll as featuring 'instrumental virtuosity, original songwriting, social criticism, a stance of anger and/or alienation' (Douglas in Auslander 1999: 69), but this required a binary polarisation between rock and pop[20] not only by reference to their racialised roots[21] but also through a legitimation of rock ideology's conservatism in its application of the principle of 'authenticity' (always already valorising 'an earlier, "purer" moment in a mythic history of the music' 1999: 69). This polarisation and the accompanying notions of authenticity have since been superseded or successfully challenged (Pattie 2007).[22] It may be tempting to think of 'punk ideology' as characteristic of British gig theatre, but I'm afraid this will amount to an erroneous and ultimately misleading contradiction in terms. Consequently, it is contradiction itself, formal counterpoint, or impossibility of semantic closure, that I take forward as the core feature of gig theatre.

An interesting example of this is contained in the works of Lucy McCormick, such as *Triple Threat* (2017) and *Post-Popular* (2019), which combine and juxtapose a strong generic allegiance to the slickness of commercial pop music in her singing and dancing style with a punk DIY visual and ideological orientation of her stagecraft (see Appendices 4.2 and 4.3). McCormick is a classically trained actor who works in mainstream theatre, but her independent output has emerged from an ideological choice to align with the new cabaret and queer performance art scene such as the Duckie and the Royal Vauxhall Tavern in London. Although McCormick does not use the label 'gig theatre' to describe her work, given the material circumstances of its production, her work seems closer to the designation of gig theatre than to commercial 'musical' which her debut *Triple Threat* – and indeed her corresponding technical prowess – evokes with deliberate irony. In her LMYE Gallery interview, McCormick explains that her DIY approach to stagecraft is indeed a result of the limited resources, but that this is also in sync with her ideological radicalism as an artist linked to relishing her authorial agency, fostering irony and incongruence, deliberately evading genre, and 'tricking the audience into watching performance art' (LMYE#1, 2021: 5). McCormick's performance idiom therefore reiterates the suggestion drawn from Bailey's and Rice's testimonies above that punk is not just a genre of music but a semantic, genealogical, ideological, and aesthetic framing orientation that can co-exist with other musical genres on stage.

For the purposes of a polyphonic historiography, gig theatre's capacity for accommodating co-existence of genres, layers of meaning and interpretive modalities (both aural and visual) is, suitably, also generative of counterpoint. The conception of genre, perpetuated by the musical industry and fan behaviours, has historically been restrictive, presupposing notions of loyalty, purity, and evaluations of authenticity (Auslander 1999). Contrary to this, theatre's expanded, dramaturgical and multimodal use of the musical genre illustrated here can also be considered emancipatory and empowering.

Historicising Gig Theatre 2: Rock Against Racism

The link between punk and comedy is not as incidental as it may seem. Both Oliver Double (2007) and Krista Bonello (2018) have conducted academic research on the cross-fertilisation and cross-referencing of the respective artforms of punk and stand-up (as documented in LMYE #4), focusing especially on the shared artistic ecology they belong to. In London itself, an interesting intersection of the alternative theatre, comedy scene, music, and activism emerged from the late 1970s onwards. A well-documented example is the formation of Rock Against Racism (RAR) in 1977, a movement initiated by the photographer/theatre-maker David Red Saunders who had been a member of Ronald Muldoon's Cartoon Archetypal Slogan Theatre (CAST) but eventually branched off with a few other CAST members into Kartoon Klowns. RAR co-founder member Roger Huddle recalls in Huddle and Billingham (2004) that, as a result of rising racism in mid-1970s London, the idea of organising a gig against racism had been explored for a while. The key event that initiated the movement happened in 1976 when Saunders wrote an open letter to Eric Clapton, denouncing Clapton's support for the racist rhetoric of politician Enoch Powell expressed at a concert in Birmingham. Saunders' letter, co-signed by a number of other Kartoon Klown members and published in the *New Musical Express*, *Melody Maker* and *Sounds*, called Clapton 'rock music's biggest colonist' implying that he downplayed the African roots of his own music. It also used the opportunity to proclaim rock's 'progressive potential' and called for a 'rank and file movement against the racist poison in rock music' (in Renton 2019: 51–2).

The letter instantaneously attracted hundreds of replies from around the country, and the first RAR gig took place in January 1977 at the London Polytechnic. The relevance of this historical circumstance is twofold in the consideration of the emergence of gig theatre specifically in the United Kingdom. In addition to the already noted aspect of RAR's inception at the intersection of theatre, live music, and activism, the second important aspect is RAR's attitude to musical genre which is less typical of musical fandom and possibly more typical of gig theatre's inclusivity.

In his recollections, while owning that most of the founder members were fans of soul, Roger Huddle emphasises the inclusivity of the movement across the divisions of musical genre: 'Reggae, Soul, Rock'n'Roll, Jazz, Funk, Punk – Our music' (2004). The anti-racist political drive of the movement as a whole resulted in an ideological move to transcend any divisions along the lines of genre allegiance on the part of the audience. Additionally, David Renton (2019) claims that the coincidence of RAR and punk helped to steer punk away from its early visual flirtations with fascism (2019: 60–3). This is corroborated by Duncombe and Tremblay (2011) in their anthology of writings about punk rock and the politics of race. In introducing an article by the famous RAR activist and physician David Widgery, the editors consider RAR to 'represent a crucial moment in punk finding its anti-racist voice' (2011: 172). Furthermore, according to Renton, by 1979 the British dub poet of Jamaican descent Benjamin Zephaniah in his poem 'Call It What Yu Like' documented an incident at Ackam Hall in Ladbroke Grove where a group of punks fended off the National Front who had 'attacked the ravers'[23] (Renton 2019: 155).

This is the period of rock's history that Kotarba (2013) links to the Birmingham School's idea of 'subculture', which, as defined by Dick Hebdige in 1979, is characterised by 'style' – a 'spectacular' communication of difference from the mainstream culture. Though Hebdige (1979) identified individual subcultures such as hipsters, beats, teddy boys, punks, and mods, for example, he was interested in the generic sociological features of subcultures as a phenomenon and further qualified them in Britain as 'predominantly working class', characterised by 'conspicuous consumption' (1979: 103), and subject to ultimate co-optation or 'incorporation' by the capitalist mainstream (1979: 94). Although RAR went on to unite various individual subcultures around a shared cause, it could be seen to have eventually been 'incorporated' into the mainstream as an idea in the form of the more globally visible Live Aid 1984, for example. With this, many of the constituent aspects of the ecology that produced RAR remained behind the scenes. Or in the words of the historian of American punk rock subculture, Kevin Mattson: 'Cultural critics often overlook "underground" cultural practices that are hard to uncover' (2001: 71). In his work, Kevin Mattson (2001, 2020) has challenged Hebdige's emphasis on style rather than the complex workings of youthful rebellion and on consumption rather than production of culture. Although allowing for the fact that aspects of the different cultural contexts (for example, class consciousness) do not directly map out across cultures, Mattson however does make several points about his case study that are applicable in reverse too. One is Mattson's emphasis on the 'spirit of Do-It-Yourself (DIY)' (which he qualifies as a form of 'folk culture'), traceable back to the now mythical three-chord drawing in an English fanzine – 'This is a chord. This is a second. This is a third. Now form a band' by Tony Moon, published in Sideburns fanzine in 1977. The second important aspect is Mattson's conceptualisation of the punk rock scene as a 'communicative network' of culture producers, creating 'musical commodities', 'innovative performances', and 'handcrafted fanzines' to oppose the commodification of culture (2001: 72). In addition, they found new spaces for performance, challenged the cult of rock stardom, and founded independent labels, facilitated by means of easily available cassette duplication (2001: 75).

On the surface level, an insight that emerges about a potential parallel between rock subculture and gig theatre is that both offer the scope for the artist to seize and deploy the means of production on their own terms and for the audience to transcend musical fandom in order to engage with something greater: a cause, a story, or an experience to be ideologically invested in. But another, more dramaturgically relevant mechanism at work is precisely the co-optation principle, traditionally maligned by the fans on account of its threat to 'authenticity', and by cultural critics on account of its economic exploitation of novelty (see also Auslander 1999/2008, Pattie 2007). On a meta-cultural level, as will be shown later, gig theatre holds the potential to co-opt the process of co-optation itself by harnessing and reframing it to achieve political empowerment for those that are marginalised.

Particularly significant for the story of gig theatre and its relation to RAR is the notion of 'scene', the term preferred by Mattson and also theorised by Kotarba as an 'ideational entity' – a place that becomes 'visible during interaction' (2013: 95). RAR emerged from a grassroots DIY scene that was a network of different kinds of artists, subcultures, genres, racial, and otherwise marginalised identities, certainly as yet insufficiently documented by historians due to the limitations and biases of pre-existing methodologies and epistemological agendas. In 2006, Sara Freeman's archival research of alternative theatre, for example, noted the existence of Joint Stock's 1987 production of the 'rap-musical' *Sanctuary* (2006: 373), staged at the time when the company briefly deployed a 'positive discrimination' policy (2006: 372). However, Mayes and Whitfield's (2021) recent digital humanities historiography of the British Musical reveals a significant erasure of the contribution of Black musical theatre-makers to the development of the form in the first half of the 20th century, showing that this contribution was not merely in the form of a subgenre but absolutely foundational to what we consider to be the mainstream musical theatre today. Similarly, existing histories of (alternative) theatre will continue to require augmentation with new evidence in order to properly reveal the hitherto invisible histories of gig theatre. It follows that in this process subcultures must be perceived as constitutive of culture not in inherently hierarchical ways, or in ways that deprive specific subsections of society from their means of cultural self-determination, and certainly not solely by reference to processes of co-optation/incorporation into the capitalist mainstream. Historiography can redress the balance by adequately establishing the extent and influence of the commonly erased contribution of subcultures to the dynamic entity that forms a heritage and a story of a culture. Perhaps a good place to start is by foregrounding the fact that popular music, a globally dominant culture of the 20th century, is axiomatically a Black American culture and entails conceptions of authorship – improvisation, collaboration, bottom-up narrative (Iyer 2004), DIY, activism, eco- rather than ego-leadership – not typical of the post-Enlightenment or Romantic Western conceptions of authorship.

Academic Katie Beswick and artist Conrad Murray – both also featured in LMYE #1 – make a powerful case in their book *Making Hip Hop Theatre*[24] for how programming politics of venues must help to resist co-optation. The specific target of their criticism is the tendency to market hip hop theatre using the more bourgeois and literary 'spoken word' designation which occludes the collaborative, community-based roots of the form and turns it into 'something capitalist and individualistic':

> Hip hop and rap remain counter cultural, even when they are part of the mainstream, because they come from grassroots collective action and are still practiced by people who believe in the power of the collective. They are free and open to anyone. This grassroots energy means hip hop is always innovating at street level; it's a living, changing form and can't be captured and pinned down. 'Spoken word' focuses on the idea of the individual genius and has been reduced to recognizable clichés. It conceals the collective nature of ideas and talent, which are always part of any creative work and visible in the result of any creative process.
>
> (2022: 205–6)

I would add that, although language is important, this is not just a matter of vocabulary. What is required is a paradigmatic change of mindset , a 'delinking' (Mignolo 2007) from the system of values that underlies the post-Enlightenment Western notions of authorship and, more specifically a recognition that the aural/oral dramaturgies, whose manifestations are now entering the mainstream, belong to a previously suppressed lineage of human creativity.

That said, some venues can and do play a positive part in ethically nurturing grassroots activity and/or fostering anti-racist allyship. One example is Battersea Arts Centre (BAC) in London, home to Beatbox Academy which Conrad Murray founded in 2008 as a weekly youth group for 12–21 year olds and whose efforts culminated in the 2016 hip hop adaptation of Mary Shelley's *Frankenstein*, that toured to Edinburgh and Adelaide and was filmed for the BBC (see LMYE Gallery#1 and Appendix 4.4). Battersea Arts Centre's extraordinary contribution to artistic, political, and cultural life of London and the United Kingdom is yet to be properly documented in academic literature. As a former South London Town Hall, and now a museum with live-in quarters for artists, a fully accessible policy, innovative creative development methodologies,[25] and multiple performance spaces on site, this arts organisation has certainly led the way for decades in rethinking what theatre can be.

Future historiographies of, specifically, anti-racist contributions to gig theatre may need to conduct a more comprehensive critical study of the London and British theatre in this respect; however, here I wish to briefly name-check two other examples of venue-based allyship adjacent to the discussion above.

One example is the work of Ronald Muldoon, a committed advocate for popular and political performance and the original founder of CAST, to which the founders of RAR had belonged. Muldoon's work is currently only documented by one academic article (McDonnell 2013) and a self-published memoir (Muldoon 2013). In 1986, Muldoon took the leadership of the Hackney Empire, the theatre at the time owned by Bingo Mecca, in order to return it to its original purpose. The fundraising efforts for the takeover were led by the chair of the Trust, poet Benjamin Zephaniah (McDonnell 2013: 103). Zephaniah, as already mentioned above, is a potentially significant figure in tracing the emergence of the lineage of gig theatre exemplified by the more recent examples of the Beatbox Academy, Kae Tempest, Brigitte Aphrodite, Debris Stevens, and Arinzé Kene (LMYE Gallery#4). Additionally, the first major success of the newly opened Hackney Empire, under Muldoon, was *Black Heroes in the Hall of Fame* by Flip Fraser in collaboration with JD Douglas and Khareem Jamal, a piece that by 1989, became the first all-Black musical to perform in the West End (https://www.blackheroesfoundation.org/black-heroes-in-the-hall-of-fame/).[26]

Another similarly relevant landmark in London's culturally diverse landscape has been the Theatre Royal Stratford East, the former home of Joan Littlewood's Theatre Workshop in East London. Philip Hedley's artistic leadership of the theatre for 25 years (1979–2004) could probably be more substantially documented in terms of its programming politics and influence. Current Artistic Director of Actors Touring Company, Matthew Xia credits Stratford East with crucial significance in his own developmental journey as a young man of a mixed-race heritage from Leytonstone. Xia had found early success as DJ Excalibah in pirate radio which led to hosting a programme on BBC 1Xtra, but having also been a member of a youth theatre group at Theatre Royal Stratford East, at the age 18, Xia joined the board of the theatre at Hedley's invitation. In 2004, the Stratford East associate theatre-maker and designer Ultz, inspired by Jay-Z's sampling of 'It's a Hard Knock Life' from the musical *Annie*, commissioned Xia to turn *The Boys from Syracuse* by Rogers and Hart into a hip hop musical (Xia in LMYE Gallery #4: 3). The result was *Da Boyz* (2004), followed by a similarly inspired adaptation of *The Blacks* (2007) based on Jean Genet's play. Continuing on this route after Xia's departure from London into regional theatre, Ultz eventually won an Olivier for *Pied Piper: A Hip Hop Dance Revolution* in 2009 also at Stratford East. However, it was not an easy win. An earlier review of the show on tour in Newcastle notes:

The whole street culture thing, with its image of grafitti and aggression and a perceived association with street crime, tends to send shivers down the spine of many in what could be called the "cultural establishment", and I certainly picked up those particular "vibes" when I mentioned what I was going to see. To be honest, I shared in them a little myself, thanks to the kind of media coverage it gets from the tabloids.

(Lathan 2009)

In the gap between the review in Newcastle and the Olivier, a subculture somehow became part of the mainstream.

Historicising Gig Theatre 3: DIY and Dramaturgy

In the year 2017, Hull-based theatre company Middle Child premiered *All We Ever Wanted Was Everything*, a piece of gig theatre for which the playtext was commissioned from playwright Luke Barnes as part of the Hull City of Culture celebration. This was not the first time gig theatre and playwriting came together. In fact, Middle Child collaborated with Barnes on *Weekend Rockstars* (2014), and nabokov theatre company, founded in 2001 in order to promote new writing, had also steered itself more explicitly towards gig theatre especially during the artistic directorship of Stef O'Driscoll (2016–19). In 2014, still under the leadership of Joe Murphy, nabokov had a gig theatre show at the Edinburgh Fringe, *Symphony*, a triptych of new writing by Ella Hickson, Nick Payne and Tom Wells (see Appendix 4.5).

All We Ever Wanted Was Everything represents a key moment for the historiography of gig theatre as Barnes' play was written in the form of 'state of the nation' play, favoured by some mainstream theatre critics (Billington 2007).[27] Arguably, this further elevated the significance and enhanced the cultural capital of gig theatre as a form. If up until then particular examples of gig theatre can be seen as an extension of the theatre-makers' personal tastes and as expression of their idiom – such as Hurley's *Beats* (2012), Ellinson, Thorpe, and Lawson's *Torycore* (2013), and Kae Tempest's *Brand New Ancients* (2012) – Middle Child and Luke Barnes' *All We Ever Wanted Was Everything* was also a way of explicitly saying something about the political moment in United Kingdom in 2017. Conceptually, the piece did this by a decade-by-decade revisiting of the incidentally intertwining life paths of a boy and a girl from different class backgrounds, both born on the same day in 1987. The respective historical contexts of their 10th, 20th, and 30th birthdays are marked through the use of popular music, each number also evoking significant political moments in the recent history of Britain (from Thatcherism in 1987, via the rise and fall of Blairism in 1997 and 2007, to Brexit Britain in 2017).

Though it was originally staged in a nightclub in Hull, the piece toured with the Paines Plough Roundabout tent to the Edinburgh Fringe in 2017, where I saw it. In performance, the immediately striking distinguishing features of this 'state of the nation' play included its in-the-round staging (not directly evocative of a gig but certainly facilitative of a gig atmosphere in a theatre), the piece being fronted by an MC/narrator (Marc Graham) whose job also included 'working the crowd', and, most notably, the seamless code-switching between the performers' roles as musicians and character-actors throughout the piece.

As elaborated in *Theatre-Making* (2013), I consider it significant for the story of innovation in theatre-making that the founder members of Middle Child, director Paul Smith and actor Marc Graham, were graduates of a university Drama department.[28] Although a convenient time could not be found for members of the company to be interviewed for the A/OD project, some relevant information about their formative years at Hull University is available from the interview with RashDash's Helen Goalen and Abbi Greenland, who were in the same year group (2006–2009) as Middle Child's Paul Smith and Marc Graham. RashDash also collaborated with Graham on their piece *Another Someone* (2009) (LMYE #1 2020). Goalen and Greenland do note that the respective career paths of the two groups of friends were quite different following graduation: Smith and Graham went on to train in London drama schools and eventually returned to Hull to base their company Middle Child there. RashDash, joined by Greenland's childhood friend Becky Wilkie, pursued a more experimental career path as a collective instead, led by their shared values, political ideals and aesthetics, and rooted in deep friendship and camaraderie. Despite these somewhat incidental differences in outlook, the two companies share significant formative influences in that drama degrees habitually tend to blur the boundaries in the division of labour, requiring everyone to take part in every aspect of making.[29] I do not wish to oversimplify the distinction between university drama departments and specialised drama school training courses; however, it is easily discernible that the two kinds of courses do have different pedagogical emphases, goals, and areas of expertise. University courses have traditionally been led by the research imperatives and intellectual or experimental investigations of the lecturers, while training courses are historically more focused on the enhancement of the technical skills and employability prospects of the students. Additionally, creative practice at university is more frequently underpinned by questions and problems informed by cross-disciplinary or theoretical inquiry. Members of Middle Child evidently embody both aspects of training in their creative practice.[30] Making theatre within the laboratory conditions of university, which frequently happens on students' own initiative both inside and outside the curriculum, where technical excellence and polish is not the main end goal, implies that material resources are potentially conceived of as perpetually scarce – sustainability is a pragmatic imperative, creative resourcefulness is key, and DIY is simply within the DNA of such theatre-making.

Legitimation of the DIY ethos and practical challenges to pre-existing modes of professionalisation are also characteristic of another contextual influence stemming from the musical scene in the UK, post-punk – a 'culture that could be at once popular, experimental and intellectually-driven' (Butt et al. 2016: 7). Kodwo Eshun, one of the co-organisers of the 2014 series of events on the subject of post-punk at Goldsmiths College, alongside Gavin Butt and Mark Fisher comments in their introductory exchange:

> Post-Punk was an amateurist and auto-didactic project that created a context for belief in your own incapacity rather than training or skill. What emerges is a drive towards self-authorisation in which people make up rules as they go.
>
> (2016: 7)

Post-punk is defined by Gavin Butt as starting with the dissolution of the Sex Pistols in 1978[31] and ending with the defeat of the miners' strikes in Britain in 1985. Additionally, Butt et al. (2016) point to post-punk's constitutive transdisciplinarity, the way the laissez-faire model of arts school training at the time meant that aspiring artists went to art school not to seek professionalisation but to join a band:

> [A]rt school was the place where you could get a local authority grant, have the costs of your tuition paid for by the government, and have three years to do whatever you wanted […] you wouldn't necessarily have to even talk to your tutor or show up in the studio.
>
> (2016: 14–5)

An emblematic example of this is Green Gartside who, having gone to arts school in Leeds, formed Scritti Politti in 1977, a band named in homage to the Marxist philosopher and political theorist Antonio Gramsci. Fisher corroborates further that the 'leading writers [in *NME*] were autodidacts who had not gone to university but who *were* nevertheless steeped in poststructuralist thought' (2016: 14, original emphasis), and credits the autodidact intellectualisation of music journalism as crucial for his own professional determination.

Echoing Hebdige's notion of the usual fate of subcultures, Fisher offers a typically pessimistic take on post-punk's demise in its co-optation by neoliberal capitalism:

> We're haunted by the failure of the left to come to some arrangement with the libertarian energies that came out of music culture [and] the right absorbed and converted the energies of the counterculture into its own project of re-individualisation'.
>
> (2016: 16)

On the other hand, however, Eshun sees the legacy of post-punk as only just maturing at the time and manifesting itself in the early 2000s through the influential music journalism of Simon Reynolds as well as the blogosphere that included Fisher's own k-punk blog as a vital and urgent force '[circulating] outside of the academy, creating a collective conversation that simultaneously functioned as libidinally charged speculation' (2016: 18). Some evidence of this influence on the generations coming of age at the time is provided by Kieran Hurley who cites Fisher's k-punk as a crucial reference in making *Heads Up* (Hurley in LMYE #3, 2021: 8). RashDash similarly cite Mike Bradwell's (2010) 'Steal a Van' article as influential. This refers to an extract in the *Guardian* from (Bradwell's 2010) memoir *The Reluctant Escapologist* where he was trying to encourage new generations of theatre-makers to make theatre 'outside the warm embrace of the theatrical establishment' by paraphrasing Tony Moon's zine graphic 'Now form a band' as: 'Find a play. Squat a building. Steal a van. Now make a show' (Bradwell 2010). Thus, Eshun's optimistic evaluation of post-punk's legacy accommodates emergence of gig theatre too, in my view.

In his summary of how the American punk rock met its own unceremonious end by co-optation into the mainstream, Mattson provides an interesting counterpoint to the story of post-punk above by diagnosing the US punk rock's anti-intellectualism – a 'divorc[e] from serious intellectual cultivation' linked to the idea that 'rebellion became more closely associated with the loud sounds' (2001: 89). Specifically, Mattson identifies the US punk rock fans' superficial interpretations of the past which they considered 'antiquated', irrelevant to their own radical endeavours, and characteristic of baby boomers who had sold out (ibid.), as well as the subculture's overemphasis of 'the authenticity of personal commitment to social change' over and above political and collective activity (2001: 91). Notwithstanding potential academic bias to these findings, Mattson's lessons reinforce the argument for a deeper understanding of the historical contingency of innovation and the significance of the collective dimension in authorisation of social change. Gig theatre is a form of theatre rather than a subculture, but its formative features belong to a variety of contextual factors.

Gig Theatre and Dramaturgy

The polyphonic take on the history of gig theatre so far highlights some generative juxtapositions of ideas around frame and genre, culture and subculture, authorisation and self-authorisation, and the construction of narratives all of which contextually inform the understanding of gig theatre specifically in the United Kingdom. In this section, I focus on the making of *Electrolyte* (2018) by Wildcard Theatre (see Appendix 4.6), whose discussion in LMYE Gallery#4 highlighted valuable insights about how specifically gig theatre represents innovation in theatre-making.

It is relevant to note that playwright/performer James Meteyard and his key creative collaborators on *Electrolyte* composer/performer Maimuna Memon and actor Olivia Sweeney all graduated from the Oxford School of Drama, although, incidentally, within a commercially unsuccessful showcase, which determined their choice of name and the decision to form a company. An interesting formative influence in Wildcard's training was the requirement introduced by the school Principal George Peck (in office 1987–2019) for every first-year student

FIGURE 4.2 *Electrolyte* (2018) by Wildcard Theatre
Photo: Joseph Dawson

to express themselves in terms of a 'self-song', individually authored and publicly performed at the end of the first term of study.[32]

In writing *Electrolyte*, Meteyard based his own explicit commitment to gig theatre on a careful consideration of the form. A key limitation he observed in other gig theatre that he wanted to transcend was the tendency of some work to place the musical genre 'on top of the story' thus appealing to a subsection of the audience whose musical taste corresponded with that of the makers. Meteyard's quest for the use of music as 'an extension of what the characters were going through' was therefore led by dramaturgical questions such as: how can the music go 'one step further than just being either a time period or a location or a vibe or nostalgic', and how can music 'be a part of the experience of the story' in the sense of the characters' emotions and emotional journeys? (2021:12)

It can be inferred from Meteyard's testimony that he considers Middle Child and Luke Barnes' *All We Ever Wanted Was Everything* a rare example of gig theatre making the shift towards a conceptual use of multiple musical genres at the service of storytelling. Meteyard wished to take this further with his collaborators and the director Donnacadh O'Briain, who was brought in to stage his text.

In the LMYE conversation about the making of *Electrolyte*, O'Briain provides a thoughtful and succinct response to how he approached the development of the piece. The first aspect of the director's contribution, noted in fact by Meteyard, was a process of 'listening' to the initial verbal and musical material and responding to the energy of the collaborators in the space, sharing their ideas. O'Briain notes that 'there was a magic available in the harnessing of that quality in the room' (the *Electrolyte* interview, LMYE Gallery #4, 2021: 10), and goes on to elaborate on this 'dramaturgy of listening' as certainly having an embodied dimension (2021: 11).[33] The next stage of the process was characterised by finding the form and 'chiselling the concept' (ibid.). Here, O'Briain charted a number of possible factors in his own dramaturgical approach. One was his previous work in autobiographical and specifically postdramatic theatre which provided a lens on 'what is possible when there's something which is true or has a lot of truth within it on stage' (ibid.). This was linked to Meteyard's intention to explore the lived experience of mental illness experienced by a close family member but also to the distinctive characteristics of a music gig, specifically: 'authenticity and immediacy and directness' (ibid.: 13). O'Briain's understanding of 'authenticity' – already considerably problematised in academic research by Philip Auslander (1999/2008) and David Pattie (2007) – allows for certain levels of theatricality in the musician's onstage persona and for the possibility that, to put it in Pattie's words, 'authenticity is *performed* in the live event' (2007: vii, my emphasis). However, the intended relationship with the audience, closer to a gig than a play, necessitated, according to O'Briain, co-presence, direct address, and trust (ibid.: 13). Hence, the process of working on *Electrolyte* as a gig theatre piece was distinctive in that it required the finding of new, 'honest' conventions, that were not theatrical conventions but that belonged in the format of a gig, 'a real event happening, and an actual group of friends' (ibid.). A prominent aspect of O'Briain's directorial approach was an inherent relationality manifesting as a sensitivity to the nature of this collaborative process, 'being careful' about 'respecting the amount of listening and learning that is available [...] in the room' (ibid.: 10). The process therefore required a renouncing of 'the conventional tools of plays', and the way the director judged authenticity, immediacy, and truth 'was very different than if [he] was doing an Arthur Miller play' (ibid.:11).

It is worth briefly pausing at these theoretically contentious notions of authenticity,[34] immediacy,[35] and truth,[36] which are the terms repeated in O'Briain's testimony, (sometimes interchangeably with other synonyms). For current discussion they could perhaps be subsumed into Kendrick's notion of aural intersubjectivity as potential qualities of the relations sound is ontologically capable of constructing; however, O'Briain's struggles in calibrating and fine-tuning these relations in the process of making the piece should not be dismissed. It is perhaps helpful to note that the notion of authenticity that is at stake here is not the kind that Stuart Fisher identifies as constituting the promise of verbatim theatre (2020: 82–4), as the issue concerned in this case is one of construction rather than transmission of authenticity.[37] In very simple terms, as a piece of theatre, *Electrolyte* primarily presents the audience with an expectation to participate in a shared act of imagination, or a process of aural co-construction of the story. In terms of the relationship between text and performance in this piece, the experience of watching the show is not dissimilar to watching a radio play being recorded, or a staged reading, only in this case the material reality of the event (the chairs in a staged reading, the recording paraphernalia in a studio) is replaced by the experiential reality and the mise-en-scene of a music gig. The latter also replaces the action characteristic of dramatic theatre. In the case of gig theatre, and especially in *Electrolyte*, the gig and the theatre unfold on parallel semantic planes and they do not aim to reiterate each other. The aural intersubjectivity facilitated by the live music helps construct our process of imaginative participation; however, this cannot be deemed sufficient by the theatre-makers whose primary focus is the dramaturgical construction that problematises our perception of mental illness.

Perhaps the idea of most relevance from David Pattie's (2007) literature review of authenticity is the notion of 'belief' derived from Richard Dyer – as 'the spontaneous expression of both the audience's and the performer's faith in the act' – forming the basis for authenticity in the performer-audience relationship (Pattie 2007: 11). Pattie goes on to argue that the main element expressed/experienced in the encounter between the star and the audience is the music itself that is perceived as carrying the 'mystical power [...] to speak truthfully' (2007: 13). Although eventually Pattie establishes that this perception of the authenticity of music is of course a myth (2007: 20), what this myth facilitates is an inherently 'contradictory' interplay of authenticity and constructedness, theatricality and spontaneity, the reality of performance, as well as the playing out of the individual and the collective identity/experience. These contradictions in fact can also be considered fundamental to our cognitive, polysubjective engagement with gig theatre.

The 'decision to completely eschew representational aesthetics' (ibid.: 11) led O'Briain to three other key decisions: to use the 'physical language of the gig', to use the microphones throughout the piece, and to tell the story of the main protagonist Jessie retrospectively (rather than in the here and now of theatrical performance). The latter decision was at first confusing to the cast, but soon it was recognised as a trope familiar through the work of musicians/storytellers such as Joni Mitchell who are 'reliving the moment through the music as they are telling the story' (Memon in LMYE Gallery#4, 2021: 11). While the act of storytelling here can be seen as an extension of amplified storytelling, *Electrolyte* develops its own bespoke conventions which productively juxtapose narrative and performance conventions. In *Electrolyte*, the main dramaturgical conceit is based on the fact that the piece makes use of our imaginative and affective participation only to eventually perform a disclosure of the narrator's unreliability, which, as we find out, is a result of her mental illness. Whereas Kieran Hurley's 'irruption of the real' in *Heads Up* is predicated on a temporary suspension of the 'fourth wall' through direct address of the audience, *Electrolyte* in the actors' performance (more so than its text) makes use of a direct address throughout, and only at the key point of the 'reveal' do the actors temporarily erect the fourth wall going off mic to perform the scene in the style of dramatic theatre. In this case, the resort to the conventions of dramatic theatre, perhaps ironically, serves to verify the 'reality' of the protagonist's life and to retroactively reveal our positioning as up until that point being *inside the head* of the main character. This is also a crucial positioning for creating empathy in the audience. Like Kieran Hurley's storyteller who abdicates his authority in *Heads Up*, Wildcard's *Electrolyte* dramaturgically reveals and reneges on its own process of co-optation of the audience's imaginative and affective investment in order to achieve its payoff[38] – this payoff being the audience's realisation of complicity with the protagonist. *Electrolyte* therefore uses gig theatre's contrapuntal multimodal workings (storytelling vs music, fourth wall vs immersion, affective vs critical engagement) to re-centre the otherwise socially stigmatised experience of mental illness. Far from being an acritical piece of theatre, *Electrolyte* engenders an implicit critique of normativity through a dialectical intersubjective engagement of the audience.

My interviewing method focusing on the formative influences in the artists' developmental journeys elicited a notable insight from O'Briain who linked his evaluations of authenticity to his class identity. Interestingly too, this background determined his dramaturgical 'lens':[39]

> I come from a working-class family, place and education, as does the protagonist Jessie – and in some way there was something about the aesthetic that comes from that, relates to that. I guess it just takes me back to this idea that getting up and pretending is just pissing about, it's kind of stupid. […] So we had to try and somehow create a production where at no point did it feel like anyone was acting, and of course the way to do that wasn't to make sure nobody was ever acting – I mean, everyone was acting all the time – but […] it was the lens which all the decisions, all the acting decisions were made via.
>
> (O'Briain in LMYE Gallery#4 2021: 10)

As intuited by O'Briain, and indeed Kendrick, this is of course evocative of the ways in which contemporary postdramatic theatre manifests Eleni Varopoulou's notion of 'musicalization of theatrical means' and, in turn, Hans-Thies Lehmann's notion of 'auditory semiotics' (Lehmann 2006: 91). However, O'Briain's testimony about the truth-seeking nature of contemporary performance points to its pre-conditioned connection to the heritage of theatrical realism. In this respect – and analogously to Lehmann's claim that postdramatic is intrinsically contingent on the dramatic tradition – gig theatre can be perceived as not a radically new form, but as a critical reconfiguration of pre-existing forms of theatre. O'Briain presupposes that the notions of authenticity, immediacy, and truth are present in his work on *Electrolyte* as much as they would be in his work on an Arthur Miller play, the main difference being the 'lens' he uses as a director, and more specifically the conventions he deploys. Gig theatre can therefore be understood as a form of postdramatic theatre which uses the frame of a gig as a way of pulling down the 'fourth wall' and letting the audience in on the multimodal processes of construction of meaning and affective critique.

Gig Theatre and (Rave) Culture

SK Shlomo's pitch for a residency with the A/OD project at the Battersea Arts Centre was outstanding. In response to the open call requesting an outline of an idea and samples of previous work, this beatboxing champion sent in a carefully edited and manually subtitled YouTube video featuring a montage of his previous collaborations with chart-topping musicians and a pitch for an autobiographical solo theatre piece about how rave helped him overcome clinical depression. The idea was that the proposed theatre show, to be directed by Matthew Xia and taken to the Edinburgh Fringe, would ultimately transform into a rave, getting the auditorium chairs out of the way and the audience up on their feet. (This pitch is included in the SK Shlomo LMYE Laboratory#4). Even if in the early 1990s the rave scene left me musically unengaged, SK Shlomo's idea completely spoke to my theatrical taste and sensibility and, as I had lived in the United Kingdom since 1993, to my political and cultural experience too. What this counterpoint crystallised for me was the way in which music itself, unlike theatre, can easily travel without translation, it can exert influence and find its fans in other cultures on the basis of taste, but the missing element in those processes of reception is the deeper appreciation of the cultural contexts of the specific music's inception. This is possibly more true of rave than of other musical genres especially as it has been narrowly, and at times mistakenly, associated primarily with acid house, techno, and the MDMA drug popularly known as Ecstasy. Although the histories of rave as a dance culture can be traced

FIGURE 4.3 SK Shlomo
Photo: Matt Forster

back to the 1950s and 1960s subcultures including the Jamaican sound systems and house parties (Deller 2019, Peter 2020), recent revisitations such as Anna Davis' (2006) BBC documentary and Gavin Watson's photo book *Raving '89* (2009) focus on the year 1989 as the year in which, according to the 'hegemonic cultural memory' (Peter 2020), the rave scene was born. However, even those documents see the birth of rave as a convergence of a number of complex sociological, political, and cultural influences. Turner Prize-winning artist Jeremy Deller's (2019) documentary for the BBC takes the form of an A-level class in political history. Here, with a group of teenagers – born well after the heyday of rave and its attempted suppression through the 1994 Criminal Justice Act documented in Kieran Hurley's *Beats* – Deller traces a number of circumstantial foundational influences in the United Kingdom and the United States: the invention of the Roland 303 synthesiser in 1981, the queer house party nightclub scene in Chicago in the 1980s, the emergence of Detroit as the first post-industrial city, the 1981 tour of the United States by the German band Kraftwork, the Afro-Caribbean house party scene in the United Kingdom, the miners' strikes, and the end of the industrial age in Britain. Deller's underlying thesis is potentially contained in the statement that when they took off in 1989, the rave parties, often occurring in disused warehouses and industrial facilities, were 'nothing less than a death ritual to mark the transition of Britain from industrial to a service economy' (35:31). Nevertheless, they also represented the 'largest mobilisation of people since the miner's strikes', admittedly for social rather than political reasons (27:07), and highlighted the new trend whereby the tools of electronic music were making the means of production available to greater numbers of people. The emergence of the DJ as a new type of music-making artist/performer in this post-industrial era is also symptomatic of the need to revisit the 19th-century processes of professionalisation and the Taylorist division of labour initiated by the needs of industrial production.

In his historiography of the DIY movement, George McKay traces the use of the term back to the jazz scene of the 1950s, and the simultaneous rise of the Campaign for Nuclear Disarmament, the alternative music scene of the 1960s (incidentally associating an early use of the term 'rave' with a Pink Floyd gig at the Roundhouse), the punk fanzines of the 1970s, the squat culture of the 1980s, ending in the road protests of the 1990s Britain in order to situate his definition of DIY there:

> DiY Culture, a youth-centred and -directed cluster of interests and practices around green radicalism, direct action politics, new musical sounds and experiences, is a kind of 1990s counterculture.
>
> (McKay 1998: 2)

Although Deller mentions the coincidence of the rave scene with the politically disenfranchised, countercultural New Age Travellers trend of the early 1990s, he keeps a strict demarcation between the political drives of those communities of activists and the pleasure- and community-seeking aspect of the rave scene itself. This is not to say that the rave scene in itself was a politically innocent movement. In fact Anna Davis' documentary clearly shows how the rave scene quickly fell under the entrepreneurial control of some of Thatcher's 'young upwardly-mobile professionals' (yuppies) thus perpetuating and potentially inventing new models of capitalist exploitation. However, by comparison to the direct-action countercultural movement invoked by McKay, rave was escapist, entertaining, resourceful, pervasive, and, according to SK Shlomo, inherently therapeutic, as well as being transgressive and intimidating in its power to assemble and unite large groups of people. Deller completes his documentary with the quote from *Raving '89* of Gavin Watson's brother Neville, a DJ:

> I loved the anarchy of the early parties. It was as if all those years we spent trying to jack the system through things like punk and aggression had had no effect, and then all these kids who'd never consider themselves political were creating this revolution. It was more punk than punk ever was.
> (Neville Watson in Deller 2019, 55:37–55:54)

In this way, 'punk' is imbued with yet another level of meaning relating to the power of music to arouse group energy to the extent that it might lead to a cultural or political change or conversely a legal ban. This power is what Julian Henriques ascribes to 'sonic dominance' (2011) – an idea based on Nancy (2007) concerning the ability of sound to affect the body but taken further in relation to Reggae dancehall and specifically the sound system culture, which, as frequently noted, forms a precursor to rave. In his sociological research, Henriques makes an important distinction to contemporary modes of listening in that the sound system places the body of the listener 'inside sound, whereas with earphone listening, it's the opposite, sound is placed inside bodies' (2011: xvi).[40] This capacity of a gig to place the body of the listener inside sound characterises the type of technology-aided group immersion that distinguishes gig theatre from other forms of amplified storytelling. But there is also another dimension to this kind of group energy available in Judith Butler's notion of 'social embodiment' – an 'unbrokered' and 'unchosen dimension to our solidarity with others' (2015: 152), which constitutes an 'enactment of popular will', more powerful than a declarative speech act (2015: 156).

It would be easy to dismiss any potential value of the forms of theatre inspired by a seemingly apolitical musical scene such as rave, or more broadly, the forms of theatre using the affective power of live music to manipulate the audience response. However this overlooks the fact that gig theatre is not a solely immersive form of theatre. The power of gig theatre is contained in an ability to deploy the appeal of popular music as an audience-development tool, as a means of integrating the marginalised into the mainstream, and ultimately as a means of raising new questions. Whether or not it brands itself as such, gig theatre is primarily a form of theatre whose juxtaposition of interpretive frames opens up space for a variety of intersubjective audience participation.

SK Shlomo connects his interest in rave and storytelling as a performer to the cultural traditions of his Iraqi Jewish ancestors which formed part of the cultural milieu that he grew up in (LMYE Gallery#3), while his chosen director Matthew Xia sees his work as a DJ and a theatre director as forms of 'political shamanism' (LMYE Gallery#4). Subjected to the rigours of dramaturgical thinking, this process never uses music (or any other element of live gig) for purely decorative or illustrative purposes but at the service of conceptual coherence, cultural connotation, and, where needed, community-building. It draws, as Pitrolo notes, on 'a historical continuum made of 3000 blissful years of dancing' (LMYE Guides 'Rave' 2022). As such, gig theatre does not only come out of fandom but out of a deep appreciation or lived experience within the wider cultural context. Conrad Murray deploys beatboxing, rap battles, and a classic novel about adolescence to give voice to council estate kids from South London (LMYE Gallery#1 see Appendix 4.4). RashDash utilise sonic dominance to ask questions about gender power imbalance (LMYE Gallery#1, see Appendix 4.7). Unfolding Theatre use participatory gig theatre as a means of finding simple joys of playing music together and overcoming grief over losses of different kinds (LMYE Laboratory#4, see Appendix 4.8). And the US queer artist Taylor Mac rewrites the entire history of America in the riotous register of popular music and durational performance (see Appendix 4.9).

This finally brings us to the question of: to what extent gig theatre is a culture-specific British phenomenon? It is evident that the term usage and the critical mass of relevant work are linked to the British music and theatre festival circuit.[41] However, Britain itself is not a monocultural, monolithic place. An interesting example of a hybridisation of influences in making gig theatre featured in LMYE Gallery#4 is *Misty* (2018) by Nigerian-born actor/playwright Arinzé Kene, commissioned and directed by Palestinian/Italian director Omar Elerian at the Bush Theatre in London. Aside from their cultural differences, Kene and Elerian also fused their distinct theatre-making sensibilities, combining hip hop, autobiography, and Lecoq into a life-affirming piece about inner city London that eventually made it to the West End and the Olivier awards. Anecdotally one hears of examples of gig theatre in other English-speaking contexts – Marcel Dorney and Brisbane-based Elbow Room's punk piece *Prehistoric* has emerged through the Australian theatre festival circuit since 2014 – and it could be speculated that this is tied in with the cultural circulation facilitated by the international festival circuit (including Edinburgh, Adelaide, Avignon, New York, and Singapore). Similarly, Rachel Chavkin's stellar success with reinventing the American musical through *Hadestown* (2006–19) and *Natasha, Pierre & The Great Comet of 1812* (2012–16) could also be partly traced back to her Edinburgh Fringe successes with her ensemble TEAM, *Mission Drift* (2011) and *Architecting* (2008). But it is also possible for gig theatre-like forms to spring up organically within other cultural contexts, as noted at the beginning of this chapter, stemming from the pervasive influence of the UK and US popular music scenes on theatre-makers internationally, especially those growing up in the 1980s onwards. An artist who came to my attention during the Covid-19 lockdown thanks to the increase in theatre streaming was the Greek actor/director Aris Biniaris. Since his production of *The Holy Billy Goat* (2011), Biniaris has experimented with fusing theatrical performance with the visual and aural aesthetics of a rock concert, a feature present in his stagings of Greek tragedy such as *The Bacchae* (2018), streamed by Onassis Stegi, Athens in April 2020. His production of *Hill 731* about a Second World War battle is entirely a rock music gig. Biniaris gave me an interview for the A/OD project (the recording of which he did not wish to be published) where he outlined the significance of punk, rock, and hip hop on his artistic idiom as a theatre-maker, as well as the influence of Grotowski, Karlos Koun and a more foundational interest in ritual, rhetoric, and rhythm inherent to ancient Greek theatre (unpublished interview, 03 June 2020). It was through his wrestling with the conventions of the ancient Greek theatre and his personal taste for rock music that Biniaris found a form that could be called gig theatre in the United Kingdom though the term is not yet used in Greece.

Along similar lines, but for very different reasons which this chapter illuminates, I included the case study of *Turbofolk* (2008) by Oliver Frljić (Figure 4.4) in LMYE Laboratory#4.

This may come across as a counter-intuitive decision – turbofolk as a music genre does not belong to the Western lineages of rock, punk, hip hop, or rave but is a popular music genre native to the Balkans. As noted in the previous chapter,

FIGURE 4.4 Turbofolk (2008) by Oliver Frljić
Photo: Screenshot from video recording of the performance

the performative and ironic coining of the term 'turbofolk' (denoting a genre of neo-folk music composed using synthesisers in 1970s and 1980s Yugoslavia) is attributed to singer Rambo Amadeus who used it as a designation for his subversive 1989 album 'Hoćemo gusle', but which has since been co-opted as a brand by the commercial mainstream. Rambo Amadeus has often been asked to define the phenomenon, and in 2005, he made a song 'Turbo folk' in response, which offers a number of possibilities for the term's definition; however, the most succinct encapsulation the artist has offered in several interviews has been that turbofolk amounts to an 'uncritical use of technology'. Here, he means the use of synthesisers which intensifies the libidinal effect of the music; however his offer also contains a Stieglerian meta-level pertaining to the prosthetic aspect of culture itself. In this respect, the emphasis of Rambo Amadeus's definition is not on the use of technology itself but on the method of its use.

Oliver Frljić's show, made as a challenge to the inherent elitism of Croatian theatre steeped in the classical bourgeois repertory system, is a piece of devised theatre using turbofolk hits as a departure point for the actors' improvisations. Far from implying a personal allegiance to the genre,[42] the production confronts turbofolk as an ideological phenomenon in its full complexity acknowledging the conservative, nationalist, and war-mongering baggage this genre of music had acquired over the years (see Gordy 1999). Being associated with the Serbian culture, turbofolk was additionally controversial in Croatia where it was unofficially banned on Croatian TV and radio in the aftermath of the Yugoslav wars (1991–95). Nonetheless, turbofolk generated a fan base and became particularly attractive to the younger generations of Croatians who listened to it in defiance of the official line. Consequently, Frljić approaches turbofolk as a culture rather than a music genre, taking into account the inherent dialectic of the form as simultaneously arousing and repulsive, conservative and emancipatory in its various manifestations. In support of the latter, Frljić notes the example that some turbofolk stars, such as Jelena Karleuša, have taken the largely unpopular but much-needed public stand in support of the LGBTQI+ rights in the Balkans (Frljić in LMYE #4: 3). *Turbofolk* (2008) was Frljić's first internationally renowned piece as a theatre director, and this recognition could have been facilitated by his chosen form requiring minimal translation while still offering ample scope for interpretation. However, *Turbofolk* (2008) and its precursor 'This is Contemporary Art' by Milica Tomić, which presented a concert of turbofolk star Dragana Mirković as a readymade at the Wienner Festwochen 2001, were perceived as problematic by Serbian and Croatian critics for promoting inferior and artistically vacuous content as a means of cultural representation. This may say more about the European cultural colonialism than about the work in question; however, the focus of this example here is its function as a potential example of gig theatre. In this respect, *Turbofolk* (2008) is an atypical example for a number of dramaturgically relevant reasons: it deploys non-Western popular musical heritage as a source of material, it removes fandom as a primary binding element of its aural intersubjectivity, and it features a very small amount of live music at the show's finale (most other iconic musical numbers in the show are played through the speakers). However, what makes it work as a notable example of gig theatre is the critically potent juxtaposition of its rousing aurality with its iconoclastic lens.[43]

Notes

1 Playwright Adriano Shaplin's definition of his ensemble, in which he also acts, as an 'intersubjective unit' (in Radosavljević 2013b) recalls some of the ideas explored in the previous chapters here too.
2 Philip Auslander offers an illuminating definition of the difference in terms: 'There is some terminological confusion in the use of the expressions "popular music" and "pop music". [...] British music commentators frequently use the term pop in a way that includes rock in that category, though the same commentators may also distinguish rock from pop in other contexts. I use "pop" to refer to rock's ideological Other and "popular music" to refer to the broader sphere that encompasses both, as well as many other genres' (Auslander 1999: 68, footnote 11).
3 This refers to the ideas developed by S.W. Taylor in his seminal 1911 text *The Principles of Scientific Management*.
4 'Once upon a time, pop's metabolism buzzed with dynamic energy, creating the surging-into-the-future feel of periods like the psychedelic sixties, the post-punk seventies, the hip-hop eighties and the rave nineties' (Reynolds 2011: x).
5 The notion of polyphony carries potential to encapsulate more broadly the nature of academic discourse. Sally Mackey has deployed the notion of 'polyphonic conversation' for example in the context of applied theatre practice as research – 'imply[ing] overlapping and concurrent voices' between 'practice, theory, reflection and action' (2016: 488).
6 *The Sligo Champion* on 1 May 2002 under the headline 'Family drama at the Glens' covers what must have been an earlier version of this piece called *The Railings*, referring to its experimental style that could be termed 'gig theatre': 'Gig theatre is the combination of the informal energy and visual enjoyment of a music gig and the dramatic storyline and emotional impact of the best of live theatre. Percussion and melody accompany the spoken lyrics and sounds, creating a sound-image extravaganza.' (No author, 'Family drama at the Glens', 2002: 8).
7 'Joycean streams of consciousness, full of echoes, soundscapes, alliterations and rhythmic repetitions.' (O'Toole 2002).
8 Also significant was the long-running tribute to Ian Dury by the Graeae Theatre company, *Reasons to be Cheerful*, about which the Graeae's artistic director, Jenny Sealey, is quoted by Williams to have said: 'I remember, on our first night at Theatre Royal Stratford East in 2010, feeling puzzled that there were so many city men in suits, but as soon as the music started they loosened their ties, took off their jackets and knew every single lyric; once a punk, always a punk' (Williams, 2016).
9 Formally, this play can also be placed within the tradition of Scottish community theatre which includes a famous 1973 precedent John McGrath's *The Cheviot, the Stag and the Black, Black Oil*, performed by 7:48 in community centres and featuring ceilidh. The play was televised by the BBC in 1974. The production is also placed within the tradition of storytelling theatre by Wilson (2006: 127).
10 This can be traced back to Greig's early collaborative work with director Graham Eatough and musician Nick Powell as part of Suspect Culture, for whom he authored a wide variety of projects including musicals (Rodríguez, 2019: 8). Furthermore, *The Strange Undoing of Prudencia Hart* (2014) and *Midsummer* (2009), even though not deliberately written as a double bill, could be perceived as dramaturgically inter-related through their shared interest in romance and Scotland by means of contrasts: while *Midsummer* is an urban love story with an electric guitar set in Edinburgh, *Prudencia Hart* is a riff on

a Border ballad set in Kelso in midwinter. In this respect, Greig is conceptually playing with the notion of genre as a playwright rather than necessarily transforming the stagecraft, even though he was also the director of the original production of *Midsummer* (2009). Holly Williams (2016) certainly credits the director of *The Strange Undoing of Prudencia Hart*, Wils Wilson with crucial contribution towards establishing gig theatre as a form in that she had directed several relevant productions (including Gruff Rhys' *Candylion* and the Welsh National Theatre, and Karine Polwart's *Wind Resistance*). Interestingly, Wilson had come to gig theatre via two decades of expertise in site-specific theatre, which is another potential line of genealogical enquiry pertaining to gig theatre.

11 Stephen Mallinder working with Jane Horrocks on the gig theatre piece *Cotton Panick* at MIF, expressed a similar enthusiasm, borne out of the opportunity that the term 'gig theatre' offers: '"Concept album" sounds so naff; "musical theatre" makes me sound like I'm in Cats! It doesn't sit in any of those boxes, particularly with the music being very electronic' (Williams 2017).

12 '"We each have in our pocket every song that's recorded, at all times – you can be absolutely entertained, constantly," points out Fink. "So the way to deal with that is to offer something you can't get from your pocket. What theatre does is offer a sense of community – and it's live." This "liveness and loudness" is crucial for [Middle Child's Paul] Smith too. "To me, gig theatre is a revolt against things like National Theatre Live [in cinemas] and Netflix and being consumed by screens. I've got no interest in making theatre that could ever be on a screen"' (Williams 2017)

13 Filter Theatre's *Twelfth Night* (2006) commissioned for the Complete Works Festival at the RSC and directed by Sean Holmes was an early atypical example of the form too, as discussed by McCourt (2021).

14 See a review here: http://fringereview.co.uk/review/edinburgh-fringe/2010/the-inconsiderate-aberrations-of-billy-the-kid/.

15 The other six characteristics of sound-based immersive/participatory theatre according to Kendrick are: 'sonic presence, lack of visual reference, sonic sensibility, non-visual spatiality, the corporeality and hapticity of audience and that sound performs' (2017: 41).

16 To encapsulate the type of shared experience at work here, Kendrick recalls William Kenney's phrase 'alone together' which he applied to the early recorded music listenership in his 1999 book *Recorded Music in American Life: The Phonograph and Popular Memory, 1890–1945*. Similarly, Ross Brown is deliberate in using the sonic 'we' within the title of his 2020 book *Sound Effect: The Theatre We Hear*. Meanwhile, in her thoughts on assembly, Judith Butler evaluates the power of the phrase 'We the people' in the US constitution, as a speech act 'that does not describe that plurality, but gathers that group together through the speech act' (2015: 175).

17 Rice discusses the music of her youth by reference to her 2008 iconoclastic production of *Don John* for Kneehigh at the RSC.

18 The work of Little Bulb also belongs to this tradition which uses music as part of storytelling for its audience-binding potential, rather than as a means of fandom-based loyalty to a particular genre. This is evident not only in their live music pieces such as the teenage romp *Operation Greenfield* (2010), the Django Reinhardt musical biopic *Orpheus* (2013) and the prog rock TED talk *The Future* (2019), but also in their very first piece *Crocosmia* (2008) which was devised around a selection of LPs from a charity shop and the memories of songs the company members taught each other as part of rehearsal (Little Bulb in LMYE #4 2021: 5). Clearly it is deep appreciation of music that informs Little Bulb's performance idiom, however this appreciation is eclectic rather than strictly reverential.

19 Both Roesner and Auslander refer their understanding of the 'frame' to Erving Goffman's 1974 seminal 'Frame analysis: an essay on the organization of experience', which as its title suggests, pertains to ethnographic work.

20 'The ideological distinction between rock and pop is precisely the distinction between the authentic and the inauthentic, the sincere and the cynical, the genuinely popular and the slickly commercial, the potentially resistant and the necessarily co-opted, art and entertainment' (Auslander 1999: 69)

21 'Rock and pop can be distinguished on a more-or-less objective basis: whereas rock derives historically from African-American roots in 1950s rock and roll, pop derives historically from the white popular music of the 1950s: Perry Como, Patti Page, and their ilk'. (Auslander 1999: 68)
22 Though Pattie (2007) examined in detail the changing conceptions of authenticity, he did not comment on Auslander's notion of 'rock ideology' in that book. He has since clarified his stance on this notion in personal correspondence to me on 1 October 2021: 'The problem with Auslander's typology is that it doesn't take account of a) the ex post facto nature of genre definitions within popular music (so the distinction between rock and pop isn't an objective one; it's a subjective distinction, made for reasons grounded in the hierarchies of popular culture), and b) fluid- so not just the immediate distinction, but the histories of rock and pop are always open to revision'.
23 This historical use of the term 'raver' indicates 'punter' and predates the 1990s musical genre.
24 This book and the accompanying collection of scripts *Beats and Elements: A Hip Hop Theatre Trilogy* (2022) by Conrad Murray and Katie Beswick, represent another excellent example of coalitional scholarship.
25 This refers to the methodology of 'scratch' noted in the Introduction(s).
26 Additionally, Jamaican farce and anti-apartheid theatre from South Africa also represented a major section of the Hackney Empire repertoire but its programming politics recognised at the time as 'wildly unorthodox' was also marked by diversity that included all ethnic and other politically oppressed subsections of its community (McDonnell 2013: 107).
27 See also Matt Trueman's denunciation of 'state of the nation' play in the *Guardian* Theatre Blog (Trueman 2011).
28 Like Smith and Graham, Middle Child's musical director James Frewer was also a University of Hull graduate though he studied music rather than drama and had probably started collaborating with Smith and Graham during their studies.
29 Though this is not exclusive to Hull Drama Department, it is also informed by my own time at Hull as a Graduate Teaching Assistant (1999–2002). At the time all first year students were assigned to multiple/rotating Assistant Stage Manager duties for main stage productions while also being free to audition for parts or propose their own projects. In addition to the staff- or older student-directed main stage productions, which followed a conventional division of labour, students could also engage in more experimental work through the studio productions and through the student-run society, Z theatre, which annually took performances to the Edinburgh Fringe.
30 Incidentally, both RashDash and Emma Frankland, who were at Hull at different times, told me on separate occasions that a significant influence on their work was the teaching of Robert Cheesemond, a lecturer who specialised in scenography.
31 This is also the moment that Renton (2019) establishes as punk's transition into a less radical and more racially diverse phase, although this is nothing to do directly with the dissolution of The Sex Pistols per se.
32 Luke Barnes, Middle Child's playwright collaborator, was also an acting graduate of the Oxford School of Drama, which may serve to establish a shared institutional influence, although he was personally not mentioned in this context.
33 The idea of the 'dramaturgy of listening' also has another manifestation in our empirical sample in the work of Christopher Brett Bailey who explains that for him, 'the instrument for writing is not the pen, it's the ear' (Brett Bailey in LMYE Gallery#4 2021: 4).
34 The turn of the 21st century saw a proliferation of academic texts on authenticity in rock music which David Pattie (2007) has helpfully summarised as dealing with: the binary between 'authentic'/ 'commercial' (Moore 2001), classifications on the basis of Romantic and Modernist notions of art (Keighley 2001), and a more fluid and relational sliding scale between modernist authorship and postmodernist pastiche constituting the polar opposites of authenticity and inauthenticity (Auslander 2003). In 2002, Moore returned to the issue to move the debate away from considerations of intention inscribed in music to considerations of perceptions ascribed to it by the audience (2002).

35 Both Freda Chapple (2006) and David Roesner (2014) offer useful evidence of how music, mediation of music in live performance (2006: 85), and musicality can function as a 'vehicle of immediacy' (Roesner 2014: 15).
36 At the time of writing, William C. Boles 'Theater in a Post-Truth World: Texts, Politics, and Performance' is forthcoming, for example.
37 The foundational interest in authenticity in theatre-making also resonates with Xia's testimony about Ultz's work: '[W]hat I love about Ultz and where his radicalism sits, is he absolutely seeks authenticity by putting real people around him. You know, have real hip hop artists around you, if you're going to try and sample, if that's your medium of choice, I guess. And he always does that [...]. I remember, you know, when he's doing design for *The Beauty Queen of Leenane*, and he calls me from the West Coast of Ireland, where he's measuring door frames in little cottages to make sure that they're exactly the same when he puts them on stage. So again this becomes part of my training about authenticity, and truth, and realness'. (Xia in LMYE Gallery#4, 2021: 4)
38 Such use of economics vocabulary, which is customary in British rehearsal room terminology, has not yet been historicised or problematised in academic literature. It is used here for consistency.
39 O'Briain's visualist term evokes Roesner's 'dispositif' and Auslander's 'frame', which is considered symptomatic of the fact that gig theatre is still primarily theatre rather than a form determined by its prevailing aurality.
40 Here the significance of rhythm becomes particularly relevant and the homology between bass (in a musical sense) and base (in a Marxist political economic sense) allows him to elevate traditionally 'low cultures' to scholarly attention.
41 One exception listed by Taylor (2016) is New Zealand-based Rochelle Bright and Kitan Petkovski' *Daffodils (A Play With Songs)*, an example of gig theatre described on its own vimeo page as 'An acclaimed New Zealand love story with a live mix-tape'.
42 In his LMYE#4 interview Frljić talks of the importance of rhythm in his directorial thinking by reference to Steve Reich and Johann Sebastian Bach. Additionally, it is in the spirit of the A/OD project to note that Frljić's development as a theatre-maker had also been informed by his initial youthful stint with a punk band Le cheval and an active engagement with student radio in Zagreb (Radosavljević and Frljić 2018).
43 For corroboration of Frljić's iconoclastic approach, please see Andrej Mirčev's 'Dissensual Politics of Performance' (2018).

Bibliography

Auslander, Philip (1999). *Liveness: Performance in a Mediatized Culture*, London and New York: Routledge.

Auslander, Philip (2003). 'Good old rock and roll: Performing the 1950s in the 1970s', *Journal of Popular Music Studies*, 15:2, 166–94.

Auslander, Philip (2012). 'Digital liveness: A historico-philosophical perspective', *PAJ* 102, 3–11.

Auslander, Philip (2021). *In Concert: Performing Musical Persona*, Ann Arbor: Michigan University Press.

Beswick, Katie, and Murray, Conrad (2022). *Making Hip Hop Theatre: Beatbox and Elements*, London: Bloomsbury Methuen.

Billington, Michael (2007). *State of the Nation: British Theatre Since 1945*, London: Faber and Faber.

Bonnello Rutter Giaponne, Krista (2018). *The Punk Turn in Comedy: Masks of Anarchy*, Cham: Palgrave Macmillan.

Bradwell, Mike (2010). 'Find a play. Squat a building. Steal a van. Now make a show', *The Guardian* Theatre Blog. https://www.theguardian.com/stage/theatreblog/2010/jun/28/theatre-outside-box-corporate-sponsorship

Butler, Judith (2015). *Notes Toward a Performative Theory of Assembly*, Cambridge, MA: Harvard University Press.
Butt, Gavin; Eshun, Kodwo, and Fisher, Mark (2016). *Post Punk Then and Now*, London: Repeater.
Cavicchi, Daniel (1998). *Tramps Like Us: Music & Meaning among Springsteen Fans*, Oxford: Oxford University Press.
Chapple, Freda (2006). 'Digital opera: Intermediality, remediation and education', in Chapple, Freda and Kattenbelt, Chiel (eds), *Intermediality in Theatre and Performance*, Amsterdam and New York: Rodopi.
Craig, Sandy (1980). *Dreams and Deconstructions: Alternative Theatre in Britain*, Ambergate: Amber Lane Press.
Davis, Anna (2006). 'The Summer of Rave, 1989', *BBC*.
Delfino, Devon (2018). 'How musicians really make their money – And it has nothing to do with how many times people listen to their songs', *Business Insider*. https://www.business insider.com/how-do-musicians-make-money-2018-10?r=US&IR=T
Deller, Jeremy (2019). 'Everybody in the place: An incomplete history of Britain 1984-1992', *BBC*.
Double, Oliver (2007). 'Punk rock as popular theatre', *New Theatre Quarterly*, 1:23, 35–48.
Duncombe, Stephen, and Tremblay, Maxwell (eds) (2011). *White Riot: Punk Rock and the Politics of Race*, London: Verso.
Dyer, Richard (1991). 'A star is born and the construction of authenticity', in Gledhill, Christine (ed.), *Stardom: Industry of Desire*, London: Routledge.
Freeman, Sara (2006). 'Towards a genealogy and taxonomy of British alternative theatre', *NTQ* 22:4, 364–78. doi: 10.1017/s0266464x06000558
Gordy, Eric D. (1999). *The Culture of Power in Serbia: Nationalism and the Destruction of Alternatives*, University Park: Pennsylvania State University Press.
Hebdige, Dick (1979). *Subculture: The Meaning of Style*, London and New York: Routledge.
Henriques, Julian (2011). *Sonic Bodies: Reggae Sound Systems, Performance Techniques, and Ways of Knowing*, London and New York: Continuum.
Huddle, Roger, and Billingham, Lee (2004). 'Anti-fascism: That was then, this is now,' *Socialist Review*. http://socialistreview.org.uk/286/anti-fascism-was-then-now
Iyer, Vijay (2004). 'Exploding the narrative in jazz improvisation'. https://jazzstudiesonline.org/files/jso/resources/pdf/IYER–Exploding%20the%20Narrative.pdf
Kaplan, E. Anne (1987). *Rocking Around the Clock: Music Television, Postmodernism and Consumer Culture*, London and New York: Routledge.
Keighley, Keir (2001). 'Reconsidering rock', in Frith, Simon, Straw, Will, and Street, John (eds), *The Cambridge Companion to Rock and Pop*, Cambridge: Cambridge University Press.
Kendrick, Lynne (2017). *Theatre Aurality*, London: Palgrave Macmillan.
Kotarba, Joseph A. (2013). *Baby Boomer Rock 'n' Roll Fans: The Music Never Ends*, Lanham, Toronto and Plymouth: Scarecrow Press.
Lathan, Peter (2009). 'Pied Piper', *British Theatre Guide*. https://www.britishtheatreguide.info/reviews/piedpiperPDL-rev
Latour, Bruno (2005). *Reassembling the Social: An Introduction to Actor-Network-Theory*, Oxford: Oxford University Press.
Lavery, Brian (2002). 'Preview of the Dublin festival', *The Irish Independent*.
Lehmann, Hans-Thies (1999/2006). *Postdramatic Theatre*, translated and introduced by Karen Jürs-Munby, London and New York: Routledge.
Mackey, Sally (2016). 'Applied theatre and practice as research: Polyphonic conversations', *Research in Drama Education: The Journal of Applied Theatre and Performance*, 21:4, 478–91. doi: 10.1080/13569783.2016.1220250

Mattson, Kevin (2001). 'Did punk matter? Analyzing the practices of a youth subculture during the 1980s', *American Studies*, 42(1), 69–97.

Mattson, Kevin (2020). *We're Not Here to Entertain: Punk Rock, Ronald Reagan, and the Real Culture War of 1980s America*, Oxford: Oxford University Press.

Mayes, Sean, and Whitfield, Sarah K. (2021). *An Inconvenient Black History of British Musical Theatre, 1900–1950*, London: Bloomsbury Methuen.

McCourt, Sarah (2021). 'Aurality and the Actor in Filter Theatre's Twelfth Night', in Pitrolo, Flora, and Radosavljević, Duška (eds) 'Aural/Oral Dramaturgies' (Special Topic), *Critical Stages*, 24., https://www.critical-stages.org/24/aurality-and-the-actor-in-filter-theatres-twelfth-night/

McDonnell, Bill (2013). 'The People's impresario: Roland Muldoon at The Hackney Empire', *Theatre Notebook*, 67:2, 103–17.

McKay, George (1998). *DIY Culture: Party and Protest in Nineties' Britain*, London, New York: Verso.

Middle Child, https://www.middlechildtheatre.co.uk/about-us/

Mignolo, Walter (2007). 'Delinking: The rhetoric of modernity, the logic of coloniality and the grammar of de-coloniality', *Cultural Studies*, 21:2-3, 449-514, DOI: 10.1080/09502380601162647

Mirčev, Andrej (2018). 'Dissensual politics of performance', *Interventions*. https://www.contemporarytheatrereview.org/2018/mircev-dissensual-politics-of-performance/

Moore, Allan (2001). 'Constructing authenticity in rock', *Performance Arts International*, 1 (Winter 2000, http://www.performanceartsinternational.net/html/Ampaper.html (now defunct).).

Moore, Allan (2002). 'Authenticity as authentication', *Popular Music*, 21: 2, 209–223.

Muldoon, Roland (2013). *Taking on the Empire: How We Saved the Hackney Empire for Popular Theatre*, Just Press.

Nancy, Jean-Luc (2007). *On Listening*, translated by Charlotte Mandell, New York: Fordham University Press.

O'Toole, Fintan (2002). 'The Hand', *The Irish Times*, https://www.irishtimes.com/culture/reviews-1.1097199

Paget, Derek (2009). 'The "broken tradition" of documentary theatre and its continued powers of endurance', in Forsyth, Alison and Megson, Chris (eds), *Get Real: Documentary Theatre Past and Present*, Basingstoke: Palgrave Macmillan.

Pattie, David (2007). *Rock Music in Performance*, Basingstoke: Palgrave Macmillan.

Peter, Beate (2020). 'Raves in the twenty-first century: DIY practices, commercial motivations and the role of technology' in Mazierska, Ewa, Les Gillon, Les, and Rigg, Tony (eds), *The Future of Live Music*, London: Bloomsbury. https://www.researchgate.net/publication/341092210_Raves_in_the_twenty-first_century_DIY_practices_commercial_motivations_and_the_role_of_technology

Radosavljević, Duška (2013a). *Theatre-Making: Interplay Between Text and Performance in the 21st Century*, Basingstoke: Palgrave.

Radosavljević, Duška (2013b). *The Contemporary Ensemble: Interviews with Theatre-Makers*, Abingdon: Routledge.

Radosavljević, Duška, and Frljić, Oliver (2018). Interview, Interventions, https://www.contemporarytheatrereview.org/2018/oliver-frljic-interviewed-by-duska-radosavljevic/

Radosavljević, Duška, and Rice, Emma (2010). 'Emma Rice in interview with Duška Radosavljević', *JAFP*, 3:1, 89–98.

Renton, David (2019). *Never Again: Rock Against Racism and the Anti-Nazi League 1976-1982*, Oxon: Routledge.

Reynolds, Simon (2011). *Retromania: Pop Culture's Addiction to Its Own Past*, London: Faber and Faber.

Rodríguez, Verónica (2019). *David Greig's Holed Theatre*, Cham: Palgrave Macmillan.

Rodosthenous, George (2011). 'I let the language lead the dance': Politics, musicality, and voyeurism. David Greig in conversation with George Rodosthenous', *New Theatre Quarterly*, 27:1, 3–13.

Taylor, Amy (2016). 'Gig theatre: Not theatre, not a gig, a movement', *The Skinny*. https://www.theskinny.co.uk/festivals/edinburgh-fringe/theatre/gig-theatre-not-theatre-not-a-gig-a-movement

Trueman, Matt (2011). 'There's no such thing as state of the nation play', *The Guardian*. https://www.theguardian.com/stage/theatreblog/2011/mar/22/state-nation-play-aleks-sierz

Wallace, Claire (2013). *The Theatre of David Greig*, London: Bloomsbury Methuen.

Watson, Gavin (2009). Raving 89, DJhistory.com

Williams, Holly (2016). 'Can the promise of a gig lure music lovers to the theatre?' *The Stage*. https://www.thestage.co.uk/features/2016/can-the-promise-of-a-gig-lure-music-lovers-to-the-theatre/

Williams, Holly (2017). 'Could playwrights save pop music? The rise of gig theatre', *The Telegraph*. https://www.telegraph.co.uk/music/what-to-listen-to/could-playwrights-save-pop-album-rise-gig-theatre/

Wilson, Michael (2006). *Storytelling and Theatre: Contemporary Storytellers and their Art*, Houndsmills: Palgrave Macmillan.

5
CONCLUSION(S)
Aural/Oral Dramaturgies in the Digital Age

The A/OD research project was designed to paradigmatically understand a selection of trends in contemporary theatre-making practice provisionally circumscribed as Post-Verbatim, Amplified Storytelling, and Gig Theatre. These trends are seen as dramaturgical innovations of the digital age connected to relevant histories of theatre-making, issues of politicity of form and content, and the technologies and (trans-)cultural contingencies of artistic expression. My intended focus on the works created at the conceptual intersection of speech-and-sound-based dramaturgies also entailed an interest in their processes of creation, hence an artist-centred research methodology informed by relational ethnography was factored in as an element of this enquiry. The project remit necessarily leaves out various other significant examples of sound-based dramaturgies considered elsewhere, such as radio dramaturgy, foley, audio walks, and/or 'theatre in the dark' (Alston and Welton 2017). Similarly this book has to leave out live art and theatre that foregrounds sound as a scenographic device: for example, the work of Ben and Max Ringham, or specific works of renowned directors such as Simon McBurney, Katie Mitchell, and Robert Lepage, or ensembles such as Rimini Protokoll, although these names remain within the project's wider citational network of influences.[1] The form of musical, music theatre more broadly, and/or 'musicality' in theatre (Bouko 2010, Roesner 2014) – while intersecting with the central interests here and acquiring an increasingly prominent role in contemporary performance[2] – are relevant themes that exceed the remit of this book. Although this work has focused on the dramaturgical affordances of aurality/orality, future work will have to account for the wider and negative aspects of the aural/oral effect, including, for example, its implicit role in sensory racism (Sekimoto and Brown 2020) or 'virtual migration' (Carrillo Rowe et al. 2013).

Research is necessarily a form of improvisation as it occurs within the space between asking a question (ideally a question not asked in the same way before)

DOI: 10.4324/9781003096337-5

and seeking to find possible answers.³ However, in its pursuit of possible answers, this research encountered the kind of obstacle whose global impact required a fundamental reconfiguration of the research design. Less than three months into the official start of the A/OD project, the Covid-19 lockdown imposed a number of parameters requiring that all research be conducted by digital means. This global cultural move created direct implications not just on the research methodology but also on the object of this research (the correlations between dramaturgy, speech, sound, and technicity) as the creative prominence of the speech-and-sound-based dramaturgies grew exponentially in this period. In the absence of opportunities to attend live performance, theatres opened up their previously publicly invisible archives to stream recordings of their productions. Some theatre artists adapted their work for the digital domain or developed ways of rehearsing digitally, as also captured in LMYE #5 Liminal Auralities (for example, She Goat, Sleepwalk Collective, sair goetz, and Oliver Zahn). As noted in the Call for Papers for a special issue of *Critical Stages* on Aural/Oral Dramaturgies, Covid-19 brought about an increased focus on born-digital theatre and performance, much of which utilised the aural dimension (Pitrolo and Radosavljević 2020). In an extension of a previous lecture performance project 'My Documents', Lola Arias commissioned Zoom lecture performances from old and new collaborators.⁴ David Rosenberg and Glen Neath's Darkfield created a series of immersive digital experiences in response to the situation. Hester Chillingworth's durational sound installation began broadcasting on the Royal Court website on 8 May 2020 and continued until 15 October 2020 (see Guy 2021). In amongst numerous, yet uncatalogued works, Stacy Makishi's *The Promise* at the Yard Online and Yannick Trapman-O'Brien's *Telelibrary* used telephone technology to create performances during the lockdown, and Toronto-based Dopolavoro Teatrale's Daniele Bartolini set up an entire festival of telephone performances Theatre-on-Call in April 2020.

The last chapter of this book serves to summarise and integrate the various findings of this research project while at the same time accounting for the unforeseen and eliciting some new insights and threads for further enquiry. The process of writing the book has also been a process of discovery. While the A/OD project was designed to evaluate the compositional acumen of speech and sound and confront the centuries-long colonisation of the field of theatre and performance by the written word, the fact that this has been conducted here somewhat contradictorily in the form of writing has also afforded insights about both registers that would not have otherwise been available. Specifically, for example, the sustained expanding linearity of the book as a form has yielded the opportunity to trace and explore some emerging themes and motifs – such as polyphony, counterpoint, intersubjectivity – from a number of perspectives and over an extended period of time. Similarly, the project as a whole has gradually embraced the combined potential of the visual and the aural for theatre-making and for knowledge production, rather than engaging in split categorical allegiances. The fact that this project has created space for oral, aural, and audio-visual testimonies and conversations has made it possible to bring to my attention so much more than would have been possible through solitary textual or aural/oral investigation alone.

Pulling the variously generated insights of the research together is not an undertaking that can easily reach completion, but this conclusionary chapter draws out a selection of resonant findings to set the scene for future conversations.

The A/OD Case Studies: Notes on a Polyphonic Methodology

As outlined in the Introduction(s), this project was initially designed to ethnographically study the creative processes of four artists selected through an open call. The A/OD Artists in Residence were the US-based sair goetz (working on an intermedial project about gender fluidity and neo-ventriloquism) and three UK-based artists: Silvia Mercuriali (working on a headphones piece for swimming pools), SK Shlomo (developing a solo piece about overcoming mental illness through rave), and Gracefool Collective (conceptualising a site-specific dance theatre piece about climate change).

When the pandemic intervened, the empirical research was redesigned to disperse and expand the project's focus on a greater cross-section of international artists while maintaining a more substantial focus on the Artists in

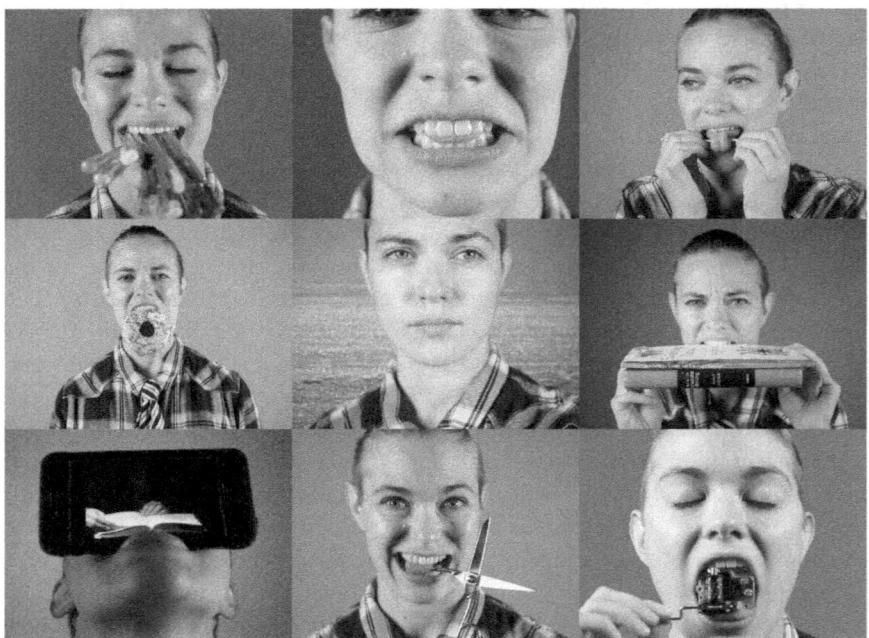

FIGURE 5.1 *Hold Yr Tongue* (2017) by sair goetz

Photo: Self-portrait montage by the artist

Conclusion(s) 163

Residence. We subsequently also included within this narrower remit Sleepwalk Collective whose ensemble work on a piece commissioned by the BAC, taking place remotely across multiple borders despite the lockdown, was deemed to be of relevance.

Each of the five artists is represented on the project website www.auralia.space through a digital package of documentation including an oral history Gallery interview, a Laboratory 'making of' documentary, and a Studio 'masterclass'.[5] Instead of the planned 'thick description' of a single process conducted according to the principles of rehearsal ethnography (McAuley 2012), this layered juxtaposition of more relational ethnographic methods reconfigures the process and the outcomes of the documentation. The inherent hegemonies of the ethnographic process are hence rebalanced through a coalitional approach to research whereby the artist is perceived as an agent in knowledge creation rather than the object of study. The multi-faceted reiterative documentation process covers the artist's work through: (1) an articulation of the performance idiom and methodology (Gallery), (2) a guided tour of the artist's personal archive concerning a specific project (Laboratory), and (3) a recorded example of transmission/dissemination of the artist's working methodology (Studio). This nascent relational ethnographic methodology, which is yet to be developed further, potentially results in polyphonic insights which cannot be deemed comprehensive or fully representative, but the networked resonances they generate and the composite effects they form help to highlight key themes about the artist's dramaturgical approach and ultimately inform the writing of this book.

The composite documentation of sair goetz's work (Figure 5.1) reveals a series of playful strategies the artist uses in exploring their voice as they gradually develop the abecedarian intermedial project *The ABCs and XYZs of LMNs*. For Gracefool Collective, this artistic and personal voice is always necessarily

FIGURE 5.2 *Re:Connect* (2020) by SK Shlomo
Photo: Screenshot from the TV video

embodied and fully vocalised through their corporeality, as illustrated in their teaching practice and previous works. In the case of SK Shlomo, the initial impulse to use live music and storytelling performance in order to turn theatre into a rave, translates, somewhat counter-intuitively but rather suitably, into a TV drama format which uses the Covid-19 lockdown as a way of turning the viewer's living room into a rave venue (Figure 5.2), in the interest of wellbeing. SK Shlomo's monologue *Re:Connect*, directed by Matthew Xia, was filmed for BBC Culture in Quarantine in 2020.

Similarly, Silvia Mercuriali applies her principle of using headphone audio as a way of reframing everyday reality by deploying the listener's gaze as a tool for the transformation of their mundane surroundings into a potentially filmic mise-en-scene. Silvia Mercuriali's headphones piece *Swimming Home* (Figure 5.3) was designed to be listened to in the audience member's bathroom (there was a version for the bath and for the shower) during the lockdown. Finally, Sleepwalk Collective's inexhaustible creative inspiration during the lockdown is captured and documented here as an unusually refreshing act of resistance and encouragement at this historically significant moment.

The potential affordances of the composite 'gestalt effect', inspired by the creative methodology of Anna Deavere Smith and highlighted by Norman Denzin (2003) as a legitimate, and potentially more valuable, ethnographic method in engendering critique in the reader/audience (see Chapter 2), can be extended to the user of the www.auralia.space website too. Organised around the chapter headings of this book, the primary materials collected in the digital database will generate various combinations of composite insights around issues of methodology (Introductions), post-dramatic use of verbatim testimonies (Post-Verbatim),

FIGURE 5.3 *Swimming Home* (2020) by Silvia Mercuriali
Photo: Susanne Dietz

the narrative role of technological developments (Amplified Storytelling), the works that deploy popular music iconography (Gig Theatre), and any further meta-discursive insights (Liminalities/Auralities/Digitalities).

This evidence-based approach, focusing on artists' testimonies, revalorises narrative over abstract epistemologies (Cavarero 1997: 3), taking into consideration a critical use of technology (to paraphrase Rambo Amadeus). As such it is complementary to relational and decolonial approaches to knowledge (Tynan 2021, Tuhiwai Smith 1999) as well as posthumanist ones (Bleeker et al. 2020, Barad 2007, Latour 2005). After Bakhtin, storytelling too can be understood as an intersubjective and polysubjective narrative mode reflective of the dialogic rather than exclusively monologic consciousness.[6] By extension, the relational, artist-centred, reparative, and dramaturgical research methodology deployed in this project, also eventually advances the notion of 'polyphonic historiography' as a more appropriate method for the historicisation of the hybrid form of gig theatre (Chapter 4).

The examples that subsequently gained analytical dominance in the process of writing the book asserted themselves on the basis of the power of insight they offered in relation to the ongoing demands of the discussion, rather than the pre-planned criteria or objective measures of significance. In the spirit of open conversation and improvisation, which has marked the delivery of this project under Covid-19, the writing follows an associative bottom-up narrative logic rather than pre-conceived agendas. Some significant and deserving examples were unintentionally left out of this discussion and will have to therefore inform future research.

The multi-faceted focus on the A/OD Artists in Residence and other artists featured in Lend Me Your Ears (LMYE) is still available to interested users and researchers within the primary research dataset of this project archived on Figshare, and on the www.auralia.space website.

Another important and particularly transformative outcome of this polyphonic work, contained in The Studio section of LMYE, includes the seven-part podcast training course 'Decolonising the Voice', created by A/OD project collaborators Jane Boston and Deelee Dubé (LMYE Studio 2022), for dissemination purposes.

Paradigmatic Questions

In summarising the A/OD project findings, it is appropriate to briefly consider the initially scoped research questions underlying this work. As originally outlined, the project envisaged a paradigmatic view of the dramaturgies of speech and sound in terms of compositional strategies (RQ1), conceptual framing (RQ2), and the role of technology (RQ3).

Possibly the first aspect to reflect on is the notion of 'paradigm' itself. Hans-Thies Lehmann has problematised applicability of this term in relation to art on the grounds that 'in the emergence of a new paradigm, the "future" structures and stylistic traits almost unavoidably appear mixed in with the conventional'

(Lehmann 1999/2006: 24) by contrast to science where looping back to outdated worldviews is not an option. Nevertheless, as noted by Catherine Bouko, Lehmann's postdramatic theatre was itself contentiously perceived as a paradigm, misapprehended, and criticised as advocating the end of drama (Bouko 2010: 76). I hope that it is now safe to assume that claims of paradigm shifts in the field of theatre and performance are no longer to be perceived in such categorical terms, but more so in relation to how dramaturgical strategies might be changing in step with technological advancements. Seda Ilter has shown in her book on the influence of mediatisation on text-based dramaturgy (2021) that technological advancements do indeed form a basis for the possibility of paradigmatic considerations of dramatic theatre itself. Ultimately, it is the task of Humanities research to always seek to 'trouble the paradigm' (Sterne 2011: 220). David Roesner's counter-suggestion to the notion of a paradigm, contained in his application of the 'dispositif' allows for the possibility of a multiplicity of overlapping, coexisting, and interacting perspectives (Roesner 2014: 11). This is an appropriate proposition for theatre and performance which is always already at an intersection of multiple research disciplines and modalities of artistic expression. Whether or not the work under consideration forms a paradigm is of a lesser significance than its ability to be effectively subjected to relevant analysis as a 'field' (Desmond 2014) or even a 'scene' (Kotarba 2013). However, the notion of multiplicity is relevant to the consideration of aural/oral dramaturgies and the theatre of speech and sound.

This investigation has resorted to the organising principle of polyphony as a way of considering the multiplicity of perspectives as polyphony also conveniently allows for the generative considerations of counterpoint, or a dialectical juxtaposition of semantic materials that engages the audience's multimodal response. The notion of polyphony is applied metaphorically rather than strictly musicologically here, but it must also be acknowledged that polyphony as a metaphor does have certain limitations in its application to theatre because it does not fully account for the non-aural aspects of theatre's multimodality, or the meaning-making mechanisms of the spoken word. The notion of counterpoint as a constitutive element of polyphony carries its own semantic potential as already explored by various cultural thinkers including Edward Said (1993),[7] Tim Ingold (2011), and Fred Moten (2017). In defining the 'field' of study for this project, I identified three emerging trends as forming a critical mass of the newly prominent dramaturgies of speech and sound in theatre: post-verbatim, amplified storytelling, and gig theatre. I have analysed each trend by reference to a number of theoretical works, composite insights resonating from curated conversations with relevant artists and scholars, and with closer attention to the dramaturgical workings of some representative examples. The emerging themes that amass, converge, and reverberate through the three chapters crucially inform this summary. While on the level of compositional strategies (RQ1), technological innovation (RQ3) can be seen to generate new ways of handling semantic, aesthetic, and mechanical material, conceptually (RQ2) the deployment of speech and sound in performance-making raises questions around different modalities of sensory perception (visual vs aural, etc.) and, ultimately, around audience reception.

'Bottom Up': Dramaturgy of Layering

One significant discovery stemming from the empirical investigations of technicity of the aural/oral dramaturgies has been the notion of 'layering'. Layering is frequently mentioned by the artists interviewed as part of the A/OD project in three significant ways: (1) metaphorically, in reference to different types of performance material; (2) as a dramaturgical method directly influenced by the workings of music-making software; and (3) conceptually, in relation to the malleability of text enabled by the digital technologies. (In the process of writing this book, for example, I am aware of how even word-processing software alone makes writing/editing more open to layering than the analogue processes of handwriting or typewriting would have done).

This dramaturgy of layering – potentially contrasting the historical linearity of writing processes – can also be perceived as being ontologically linked to a DIY ethos of performance-making. Even before the advent of the digital technologies, the specialised analogue technologies linked to popular music culture such as pedals, synthesisers, and amplifiers created the conditions for an emergence of newly specialised creative artists such as DJs, thus complicating the pre-existing divisions of labour in musical performance and production. The digital technologies further enabled a wider access to the previously highly professionalised modes of labour, such as musical composition. Several artists interviewed as part of the A/OD project and featured in Lend Me Your Ears (Matthew Xia, Quote Unquote, Melanie Wilson) have testified to composing music digitally despite the absence of formal training in musical composition. Combined with the formatively influential 1980s legacy of post-punk and its promotion of self-authorisation, auto-didacticism, and DIY, the post-industrial digital means of production enable the contemporary theatre-makers to conceive of their work in an increasingly deprofessionalised, generically fluid, and creatively emancipated ways. In some cases, such as Kieran Hurley's *Beats*, the input of a DJ was fundamental to the dramaturgy of the piece, in others, such as the work of Matthew Xia, the DJing expertise informs the conception of the theatre-making process as a community-building activity. This form of community-oriented, post-industrial, digitally-aided deprofessionalisation reconnects contemporary theatre and performance-making with 'grassroots collective action' (Beswick and Murray 2022), 'bottom-up views of narrativity' (Iyer 2004), and 'thinking through sound' (Henriques 2011), as well as the improvisatory practices inherent to Black American musical culture that forms the basis of much popular music of the 20th century. Via the influence of the popular music of the 20th century, contemporary aural/oral dramaturgies can be seen as deeply rooted in the Black American (and other non-Western) cultural conceptions of authorship gradually updated and modified by technological developments outside of institutional structures, and mostly tangential to the post-Enlightenment Western European ones.

When it comes to the role of technology in aural/oral dramaturgies, hardware such as microphones and headphones can resource another significant dramaturgical layer too. In addition to the well-observed associated contemporary performance trends of 'transmission' and 'channelling' (Parker-Starbuck 2017) and the move towards the 'somatosensory modalities' (Klich 2017) that the contemporary technologies facilitate, my field research records a growing interest in a more playfully poetic remediation of the effect of amplification (Dead Centre, Kate Hunter, Sleepwalk Collective), as well as an incorporation of full accessibility strategies into the core dramaturgy of the work (She Goat, The Unspoken Project). In the new materialist ways proposed by Karen Barad (2007) and Bruno Latour (2005), loop pedals and recording devices are also treated as collaborators in the creative processes of the interviewed artists (SK Shlomo, Maya Krishna Rao, Kate Hunter), while during the Covid-19 lockdown, computer screens in fact became the stage (Oliver Zahn, Lola Arias) in ways exceeded by Brenda Laurel's conception of this analogy in *Computers as Theatre* (1991).

The Disruption of Closure: Dramaturgy of Methexis

On the conceptual level, speech and sound are evidenced to carry their own affordances in relation to making theatre. Adriana Cavarero's (2005) idea of speech insists on the primacy of the vocalic over the semantic, emphasising the sonorous materiality of voice which leads to a relational and ultimately political potential. Similarly, Jean-Luc Nancy qualifies the sonorous as 'tendentially methexic (that is, having to do with participation, sharing, or contagion)' as opposed to the mimetic tendency of the visual, although he notes that the two do not exclude the possibility of intersection (2002/2007: 10). On further reflection, the methexic by comparison to the mimetic might be understood as an immaterial process of engendering meaning – an apprehension of meaning by affect or intuition, perhaps – as opposed to that which can be perceived through visual representation/imitation. Much of this requires categorical rethinking and rearticulation to be pursued beyond the confines of this volume, however, key findings of the A/OD project point to the integral and costitutive status of reception processes within the dramaturgies of speech and sound.

Significant insights about the dramaturgies of speech and sound in this book converge around the productive potential of the dialectical layering mechanism of counterpoint in engaging the audience intersubjectively. Furthermore, 'self-disclosure and vulnerability', noted by Dwight Conquergood as constituent requirements of 'the praxis of speaking and listening – conversation', are set in opposition to the notion of 'closure' characteristic of the 'gaze' (2013: 87). Both self-disclosure and vulnerability are at work simultaneously in the intersubjective theatre of speech and sound predicated on the simultaneous existence and removal of the fourth wall, as shown in Chapter 4. The effect of 'vulnerability' ensues by exposure to sound whose immersive capacity gives rise to concerns about potential co-optation of the audience 'by profit-making enterprises' (Alston 2013: 13). Co-optation is also a problem we encounter in relation to the unfortunate fate of subcultures which begin their life through 'spectacular' communication of difference from the mainstream culture (Hebdige 1979) only to end in a process informally known as 'selling out' (Mattson 2001). These are two different manifestations of co-optation which as a term is ultimately defined by a power imbalance between a bigger and a smaller entity and a loss of agency of the latter in exchange for some other kind of compensation. While the commercial exploitation of the co-opted is a serious political problem – especially when full awareness of the fact of exploitation is occluded through affective subjugation of the latter – theatre as a meta-political microcosm also has the potential to dramaturgically co-opt, illuminate and disclose the co-optation principle. The empowering efficacy of Marxist critique contained in the uncovering of the hidden workings of ideology can foreclose the possibility of dialectically perceiving the emancipatory potential of the processes under critique. Hence, vulnerability, on the other hand, is a 'mode of relationality' that, according to Judith Butler, can lead to solidarity, political collections, and coalitions (Butler 2015: 130).

The dramaturgies of speech and sound present an opportunity to re-examine the applicability of the pre-existing critical tools because the ontological features of speech and sound in the first place problematise the applicability of the entire metaphysical tradition of the West as shown by Cavarero (2005) and corroborated in various ways by Conquergood (2013), Feld (2015), Henriques (2011), Iyer (2004), Kendrick (2017), Nancy (2002/2007), Robinson (2020), Ngũgĩ (2012), and others. As illustrated by the example of Serbian orature, explored in Chapter 3, this does not mean that non-Western heritage necessarily provides readymade alternatives – criticality towards the hegemonic processes of tradition itself remains a necessary ingredient in decolonial deployment of epistemological alternatives. Hence, some key ontology-related aspects of the dramaturgies of speech and sound that have emerged as significant throughout the discussion here include dialectically layered insights concerning ocular-centricity vis-a-vis aurality/orality, politicity of form and content, audience reception (immersivity, relationality, methexis, aural intersubjectivity, and polysubjectivity), im-provisation,[8] critical resistance to pre-ordained orders/hierarchies/modes of marginalisation, and disruption of closure.

The 'disruption of closure' is probably the closest one gets to a definitionally coherent designation pertaining to the methexic dramaturgies of speech and sound. This syntagm evokes Lehmann's original use to contextualise the post-dramatic procedures of 'disruption' to the 'fictive cosmos' of dramatic theatre (1999/2006: 100), as well as integrating Conquergood's negation of the possibility of 'closure' in the processes of listening (2013:87). It additionally extends my own discussion in *Theatre-Making* concerning the difficulty experienced by the audience in attaining semantic closure in the course of watching Tim Crouch's *The Author* (2009). This piece is constructed in such a way that the primary engagement of the audience in the course of attending is affectively challenging, which causes semantic closure (or making sense of the work) to be only 'attainable *post hoc*, in the process of reflection' (Radosavljević 2013: 196, original emphasis). In this case, the audience are denied a reflective distance in the process of watching – and, in fact, they are not 'watching' but mostly listening/experiencing/imagining/ cognitively participating in the piece – which simultaneously denies or postpones the semantic closure. On further reflection, Tim Crouch's *The Author* (2009) can also be perceived as foregrounding methexis/the intersubjective dramaturgy of speech and sound ('tell rather than show') over mimesis/the representational dramaturgies of dramatic theatre ('show rather than tell').

Enmeshment vs Immersion: Dramaturgy of Intersubjectivity

If these findings seem overly dispersed or meanderingly interconnected, this too is related to the ontological nature of speech and sound which collapses mimesis into methexis. Following in the footsteps of Milman Parry and Albert Lord, the oral composition scholar John Miles Foley (1947–2012) in his swan song book/ website *Oral Tradition and the Internet* (2012) contrasts the 'fixed, spatial linearity' of the book to the oral tradition (OT) and the internet (IT) as the twin technologies that '*mime the way we think* – by navigating along pathways within an interactive network' (Foley 2012: 8, original emphasis). This choice of terms represents a different, non-Aristotelian conception of 'mimesis' – a mimesis of the thinking/speaking process itself – that can be perceived to exist, not in opposition to, but at the core of the methexic dramaturgies of speech and sound.

Foley elaborates that the oral tradition and the internet 'do not operate by spatializing, sequencing, or objectifying', but instead 'they invite and require active participation and support a rich diversity of individual, one-time-only experiences' (ibid.). In this way, they 'do not fossilize ideas into freestanding museum exhibits [...] as books typically do' (ibid.). Foley's theorising is founded on a categorical juxtaposition between orality and textuality and therefore does not fully account for the possible third dimension of live performance of speech and sound which may indeed entail spatialising or objectifying implications, in an expanded, more fluid sense. Additionally, he ignores the hybridity of hypertext and 'oral textuality' noted by Steve Dixon as a function of the 'changing nature of language and linguistic creativity' in the digital culture (2007/2015: 485–6). However, Foley's emphasis on 'pathways' is in sync with Latour's emphasis on 'relations' over causalities that networks as organising structures enable. Both thinkers' ideas are rooted in a favoring of heterarchies rather than traditional hierarchies of value. In her 2015 rethinking of formalism with a view to highlighting political affordances of form, literary critic Caroline Levine identifies 'network' as one of the four prevalent forms in contemporary cultural studies. Formally, she sees this as a recognition of the fact that the world is 'much more chaotic and contingent [...] than Foucault imagined' (2015: xiii) and defers instead to his successors Gilles Deleuze and Félix Guattari's idea of the 'rhizome' as a more potent conceptual analogy than the 'unifying form of the tree' at the base of Foucault's 'genealogy'. Having begun with Foucault, my own investigation in this book arrives at the point where, for a number of noted conceptual and methodological reasons, it becomes clear it is necessary to uphold the prevalence of networked rhizomaticity in relation to the dramaturgies of speech and sound.[9]

All of the above allows me to postulate that in attending theatre and performance that prioritises speech and sound, the audience is therefore *enmeshed* in a complex process of reception that entails multimodal sensory perception (show-*and*-tell), and a mimesis of the thinking process itself (especially perhaps the intersubjective, collective kind characteristic of theatre attendance). The notion of enmeshment, vis-a-vis 'immersion' problematised in the Introduction(s), points to the fact that different meaning-making modalities are not necessarily in a hierarchical relationship to each other, and that the audience is not entirely submerged or disempowered in the experience or deprived of their meta-critical reflection. Even if the full meaning-making closure might not be available in the course of experiencing the piece, if it might be substituted with primarily affective engagement, or subject to delay to a post hoc moment,[10] the audience member's intersubjective involvement is always contingent on a number of variables rather than being fully open to totalisation, transgression, or cynical exploitation.[11] Furthermore, artists' testimonies (for example, Valentijn Dhaenens in LMYE Gallery#2, Donnecadh O'Briain in LMYE Gallery#4) reveal that the way in which the aural/oral dramaturgy work opens itself up to intersubjective interaction demands more consideration of the formal conventions and the audience's role than the case might have been in dramatic theatre whose terms of engagement are relatively clearly set and where both sides are comparatively free from the need to improvise.

As noted in Chapter 2, in relation to the audience reception, I am particularly interested in the semantic gap created through counterpoint in the polyphonic multimodalities of the theatre of speech and sound. This semantic gap, or a space for reflection as I have also called it, is an opportunity provided within the piece for the audience's reckoning between different levels of meaning contained in a simultaneous layering/juxtaposition of the various meaning-making modalities (or technicities of representation including speech, sound, body, voice, gender, movement, or scenic design). This is well illustrated by post-verbatim theatre which, contrary to verbatim theatre's presumption of faithful transmission of the documented speech, proceeds to theatricalise the original testimony by subjecting it to a multimodal process of translation, interpretation, and critical intervention. In the case of Nic Green's *Cock and Bull* (2015), the deliberate deployment of counterpoint between the intended meanings of the spoken words and their rendering in dance performance engenders an act of collective affective critique whereby the audience is co-opted as an ally (rather than being treated as the recipient of transmission, or witness, as is more common in verbatim theatre).

In Chapter 3, I showed how the artist can use technological tools to politicise content through formal innovation when the form and content remain fossilised in performance. As shown on the example of Rambo Amadeus, the apparent incongruence that technological innovation offers in a juxtaposition of content and its performance (to put it simply but not reductively as 'amplification of storytelling') prompts an intersubjective meaning-making involvement of the audience. Once again, the immediate affective response might be humor or wonder, curiosity or confusion, but the takeaway effect is the post hoc semantic closure that might follow. Another takeaway, from the point of view of the artist, is a diversification of dramaturgical means.

Lucy McCormick exemplifies the deployment of incongruence well in her unique juxtaposition of genres of performance and different aesthetic frames in 'tricking the audience into watching performance art' (LMYE Gallery#1). Incongruence is by no means characteristic of all of gig theatre explored in Chapter 4, but McCormick's example does highlight the inherent multimodal potential of gig theatre to accommodate contrasting musical and scenic content because it recognises the distinctions between theatre audiences and music fans and their respective expectations. Gig theatre may use fandom as a semantic and cultural reference – and it might appeal to the audience's own social role as popular music consumers, or to the capacity of amplified music to generate the effect of 'sonic dominance' (Henriques 2011) and 'unchosen solidarity' or 'coalition' (Butler 2015) – but it does not seek to reproduce fan behaviors. Instead, it anticipates a sustained imaginative and meaning-making enmeshment of the audience in the world-making (Voegelin 2014, Kondo 2018) capacity of theatre in conjunction with speech and sound.

Epilogue: Liminalities

On 20 May 2020, The Theatre Times International Online Festival of Theatre streamed Annie Dorsen's piece *Hello Hi There* (2010), accompanied by a live Q and A between academic/dramaturg Tom Sellar and the theatre-maker herself. Although Dorsen had spent years thinking and writing about her idea of 'algorithmic theatre', when her piece first premiered ten years previously in a theatre in Austria, she was concerned about its potential reception. Scenographically, *Hello Hi There* (2010) consisted of computer and TV screens laid out on an astroturf. There were no actors. Taking as its points of inspiration a 1971 recording of a TV debate between Michel Foucault and Noam Chomsky, and Alan Turing's 1950 essay 'Computing Machinery and Intelligence', the piece was an examination of whether a meaningful communication through language without thinking is possible. The result was a Beckettian framework within which the artist attempted to achieve plausibility and a convincing effect of communication between machines. Whereas Dorsen might have been nervous about the potential reception of this piece in a theatre auditorium in 2010, under the Covid-19 global lockdown, where all theatre was streamed through our TV or computer screens – this piece about the performativity of the digital, was in fact the most effective medium-specific theatre available.

Conclusion(s)   **173**

The A/OD project includes the designation 'digital age' in its long title. It is therefore appropriate to also ask what the confinement of theatre to the solely digital realm caused by Covid-19 brought about that was of relevance to the investigation?

Two other particularly effective examples I saw in this context included Filippo Michelangelo Ceredi's piece *Between Me and P.* (2016) and Oliver Zahn's piece *In Praise of Forgetting II* (2020). The first had been made as a multimedia piece performed in theatres before the pandemic. In it Ceredi projects selected digitised items from his personal archive (conversations, photographs, pieces of music) in order to conjure up a 'digital double' (Dixon 2007: 241) of his older brother who had been missing since 1987. The second piece was an adaptation for Zoom of a theatre performance Zahn had made using an oral ethnographic archive that documents the experience of the Germans expelled from the non-German lands following World War Two. Unfolding entirely via the screen-share function on Zoom, *In Praise of Forgetting II* (2020) consists of a choreographed operation of text boxes, jpegs, and sound and video files, accompanied by live writing. Neither performer used any spoken commentary in their performance.

As performativity of the desktop proliferated,[12] what Covid-19 highlighted were aural/oral dramaturgies that manifested through absence – of the theatre space and of live speech and sound. Following Ong (1982), one might speculate about the 'tertiary orality', carried out by non-verbal means.

In a way that collapses form and content into each other, it is archive itself that emerges instead as a theme of the final issue of Lend Me Your Ears, the digital repository of the A/OD project. Oliver Zahn's *In Praise of Forgetting II* (2020) and Filippo Michelangelo Ceredi's *Between Me and P.* (2016) perform different kinds of archives and are featured in the Gallery section as examples of the dramaturgies using speech and sound documents in their inception. Found recordings and associated documents become a basis for works made by the means of 'assemblage' (Thomaidis LMYE Salon#2), rather than transmission. Flora Pitrolo's inspired naming of the Salon conversation between Robert Icke and Anne Washburn (concerning their 2014 collaboration *Mr Burns: A Post-Electric Play*), as 'Oral/Aural Remains' also brought to mind Rebecca Schneider's seminal 2001 essay which acquired new meanings in the period of lockdown when all we had available were the archives of performance rather than live events.[13] Archaeology is not so far from archives, at least in name, and so Annie Goh and Miriam Kolar's fascinating Salon conversation about performing archaeoacoustics also found its place here. By association of ideas, another interdisciplinary excursion of this final issue was a Salon conversation by Danilo Mandic and Sara Ramshaw deliberating about the relationships between law and justice, structure and form, listening and hearing, improvisation and composition, and machine listening.

In parallel, LMYE#5 explores the theme of technicity – Worthen's 2020 book is featured in Library #5 and Maria Kapsali's practice research project on movement sonification in this issue matches and extends Library#4's outing into formal experimentation in academic research (exemplified by A.D. Carson's peer-reviewed album 'i used to love to dream' (2020) published by the University of Michigan Press). Furthermore, She Goat's Laboratory recording takes the viewer through the intricacies of making a Covid-induced adaptation of a theatre performance into a sound podcast, while Hanna Slattnë and Shannon Yee reverse engineer the making of *Reassembled, Slightly Askew* (2015), a piece of headphones theatre that takes the audience inside the head of a patient with brain injury.[14] sair goetz's Laboratory, in conjunction with their Gallery interview, offers a network of insights into their specific poetics manifesting liminality of different kinds – formal, intermedial, gen(d)eric. Cultural liminality too is explored and expressed in this context through She Goat and Sleepwalk Collective's Gallery interviews. Thus the final issue of Lend Me Your Ears is named 'Liminal Auralities' in order to embrace the full breadth of these emerging themes. The idea of liminality at the core of this selection can still be related back to Susan Broadhurst's (1999) definition of liminal performance as a 'marginalised form', characterised by experimentation, embrace of technology, innovation, heterogeneity, and the 'collapse of the hierarchical distinction between high and popular culture' (1999:1).

As shown in this book, this 'collapse' of hierarchies characterises most of the work explored as part of the A/OD project. The LMYE Editorial #5 further proposes that Broadhurst's definition of the 'liminal' may now be expanded to include other changes, transitions, and non-binaries highlighted by our interlocutors, including gender fluidity, genre fluidity, trans-cultural liminality, centring of accessibility, and digitality within the continuum of technological developments, as well as the search for new languages of performance and discourse. Thus, ontological liminality of the aural/oral dramaturgies – also denoted in this book as inherently intersubjective, relational, polyphonic, multimodal, layered, enmeshing, and resistant to closure – precipitates a kind of conclusion that must remain 'open-ended, anticipatory and dehegemonising' (Editorial LMYE#5).

Notes

1. For example, Katie Mitchell's collaborator Melanie Wilson is interviewed for Lend Me Your Ears and Simon McBurney's *The Encounter* is frequently mentioned in interviews and explored in Lynne Kendrick's book *Theatre Aurality* (2017). Robert Lepage's collaborators on *Lipsynch* (2008) John Cobb and Sarah Kemp were interviewed as part of this project although their interview was not featured in Lend Me Your Ears.
2. The *Guardian* review of Katie Mitchell and Miriam Batty's adaptation of Rebecca Watson's novel *Little Scratch* (2021) at the Hampstead Theatre refers to it as an 'arrangement', a term seen as doing 'better justice to this contrapuntal treatment of the text, which has a musical precision' (https://www.theguardian.com/stage/2021/nov/12/little-scratch-review-rebecca-watson-katie-mitchell).
3. This was also pointed out by dancer Kent de Spain who conceives of improvisation as 'another way of "thinking" […] that produces ideas impossible to conceive in stillness' (2003: 27).
4. Clio Unger (2021) problematised this project in an award-winning article about lecture performances in the context of post-Fordist commodification of knowledge.

5 The only exception is SK Shlomo who is not featured in the Studio due to constraints on his time.
6 In this context, Norman Denzin understands the method of interview as a 'ubiquitous method of self-construction' (2003: 57) in an increasingly mediatised and inherently dramaturgical society, that however has the potential to 'uncover structures of oppression' and 'critically promote the agendas of radical democratic practice' (2003: 75).
7 See also Capitain (2020) analysing the use of 'counterpoint' by Said throughout his body of work, focusing especially on various drafts of *Culture and Imperialism* (1993).
8 This spelling wishes to draw attention to the Latin etymology of the term indicating the impossibility of seeing ahead.
9 In their recent anthology, Fisher and Gotman place Foucault's theatrical conception of his own metaphysics within the ocular-centric tradition: '[W]hat we aim to do here is draw attention to the vectors of sight – the gazes and the performances – by which these discourses come to appear. These forms of visibilisation are, then, inherently theatrical: and Foucault's work, we therefore contend in this volume, must be read in this light' (Fisher and Gotman 2020: 19).
10 Ontroerend Goed's *Internal* (2009), which was perceived as ethically problematic not necessarily because it exploits the audience for commercial gain but for the reasons of betraying the audience's confidence, resulted in extended self-motivated conversations among audience members in pursuit of semantic closure for hours, days, weeks, and sometimes years afterwards within online forums or festival contexts. I understood this phenomenon as a formation of 'discursive communities' around a show (Radosavljević 2015); and the process of seeking semantic closure in relation to this show continued for me via the writing of the book and thinking about the show for years afterwards.
11 This does not deny the possibility that some immersive theatre may indeed be driven primarily by commercial gain in exchange for delivering uncritical ludic entertainment, but this is not necessarily a characteristic of all immersive theatre, or the dramaturgical apparatus at its core.
12 This performativity of the desktop is quite different from the form defined as 'desktop theatres' (Dixon 2007: 488–91) which occurs instead in the cyberspace, using chatrooms and textual MOOs.
13 As noted in the Editorial for Lend Me Your Ears, Issue #5: far from following the imperative of 'imperialism inherent in archival logic' (Schneider 2001: 101), the interviews collected within LMYE followed the impulse instead 'to stay connected, share, partake, host, amplify, relate and ultimately amass shared input and wisdom, assemble a community, and outline an ecology suitable for acoustemological (Feld 2015) investigation'.
14 Slattnë corroborates further on her dramaturgical methodology in this work in the Aural/Oral Dramaturgies issue of *Critical Stages* (2021).

Bibliography

Alston, Adam (2013). 'Audience participation and neoliberal value: Risk, agency and responsibility in immersive theatre', *Performance Research: A Journal of the Performing Arts*, 18:2, 128–38, https://doi.org/10.1080/13528165.2013.807177

Alston, Adam, and Welton, Martin (eds) (2017). *Theatre in the Dark: Shadow, Gloom and Blackout in Contemporary Theatre*, London: Bloomsbury.

Barad, Karen (2007). *Meeting the Universe Halfway. Quantum Physics and the Entanglement of Matter and Meaning*, Durham, NC: Duke University Press.

Beswick, Katie, and Murray, Conrad (2022). *Making Hip Hop Theatre: Beatbox and Elements*, London: Bloomsbury Methuen.

Bleeker, Maaike, Verhoeff, Nana, and Werning, Stefan (2020). 'Sensing data: Encountering data sonifications, materialization, and interactives as *knowledge objects*', *Convergence: The*

International Journal of Research into New Media Technologies, 26:5–6, 1–20 (online-generated pdf). doi: https://doi.org/10.1177/1354856520938601

Bouko, Catherine (2010). 'Musicality in postdramatic theatre: the opacity of auditory signs and the model of the iconic thought', *Studies in Musical Theatre*, 4(1), 75–87.

Broadhurst, Susan (1999). *Liminal Acts: A Critical Overview of Contemporary Performance and Theory*, London and New York: Cassell.

Butler, Judith (2015). *Notes Toward a Performative Theory of Assembly*, Cambridge, MA: Harvard University Press.

Capitain, Wouter (2020). 'From counterpoint to heterophony and back again: Reading Edward Said's drafts for culture and imperialism', *Journal of Musicological Research*, 41:1, 1–22. doi: 10.1080/01411896.2020.1787793: https://doi.org/10.1080/01411896.2020.1787793

Carrillo Rowe, Aimee, Malhotra, Sheena, and Pérez, Kimberlee (2013). 'Answering the call: Virtual migration in Indian call centres', *Comparative American Studies an International Journal*, 12:1–2, 51–70. doi: 10.1179/1477570014Z.00000000068

Cavarero, Adriana (1997/2000). *Relating Narratives: Storytelling and Selfhood*, translated and with an introduction by Paul A. Kottman, London, New York: Routledge.

Cavarero, Adriana (2005). *For More than One Voice: Toward a Philosophy of Vocal Expression*, Stanford: Stanford University Press.

Conquergood, Dwight (2013). *Cultural Struggles: Performance, Ethnography, Praxis*, edited and introduced by Johnson, E. Patrick, Ann Arbor: University of Michigan Press.

De Spain, Kent (2003). 'The cutting edge of awareness: Reports from the inside of improvisation', in Cooper Albright, Ann and Gere, David (eds), *Taken by Surprise*, Connecticut: Wesleyan University Press.

Denzin, Norman (2003). *Performance Ethnography: Critical Pedagogy and the Politics of Culture*, Thousand Oaks: SagePrint.

Desmond, Matthew (2014). 'Relational ethnography', *Theory and Society*, 43:5, 547–79.

Dixon, Steve (2007/2015). *Digital Performance: A History of New Media in Theater, Dance, Performance Art, and Installation*, Cambridge, MA: MIT.

Feld, Steven (2015). 'Acoustemology' in Novak, David and Sakakeeny, Matt (eds), *Keywords in Sound*, Durham, NC: Duke University Press.

Felski, Rita (2015). *The Limits of Critique*, Chicago: University of Chicago Press.

Fisher, Tony, and Gotman, Kélina (2020). *Foucault's Theatres*, Manchester: Manchester University Press.

Foley, John Miles (2012). *Oral Tradition and the Internet: Pathways of the Mind*, Urbana, Chicago, and Springfield: University of Illinois Press.

Guy, Georgina (2021) 'Staged installation, reported speech, and syndemic images in blindness and caretaker', Pitrolo, Flora, and Radosavljević, Duška (eds) 'Aural/Oral Dramaturgies' (Special Topic), *Critical Stages*, 24. https://www.critical-stages.org/24/staged-installation-reported-speech-and-syndemic-images-in-blindness-and-caretaker-2020/

Hebdige, Dick (1979). *Subculture: The Meaning of Style*, London and New York: Routledge.

Henriques, Julian (2011). *Sonic Bodies: Reggae Sound Systems, Performance Techniques, and Ways of Knowing*, London and New York: Continuum.

Ilter, Seda (2021). *Mediatized Dramaturgy: The Evolution of Plays in the Media Age*, London: Bloomsbury Methuen.

Ingold, Tim (2011). *Being Alive: Essays on Movement, Knowledge and Description*, London, New York: Routledge.

Iyer, Vijay (2004). 'Exploding the narrative in jazz improvisation'. https://jazzstudiesonline.org/files/jso/resources/pdf/IYER-Exploding%20the%20Narrative.pdf

Kendrick, Lynne (2017). *Theatre Aurality*, London: Palgrave Macmillan.
Klich, Rosemary (2017). 'Amplifying sensory spaces: The in- and out-puts of headphone theatre', *Contemporary Theatre Review*, 27: 3, 366–78. doi: https://doi.org/10.1080/10486801.2017.1343247
Kondo, Dorinne (2018). *Worldmaking: Race, Performance, and the Work of Creativity*, Durham, NC: Duke University Press.
Kotarba, Joseph A. (2013). *Baby Boomer Rock 'n' Roll Fans: The Music Never Ends*, Lanham, Toronto and Plymouth: Scarecrow Press.
Latour, Bruno (2004). 'Why has critique run out of steam? From matters of fact to matters of concern', *Critical Inquiry*, 30:2, 225–48.
Latour, Bruno (2005). *Reassembling the Social: An Introduction to Actor-Network-Theory*, Oxford: Oxford University Press.
Laurel, Brenda (1991/2013). *Computers as Theater*, Reading, MA: Addison-Wesley.
Lehmann, Hans-Thies (1999/2006). *Postdramatic Theatre*, translated and introduced by Karen Jürs-Munby, London and New York: Routledge.
Levine, Caroline (2015). *Forms: Whole, Rhythm, Hierarchy, Network*, New Jersey: Princeton University Press.
Mattson, Kevin (2001). 'Did punk matter? Analyzing the practices of a youth subculture during the 1980s', *American Studies*, 42(1), 69–97.
McAuley, Gay (2012). *Not Magic but Work: An Ethnographic Account of a Rehearsal Process*, Manchester: Manchester University Press.
Moten, Fred (2017). *Black or Blur: Consent Not to Be a Single Being*, Durham, NC: Duke University Press.
Nancy, Jean-Luc (2007). *On Listening*, translated by Charlotte Mandell, New York: Fordham University Press.
Ngũgĩ Wa Thiong'o (2012). *Globalectics: Theory and Politics of Knowing*, New York: Columbia University Press.
Ong, Walter (1982/2002). *Orality and Literacy: The Technologizing of the World*, London and New York: Routledge.
Parker-Starbuck, Jennifer (2017). 'Karaoke theatre: Channelling mediated lives', *Contemporary Theatre Review*, 27:3, 379–90. doi: https://doi.org/10.1080/10486801.2017.1343243
Pitrolo, Flora, and Radosavljević, Duška (2020). 'Call for papers and essays', *Critical Stages*. https://www.critical-stages.org/21/aural-oral-dramaturgies/
Pitrolo, Flora, and Radosavljević, Duška (eds) (2021) 'Editors' introduction: Aural/Oral Dramaturgies' (Special Topic), *Critical Stages*, 24. https://www.critical-stages.org/24/aural-oral-dramaturgies-editors-introduction/
Radosavljević, Duška (2013). *Theatre-Making: Interplay Between Text and Performance in the 21st Century*, Basingstoke: Palgrave.
Radosavljević, Duška (2015) 'The machinery of democracy', *Exeunt*. http://exeuntmagazine.com/features/the-machinery-of-democracy/
Robinson, Dylan (2020). *Hungry Listening: Resonant Theory for Indigenous Sound Studies*, Minneapolis: University of Minnesota Press.
Roesner, David (2014). *Method and Metaphor in Theatre-Making*, Farnham/Burlington: Ashgate.
Said, Edward (1993). *Culture and Imperialism*, London: Chatto & Windus.
Schneider, Rebecca (2001). 'Performance remains', *Performance Research*, 6:2, 100–108. doi: 10.1080/13528165.2001.10871792
Sekimoto, Sachi, and Brown, Christopher (2020). *Race and the Senses: The Felt Politics of Racial Embodiment*, Abingdon: Routledge.

Slattnë, Hanna (2021) 'Dramaturging from within: The dramaturg as first experiencer in immersive audio', in Pitrolo, Flora, and Radosavljević, Duška (eds) 'Aural/Oral Dramaturgies' (Special Topic), *Critical Stages*, 24. https://www.critical-stages.org/24/dramaturging-from-within-the-dramaturg-as-first-experiencer-in-immersive-audio/

Sterne, Jonathan (2011). 'The Theology of Sound: A Critique of Orality', *Canadian Journal of Communication*, 36, 207–25.

Tuhiwai Smith, Linda (1999). *Decolonizing Methodologies: Research and Indigenous Peoples*, London and New York: Zed Books Ltd.

Tynan, Lauren (2021). 'What is relationality? Indigenous knowledges, practices and responsibilities with kin', *Cultural Geographies*, 28(4), 597–610. https://doi.org/10.1177/14744740211029287

Unger, Clio (2021) 'Share your work: Lola Arias's lecture performance series and the artistic cognitariat of the global pandemic', *Contemporary Theatre Review*, 31:4, 471–95. doi: 10.1080/10486801.2021.1976166

Voegelin, Salomé (2014). *Sonic Possible Worlds: Hearing the Continuum of Sound*, London: Bloomsbury.

APPENDICES

Enclosed in the Appendices are reviews of performances I attended between 2010 and 2020 in Edinburgh and London. These texts were written for a variety of publications and were aimed at a general, non-academic readership. Their respective lengths and tone are determined by the house styles of the publications they belong to, but they have been lightly edited here for stylistic and typographic consistency with the rest of this publication. Occasional use of the pronoun 'we' still remains within these texts as it mostly refers to elements of the dramaturgical construction intended to be experienced collectively by the theatre audience. Although most of the reviews were published online, at the time of writing this book, not all of the web addresses are active so those links are not included. Cumulatively, these texts represent accompanying documentation of the emergence of the A/OD project.

Appendix 2.1 Anna Deavere Smith: *Notes from the Field*

(Royal Court Theatre, London)

Anna Deavere Smith literally steps into another pair of shoes to channel one of her many real-life characters onto the stage. Sometimes she remains barefoot, and sometimes she surreptitiously adds small garments to suggest archetypes – such as a cloak for a pastor or a hoodie for a street protester. Throughout most of the first half of this show, she also wears brocade trousers with sewn-on patches down the front of her legs. The patches, made of the same material as the trousers, are quite conspicuous, almost ornamental. This approach to costuming choices (designed by Ann Hould-Ward) acts as a kind of metaphor for the author's methodological approach too – dynamic, versatile, exact, raw, and stylistically detailed.

It's just over 25 years since Anna Deavere Smith invented a way of making performance that ushered in a wave of verbatim and documentary theatre around and beyond the English-speaking world. Her pieces *Fires in the Mirror* and its sequel *Twilight: Los Angeles 1992*, both prompted by racial riots in New York and LA, respectively, took a multi-perspective approach to these complex events, involving the viewpoints of various officials, the judiciary and the police as well as the rioters and the relatives of the victims at the centre of each case. Both of these works have received multiple accolades and awards, and *Twilight* has been named one of the best plays of the last 25 years by the *New York Times*.

Like the title of her latest piece suggests, Anna Deavere Smith's work is often ethnographic in its nature and based on substantial research conducted over an extended period of time. *Notes from the Field* forms part of a larger project by the author, known as the Pipeline Project, in which the aim is to investigate the so-called 'school-to-prison pipeline' – the link between formal education and incarceration – afflicting America's racial minorities in particular.

The two hours of performance material, edited down from over 250 interviews, are organised into a five-act structure, focusing on a combination of case studies and thematic segments. The case of Freddie Gray, who in 2015 died in police custody in Baltimore, opens the evening; we then travel across America, meeting various individuals relevant to the project until, half-way through, we settle again on Shakara, a school-girl from Columbia, whose mistreatment in the hands of a policeman, in her own classroom at Spring Valley High School, was caught on a phone camera and subsequently went viral. The final sections of the piece focus on the broader themes of trauma and hope.

There are 17 monologues in this final version of *Notes from the Field*, accompanied live at times by the double bass player Marcus Shelby and his warm smiles. Earlier versions of the piece featured an attempt to stage an audience discussion on some of the central themes following the interval. The participation element of the current version is contained in a short and rather powerful moment in the show's finale in which [spoiler alert] the audience is inspired and maybe even tricked into singing together. The song is one which works even if, and particularly if, sang below one's breath ['Amazing Grace'], so the ask is really modest, especially in the context where we are in the author's debt in terms of the amount of hard work and harrowing insight we have witnessed up until that point in time.

Notes from the Field is certainly a test of stamina for both the performer and the audience, even though Smith's virtuosic artistry provides much to be admired throughout the evening as a whole. Her approach, distinguished by an extraordinary skill of mimicry, is also characterised by certain discrete and judicious exaggerations – a kind of framing of the idiolectic detail found in her interlocutors which reveals deeper layers of meaning than those ordinarily available in the real-life encounter. Hesitations, false starts, speech cadences and moments of laughter are performed as if part of a music score to reveal the emotional state of the speaker, or specific regional or cultural accents are exaggerated for added effect. This is a method already familiar to us from much of the rest of verbatim theatre we have seen over the years, however, in the case of Smith's distinctive approach, we really see these technical workings as if for the first time.

There is also a real literary or, more specifically, oratory beauty in many of the conveyed testimonies. 'The camera is the only weapon that we have', 'we can't wait for the leaders to make it better', and 'I don't know how you can be black in America and be silent' are just some of the introductory aphorisms ringing in the audience's ears long after the show is over. Some epitomise the form of the show itself ('I always talk in stories because I think it illustrates points'); some are potent (self)-indictments ('I think we judges fell asleep at the job'); and some – like the entire testimony of former lawyer Bryan Stevenson – get to the real heart of the profound poetics of real life that this specific method illuminates: 'the broken among us teach us to be human'.

Though we might be lacking the rousing sense of novelty that Smith's early works must have engendered, *Notes from the Field* carries instead the authority of an expertly constructed piece of theatre that quite deservedly gets the audience up to its feet in the end. It's not solely and entirely an ovation that comes from the gut, but it is infectious, and certainly part of the testament to Smith's own brand of magic.

Published 19 June 2018
http://exeuntmagazine.com/reviews/review-notes-field-royal-court-theatre/

Appendix 2.2 SKaGeN: *Pardon/In Cuffs*

(Traverse Theatre, Edinburgh)

Edinburgh audiences have previously had a chance to see the work of Belgian SKaGeN theatre company mostly through the solo work of Valentijn Dhaenens – specifically his shows *BigmoutH* and *SmallWaR*. Dhaenens is a talented and hugely charismatic performer, whose forte, as seen in these two productions, could be best described as voice art. On both occasions his departure point had been samples of found text, largely oral testimonies and records of public speeches. What distinguishes Dhaenaens' approach from the form we have come to call verbatim theatre, is his deliberate emphasis on the potential artistry of this genre rather than its apparent documentariness. In the first instance, his verbatim piece became a complex sound installation, and in the second, a choir of video screens – a sophisticated technological multiplication of his own resources as an individual artist was deployed in both cases to push the boundaries of the form he was working with.

In his latest piece, Dhaenens returns to the more traditional technologies of theatre-making: a table, two chairs, a revolving podium and the intermittent live musical accompaniment. More strikingly, we also get to meet two other co-founder members of SKaGeN – equally captivating performers Clara van den Broek and Korneel Hamers – and witness the seamlessness and elegance of their ensemble play. The content this time is testimonies collected from the initial hearings of petty criminals in the public prosecutor's office, moments after they had been caught in the act and some days before they formally entered the court. Narratively, the piece is a panoply of character portraits, their quirks and vulnerabilities, and the various ways in which they choose to explain their actions before the law – sometimes resigned, sometimes desperate, charming, deceitful, fearful, often, though not always, fighting for survival.

The crucial aspect of this production is the acute and explicit severance of the style of the text from the style of its theatrical representation. In the initial scene, the public prosecutor played by van den Broek is wearing an elegant satin gown. Incrementally, throughout the show, the actions accompanying the naturalistic dialogues are purposeful and surreal exaggerations of the potential subliminal content – a con artist is doing a three-point shuffle as he delivers his testimony, a prosecutor tenderly kisses a criminal to whom she has taken a liking – to the extent where they become pure metaphor. Complex dances, wrestling matches, and illusionist acts emerge from these seemingly prosaic exchanges with such appeal and lyrical finesse that they certainly make the audience more elated than they could have hoped given the subject matter of the piece.

Pardon/In Cuffs appears a little less ingenious, less flashy, and mind-blowing than Dhaenens' previous creations. However, for the existing fans, this show will serve as a useful primer for understanding the key underlying principles of Dhaenens' theatricality, showing that the high-tech nature of his other work is largely instrumental rather than being its defining feature. And if this is your first encounter with SKaGeN's work, you are guaranteed to be suitably enraptured, and you might even find yourself letting out a little gasp of delight by the end.

Published 19 August 2015
http://exeuntmagazine.com/reviews/pardon-in-cuffs/

Appendix 2.3 Dead Centre: *Lippy*

(Young Vic Theatre, London)

Seemingly intent on questioning and subverting the trend of verbatim theatre, the young Irish company Dead Centre is also resolute in restoring visual artistry to the notion of (documentary) theatre. Indeed, the piece begins with a staged Q and A: we all pretend – the audience loves it! – that we are in a post-show discussion. This allows for the conceptual framework of the piece to be introduced in a gentle and predominantly entertaining way – the piece is interested in the 'voice as a site of meaning and site of power', in the unreliability of 'lip-reading', and in the fusion and separation of the seen and the heard in theatre.

The discussion is facilitated by Bush Moukarzel – the actual author of the piece – although he introduces himself as a supporting actor, previously employed by the company. The set-up allows for some irony and playful digs at the director Ben Kidd, but it also reveals Moukarzel as a skilled and likeable actor whose conversational chatter is still convincing despite the well-lived-in, well-travelled nature of this particular festival piece (shown previously at Dublin, Wiesbaden and Edinburgh). Eventually, the curtain lifts and we are given the opportunity to see the piece that we have only heard about.

Its subject matter is a dark one – the production is about four women engaged in a suicide pact by starvation which lasted for 40 days and took place in an Irish village in 2000. But it is also dreamlike, imaginative, provocative – a series of stark, poignant, highly lyrical vignettes, presented apparently in a reversed order, and then disrupted further by flights of fancy. The four women – chosen perhaps to represent a wide range of Irish female physicality – are extraordinarily watchable. Former ballet dancer Joanna Banks plays the eldest of those who committed suicide, the aunt to the three nieces. Her death is imagined in a way that resembles a leaf in the autumn wind. The set, consisting mostly of poeticised debris, is designed by a sculptor; the engulfing soundscape by an actor – the piece as a whole is commendable in its multi-faceted ambitions.

Most intriguingly, the publicity for the show declares that this is a play about authorship and 'the role of the writer', but disappointingly, the piece does not consciously cast any more light on this question other than to allude to Samuel Beckett as the ultimate theatre author. It is a company clearly capable of taking its heritage into the 21st century, and it remains to be hoped that they will continue to do so.

Published 27 February 2015
http://exeuntmagazine.com/reviews/lippy-3/

Appendix 2.4 Milo Rau: *Five Easy Pieces*

(Unicorn Theatre, London)

It's not often that a children's theatre features a piece about a paedophile and child murderer in its repertoire. But on rare occasions when vision, intelligence, and courage align, this kind of programming can change lives.

Last week, Swiss director Milo Rau's piece, made by commission for Ghent's Campo theatre and dealing with the Belgian child murderer Marc Dutroux, was shown at London's Unicorn theatre for two nights. No less than nine institutions from Europe and Singapore are listed as co-producers of this extraordinary theatrical experiment which has already been on tour for a couple of years. Although it is performed by a cast of seven pre-pubescent children and one adult, this piece is not primarily aimed at a young audience, and it is not easy viewing for adults either – especially not the parents of young children. As a matter of fact, there is nothing easy about it at all.

The Dutroux case has been weighing on the Belgian national psyche for more than two decades. Though the young cast here doesn't have living memories of the events, the parents of the six victims are still grieving and, as it happens, Dutroux's own father is still living with the difficult legacy of the case too. Rau's sociological approach to making theatre entails an all-encompassing inquiry, so the first of the five scenes forming part of this probing 90 minutes, interestingly, focuses on Dutroux senior and his own memories. The stories span decades and continents, charting the days of the Belgian empire – another difficult topic for Campo's original audience. The old man is played by a ten-year-old boy, wearing just enough makeup to add a layer of make believe but not too much to suggest a caricature. He speaks to a camera and we can simultaneously watch the way in which the scene is constructed on stage and the way in which it is mediated on screen. The gap creates a space for reflection, and this is basically an encapsulation of the method of the piece as a whole.

There is an outer framing to the five scenes giving us an opportunity to meet the child performers and find out about their interests, biographies, and their own thoughts about life and death. They are gently coached through this process by adult actor Peter Seynaeve, who has also worked as Rau's assistant on the piece. This initial overture takes the form of a casting session therefore, led by Seynaeve. A happy balance of humour and philosophy makes up this outer frame, leading us safely into the more uncomfortable territory of sheer torment and suffering. Later scenes, for example, feature a close-up on a semi-naked eight-year-old girl, speaking the 'letters to her family' from the dark depths of captivity, followed by a blow-by-blow account of a father's story of loss. The procedure is carried out with clinical, almost surgical, precision – and as the case might be within a medical context, there is no space for sentimentality in it. In a post-show discussion afterward, we find out that the work was largely motivated by a desire to address and deal with the key national traumas of Belgium's recent past as a means of achieving healing and moving on. And a child psychologist was involved in this process too.

Despite the many ethical questions that an undertaking such as this one might raise in a theatre context – why is an outsider digging through the painful history of a nation; how can the use of children be justified in this context – the main redeeming feature of the work is contained precisely in its cold scientific method. A convention deployed throughout, and further justifying the use of video technology on stage, is that many of the chosen protagonists in the piece are represented by adult actors in pre-recorded scenes on the screen before they are played by the children on stage. This method, which can be seen to follow in the tradition of performance re-enactment, has a pragmatic didactic purpose too – evoked by the title itself, borrowed originally from Stravinsky but also, in turn, from Marina Abramović and others who have quoted or paraphrased it before. Acknowledging their natural lack of emotional experience, the child actors are prompted to use and practise the basic skills of mimicry as a means of learning how to be adults, both for the needs of the stage and as a means of their own personal growth. Other skills covered by these theatrical drills include studies of power, subjection, imagination, etc. The piece also sees itself as following in the footsteps of Tim Etchells' and Gob Squad's previous work with children.

London's Unicorn theatre was founded in 1947. Throughout its history, it has combined a children's repertoire by day with an adult repertoire by night as a means of financial survival. In 2005, it moved from the West End's Arts Theatre to its new award-winning home in London Bridge. For the last six years, under the leadership of Purni Morell, it has been characterised by bold and adventurous programming which treats children with respect and bestows them with civic responsibility. The jewels of British and European theatre such as Ignace Cornelissen, Ellen McDougal, Tim Crouch, Ontroerend Goed, and Marius von Mayerburg have all had the platform to inspire and engage local audiences aged 0 and above. I have rarely seen a children's theatre filled up with excited audiences of all ages – and at the same time, incidentally rubbing shoulders together with the who's who of London theatre – as often as I have witnessed this at the Unicorn in recent years. The same was the case on the night of *Five Easy Pieces*, though not without a certain sense of impending loss as Morell passes the baton on to her successor Justin Audibert as the new Artistic Director of the theatre. Audibert is bound to continue to rock, if his recent track record is anything to go by, but it is hard not to read the timing of Morell's decision in sync with the changing climate in the pre-Brexit Britain. How long before this sort of programming becomes consigned to history?

Published 15 May 2018
https://thetheatretimes.com/five-easy-pieces/

Appendix 2.5 Lola Arias: *Minefield*

(Royal Court Theatre, London)

Every soldier has a story to tell – sometimes a joke, sometimes a parable, often a tragedy. The simple genius of Lola Arias's *Minefield* is that it gathers together and places on stage the stories of six veterans from two opposing sides. Even the fact that theatre can make this possible is enough to send tingles down your spine. But then there is more: soldiers, like actors, are likely to have quite a bit of physical prowess to put to good use in a theatrical performance, and – to make more of another cliché – they often play music too. The latter will gradually become a secret ingredient that really makes this show stand head and shoulders above many others.

But to start from the beginning: for the last ten years, Argentinian theatre-maker Lola Arias has built an international reputation as an artist who places real life on stage: beggars, prostitutes, and street musicians of Bremen in *The Art Of Making Money* (2013), for example, but also her own and her collaborators' autobiographies in other multiple works. She is also known as a poet, a visual artist, and a musician, all of which inform her theatre work. Though she has worked extensively in Europe, *Minefield*, made in collaboration with LIFT festival, Brighton Festival, and the Royal Court, was her first major British collaboration in which she revisits the events of the 1982 Falklands/Malvinas war between the UK and Argentina. Following the initial sell-out run in 2016, the show is back on at the Royal Court for a brief reprise.

The piece has a very straightforward and seemingly unambitious structure – the soldiers start by telling us about who they are, how they became soldiers, and then how they entered into the war. The delivery is dynamic and although they are not trained performers, the unlikely ensemble members have clearly been taught various storytelling and performance techniques during the year-long development process. They have been asked to keep diaries of the rehearsal process, and at times they share small extracts with us in spare, but well-placed, moments of metatheatrical commentary.

The centrepiece of Mariana Tirantte's set is a curved projection screen, made to resemble an open book, perhaps. This is where photographs and complementary footage of landscapes are projected. On the right there is a desk with a suspended camera connected to the projection screen via live feed, so the performers can display their personal documents, maps, props, or manipulate toy soldiers in the process of evoking memories. On the left – a drum kit, and some everyday objects which are used to create foley sound effects at suitable dramatic moments. Newspaper cover stories are literally brought to life here; documentary footage of politicians' speeches (Margaret Thatcher's and Leopoldo Galtieri's) is lip-synched to by the performers wearing full-head masks, representing these real-life protagonists; death is recounted first-hand. Like many previous artworks about war, this one also makes the point that war more easily happens between groups manipulated by power figures rather than between living, breathing individuals. So if, like Marcelo Vallejo, one always dreamt of meeting a representative of the other side to take their anger out on them in person, they soon found out that eye to eye – and heart to heart – contact made this compensation impossible.

Nevertheless, it's not so much the stories of combat, different sides of history or even ultimate reconciliation that this show is about. The somewhat seemingly clunky sequence of scenes covering each soldier's time in the war from arrival, via the sinking of the Belgrano ship and other significant military or personal moments, to their eventual homecoming, is only a preamble to the final and most significant part of the show in which the soldiers explore the personal after-effects of their military experience. Many were still in their early twenties when they returned and so the war was only the beginning of the rest of their lives. Variously, they dealt with the post-traumatic disorder by taking drugs, or isolating themselves, or travelling, receiving therapy, and even learning to give therapy to others. Today, as men in their 50s and 60s, they have other professional identities, hobbies, and occupations – doing sports and music, psychology, or criminal law – but all the same, the memories remain.

In putting many disparate aspects of this complex and deeply conflicted shared life experience together, Lola Arias's craftsmanship is truly remarkable. The choice of a very linear dramaturgy serves to open the space for real-life stories and real-life performers to find their own way to the audience. Meanwhile, the director provides carefully chosen tools for performative storytelling to take place, taking care of the overall rhythm of the piece and making sure moments of humour, feeling, and reflection succeed each other in equal measure throughout the piece. In shaping the material, Arias's contribution is comparable to that of a musical composer, which is no mean feat in this particular kind of symphonic context.

My Swiss companion on this occasion, who happens to be more familiar with Arias's earlier works, described the director's approach as a 'punk aesthetic'. This rings true on the level of the musical content of the piece, but it is even more accurately reflective of the iconoclastic, angry and impassioned prioritising of raw matter over any kind of virtuosity or artifice. The six men simply come before us with who they are and what they have, warts and all; they bleed and they cry and they grit their teeth, and they shine too! Especially when they drop their weapons and pick up their guitars, drumsticks, and microphones to play music together. This is where each one of them is at their absolute natural best – and it just goes to show that if there is ever a way to achieve world peace, rock'n'roll must have something to do with it!

Published 11 Nov 2017
https://thetheatretimes.com/minefield-review-stories-soldiers/

Appendix 3.1 Kieran Hurley: *Heads Up*

(Summerhall, Edinburgh)

There was a time when some predominantly verbal theatre might have prompted the question of what makes it stage rather than radio-worthy. Not so in the case of Kieran Hurley's work, even though he spends most of his stage time seated at a desk.

It has been a few years since Hurley distinguished himself as an exciting new voice from Scotland. His award-winning piece from 2012, *Beats*, featuring a live accompaniment from a DJ and dealing with the criminalised rave scene of the 1990s, could be seen as an early prototype of the newly emerging genre of gig theatre.

Like *Beats*, this new piece, *Heads Up*, has a poetic virtuosity and intrinsic musicality amplified by a carefully designed soundscape. The latter, however, is much more ambitious both in terms of content and form. While reading, Hurley also operates his own sound cues, his besuited seated figure carefully lit to reveal meaningful gestures as well as his bare feet engaged in subtle characterisations of their own. It is a case of hip hop-style sampling, on more levels than one.

Although his blurb lists more, four meticulous portraits from the show linger in memory, not least because of Hurley's considered rendition – futures-dealer Mercy, sexually awakening 13-year-old Ash, ditzy pop star-turned-father Leon, and mortified barista Abdullah. They are drawn to ring bells for us, whichever city we happen to come from, and to bear resonances of some more epic archetypes. It is the kind of material that mixes the urban and the mythical in the way that Kate Tempest has also done, although each artist's execution is singular in tone and timbre.

The fact that, as modern-day storyteller, Hurley opts for a second-person narrative is justified by an apparent thematic focus on empathy, signalled in the first act. The piece ruptures half-way through, possibly in a deliberate attempt to simulate a terror attack? This, after all, is a story about the end of the world as we are told from the outset. However, this somewhat forced dramaturgical intervention results in an apparent loss of the storyteller's command over the material, the latter end seeming a little too dispersed to culminate in a satisfyingly cogent finale. Perhaps this is part of the point – for each of us the end of the world will mean something different after all. But if you find yourself holding your breath for a punchline, you might be a little disappointed.

Published 22 August 2016
http://exeuntmagazine.com/reviews/review-heads-summerhall/

Appendix 3.2 Kieran Hurley: *Beats*

(Soho Theatre, London)

The most intriguing things in British theatre often come from the least expected places. This one hails from a small Scottish town at a particular cultural moment in 1994 when public gatherings around amplified music featuring 'a succession of repetitive beats' became outlawed by a Criminal Justice Act.

At first glance, the story focuses on Johnno McCreadie, a 15-year old 'disappointed with the world, and terrified of his own place in it', whose first experience of an illegal rave leaves him with the police-inflicted bruises but awakens to the ultimate freedom of his imagination. At the heart of it, however, this is a piece of poetic activism, concerned with the potential of any younger generation to change the world they happen to have inherited from their parents.

Having garnered numerous accolades and charmed the Edinburgh Fringe audiences for the last two years, Kieran Hurley's inventive fusion of storytelling and technology is poised for a national tour, following its current run at London's Soho Theatre.

It is a simple piece in terms of stagecraft – Hurley is seated at a desk lit by a lamp at one end of the stage, while a Hushpuppy DJ live-mixes a soundtrack at the other end. They are both illuminated by club lights and a backdrop of the 1990s-style psychedelic visuals.

One might wonder whether, with such an emphasis on sound, this needs to be a theatre rather than a radio piece. However, both in terms of its style and content, Hurley's creation seems to offer a different take on the notion of 'immersive theatre'.

At the outset, his script invites us to 'fill in the gaps' in the story that is about to unfold before us. But the production creates a physical gap too, positioning the audience at the point of being moved to action. The fact that you are denied the actual possibility of taking to the dancefloor might just mean you leave the show energised to take on the world.

An opportunity not to be missed, at the Soho, or when it gets to your local venue.

Published October 2013
http://theatreguidelondon.co.uk/reviews/beats13.htm

Appendix 3.3 Nassim Soleimanpour: *Blind Hamlet*

(Assembly Roxy, Edinburgh)

The audience members pour out, elated after this show. 'That was amazing,' one of them enthuses – incidentally, the one who has actually taken part on the stage. 'It's one of those shows that's going to be difficult to describe to people,' says his friend. 'One of those indie shows,' they conclude.

Those already familiar with Nassim Soleimanpour's 2012 hit *White Rabbit Red Rabbit* – which saw various famous actors take part without any rehearsal whatsoever – may not be surprised to learn that this piece too will keep us all on our toes. This time, however, the Iranian playwright and the British director Ramin Gray contrive to turn the audience members into the main actors, helped along by a lone stage manager. The author is present as a recorded voice played back for the duration of most of the show. This provides the story of a man with deteriorating eyesight trying to read *Hamlet* before he goes blind, interspersed with instructions for some games he has devised for the audience to play (often with their eyes closed).

This type of work is not entirely new in the UK – Rotozaza and Tim Crouch have played with similar conventions, moving the boundaries of what the audience might have thought possible in theatre and live performance. The interplay between the pre-recorded and the live, the preplanned and the spontaneous, creates suspense and keeps the audience invested and involved. The point is that the result of this kind of experience strips the notion of theatre-going to its bare bones – imagination, conflict, play – elements which have been there for ever.

So the most important thing to say when describing this show to your friends is that this is a kind of theatre which restores joy to the often dreaded act of audience participation. And the reason is that most of us go to the theatre wanting what we are seeing to succeed. Soleimanpour and Gray show us that if you lead the audience to believe that the success of the show really depends on them, they will be more than willing to help along.

Blind Hamlet is not entirely flawless – its narrative flow is occasionally contrived, and sometimes the pre-recorded voice is pitched precariously between its desire to communicate ('I wish I could see your face' is the refrain of the opening section) and a radio drama style introversion. But its ambition and its overall achievement outweigh this.

Published 7 August 2014
http://totaltheatre.org.uk/actors-touring-company-blind-hamlet/

Appendix 3.4 Rachel Mars: *Our Carnal Hearts*

(Summerhall, Edinburgh)

There is so much to admire in Rachel Mars's show. Fans of her writing and wry comedy are treated to another exquisitely sharp satire on social media-induced envy. Those new to the work are provided with a rousing initiation ritual. Musically inclined audiences get to encounter an altogether new take on the notions of recital, choir, and pop. And there's even something there for older siblings, coffee enthusiasts, and seekers of inner peace.

Dramaturgically, it is a complex but clear construction consisting of several intersecting planes: there is Mars the parody preacher delivering a sermon on envy, there is Mars the delicate prose writer lurking in the shadows, and Mars the comedy storyteller narratively holding the whole thing together with the question: what if a fairy came to you in the middle of the night promising anything you want, on condition your neighbour got twice as much of the same thing?

But this is not a mere solo show. Theatrically, Mars has collaborated with an all female ensemble to create a live choral soundscape for her piece. Sh!t Theatre's Louise Mothersole has composed and created the musical arrangements that form this intricate, playful, and sturdy container for Mars's meditation, though the transitions between these different elements of the show's content are often entirely seamless. As such, this show is definitely more than the sum of its parts. In terms of its crafting, *Our Carnal Hearts* is something quite new and unique and fascinating. (Enough to turn anyone's rivals quite green with envy too.)

Even the choice of the venue on this occasion – the Dissection room at Summerhall – seems significant and is acknowledged as such. And then there are other perks too, like the chorus of Spandau Ballet's 'Gold' repurposed as a personal affirmation and turned into an earworm you will struggle to shake off for at least 24 hours.

Invited to welcome the ugly part of ourselves, we, the audience, definitely get our various buttons pressed – we laugh, we think, we question, we sing, we admire, we envy, we make confessions, we congratulate our rivals on their success (and learn to mean it), we exorcise our own demons, and ultimately, we emerge out of this show lighter and with a spring in our step. If it sounds like therapy, it's even better than that. Go and see for yourselves.

Published 25 August 2017
http://exeuntmagazine.com/reviews/edinburgh-fringe-review-carnal-hearts/

Appendix 3.5 Ontroerend Goed: *World Without Us*

(Summerhall, Edinburgh)

With every new project, the Belgian company Ontroerend Goed never fails to inspire excitement and wonder, even if their chosen subject might be as bleak as the world after the apocalypse. The content of their new piece is completely and quite literally contained in its title. For just over an hour, a performer – Valentijn Dhaenens and Karolien De Bleser take it in turns on alternate dates – speaks, frequently in complete darkness, a sequence of verbal articulations of what that world might look like, each sentence beautifully honed, each mental image almost visibly sparking off thoughts in the heads of the audience.

As ever, it is the clarity, simplicity, and brilliance of the form found in order to express specific content that dazzles when it comes to Ontroerend Goed's work. This is not the kind of theatre that is interested in displaying the vocal or physical virtuosity of the actor. It is rather the imaginative virtuosity of the ensemble as a whole (including the audience) that is at the centre of its accomplishments. There is a sense of complete and utter commitment to the task the company has set themselves – the act of imagining a world without us.

It starts off simply, in the here and now, and zooms out to take in a bigger picture: a rat, until recently hiding somewhere in the theatre building, will come out and munch on a biscuit lying in somebody's bag; our technology will outlive us for the duration of its battery power; the natural world will carry on without us despite the fact that everything is radioactive and 'no one will complain'. There are scenarios of how much better off and how much worse off things might be without human intervention and then in characteristic OG fashion, the thought is taken to its ultimate logical conclusion. What the world will be like without us won't even matter without human consciousness. But there is a sting in the tale too, this piece of theatre in fact is not just blue-sky thinking, it is directly related to the existence of specific material that may or may not one day in the future become 'found material'. For the Voyager spaceship has just left the solar system, together with our messages...

According to director Alexander Devriendt, each one of Ontroerend Goed's pieces aims to answer a difficult question the makers set themselves. With *Internal*, the question was 'how quickly can you establish a meaningful connection with a stranger?'; with *Teenage Riot*, 'is a riot still possible?'. *World Without Us* contains within itself not only the obvious question of what the world would be like if we all instantaneously disappeared, but also a much deeper one – the possible meaning of our existence in the universe. Like many of its precursors, this OG show opens up conversations between audience members on their way out, then flows on further into discussions with those who have not even seen it yet. Above all, however, it shows how crucial and how yielding a good question can be in a theatre-making process.

Additionally, if you have ever wondered what 'dramaturgy' is, there is seldom a better opportunity to have this question answered in very practical terms. This is the kind of theatre that is luminous and pristine in the way it makes its inner workings the core of its content, while at the same time pushing the boundaries of theatre and live performance a little bit further. This time, like every time before.

Published 26 August 2016
http://exeuntmagazine.com/reviews/review-world-without-us-summerhall/

Appendix 3.6 Dead Centre: *Chekhov's First Play*

(Battersea Arts Centre, London)

Also known as *Platonov* or the *Play Without a Title*, Chekhov's first playtext, written when he was 18 and never published during his lifetime, is a complex prototype version of all of his four most famous plays. It is a play with some production history in the English-speaking world (sometimes in Michael Frayn's adaptation as *Wild Honey*), though not one that has any particularly memorable precursors in recent years. It is a problem play, often chosen by adaptors and directors for its problem-solving potential.

Dead Centre's version is different. It is smartly named *Chekhov's First Play*, and the textual authorship credit is apportioned between Chekhov and the directors Kidd and Moukarzel, making it clear this is no one's vanity project. Neither is this an act of directorial assertion of authorship over the original text, nor a clumsy suggestion of an adaptation. Instead, one could qualify it as a three-way conversation with the original – a collaboration of sorts, an ensemble riff on beginnings.

The play opens with a direct address from director Bush Moukarzel standing on stage and speaking through a microphone that feeds into the headphones provided at each seat. Worried that we won't understand Chekhov's youthful ramblings, now additionally removed from us by history and geography, the director will give us a helpful DVD-style running commentary.

'For those who are used to having a voice in their head, this is like having two voices in your head.'

Game on – the audience is immediately up for it.

Moukarzel informs us of the finer details of the plot, subtext, cuts he has made, casting, and even some inter-personal gossip regarding his company. Property and greed are foregrounded as the main themes of Chekhov's play, and later we will be offered ways of reading these themes in relation to the times we live in and present-day Ireland, the home of Dead Centre as a company.

The Irish connection seems important to note here on a number of levels. Moukarzel speaks with an English accent; however, he has made Ireland his base, and the same is the case with his directorial partner Ben Kidd with whom he co-founded Dead Centre in 2012. Their early piece, *Lippy* (2013), was an understated tribute to Beckett, displaying a strong commitment to a fusion of the verbal, the visual, and conceptual in their engagement with stagecraft – an approach still underlying the company's work.

On this occasion too, every aspect of the design is meticulously thought-through in relation to the central concept – the idea that ultimately less is more. And this idea is taken to extremes – silence-noise, presence-absence, possession-dispossession, comedy-tragedy, simplicity-complexity, life-death. Somewhere along the line, in this process of calibration, poignant moments of beauty and insight elegantly shine through.

It is an extraordinarily rich and layered piece which requires more than one viewing to properly appreciate its facets. It's as though, in condemning greed, Kidd and Moukarzel's work creates a sense of aesthetic insatiety itself.

Describing the work's various moments of poetry and wit, therefore, does not do it justice, as the piece is primarily designed to be experienced. But I will say this: it is Chekhov like you have never seen it in the English-speaking world before. Totally true to its source, totally original in its execution. Although at times *Chekhov's First Play* may resemble the regietheater of the German tradition, it is, in fact, an entirely autonomous achievement, whose aesthetic completely clearly emerges from its own deliberations.

This is where my review, like most others, has to stop short of revealing the central dramaturgical decision the work is based on. However, for the sake of posterity, I will add a spoilery post-scriptum – only for those who have already seen the show or are not in a position to ever see it again.

What I have described above regarding the director's DVD commentary to the piece turns out to be only a smart overture to the piece. Most of the first act of Chekhov's *Platonov* serves to set up the mysterious title character's arrival. Everyone's third-person account of Platonov adds to this sense of anticipation – and this, the directors seem to have decided, is the play's only most interesting feature.

Halfway through Dead Centre's version, Moukarzel reminds us of his own (and indeed Chekhov's) authorial ambitions for new forms of theatre and new ways of connecting to audiences; at this point, the conceit that has been painstakingly established is smashed with a burning cannonball flying through the set. A light shines on an audience member, who rises from his seat, a hypnotic score drowns out Moukarzel's voice, and from this point on, we are sucked into a dreamlike state in which we witness our representative (the randomly chosen audience member) walk and dance and play their way through the piece, the only competence for their actions seemingly drawn from the director's voice that must still be coming through their headphones.

The effect is a strange combination of reality and construct, the kind Chekhov must indeed have been aiming for but never thought possible with the available technology of his age. Platonov's expositional absence is fully justified by this surprising entrance from the end of the auditorium elided into oblivion by the proverbial fourth wall. As we approach the end, in which the ensemble has reached a Russian roulette moment, Moukarzel speaks to us again. There is that famous quotation of Chekhov's which he is yet to finish – that if you see a gun at the opening of act one, by the end of the play it must be fired. But wait for this – all of Chekhov's plays except the last one, Moukarzel informs us, have a gun in them:

'He wrote away the gun – his characters needed to learn to do something worse than dying.'

More a philosophical treatise than a straightforward theatre production, Kidd and Moukarzel's fun-filled creation is both a contribution to the glittering annals of Chekohvian production histories and to the proliferating genre of immersive performance, but above all a key benchmark for any aspiring theatre-maker to see and think about.

Published 11 November 2018.
https://thetheatretimes.com/dead-centres-chekhovs-first-play/

Appendix 4.1 RashDash: *Another Someone*

(Bedlam, Edinburgh)

If you are after something young and refreshing, unpretentious and uplifting – go and see this show. Even though it probably defies most neat categorisations – being both a contemporary dance with words and a musical with storytelling – this little show about happiness could probably pass for a piece of easy audience therapy too.

The fact that it doesn't try too hard to be older or cleverer than it is probably lets this piece get away with occasional narrative flaws. And the creators make these work by flaunting them.

Becky Wilkie's thoroughly enchanting music makes the whole thing bind seamlessly together, and she appears in the triple role of a composer, musician, and narrator. RashDash's founders Helen Goalen and Abbi Greenland as well as their new member Marc Graham are all talented singers and dancers too, making it feel as though this quartet redefines the notion of a triple-threat.

Not only that, but they genuinely threaten to break new ground and bring about a whole new brand of music theatre – if not an album or two as well. So do go and see them while they are such amazing value for money. Happiness guaranteed.

Published August 2010
The Stage

Appendix 4.2 Lucy McCormick: *Triple Threat*

(Soho Theatre, London)

There are some shows that can simply never be made by men. I don't mean in the sense of subject matter. I mean in the sense of the means of production. And biology.

Bear with me.

In 2010, performer Lucy McCormick became one of the three co-founder members of an all-female company Get In The Back Of The Van. Combining live art, writing, low-key banter, cabaret, and theatre, the company proceeded to make a series of performances, installations, and curated projects existing within an intersection of art forms, genres, and – often feminist – topics.

In some ways, Lucy McCormick's independent project, *Triple Threat*, does build on this legacy – in others, it pushes forth in its own way.

As promised by the title, McCormick is a consummate and virtuosic performer as a singer, dancer, and actor. However, her display is frequently a tongue-in-cheek attempt at self-parody of a kind, testifying that her fourth and overriding talent is that of comic performance. As with Chaplin and Baron-Cohen, for example, there is something utterly authentic in her particular brand of pushing the boundaries of the acceptable to the point of unnerving cringe-worthiness and still staying on the safe side of comedy. In this particular show, self-branded as 'post-popular, trashstep, dubpunk, experiential morality play' and re-enactment, which repackages the story of Jesus Christ in the style of a series of MTV videos, there is a moment in which McCormick, following an act of physical over-exertion, downs a bottle of redberry Innocent smoothie, followed by the one-liner 'That was a scene of Herod massacring the innocent.' And it works.

That said, McCormick's comic style does not really withstand comparison to any existing male – or even female – comedian. Over the decades, we have become familiar with a number of deliberately provocative tropes in male stand up which female comedians have often ended up adopting for a similar effect – I'm thinking of endless stories of masturbation, for example. McCormick's own show opens in medias res – actions rather than words – taking this trope as an initial cue but turning it into something more substantial, and into the very dramaturgical core of this piece. Without giving too much away, it would be safe to say perhaps that the explicit use of genitalia will acquire various additional levels of meaning in the course of this performance.

In this respect, the spirit, though not necessarily the look, of McCormick's show might also be seen to fit in with the traditions of feminist live art and neo-burlesque. However, what once again distinguishes this particular artist is that her demeanour, aided by her technical accomplishment and Ursula Martinez's subtle direction, is less concerned with making an explicit political statement than with truly entertaining the audience. She bares all with the earnestness – and self-consciousness – of a four-year-old. The same applies to the way in which she bosses around her two helpers – Sam Kennedy and Ted Rodgers – backing dancers and vocals, players of bit parts and part-time angels in Calvin Klein pants. It is disarming, often just sweet, and largely forgivable.

Under the veneer of messiness, irreverence, and faux naivete, there is certainly a kind of mad genius at work here. The choice of each pop hit, from Justin Bieber to Christina Aguilera, though seemingly selected for the singer's own self-indulgent reasons, is actually carefully chosen to sit at a particular narrative point of the proceedings and thus gain a new kind of significance in turn. The show benefits from tremendous clarity and integrity in terms of the paradigm of artistic choices it draws from. For example, its entire props list could be sourced from a couple of supermarket aisles. However, all the foodstuffs – including Nescafe Gold, frankfurters, and meringue at the birth of Christ (get it?) – have been clearly submitted to rigorous scrutiny for narrative, aesthetic, and sequencing effect before being deployed in the show (you'll long remember the use of Nutella in this particular production).

Far from wishing to sound twee, this really is a show which gives another meaning to the proverbial putting of one's whole being on the altar of one's art. And the triple threat of the title may as well be read as clever, brave, and funny.

Published 27 December 2017
https://thetheatretimes.com/lucy-mccormick-triple-threat/

Appendix 4.3 Lucy McCormick: *Post-Popular*

(Soho Theatre, London)

Lucy McCormick specialises in historical re-enactments, she tells us, and she is here to play all the women of history, as a means of finding her hero. All this – within about one hour, and with enough time for a snack break in the middle. What ensues is a joy ride in parody, politics, and passionate silliness.

Somewhat predictably, the women featured in the show are the English history books regulars – Eve, Boudicca, Anne Boleyn, Florence Nightingale, the Suffragettes – that's it. And the brevity of the list is part of McCormick's point – whoever can still take such grossly unbalanced history books seriously? But *Post-Popular* has a subplot concerning heroism and food, and a punchline finale that this is all leading towards.

It's worth remembering briefly McCormick's previous show *Triple Threat* from 2016. This was an absolute game changer on a number of fronts – alternative entertainment, comedy, musical, live art, gig theatre, neo-burlesque and nativity play would never be the same again! A DIY story of the birth of Jesus Christ, *Triple Threat* was told through the medium of pop music and supermarket groceries. Its showstopping moments came from McCormick's boundary-busting attitude to body politics and included naked crowd-surfing and a performative use of the vagina. The latter choice is not without its precedents – Carolee Schneemann's performance art piece *Interior Scroll* (1975) and Ursula Martinez's cabaret number *Hanky Panky* (2004) had been there before, and, undoubtedly, McCormick is well aware of this lineage. Both *Triple Threat* and *Post-Popular* were directed by Martinez, and by now the vagina trick can be considered a regular part of McCormick's repoertoire.

As the title suggests, the new show carries elements of the 'difficult second album' syndrome. Structurally, *Post-Popular* could also be seen as a kind of a re-enactment of *Triple Threat* itself – the backing dancers, the crowd surfing, the jokes, the supermarket goods, the song and dance routines, and the vagina trick are all back in again, with some slight variations. Content-wise, what makes *Post-Popular* most eminently enjoyable on its own terms, however, is McCormick's virtuosity as a singer, dancer, and comedian. She has the whole audience in the palm of her hand throughout, so much so that you might find yourself tricked into laughing at morally dubious things. This does not necessarily refer to the explicitly parodic and totally hilarious beheading of Anne Boleyn, but to the moments of horror that McCormick relishes leading you towards, especially when the boundaries between the real and the fictional or the sublime and the ridiculous get erased suddenly and quite deliberately in order to create an insight. In this respect, McCormick's work reminds us of its deeply political nature too.

The answer is simple: if you have missed *Triple Threat*, do see *Post-Popular* and you'll get the idea of McCormick's uniquely world-changing approach. If you did see the earlier show, then just see *Post-Popular* for the sheer fun of it. In any case, McCormick is one to watch for every reason imaginable.

Published 21 December 2019
https://thetheatretimes.com/lucy-mccormick-post-popular-at-soho-theatre/

Appendix 4.4 Beatbox Academy: *Frankenstein*

(Battersea Arts Centre, London)

Part of the Phoenix Season at the newly re-opened Grand Hall at Battersea Arts Centre is also BAC Beatbox Academy, a host of homegrown talent celebrating the tenth anniversary of its increasingly stellar existence. Led by Conrad Murray and David Cumming, the group, originating from south London's estates, meets at BAC on Thursdays to nurture the music-making and spoken word affinities of its members, aged 0–29. Over the last ten years, BAC Beatbox Academy has toured nationally, headlined the Royal Festival Hall and been shortlisted as the finalists of the BBC2 television series *The Choir*. Certainly, a story worthy of the Phoenix title.

There is more to this, however, as their show *Frankenstein: How To Make A Monster* sets a new benchmark not only for community theatre itself but for British contemporary theatre as a whole. There is much that can be learned from the BAC Beatbox Academy about audience rapport and performance prowess, but, chiefly, about the art of stage adaptation itself. The age-old problem that theatre-makers constantly encounter around fidelity to the original text is on this occasion handled with quiet elegance and artistic integrity, ultimately revealing a new reading and a new method of reading of the original text, and hopefully settling the question once and for all.

The evening is framed in the spirit of a slam. It opens with director Conrad Murray's lively address, giving some background info on the project. With the main actors patiently seated on the stage in a cloud of haze and under the canopy of hanging LED lightbulbs, Murray brings on some younger members of the Beatbox Academy to warm us all up – it's lucky it is half-term in London, so those primary schoolers can stay up late. The tone for the evening is set through rap numbers about the history of London riots, and some rousing aphoristic verse concluding in the declaration that 'we can do it!' and 'you can do it!' We are promised more spoken word, rap, and beatbox battles following the end of the actual performance.

The show begins with a soundscape evocative of a countryside: birds chirping, breeze, a running brook perhaps. We are informed that all the sounds we hear tonight are made live on the stage using the performers' mouths and microphones alone, and are then transported into a busy urban soundscape – mobile phone gossip, traffic, noise. Having established the atmosphere and the basic theme of the show (nature vs. technology), the ensemble introduces themselves: six performers' true personalities ranging from genius and angelic to cheeky and self-deprecating. The individuals work deftly together to bricolage fleeting but relevant musical references into stunning harmonies as a means of developing their show's narrative and captivating the broadest range of audience: Prodigy, James Brown, as well as some more up-to-the minute soul and rap hits, get wittily cited within the show to delighted laughter of recognition. And then there are original numbers too, that have grown out of rehearsal jams and improvisations.

The performance is organised into five chapters, titled The Tower of Knowledge, How to Make a Monster, Growing Pains, The World Uncensored, and Descent. Rather than attempting literal storytelling or representation of Mary Shelley's novel in any way, the company works to interpret its deepest meanings as they relate to our day and age. As such, the monster we have collectively created lives within the world of social media and within the world of impossible beauty ideals, shaped by narrow consensus and leading to bullying.

There is true ire and sass, some flirting and teasing of the audience, as well as genuine pathos within these two hours on the stage, but the overwhelming feeling on the audience's part is one of complete awe in relation to the dedication and the cumulative achievement of these young people.

The evening does conclude with the promised battles giving us more of a glimpse into the company as a whole, their way of working and the joy they generate by simply being together. It is a deeply infectious kind of joy summoned out of nothing other than the human voice and the sense of community it can generate, but BAC Beatbox Academy's show sends the audience away on such a high that most lavishly produced West End musicals would fail to match.

Published 27 October 2018
https://thetheatretimes.com/frankenstein-how-to-make-a-monster-at-battersea-arts-centre/

Appendix 4.5 nabokov: *Symphony*

(Assembly George Square Gardens, Edinburgh)

It's not often that you walk into a music gig headlining a playwright. Or three. Although if you ask me, I would bet my bottom dollar most successful theatre people were at one point or another wannabe rock stars. Often they simply took that energy and transferred it into the language of theatre, never again getting the chance to brandish their electric guitars, drum sticks, or microphones; but here is finally a welcome exception. A band of three writers (Tom Wells, Ella Hickson, Nick Payne), a composer (ED Gaughan), a director (Joe Murphy), and four excellent multi-skilled multi-tasking actors (Jack Brown, Katie Elin-Salt, Liam Gerrard, and Iddon Jones) showing us just how much great ensemble work owes to music itself.

The set consists of three stories, mostly underscored and interspersed with narrative-driven songs, deftly woven together into a single piece which coheres around its symphonic throughlines rather than a single theme as such. Though if a theme does emerge, it has a lot to do with overcoming loneliness. In the first story, a 15-year-old asthmatic boy Jonesy resolves to overcome his isolation by becoming a sporting hero; in story number two an awkward Londoner loses a fellow commuter he secretly fancies to another guy; while the finale is a classic will-they-won't-they get it together love story conceived in the loo of a nightclub. This sort of narrative range also provides scope for similarly broad musical display covering anything from humorous ditties and silly dance numbers to heart-rending power ballads. The obvious showcasing is probably the only thing detracting from the show's genuine brilliance. But the line up as a whole is truly thrilling, its inner magic achieved through the notion of the whole being greater than the sum of its parts.

I will not search for musical references that might entice you to see this show. Suffice it to say that the rhythm section grips you from the start and never lets go – even when the band members begin to rotate their way through the various instruments on stage. If you love theatre and have ever had a band you loved, this is a show for you.

Published 7 August 2014
http://totaltheatre.org.uk/nabokov-symphony-by-ella-hickson-nick-payne-and-tom-wells/

Appendix 4.6 Wildcard Theatre: *Electrolyte*

(Pleasance, Edinburgh)

The sound check is still on as the audience shuffles in from the rain. The band members smile gently while tuning their instruments, exchanging personal remarks, or chatting in a laid back way to familiar faces in the crowd. There's a person in the front row watching the show for the eight time. Olivia Sweeney, the apparent front woman of the band, narrator and performer who will be playing the central character Jessie in the story, informally plans a pre-show party for this fan's tenth return visit to the show.

This deliberate (though somewhat counter-intuitive) removal of the fourth wall is a well placed device which serves to get us all off to a shared start and ensure we travel a longer distance together than might have been possible if we had just walked into a pre-set world. If this were just a theatre show, and the actors were on stage already, we might have expected to walk into an already created atmosphere. If it were a gig, we'd either be waiting for a while in vacuous suspense for the band members to take their positions, or at least they'd have warmed up already.

But this is not just a mere gig or a straightforward theatre show, and no one is a single star here – instead, what the gig theatre format makes possible is a subtle actualisation of the piece's central claim that 'we are all stardust and dreams'!

It is not hard to see how *Electrolyte* became a multiple-award-winning smash hit of the Edinburgh Fringe 2018. The production teems with talent and thrills, twenty-something-olds' anguish, and the ultimate hard-earned feelgood factor.

The story, rendered in verse, is a rollercoaster ride courtesy of Leeds-based party girl Jessie. A girl crush on an other-worldly musician Allie Touch (played by the equally other-worldly performer that is the show's composer Maimuna Memon), a surprise letter from her estranged mother, a fall out with her best friend – we follow closely as Jessie lives through a quick succession of seemingly life-changing events, catapulting her on an ill-judged adventure to London.

Various band members step in and out of multiple roles. Besides Memon, Wildcard's co-artistic director and the show's playwright James Meteyard is also part of the band and playing Jessie's eventual love interest Jim.

There is so much in store in this show that is hard to sum up in other words than to say: just like the eight-times fan from the start, you'll most likely be wanting to come back too. At the risk of giving spoilers away, it cannot be omitted that *Electrolyte* is ultimately a piece about our fundamental significance to each other – as loyal friends, unexpected lovers, as strangers who make up a community – in ensuring mental wellbeing and survival. That is where its secret power lies, and as such, there are few better ways of ensuring togetherness than in an immersive form of a gig theatre piece.

Published 13 August 2019
http://exeuntmagazine.com/reviews/edinburgh-fringe-review-electrolyte/

Appendix 4.7 RashDash: *Two Man Show*

(Soho Theatre, London)

Over the last ten years, a new form has evolved on the British stage, rather simply referred to as 'gig theatre'. Though one could trace its origins to the tents of the Latitude and Edinburgh Fringe festivals, this year the genre has even reached the Manchester International Festival, prompting speculation of its debt to the dying recorded music industry.

The use of live music in theatre is not so new. Brecht was an early advocate. In the UK, Kneehigh Theatre made it fashionable in the last twenty years, inspired by a mix of Grotowskian and rural English community theatre influences. However, the newest generation of gig theatre-makers is doing something slightly different with it – creating a form where the performers themselves play instruments rather than having an accompanying band on stage, and in this way, they make music part of the dramaturgical fabric of the piece rather than just a complementary underscore.

Early pioneers of this genre include RashDash, a company of Hull University graduates based in Leeds, led by the female tandem Abbi Greenland and Helen Goalen. Their first show, *Another Someone,* opened at the Edinburgh Fringe in 2010. It was an ensemble piece about happiness, combining original music, movement, and drama on a shoestring budget – a bit messy and rough at the edges, but self-assured, refreshing, and completely compelling. This won them a following and a tour, and they have moved from strength to strength ever since.

Their latest – *Two Man Show* – is a co-production with Northern Stage in association with Soho Theatre. It also opened in Edinburgh, in 2016, and is on the road again for the third time with plenty of mileage left in it. In theatre terms, *Two Man Show* is a ground-breaking marvel on many levels. Style-wise, what originally might have seemed a fusion of talent and skills picked up from a university drama department (a bit of acting, a bit of movement, a bit of playwriting, a bit of research, a bit of music) has been refined into a distinctive performance idiom. Greenland and Goalen make no excuses for their bold artistic choices: the fact that this show has resulted in a script published by Oberon with only RashDash credited as its author, or the meshing of the visceral and the intellectual throughout the piece, or the deliberately stark juxtapositions of the heard and the seen. Slowly but surely, it pushes at the boundaries of what has been deemed possible within any particular performance genre. There are moments in this show that will make a lasting impression on the audience in a way that resists mere verbalisation. (Interestingly too, the impossibility of verbalisation is one of the show's own main themes). It is a work that needs to be experienced.

In very basic terms, this is a piece about patriarchy and its effects on gender in its various manifestations. To begin with, the two women, accompanied by musician Becky Wilkie, revisit the ancient history of gender anthropology to frame a sequence of dramatic scenes in which they play John and Dan, two brothers faced with caring responsibilities of different kinds. The delivery is punctuated with musical interludes, the percussion instruments on stage and mics with various filters serving as indispensable props. Utter conviction and artistic rigour underlie this work that could, on its face, be mistaken for trendy posturing. This is by no means just another piece of feminist activism. Greenland and Goalen shed real sweat as they dig for answers. They strip themselves – literally – of all possible layers to get to the heart of the matter. The results are striking: explicitly female bodies displaying masculine strength and gait, evocative and often entertaining characterisations deliberately devoid of any attempt at naturalism. In the first scene concerning the brothers, the women are wearing evening gowns and sitting quietly throughout what sounds like a dynamic encounter. Later, they will play out fraternal fights at a funeral, wearing nothing but boxer shorts. The atmosphere is thick with irony, anticipation, hard work, vulnerability, brutal honesty, and occasional mischief, not to mention the customary immersive vibe of a live music gig. At Soho Theatre, it is still a relatively intimate encounter for less than a 100 audience members at a time, but RashDash are true rock stars of British theatre, and you should get up close while you still can.

Published 25 October 2017
https://thetheatretimes.com/rashdash-two-man-show/

Appendix 4.8 Unfolding Theatre: *Putting the Band Back Together*

(Summerhall, Edinburgh)

There is a moment in this show when two actors in a tableaux give voice to a clarinet which has been boxed up and forgotten for 20 years. As it pleads to be picked up again, the clarinet tells us that 'physically AND metaphorically it is in pieces'. This moment tells you quite a lot you need to know about Unfolding Theatre's new piece, but I feel compelled to say more.

This is not a review. Or a dramaturgical essay. It is maybe a personal/professional reflection, a reminiscence, or a piece of learning. It is, in the spirit of the show itself, a sharing. An act of community-practice, if I might coin a phrase. And no one in the UK does community-practice better than a Geordie. I say that as someone – a stranger – who lived in Newcastle for a bit.

You might have heard of Annie Rigby's show, on at Northern Stage at Summerhall this August. It's a show that gives audience members an opportunity to pick up again an instrument they might have left behind, for whatever reason. At 3 pm every day, those interested in being in the show meet up for a bit of practice with the cast members, and off they go on stage for that evening's gig two hours later. That in itself is a brilliant act of sharing, an empowering, generous, life-affirming gesture, forming the premise for a theatrical interaction. Interactivity has become a thing in theatre in recent years, but this show is so much more. It is a cross between interactive, gig theatre, storytelling and real life. Above all, it is a homage to the healing power of music.

The initial idea for the show presented itself when director Annie had a drink with someone in a pub and discovered a sense of regret for having abandoned her accordion at the age of 20. But the show's main subject – the 'core' – is Mark Lloyd, an actor and musician from Newcastle, played here by his colleague and friend Alex Elliot. The other performers are musician Ross Millard, actor Maria Crocker, and director Annie Rigby herself, as well as, to various degrees – us, the audience.

Even though we start out on a relatively innocent journey of putting a band together, as the show progresses, we find ourselves sharing in so much more together. For those who happened to know Mark Lloyd, it is also about sharing bereavement.

I knew Mark Lloyd. He and his wife Kylie, who is another invisible heroine of this piece, as well as Annie and Alex and I all used to work together at Northern Stage in Newcastle-upon-Tyne in the early 2000s. This was the time of the Northern Stage Ensemble, a big dream that Alan Lyddiard made come true for a bit. Mark was one of a dozen actors forming the permanent ensemble, most of whom were also musically accomplished. Even though, as a company dramaturg for three years, I was a relative outsider for much of the time, my time with Northern Stage was so intense that it felt to me like I had packed at least ten years into it. As a result, watching *Putting the Band Back Together* was a peculiar experience, one of those which prompts a simultaneous mental reel of flashbacks: Mark as the groom in the Gypsy piece, Annie's thinking expression, Mark as a 19th century Russian doctor having the idea of a heart transplant, coffees with Kylie in Edinburgh, Mark and Kylie snuggled together in the theatre foyer, Annie's buoyant hugs, Kylie's efficiency, dinner parties, wedding photos, Mark as a bus driver learning Sanskrit in a vision of Newcastle modelled on Barcelona. We also did a few play readings together, one of them even in the form of a gig! I can't claim we were close friends, but I do cherish Mark's trademark greeting to me: 'You are my favourite dramaturg!'. It was a running joke, because – how many dramaturgs do you know? How many do you think might have existed in Newcastle in the early 2000s? But when I do think back to my humble career beginnings – like this show has made me do – the main thing I think is: I wish I could have been more generous more often. As a dramaturg, your job is simply to be rigorous, to be critical, to be the purveyor of tough love. When someone has gone for ever, you wish there was just love. Pure and simple.

Two years ago, Mark was diagnosed with pancreatic cancer. I am not giving anything away, this is pretty much the inciting incident of this piece. In May this year, Mark passed away. Annie has been making this piece for two years, with Mark (and Alex and Ross and Maria as well as writer Chloe Daykin and designer Lily Arnold), probably knowing that this was going to be Mark's swan song. Or more precisely – an (concept) album. Deep, haunting, opulent in its range.

Putting the Band Back Together is a show about loss and hope. In another memorable moment, Mark is writing an email to a bandmate of his he hadn't been in touch with for twenty years because he wants to do a charity gig together. It is a classic 'where do I start' sort of palimpsest of false starts. It also encapsulates another one of the show's underlying themes: the remorse you might feel about having dropped something or someone for no particular reason (other than maybe self-doubt) can also be easily overcome. Face up to and just pick it up again. Or let it pick you up.

So ultimately, *Putting the Back Band Together* is a masterful study of acceptance and an understated act of grief, with not a drop of cheap sentimentality in it. It has clarity, it has depth, it has humour in abundance, and above all – it has genuine warmth for everyone involved. Both physically AND metaphorically, it guides us through the process of picking up the pieces in order to find happiness.

Published 26 August 2016
http://exeuntmagazine.com/features/putting-band-back-together/

Appendix 4.9 Taylor Mac: *A 24-Decade History of Popular Music: The First Act*

(Barbican Theatre, London)

There isn't an easy way to write about Taylor Mac's work. Founded on the principle of deliberately resisting categorisation – while at the same time parodying everything, including the processes of its own reception – Taylor Mac's method is an often lethal mix of wit, music, visual art, and audience participation. On this occasion, we get to sample Mac's latest creation – a 24-hour-long history class served as a cross between a musical, a fashion show, and a kind of love-in. Though it brands itself as a show about the history of popular music, it is in fact an alternative history of American politics itself, starting as it does in 1776.

The three-hour section, presented here simultaneously as part of the LIFT festival and the Barbican's own The Art of Change Season, covers only a tiny sliver (the three concluding decades of the 18th century) of the show as a whole. Nevertheless, this is more than enough to take the audience on an exhilarating ride from the raucous and the ridiculous to the edifying and the sublime.

For those who remember Mac's performances at the Royal Vauxhall Tavern or the Edinburgh Fringe some 10–15 years ago, the change in scale will feel monumental. Gone is the besequinned waif, quipping and strumming pensively on a ukulele to an audience of confidantes. Years of hard work and numerous awards later, Mac has blossomed into a full scale diva with the kinds of frocks and headdresses that require a temple. Nevertheless, the overwhelming impression is that in the process, Mac has left none of the old friends behind. This epic new show has scores of musicians, singers, chorus members, and other kinds of collaborators on board – fondly referred to as the Dandy Minions. And the loyal audiences have followed too. That said, the point of the show is to blur the boundaries between the mainstream and the queer, making us all feel equally at home together – and this it does extremely well!

'How do we build ourselves when at the same time we are torn apart?' – is the central question of the show which, amongst other things, takes the tracts, pamphlets, and revolutionary articles from the historical archives just as seriously as the range of folk ballads, nursery rhymes, and drinking songs which form the backbone of the show. Mac honours these original songs by at the same time, questioning, interpreting, dissecting, fantasising and extemporising around them – all in the interest of mining their latent political function. At times, audience members are roped into impromptu role-play exercises stemming from the song lyrics and other material, giving Mac the air of a crazy kindergarten teacher. ('Crazy', by the way, is an adjective voraciously claimed by Mac, and there is a whole story to warm your cockles on that subject alone.)

It is an extraordinarily rich show. Quite explicitly concept-led, it foregrounds the process rather than the product, the 'making rather than the shopping', and its own political provenance as a left-field, anti-capitalist, anti-colonialist, and, chiefly, feminist show. That this is not a token is demonstrated by a sort of generosity of spirit that permeates every fibre of its being (and despite the fact that generosity traditionally feels a bit out of place in a show like this). The female backing vocals and musicians are frequently transformed into truly stunning soloists here. Deliberate, carefully orchestrated, chaos is unleashed on the auditorium at times: ping pong balls, cans of beer, and apple cadavers will grace every crevice of the auditorium by the end of this so-called 'first act', but this too will feel like a relic of a performance art piece rather than a mere aftermath of a carnival.

That we are indeed in the hands of a 'Genius' – crowned as such by the 2017 MacArthur Foundation award – becomes clear towards the end of this three-hour piece as Mac follows up the singing of drinking songs by having the audience tell 'puking stories' to each other. ('Because everyone has one!') The accompanying injunction to physically comfort each other in response becomes not only a matter of common sense, but also helps to bathe the audience in a pool of empathy and resulting elation, before they are allowed to depart home, following what has evidently unfolded as a ritual (as promised at the beginning), rather than simply an evening of entertainment (as it seemed all along). The notion of theatre as a kind of utopia, once famously theorised by Jill Dolan, certainly suggests itself here anew.

Though much of this is delivered tongue in cheek and with spine-tingling amounts of irreverent playfulness, it must be said that at the core of the piece is certainly Taylor Mac, the consummate poet and truly accomplished singer. Ultimately, however, Mac's creation on this occasion is a kind of history class that must urgently find its way onto every high school curriculum.

Published 2 July 2018
http://exeuntmagazine.com/reviews/review-taylor-mac-24-decade-history-popular-music-first-act-barbican/

LEND ME YOUR EARS COLLECTION

These are the individual interviews made as part of the A/OD field research. Most were recorded on Zoom during the Covid-19 pandemic in 2020 (except for RashDash which was recorded in person in January 2020).

The original research design envisaged a 12-part podcast series Lend Me Your Ears to be hosted on the Digital Theatre website. This aspect of the research grew in scope and magnitude as a result of the changed circumstances during the pandemic. We therefore decided to build a bespoke website on which to host all the recordings. Eventually, we loosely organised the content around the planned chapter structure of this book so that the website serves as a companion to this discussion. Each LMYE issue is marked with a #number corresponding with the book chapter number; although this is not a strict correlation – within discussion throughout the book I refer to #issue numbers across the board as required. Also, not all of the items are necessarily referred to in the corresponding chapter.

Four audio-visual formats were curated in the Lend Me Your Ears (LMYE) Collection throughout 2020: the Gallery (Interviews with Artists) and the Salon (Conversations about Sound) items are sound-only recordings; and the Laboratory (Creative Practices) and the Library (Oral Introductions) are video recordings. In 2021, the Studio recordings of courses and masterclasses were added. All recordings were edited and made accessible through captions or transcripts.

All individual items have been archived on Figshare to generate a DOI number, as well as being presented in a more navigable format on www.auralia.space, designed by Beatriz Cabur. Each recording in the Gallery, Salon, Laboratory, and Library has an accompanying transcript which is scrollable on the website, or downloadable on www.auralia.space and on Figshare. The Studio Masterclasses have YouTube-generated captions and no downloadable transcripts, but the 'Decolonising the Voice' podcast training course is equipped with transcripts, which can also serve as worksheets when downloaded or printed out. Also listed here are Flora Pitrolo's LMYE Guides – a set of short essays on chosen topics charting the resonance of certain themes throughout the collection – they too carry their individual DOI numbers and are available in a portable form.

The Figshare website (https://rcssd.figshare.com/account/home#/projects/75384) generates citations for each item including the DOI number. The citations given in Figshare (or those given in a slightly modified version at the end of each recording's accompanying pdf) are offered to be used in future referencing of these materials.

Because of the way in which the Figshare interface is set up, the citations are automatically generated in this format:

> Radosavljević, Duška; Pitrolo, Flora; Bano, Tim; McCormick, Lucy (2020): LMYE Gallery #1: Tricking the Audience into Watching Performance Art - An Interview with Lucy McCormick. The Royal Central School of Speech and Drama. Media. https://doi.org/10.25389/rcssd.12554738.v7.

This format acknowledges all the people involved in creating each item (including Flora Pitrolo as the PDRA and website curator, Tim Bano as sound editor, Juan Felipe Salazar Cordona as the video editor as well as the interviewed artists); however, to avoid repetition and save space, I have truncated these citation formats to foreground the interviewed artists and scholars in each case and also in order to make the cross-referencing with the main discussion in the book easier. In the main discussion, I refer to each recording by citing the name of the interviewee, the category and issue number of LMYE the recording belongs to (e.g. LMYE Laboratory#3), the year of publication, and, where relevant, the page number of the pdf (e.g. McCormick in LMYE Gallery#1 2020: 3).

In the list below, I have included the DOI numbers as well as the html links for all individual items on www.auralia.space. At the time of writing, the hosting on www.auralia.space has been paid for until 2023, whereas the DOI links on Figshare are permanent and can be used for reference purposes indefinitely. Accompanying pdf transcripts are also archived with each recording on Figshare.

LMYE#1

Gallery#1

JQ (2020) 'LMYE Gallery #1: Theatre as a Sample-Based Artform - An Interview with JQ (Q Brothers)', Royal Central School of Speech and Drama, https://doi.org/10.25389/rcssd.12982277.v7. Also: https://www.auralia.space/gallery1-jq/.

Krishna Rao, Maya (2020) 'LMYE Gallery #1: The Chord that Opens Up the Subconscious - Interview with Maya Krishna Rao', https://doi.org/10.25389/rcssd.13027361.v7. Also: https://www.auralia.space/gallery1-mayakrishnarao/.

McCormick, Lucy (2020) 'LMYE Gallery #1: Tricking the Audience into Watching Performance Art - An Interview with Lucy McCormick', https://doi.org/10.25389/rcssd.12554738.v7. Also: https://www.auralia.space/gallery1-lucymccormick/.

Mercuriali, Silvia (2020) 'LMYE Gallery #1: Putting a Different Spin on the World - An Interview with Silvia Mercuriali', https://doi.org/10.25389/rcssd.12764300.v7. Also: https://www.auralia.space/gallery1-silviamercuriali/.

Murray, Conrad (2020) 'LMYE Gallery #1: All From the Mouth - An Interview with Conrad Murray', https://doi.org/10.25389/rcssd.13026971.v6. Also: https://www.auralia.space/gallery1-conradmurray/.

RashDash (2020) 'LMYE Gallery #1: Between the Big and the Small Picture - An Interview with RashDash', https://doi.org/10.25389/rcssd.12744836.v7. Also: https://www.auralia.space/gallery1-rashdash/.

Salon#1

Beswick, Katie, and Johnson, Javon (2020) 'LMYE Salon #1: Katie Beswick & Javon Johnson - Sounds of the City', https://doi.org/10.25389/rcssd.13017659.v7. Also: https://www.auralia.space/salon1-katiebeswick-and-javonjohnson/.

Finer, Ella, and Shirhan, Urok (2020) 'LMYE Salon #1: Ella Finer & Urok Shirhan - Companion Sounds', https://doi.org/10.25389/rcssd.13017653.v6. Also: https://www.auralia.space/salon1-ellafiner-and-urokshirhan/.

Henriques, Julian, and Mircev, Andrej (2020) 'LMYE Salon #1: Andrej Mircev & Julian Henriques - Dramaturgy as Sonic Warfare', https://doi.org/10.25389/rcssd.13017644.v8. Also: https://www.auralia.space/salon1-andrejmircev-and-julianhenriques/.

Laboratory#1

Mercuriali, Silvia (2020) 'LMYE Laboratory #1: Silvia Mercuriali - The Making of Swimming Home (2020)', https://doi.org/10.25389/rcssd.13065923.v6. Also: https://www.auralia.space/laboratory1-silviamercuriali/.

Sleepwalk Collective (2020) 'LMYE Laboratory #1: Sleepwalk Collective - The Making of Swimming Pools (2020)', https://doi.org/10.25389/rcssd.13066049.v5. Also: https://www.auralia.space/laboratory1-sleepwalkcollective/.

Library#1

Hunter, Lynette (2020) 'LMYE Library #1: Lynette Hunter - Politics of Practice (2019)', https://doi.org/10.25389/rcssd.13034591.v6. Also: https://www.auralia.space/library1-lynettehunter/.

Jestrovic, Silvija (2020) 'LMYE Library #1: Silvija Jestrovic - Performances of Authorial Presence and Absence (2020)', https://doi.org/10.25389/rcssd.13034456.v6. Also: https://www.auralia.space/library1-silvijajestrovic/.

Kendrick, Lynne (2020) 'LMYE Library #1: Lynne Kendrick - Theatre Aurality (2017)', https://doi.org/10.25389/rcssd.13034768.v7. Also: https://www.auralia.space/library1-lynnekendrick/.

LMYE#2

Gallery#2

Arias, Lola (2021) 'LMYE Gallery #2: Storytelling as Survival - An Interview with Lola Arias', https://doi.org/10.25389/rcssd.14013182.v2. Also: https://www.auralia.space/gallery2-lolaarias/.

Dead Centre (2021): LMYE Gallery #2: Poets of the Digital Age - An Interview with Dead Centre. The Royal Central School of Speech and Drama. Media. https://doi.org/10.25389/rcssd.14013311.v2. Also: https://www.auralia.space/gallery2-deadcentre/.

Dhaenens, Valentijn (2021) 'LMYE Gallery #2: Changing the World by Opening Your Mouth - Valentijn Dhaenens', https://doi.org/10.25389/rcssd.14013371.v2. Also: https://www.auralia.space/gallery2-valentijndhaenens/.

Gracefool Collective (2020) 'LMYE Gallery #2: Finding the Dancer's Voice - An Interview with Gracefool Collective', https://doi.org/10.25389/rcssd.12764333.v6. Also: https://www.auralia.space/gallery2-gracefoolcollective/.

Hunter, Kate (2020) 'LMYE Gallery #2: This Language That is Our Lives - An Interview with Kate Hunter', https://doi.org/10.25389/rcssd.12764276.v7. Also: https://www.auralia.space/gallery2-katehunter/.

Salon#2

Dwyer, Paul, Ginters, Laura, and McAuley, Gay (2021) 'LMYE Salon #2: Paul Dwyer, Laura Ginters & Gay McAuley - Rehearsal as an Oral Space', https://doi.org/10.25389/rcssd.14013482.v2. Also: https://www.auralia.space/salon2-pauldwyer-lauraginters-and-gaymcauley/.

Fleishman, Mark, and Muyanga, Neo (2021) 'LMYE Salon #2: Mark Fleishman & Neo Muyanga - The Third Character', https://doi.org/10.25389/rcssd.14013428.v2. Also: https://www.auralia.space/salon2-markfleishman-and-neomuyanga/.

LaBelle, Brandon, and Thomaidis, Konstantinos (2021) 'LMYE Salon #2: Brandon LaBelle & Konstantinos Thomaidis - Vocal Positionings', https://doi.org/10.25389/rcssd.14013566.v2. Also: https://www.auralia.space/salon2-brandonlabelle-and-konstantinosthomaidis/.

Laboratory#2

Frankland, Emma (2021) 'LMYE Laboratory #2: Emma Frankland - The Making of Hearty (2018-2020)', https://doi.org/10.25389/rcssd.14013854.v2. Also: https://www.auralia.space/laboratory2-emmafrankland/.

Green, Nic (2021) 'LMYE Laboratory #2: Nic Green - The Making of Cock and Bull (2015)', https://doi.org/10.25389/rcssd.14013647.v2. Also: https://www.auralia.space/laboratory2-nicgreen/.

The Fall Collective (2021) 'LMYE Laboratory #2: The Fall Collective - The Making of The Fall (2016)', https://doi.org/10.25389/rcssd.14013752.v2. Also: https://www.auralia.space/laboratory2-thefallcollective/.

Library#2

Finer, Ella (2021) 'LMYE Library #2: Ella Finer - Acoustic Commons', https://doi.org/10.25389/rcssd.14014166.v2. Also: https://www.auralia.space/library2-ellafiner/.

Soltani, Farokh (2021) 'LMYE Library #2: Farokh Soltani - Radio/Body (2020)', https://doi.org/10.25389/rcssd.14014055.v2. Also: https://www.auralia.space/library2-farokhsoltani/.

Spatz, Ben (2021) 'LMYE Library #2: Ben Spatz - Making a Laboratory (2020)', https://doi.org/10.25389/rcssd.14013941.v2. Also: https://www.auralia.space/library2-benspatz/.

LMYE#3

Gallery#3

Hurley, Kieran (2021) 'LMYE Gallery #3: Storytelling as Sonic Conjuring - An Interview with Kieran Hurley', https://doi.org/10.25389/rcssd.14014658.v2. Also: https://www.auralia.space/gallery3-kieranhurley/.

Kalman, Eszter (2021) 'LMYE Gallery #3: Non-Verbal Narratives - An Interview with Eszter Kalman', https://doi.org/10.25389/rcssd.14014589.v2. Also: https://www.auralia.space/gallery3-eszterkalman/.

Quote Unquote (2021) 'LMYE Gallery #3: Learning by Ear, Painting by Voice - An Interview with Quote Unquote', https://doi.org/10.25389/rcssd.14014787.v2. Also: https://www.auralia.space/gallery3-quoteunquote/.

Shlomo, SK (2020) 'LMYE Gallery #3: To Unite in the Groove - An Interview with SK Shlomo', https://doi.org/10.25389/rcssd.12764285.v7. Also: https://www.auralia.space/gallery3-skshlomo/.

Wilson, Melanie (2021) 'LMYE Gallery #3: Sound is a Plastic Art - An Interview with Melanie Wilson', https://doi.org/10.25389/rcssd.14014859.v2. Also: https://www.auralia.space/gallery3-melaniewilson/.

ZU-UK (2021) 'LMYE Gallery #3: Slippages in Perception - An Interview with ZU-UK', https://doi.org/10.25389/rcssd.14014724.v2. Also: https://www.auralia.space/gallery3-zuuk/.

Salon#3

Boston, Jane, and Mills, Matthew (2021) 'LMYE Salon #3: Jane Boston & Matthew Mills - To Sound Ourselves', https://doi.org/10.25389/rcssd.14015243.v2. Also: https://www.auralia.space/salon3-janeboston-and-matthewmills/.

de Senna, Pedro, and Svich, Caridad (2021) 'LMYE Salon #3: Caridad Svich & Pedro de Senna - Ramble Dramaturgies', https://doi.org/10.25389/rcssd.14015357.v3. Also: https://www.auralia.space/salon3-pedrodesenna-and-caridadsvich/.

Laboratory#3

Gracefool Collective (2021) 'LMYE Laboratory #3: Gracefool Collective - The Making of This is Not a Wedding (2019)', https://doi.org/10.25389/rcssd.14025854.v2. Also: https://www.auralia.space/laboratory3-gracefoolcollective/.

The Unspoken Project (2021) 'LMYE Laboratory #3: The Unspoken Project - The Making of The Voice Monologues (2018)', https://doi.org/10.25389/rcssd.14025452.v2. Also: https://www.auralia.space/laboratory3-theunspokenproject/.

Library#3

Brown, Ross (2021) 'LMYE Library #3: Ross Brown - Sound Effect (2020)', https://doi.org/10.25389/rcssd.14026373.v2. Also: https://www.auralia.space/library3-rossbrown/.

Kochhar-Lindgren, Kanta (2021) 'LMYE Library #3: Kanta Kochhar-Lindgren - Hearing Difference (2006)', https://doi.org/10.25389/rcssd.14026097.v2. Also: https://www.auralia.space/library3-kantakochharlindren/.

Lech, Kasia (2021) 'LMYE Library #3: Kasia Lech - Dramaturgy of Form (2021)', https://doi.org/10.25389/rcssd.14026700.v2. Also: https://www.auralia.space/library3-kasialech/.

LMYE#4

Gallery#4

Brett Bailey, Christopher (2021) 'LMYE Gallery #4: Forever at This Volume - An Interview with Christopher Brett Bailey', https://doi.org/10.25389/rcssd.14027066.v2. Also: https://www.auralia.space/galley4-christopherbrettbailey/.

Elerian, Omar, and Kene, Arinze (2021) 'LMYE Gallery #4: Pushing the Boundaries of Storytelling - The Misty Interview', https://doi.org/10.25389/rcssd.14027606.v2. Also: https://www.auralia.space/gallery4-misty/.

Little Bulb (2021) 'LMYE Gallery #4: Taking Music Up a Level - An Interview with Little Bulb', https://doi.org/10.25389/rcssd.14027885.v2. Also: https://www.auralia.space/gallery4-littlebulb/.

Meteyard, James, Memon, Maimuna, and O'Briain, Donnacadh (2021) 'LMYE Gallery #4: Harnessing the Magic of the Gig - The Electrolyte Interview', https://doi.org/10.25389/rcssd.14027063.v2. Also: https://www.auralia.space/gallery4-wildcard/.

Xia, Matthew (2021) 'LMYE Gallery #4: The Political Shaman - An Interview with Matthew Xia', https://doi.org/10.25389/rcssd.14028077.v2. Also: https://www.auralia.space/gallery4-matthewxia/.

Salon#4

Brooks, Daphne, and Skantze, P.A. (2021) 'LMYE Salon #4: Daphne Brooks & P.A. Skantze - A Playlist for Encouragement', https://doi.org/10.25389/rcssd.14060846.v2. Also: https://www.auralia.space/salon4-daphnebrooks-paskantze/.

Double, Oliver, and Long, Josie (2021) 'LMYE Salon #4: Olly Double & Josie Long - Finding Your Favourite Band in Comedy', https://doi.org/10.25389/rcssd.14060861.v2. Also: https://www.auralia.space/salon4-oliverdouble-josielong/.

Roesner, David, Rost, Katharina, and Stemann, Nicolas (2021) 'LMYE Salon #4: Roesner, Rost & Stemann - The Dirty Noise of Theatre', https://doi.org/10.25389/rcssd.14028248.v2. Also: https://www.auralia.space/salon4-davidroesner-katharinarost-nicolasstemann/.

Laboratory#4

Frljić, Oliver (2021) 'LMYE Laboratory #4: Oliver Frljic - The Making of TURBOFOLK (2008)', https://doi.org/10.25389/rcssd.14060933.v3. Also: https://www.auralia.space/laboratory4-oliverfrljic/.

Shlomo, SK (2021) 'LMYE Laboratory #4: SK Shlomo - The Making of Reconnect: Digital Raving (2020)', https://doi.org/10.25389/rcssd.14060999.v4. Also: https://www.auralia.space/laboratory4-skshlomo/.

Unfolding Theatre (2021) 'LMYE Laboratory #4: Unfolding Theatre - Putting the Band Back Together (2016)', https://doi.org/10.25389/rcssd.14060975.v3. Also: https://www.auralia.space/laboratory4-unfoldingtheatre/.

Library#4

Bonello Rutter Giappone, Krista (2021) 'LMYE Library #4: Krista Bonello Rutter Giappone - The Punk Turn in Comedy (2018)', https://doi.org/10.25389/rcssd.14061029.v4. Also: https://www.auralia.space/library4-kristabonello/.

Carson, A.D. (2021) 'LMYE Library #4: A.D. Carson - i used to love to dream (2020)', https://doi.org/10.25389/rcssd.14061041.v3. Also: https://www.auralia.space/library4-adcarson/.

LMYE#5

Gallery#5

Ceredi, Filippo Michelangelo (2020) 'LMYE Gallery #5: The Rhythm of the Archive - An Interview with Filippo Michelangelo Ceredi', https://doi.org/10.25389/rcssd.12593750.v7. Also: https://www.auralia.space/gallery5-filippomichelangeloceredi/.

goetz, sair (2021) 'LMYE Gallery #5: sair goetz - The Voice I Want for Myself', https://doi.org/10.25389/rcssd.14061197.v2. Also: https://www.auralia.space/gallery5-sairgoetz/.

Metcalfe, Sammy (Sleepwalk Collective) (2021) 'LMYE Gallery #5: Sammy Metcalfe (Sleepwalk Collective) - The Sound That You Feel', https://doi.org/10.25389/rcssd.14061113.v2. Also: https://www.auralia.space/gallery5-sammymetcalfe/.

Pastor, Eugenie, and Turner, Shamira (2021) 'LMYE Gallery #5: She Goat - Everything in Harmony', https://doi.org/10.25389/rcssd.14061131.v2. Also: https://www.auralia.space/gallery5-shegoat/

Zahn, Oliver (2021) 'LMYE Gallery #5: Oliver Zahn - Pointing at Things and Saying What They Are', https://doi.org/10.25389/rcssd.14061095.v2. Also: https://www.auralia.space/gallery5-oliverzahn/.

Salon#5

Goh, Annie, and Kolar, Miriam (2021) 'LMYE Salon #5: Annie Goh & Miriam Kolar - Performing Archaeoacoustics', https://doi.org/10.25389/rcssd.14061611.v2. Also: https://www.auralia.space/salon5-anniegoh-miriamkolar/.

Icke, Robert, and Washburn, Anne (2021) 'LMYE Salon #5: Robert Icke & Anne Washburn - Oral/Aural Remains', https://doi.org/10.25389/rcssd.14061530.v2. Also: https://www.auralia.space/salon5-annewashburn-roberticke/.

Mandic, Danilo, and Ramshaw, Sara (2021) 'LMYE Salon #5: Sara Ramshaw & Danilo Mandic - Law as Sonic Performance', https://doi.org/10.25389/rcssd.14061674.v2. Also: https://www.auralia.space/salon5-danilomandic-sararamshaw/.

Laboratory#5

goetz, sair (2021) 'LMYE Laboratory #5: sair goetz - The Making of THE ABCs AND XYZs OF LMNs (2020-2021)', https://doi.org/10.25389/rcssd.14061770.v3. Also: https://www.auralia.space/laboratory5-sairgoetz/.

Pastor, Eugenie, and Turner, Shamira (2021) 'LMYE Laboratory #5: She Goat - The Making of The Undefinable (2019-2020)', https://doi.org/10.25389/rcssd.14061716.v2. Also: https://www.auralia.space/laboratory5-shegoat/.

Slattne, Hanna, and Yee, Shannon (2021) 'LMYE Laboratory #5: Shannon Yee & Hanna Slattne - Reassembled, Slightly Askew (2015)', https://doi.org/10.25389/rcssd.14061746.v3. Also: https://www.auralia.space/laboratory5-shannonyee-hannaslattne/.

Library#5

Kapsali, Maria (2021) 'LMYE Library #5: Maria Kapsali - Movement Sonification and its Application in Pedagogical and Artistic Contexts (2014-2019)', https://doi.org/10.25389/rcssd.14061818.v2. Also: https://www.auralia.space/library5-mariakapsali/.

Worthen, W.B. (2021) 'LMYE Library #5: W.B. Worthen - Shakespeare, Technicity, Theatre (2020)', https://doi.org/10.25389/rcssd.14061800.v2. Also: https://www.auralia.space/library5-wbworthen/.

LMYE Guides

Pitrolo, Flora (2022) LMYE Guides: Genre, Auralia.Space, Royal Central School of Speech and Drama, https://doi.org/10.25389/rcssd.17259614. Also: https://www.auralia.space/lmye-guides-genre/.

Pitrolo, Flora (2022) LMYE Guides: In the Archives, Auralia.Space, Royal Central School of Speech and Drama, https://doi.org/10.25389/rcssd.17259701. Also: https://www.auralia.space/lmye-guides-in-the-archives/.

Pitrolo, Flora (2022) LMYE Guides: Queer Sonics, Auralia.Space, Royal Central School of Speech and Drama, https://doi.org/10.25389/rcssd.17259734. Also: https://www.auralia.space/lmye-guides-queer-sonics/.

Pitrolo, Flora (2022) LMYE Guides: Radio, Auralia.Space, Royal Central School of Speech and Drama, https://doi.org/10.25389/rcssd.17259788. Also: https://www.auralia.space/lmye-guides-radio/.

Pitrolo, Flora (2022) LMYE Guides: Rave, Auralia.Space, Royal Central School of Speech and Drama, https://doi.org/10.25389/rcssd.17260484. Also: https://www.auralia.space/lmye-guides-rave/.

Pitrolo, Flora (2022) LMYE Guides: The Politics of Voice, Auralia.Space, Royal Central School of Speech and Drama, https://doi.org/10.25389/rcssd.17260532. Also: https://www.auralia.space/lmye-guides-the-politics-of-voice/.

The Studio: Courses and Masterclasses

https://www.auralia.space/lend-me-your-ears/the-studio/

In addition to the Lend Me Your Ears (LMYE) Collection created in 2020, the www.auralia.space features The Studio – a selection of masterclasses commissioned from some of the artists above and a podcast training course 'Decolonising the Voice' created by Jane Boston and Deelee Dubé. All of these items were created in 2021 and 2022 and are also archived on Figshare.

'Decolonising the Voice' Podcast Training Course

Boston, Jane, and Dubé, Sitandile (2022) LMYE Studio: Decolonising the Voice 1 - Diasporic Voices, Auralia.Space, Royal Central School of Speech and Drama, https://doi.org/10.25389/rcssd.17259227.

Boston, Jane, and Dube, Sitandile (2022) LMYE Studio: Decolonising the Voice 2 – Estranged Voices, Auralia.Space, Royal Central School of Speech and Drama, https://doi.org/10.25389/rcssd.17259320.

Boston, Jane, and Dube, Sitandile (2022) LMYE Studio: Decolonising the Voice 3 – Gendered Voices, Auralia.Space, Royal Central School of Speech and Drama, https://doi.org/10.25389/rcssd.17259383.

Boston, Jane, and Dube, Sitandile (2022) LMYE Studio: Decolonising the Voice 4 - Historical Vocalities (part 1), Auralia.Space, Royal Central School of Speech and Drama, https://doi.org/10.25389/rcssd.17259458.

Boston, Jane, and Dube, Sitandile (2022) LMYE Studio: Decolonising the Voice 5 - Historical Vocalities (part 2), Auralia.Space, Royal Central School of Speech and Drama, https://doi.org/10.25389/rcssd.17259503.

Boston, Jane, and Dube, Sitandile (2022) LMYE Studio: Decolonising the Voice 6 - Tonalities and Tunes, Auralia.Space, Royal Central School of Speech and Drama, https://doi.org/10.25389/rcssd.17259533.

Boston, Jane, and Dube, Sitandile (2022) LMYE Studio: Decolonising the Voice 7 – Repositioned Voices and Affirmations, Auralia.Space, Royal Central School of Speech and Drama, https://doi.org/10.25389/rcssd.17259581.

Masterclasses (Video Recordings)

Radosavljević, Duška, Boston, Jane, and Dube, Sitandile (2021) LMYE Studio: Jane Boston and Deelee Dube - Decolonising the Voice Masterclass. The Royal Central School of Speech and Drama. Media. https://doi.org/10.25389/rcssd.16814950.v1. Also: https://www.auralia.space/jane-boston-and-deelee-dube-decolonising-the-voice/

Radosavljević, Duška, and goetz, sair (2021) LMYE Studio: sair goetz - PlayVox. The Royal Central School of Speech and Drama. Media. https://doi.org/10.25389/rcssd.16815019.v1. Also: https://www.auralia.space/sair-goetz-playvox/

Radosavljević, Duška, and Gracefool Collective (2021) LMYE Studio: Gracefool Collective - Embracing Failure; And Approach to Movement, Sound and Voice. The Royal Central School of Speech and Drama. Media. https://doi.org/10.25389/rcssd.16814908.v1. Also: https://www.auralia.space/gracefool-collective-embracing-failure-an-approach-to-movement-sound-and-voice/

Radosavljević, Duška, and Krishna Rao, Maya (2021) LMYE Studio: Maya Krishna Rao - The Solo Devising Performer; Pathways into Imagination and Process. The Royal Central School of Speech and Drama. Media. https://doi.org/10.25389/rcssd.16814998.v1. Also: https://www.auralia.space/maya-krishna-rao-the-solo-devising-performer-pathways-into-imagination-and-process/

Radosavljević, Duška, and Lech, Kasia (2021) LMYE Studio: Kasia Lech - Performing Verse Structure through Body, Voice and Technology. The Royal Central School of Speech and Drama. Media. https://doi.org/10.25389/rcssd.16814989.v1. Also: https://www.auralia.space/kasia-lech-performing-verse-structure-through-body-voice-and-technology/

Radosavljević, Duška, and Mercuriali, Silvia (2021) LMYE Studio: Silvia Mercuriali - Immersive Theatrical Experiences in Public Spaces. The Royal Central School of Speech and Drama. Media. https://doi.org/10.25389/rcssd.16815037.v1. Also: https://www.auralia.space/silvia-mercuriali-immersive-theatrical-experiences-in-public-spaces/

Radosavljević, Duška, Pitrolo, Flora, and Bamba, Rokia (2021) LMYE Studio: Rokia Bamba - Creating Your Trademark. The Royal Central School of Speech and Drama. Media. https://doi.org/10.25389/rcssd.16815013.v1. Also: https://www.auralia.space/rokia-bamba-creating-your-trademark/

Radosavljević, Duška, and Sleepwalk Collective (2021) LMYE Studio: Sammy Metcalfe - Conversations with Objects. The Royal Central School of Speech and Drama. Media. https://doi.org/10.25389/rcssd.16815025.v1. Also: https://www.auralia.space/sammy-metcalfe-conversations-with-objects/

INDEX

AAC 39, 91–92, 115
Abramović, Marina 46, 184
accessibility 43, 109, 127, 137, 168; centring of 174
acoustemology 17–18, 56, 58, 72, 176
adaptation 6, 74, 102, 120, 130, 137, 138, 161, 173, 174, 192, 197
affect 8, 31, 32, 40, 50, 59, 71, 72, 74–75, 76, 77, 81, 84, 86, 87, 96, 97, 101, 114, 122, 145–146, 149, 168, 169, 170, 171, 172; affective critique 39, 85, 146, 171
Africa 50, 63, 85, 155; African 23, 134; African-American 110, 123, 155; South Africa 63, 85, 89, 155
agency 11, 14, 29, 36, 37, 49, 53, 71, 81, 92, 100, 114, 134, 169; agential entanglement 13, 22, 26, 52
allyship 36, 137, 138, 171
Alston, Adam 30–31, 51, 53, 54, 160, 169, 175
American ix, 11, 18, 19, 49, 52, 65, 68, 86, 87, 102, 123, 130, 131, 135, 137, 142, 150, 154, 176, 177, 204; *see also* Africa, African American; Black (culture); United States
amplification 85, 94, 107, 115, 168, 172; amplified storytelling 5, 38, 39, 40, 41, 91–121, 145, 149, 165
ANT (actor network theory) 13, 35, 57
anthropology 7, 8, 17, 33, 56, 58, 59, 119, 201
antiphony 71, 110
archive 12, 44, 46, 53, 119, 125, 161, 163, 173, 204, 212, 213

Argentinian 84, 185–187
Arias, Lola 5, 84, 85, 123, 161, 168, 185, 208
artefact 9, 13, 46
artform 72, 100, 111, 112, 131, 134, 194, 207
articulation 24–26, 28, 42, 46, 65, 73, 163, 168, 190
artist and creation of knowledge 10, 13, 22, 26, 36–37, 41, 44–45, 163; artist-centred research 36, 65, 128, 160, 165; artistic expression 92, 121, 160, 166; artistic idiom 130, 151; artistic process 13, 26, 36, 37, 65, 84; artistic research 48, 90; artist in residence 41, 44, 162–165
assemblage 73, 173
assembly 52, 55, 116, 128, 154, 157, 176
audience xi, 2–5, 8, 14, 16, 17, 23, 26, 30, 31, 39, 40, 51, 52, 53, 60, 61, 62, 64, 66–68, 70–72, 75–78, 79, 81, 83, 85, 87, 88, 90, 92, 95–96, 97, 98, 100, 101, 102, 109–110, 112, 113, 114, 117, 122, 125–126, 127, 129, 132, 134, 136, 143, 144, 145, 146, 147, 149, 150, 154, 164, 168–170, 171–172, 174, 175, 179, 180, 181, 182, 183, 188, 189, 190, 191, 192, 193, 194, 195, 196, 197, 198, 199, 201, 202, 204, 205, 207; fandom 117, 122, 131, 135, 136, 150, 152
aural/oral dramaturgies 3–4, 6, 14, 15, 36, 47, 59, 103, 124, 158, 137, 160, 161, 166, 167, 168, 171, 173, 174; A/OD project 3–4, 5–6, 7, 13, 22,

25, 28, 30, 32–35, 36–38, 40–46, 68, 82–83, 93, 107, 110, 124–125, 129, 140, 147, 151, 160–165, 167, 168, 173–174; www.auralia.space xvi, 2, 35, 39, 45, 47, 53, 78, 117, 163, 164, 165, 206–214
aurality 14, 17, 23, 31, 46, 47, 51, 57, 128, 129, 153, 156, 157, 158, 160, 169, 174, 177, 208
Auslander, Philip 50, 54, 128, 132, 133, 134, 136, 144, 153, 154, 155, 156
Australia 63, 64, 82, 88, 90, 116, 150
author viii, x, 8, 19, 24, 26, 29, 30, 46, 50, 51, 54, 56, 60, 68, 69, 71, 87, 89, 97–99, 101, 105, 111, 115, 116, 119, 120, 130, 153, 169, 180, 182, 183, 189, 201; 'author function' 8, 24; authorial 29, 31, 43, 68, 69, 84, 89, 97, 100, 116, 119, 134, 193, 208; authority, 2, 4, 5, 11, 37, 60, 62, 67, 68, 75, 76, 85, 90, 116, 120, 141, 146, 181
authorship ix, xii, 4, 6, 19, 24, 30, 41, 45, 46, 58, 61, 63, 68, 70, 93, 97–100, 109, 116, 119, 122, 137, 155, 167, 183, 192; collective authorship 63, 97, 116
auto-didactic viii, 141, 167

Bailey, Christopher Brett xvi, 5, 125, 130, 131, 155, 211
Bakhtin, Mikhail 67, 69, 70–72, 88, 90, 93, 97–99, 118, 120, 129, 165; bakhtinian 73, 74, 97, 98, 100, 129
Balkan(s) ix, 23, 46, 58, 95, 120, 151, 152
Balkanism 50, 94
Barad, Karen 13, 31, 52, 54, 165, 168, 175
Barthes, Roland 8, 29, 47, 51, 54
Battersea Arts Centre (BAC) xv, 40, 41, 52, 54, 131, 137, 147, 163, 191, 197
Beatbox(ing) 118, 137, 147, 150, 156, 176, 197, 198; Beatbox Academy 137, 138, 197, 198
Beckett, Samuel 79, 183, 192; Beckettian 79, 80, 172
Bennett, Susan 1, 16, 17, 54
Beswick, Katie 44, 102, 117, 118, 137, 155, 156, 167, 175, 208
Black (culture) 55, 102, 110, 120, 136, 137, 138, 158, 167, 181
Bleeker, Maaike 12, 13, 22, 52, 54, 165, 175
body 14, 46, 59, 60, 82, 87, 88, 89, 97, 112, 113–114, 149, 171, 196, 209, 214; see also embodiment, embodied
Bonello, Krista 134, 211
Bouko, Catherine 14, 15, 54, 160, 166, 176

Bowring, John x, xvi, 95, 96, 98, 101, 116, 119
Brecht, Bertolt 64, 87, 90, 200
Bristol (Bristol University) 8, 9, 117
British, 5, 28, 47, 48, 51, 61, 63, 79, 84, 86, 89, 93, 99, 121, 124, 125, 130, 132, 133, 135, 136, 138, 150, 153, 156, 157, 158, 185, 188, 189, 197, 200, 201; see also United Kingdom
Brown, Ross xv, 1, 14, 18, 30, 47, 55, 154, 210
Butler, Judith 52, 55, 128, 154, 157, 169, 172, 176
Butt, Gavin 55, 140, 141, 157

cabaret 133, 194, 195
camera 45, 82, 104, 105, 109, 117, 180, 181, 184, 186
Canada 85; Canadian 5, 19, 49, 59, 108, 114, 131, 178
canon ix, xii, 6, 11, 94, 99, 101, 109, 116
Caryer, Kate 91, 92, 115
CAST 134, 138
Cavarero, Adriana 15, 21, 22, 23, 30, 31, 38, 43, 49, 55, 67, 71, 94, 98, 101, 114, 115, 118, 119, 165, 169, 176
Ceredi, Filippo Michelangelo 173, 212
character 60, 62, 64, 65, 68, 70, 74, 78–79, 86, 114, 117, 140, 146, 181, 209
choreography 74, 75, 77, 89, 173
class 92, 115, 135, 139, 146
climate change 41, 60, 162
closure 32, 38, 72, 87, 133, 171, 172, 174, 175; disruption of closure 40, 112, 168–170
coalition 36, 37, 56, 169, 172; coalitional research methodology 13, 36, 39, 155, 163
Cock and Bull 39, 72, 73–80, 90, 171, 209
code-switching ix, 25, 37, 51, 122, 140
collaboration 6, 30, 31, 36, 37, 54, 58, 59, 120, 127, 128, 129, 137, 138, 173, 185, 192; collaborative 13, 28, 37, 67, 121, 130, 137, 144, 153
collage 67, 68, 73, 78, 82
collective 18, 33, 47, 67, 75, 82, 85, 87, 88, 97, 98, 100, 101, 112, 129, 137, 142, 145, 167, 171; collective body 97; collective consciousness 100; collective critique 39, 67, 69, 75, 82, 85, 171; see also authorship, collective authorship; Gracefool Collective; Little Bulb; Ontroerend Goed; SKaGeN Theatre; Sleepwalk Collective; RashDash; The Fall

Collective; The Unspoken Project; Wildcard Theatre; ZU-UK
Coltrane, John 109, 110
comedy 83, 131, 134, 156, 189, 190, 192, 195, 196, 211
community 17, 26, 34, 36, 44, 45, 48, 51, 52, 58, 93, 98, 113, 122, 128, 129, 130, 132, 137, 149, 150, 153, 154, 155, 167, 175, 197, 198, 200, 202; incidental community 36, 45
composition ix, xi, xii, 19, 47, 70, 71, 83, 92, 95, 97, 99, 100, 108, 109, 110, 118, 167, 170, 173; compositional ix, 2, 4, 5, 17, 40, 47, 62, 70, 72, 77, 82, 83, 90, 95, 97, 118, 123, 161, 165, 166; compositionality principle 27
Conquergood, Dwight 32, 33, 38, 51, 52, 55, 57, 168, 169, 176
consciousness 7, 20, 21, 29, 65, 68, 69, 98, 99, 100, 104, 135, 153, 165, 191, 195
contradiction xiv, 16, 24, 28, 30, 31, 32, 73, 80, 124, 133, 145
conversation 32, 34, 35, 38, 40, 41, 42, 43, 44, 46, 52, 53, 57, 62, 76, 82, 89, 125, 141, 143, 153, 157, 159, 162, 166, 168, 173, 175, 191, 192, 206, 214
context(s) 3–4, 5, 9, 11–12, 14, 18, 20, 26–27, 29, 30, 36, 39, 40, 48, 50, 55, 78, 81, 85, 100, 102, 103, 104, 112, 121, 124, 126, 128, 130, 135, 139, 141, 147, 150, 153, 175, 184, 186, 212
contingency 20, 25, 37, 38, 82, 84, 85, 124, 142, 160
co-optation 11, 30, 31, 83, 85, 129, 135, 136, 137, 141, 142, 146, 152, 154, 169, 171
counterpoint 39, 62, 69–73, 75, 77, 78, 79, 81, 82, 83, 85, 87, 88, 92, 97, 106, 107, 109, 124, 133, 134, 142, 147, 161, 166, 168, 171, 175, 176; contrapuntal 39, 71, 73, 78, 81, 85, 92, 100, 146, 174
Covid-19 xiv, 4, 6, 10, 12, 34, 40–46, 151, 161, 164, 165, 168, 172, 173, 174, 206
craft 7, 9, 18, 186, 190
critic 11, 26, 29, 37, 50, 51, 61, 67, 68, 75, 86, 97, 99, 170; Critical Stages xvi, 2, 46, 54, 59, 158, 161, 175, 176, 177, 178; critical theory 7, 16; critical tools 81, 110, 169; criticality 30, 31, 109, 169; criticism 2, 11, 24, 29–31, 35, 36, 51, 55, 86, 92, 110, 116, 133, 137, 171; critique 8, 10, 11, 12, 21, 26, 29, 31, 32, 35, 39, 40, 54, 56, 57, 59, 63, 66, 67–69, 74, 75, 76, 81, 82, 84, 85, 86, 87, 104, 146, 164, 169, 171; reparative critique 35; *see also* affect, affective critique; collective, collective critique; post-critique
Croatia viii, 26, 51, 115, 116, 152
Crouch, Tim 26, 50, 87, 88, 169–170, 185, 189
culture ix, 2–4, 18, 28, 34, 37, 48, 52, 55, 64, 84, 85, 87, 92, 94, 95, 102, 122, 137, 140, 142, 147, 148, 152, 158, 176; counter-culture 65, 93, 137, 148, 149; cultural context 5, 26, 29, 30, 40, 48, 78, 85, 102, 122, 124, 135, 147, 150; cultural contingency 82, 84, 85, 124; cultural consumption xiii, 127, 135; cultural critique 67–68; cultural history viii–xiv, 15, 16, 18, 19, 20, 24, 25, 84, 94; Cultural Materialism 8; cultural production 8, 15, 19, 28, 29, 105, 126, 135–136; cultural value 49, 129; digital culture 170; festival culture 126; folk culture 93, 132, 135; mainstream culture 135, 137, 169; rave culture 110, 147–150; rock culture 117, 131; subculture 123, 124, 135, 136, 137, 139, 141, 142, 148, 157, 158, 169, 176; sociology of culture 122–123; trans-cultural 82, 85, 160, 174; *see also* popular culture

dance 5, 14, 41, 54, 55, 73, 74, 75, 77, 78, 83, 87, 119, 132, 138, 147, 159, 162, 171, 176, 193, 194, 196, 199
Dead Centre (Ben Kidd, Bush Moukarzel) 79–81, 82, 112, 113, 168, 182–183, 191–193, 209
decolonisation 2, 4, 12, 15, 16, 17, 22, 23, 31, 37, 50, 58, 95, 165, 169, 85, 94; Decolonising the Voice 46, 206, 213–214
Deleuze, gilles, 21, 170
Deller, Jeremy 148–149, 157
Denzin, Norman 32, 55, 62, 66–68, 73, 74, 82, 86, 87, 88, 164, 175, 176
deprofessionalisation 28–30, 51, 55, 122, 167; multiprofessionalisation 51
Derrida, Jacques 21–22, 47, 50, 54, 55
design xi, 4, 5, 6, 9, 14, 31, 32–34, 41, 44, 45, 49, 51, 56, 62, 121, 138. 156, 161, 162, 164, 171, 179, 183, 187, 192, 203, 206
Desmond, Matthew 33–34, 37, 52, 55, 166, 176
devising 14, 25, 57, 78, 82, 131, 152, 154, 214

Dhaenens, Valentijn 5, 78–79, 82, 107, 123, 171, 181–182, 190, 209
dialectic 28–31, 49, 51, 65, 69, 70, 73, 81, 105, 119, 146, 166, 168, 169
dialogic xi, 67, 68, 69, 72, 76, 82, 88, 95, 97, 99, 105, 110, 112, 165
digital xiv, 2, 3, 4, 8, 12, 14, 19, 23, 27, 32, 35, 37, 40, 44, 45, 49, 50, 52, 54, 55, 57, 58, 79, 88, 94, 109, 120, 128, 156, 157, 160, 161, 163, 164, 167, 170, 172, 173, 209, 211
digital humanities 11–12, 53, 55, 59, 136
Digital Theatre xvi, 41, 206
direct address 83, 100, 105, 109, 112, 127, 144, 145, 192
disability 41, 92, 115, 118, 119
division of labour 28, 99, 121, 140, 148, 155
Dixon, Steve 170, 173, 175, 176
DIY 45, 83, 102, 121, 124, 133, 135, 136, 137, 139, 140, 148, 158, 167, 196
DJ (DJing) 102, 111, 138, 148, 149, 150, 167, 187, 188
documentary 5, 39, 61–66, 68, 71, 72, 73, 75, 78, 79, 83, 86, 89, 92, 106, 148, 149, 158, 163, 179, 182, 186
documentation 9, 34, 40, 41, 45, 46, 52, 65, 71, 73, 163, 179
Dorsen, Annie 88, 172
Double, Oliver 44, 134, 211
DV8 5, 74–75

ecology 14, 17, 29, 37, 45, 122, 134, 135, 175; ecological 15; eco-leadership 137
Edinburgh Fringe 40, 111, 121, 126, 128, 137, 139, 147, 150, 155, 159, 179, 181, 182, 187, 188, 189, 190, 194, 198, 199, 200, 201, 202, 203, 204
editing 42–43, 46, 53, 61, 66, 93, 108, 167
education 8, 9, 10, 28, 51, 52, 55, 57, 93, 107, 119, 146, 157, 180
Eisenstein, Sergei 104, 106
Electrolyte 40, 125, 128, 142–146, 199
Elerian, Omar 150, 211
Elevator Repair Service 14
embodiment 8, 32, 54, 78, 112, 149, 177; embodied 9, 15, 51, 65, 67, 71, 72, 74, 77, 82, 86, 110, 112, 144, 163; *see also* body
engagement 1, 4, 27, 30, 31, 40, 43, 45, 55, 61, 62, 67, 74, 75, 77, 81, 83, 84, 88, 93, 98, 112, 113, 126, 132, 145, 146, 169–170, 171, 192
enlightenment viii, 6, 68, 95, 137, 168
enmeshment 34, 37, 40, 46, 65, 170–172, 174

ensemble 1, 5, 27, 42, 47, 50, 52, 56, 58, 91, 121, 122, 150, 153, 158, 160, 163, 181, 186, 190, 191, 192, 193, 198, 201, 202
entanglement 13, 22, 26, 52, 54
entrainment 71, 87, 88, 90, 101
episteme 9, 22, 48
epistemology 6–13, 18, 22, 24, 26, 30, 31, 34, 36, 37, 56, 62, 67, 68, 94, 95, 98, 102, 109, 136, 169
ethics 9, 15, 25, 26, 43, 44, 48, 50, 53, 69, 74, 80, 82, 85, 87, 98, 137, 175, 184
ethnography x, 5, 18, 24, 25, 33, 34, 35, 37, 39, 40, 50, 51, 55, 63–65, 67, 85, 88, 94, 101, 116, 154, 163, 164, 173, 176, 180; performative ethnography 62, 66–69; rehearsal ethnography 33, 37, 40, 44, 52, 57, 163, 176; relational ethnography 32–35, 55, 160
experience 3, 7, 8, 17, 19, 20, 30, 31, 34, 49, 50, 53, 54, 62, 67, 68, 69, 72, 75, 83, 85, 87, 93, 98, 101, 108, 109, 114, 115, 118, 129, 136, 143, 144, 145, 146, 147, 150, 154, 171, 173, 184, 186, 188, 189, 195, 202
experiential turn 8, 48
experimental 79, 88, 111, 124, 128, 131, 140, 153, 155

Feld, Steven 17–18, 23, 31, 56, 72, 169, 175, 176
Felski, Rita 10–11, 35, 54, 56, 67, 89, 176
festival 41, 52, 121, 122, 126, 127, 129, 150, 161, 172, 175, 182, 185; Complete Works Festival 154; Dublin Festival 125–126, 157; GIFT 44; Glastonbury 121, 126; Latitude Festival 121, 126, 200; LIFT 185, 204; Manchester International Festival 127, 200; *see also* Edinburgh Fringe
field 6–12, 14, 16, 19, 31, 34–35, 36, 37, 39, 41, 45, 47, 48, 50, 51, 57, 62, 64, 67, 82, 100, 107, 118, 161, 166, 168, 206; field recording ix, 17; fieldwork 39, 40, 45, 95; *Minefield* 84, 121, 185–187; *Notes from the Field* 39, 62–63, 179–181
Fisher, Mark (k-punk) 111, 119, 141
Foley, John Miles 170, 176
folk ix, xiv, 105, 119, 127, 132, 152, 204
folklore 7, 19, 105, 129, 132; *see also* culture, folk culture; turbofolk, *Turbofolk*
form 2, 3, 5, 23, 27, 29, 40, 43, 46, 52, 61, 62, 63, 64, 65, 67, 69, 73, 78, 79, 81–86, 87, 88, 89, 94, 98, 100–115, 117, 119, 120, 121, 123, 124, 126, 127, 128,

132, 136, 137, 139, 142, 143, 144, 146, 150, 152, 154, 156, 160, 161, 165, 167, 169, 170, 171, 173, 174, 175, 181, 187, 191, 200, 203, 210
Foucault. Michel 8, 24, 25, 29, 30, 47, 50, 56, 57, 170, 171, 172
frame 40, 132–133, 142, 146, 154, 156, 184
Frankland, Emma 85, 155, 209
Frljić, Oliver 105, 123, 151, 152, 156, 158, 211
fourth wall 5, 30, 100, 145–146, 147, 193, 199

gender xi, 41, 52, 55, 85, 150, 162, 171, 174, 201, 213
genealogy 6, 7, 24, 25, 26, 45, 46, 48, 50, 62, 63–66, 70, 86, 124, 130, 157, 171
genre xi, 22, 40, 64, 65, 98, 105, 123, 127, 129–134, 135, 142, 143, 151, 152, 154, 155, 174, 181, 187, 193, 200, 201, 213; *see also* culture; folk; hip hop; punk; rap; rave; reggae; rock music; techno
German x, 7, 8, 48, 68, 70, 84, 86, 90, 98, 104, 105, 131, 148, 173, 193; Germany 9, 28, 63, 85, 93
gestalt 67, 68, 75, 78, 82, 94, 98, 164
goetz, sair xvi, 41, 161, 162, 163, 174, 212, 214
Goh, Annie 49, 56, 173, 212
Gracefool Collective xvi, 41, 83, 84, 108, 162, 163, 209, 210, 214
Green, Nic xvi, 5, 39, 72, 73, 75–77, 79, 80, 82, 85, 88, 90, 108, 123, 171, 209
Greig, David 127, 128, 153, 154, 158, 159
gusle x, xi, xvi, 94, 95, 96, 100, 102, 104, 105, 109, 116, 117, 118, 152

headphones 93, 113, 114, 162, 168, 192, 193; headphone theatre 5, 41, 52, 57, 114, 119, 164, 174, 177; headphone verbatim 64, 86, 88, 90
Hebdige, Dick 123, 135, 141, 157, 169, 176
Hegel, Georg 98, 106, 119; Hegelian 71, 100, 107
hegemony 2, 8, 11, 14, 15, 20, 29, 33, 50, 68, 70, 85, 148, 163, 169
Henriques, Julian 18, 23, 56, 71, 149, 157, 167, 169, 172, 176, 208; *see also* sonic, sonic dominance
heterarchy 5, 58, 82, 170
heteroglossia 69, 70, 73, 74, 75, 88, 97, 109
hierarchy 5, 9, 13, 16, 36, 68, 70, 95, 99, 136, 155, 169, 170, 171, 174, 177

hip hop xiii, 102, 103, 117, 118, 123, 131, 137, 138, 150, 151, 153, 155, 156, 175, 187
history xiv, 7, 9, 11, 12, 15, 16, 17, 18, 20, 24, 40, 42, 46, 49, 53, 56, 57, 65, 69, 78, 86, 87, 89, 90, 91, 99, 101, 102, 116, 118, 124, 133, 135, 136, 139, 142, 147, 148, 150, 155, 157, 158, 161, 163, 176, 184, 185, 186, 192, 193, 196, 197, 201, 203, 204, 205; historiography xi, 20, 25, 57, 95, 100, 123, 124, 129, 134, 136, 137, 139, 148, 165; oral history 46, 65, 89, 90, 163
Home-Cook, George 1, 3, 14, 15, 30, 31, 49, 56, 71, 72, 89
Hull 128, 139, University of Hull 140, 155, 200
Humboldt, Wilhelm von 7, 10
Hunter, Kate 82, 88, 122, 168, 209
Hurley, Kieran xvi, 93, 107, 110, 111–112, 118, 119, 126, 128, 130, 131, 139, 142, 145, 146, 148, 167, 187, 188, 210

idiom 25, 26, 27, 32, 37, 38; *see also* performance idiom
immersion xiii, 4, 18, 30, 31, 32, 33, 34, 40, 45, 122, 131, 146, 149, 170, 171;
immersivity 5, 14, 30, 32, 45, 75, 112, 169, 201; immersive theatre 8, 30, 31, 51, 53, 54, 57, 60, 128, 129, 149, 154, 161, 175, 178, 188, 193, 200, 214
imperialism 33, 87, 90, 94, 119, 175, 176, 177; anti-imperialism 50
improvisation 25, 26, 45, 46, 55, 67, 84, 95, 104, 110, 119, 120, 130, 137, 152, 157, 160, 165, 169, 173, 174, 176, 198
Indian 82, 176
Indigenous 15, 31, 59, 60, 85, 120, 177, 178
industrial 7, 22, 28, 93, 94, 148, 167
innovation 2, 6, 8, 12, 29, 31, 35, 46, 62, 79, 81, 93, 98, 104, 121, 126, 140, 142, 166, 171, 172, 174; innovatory 7, 13, 26, 29, 37
institutions 29, 34; institutional 6–13, 43, 49, 56, 132, 133, 155, 168
intersubjectivity 40, 56, 62, 70, 72, 75, 76, 87, 92, 93, 94, 98, 99, 100, 109, 114, 115, 129, 132, 144, 145, 146, 150, 152, 153, 161, 165, 168, 169, 170–172, 174; *see also* polysubjectivity
intertextuality 77, 78, 104, 117
intuition 31, 72, 73, 82, 168
Ireland 120, 156, 192; Irish 79, 80, 89, 125, 126, 157, 158, 182, 183, 192

Iyer, Vijay 110, 112, 119, 137, 157, 167, 169, 176

Jackson, Shannon 6, 47, 48, 51
Jamaican 18, 48, 135, 148, 155
jazz 54, 67, 68, 109, 110, 112, 119, 120, 135, 148, 157, 176
Jestrovic, Silvija xvi, 70, 89, 97, 99, 101, 116, 119, 208
juxtaposition xiv, 40, 65, 69, 71, 72, 92, 103, 104, 109, 117, 133, 142, 145, 150, 153, 163, 166, 170, 171, 172, 201

Kant, Immanuel 7, 16, 68, 80, 106
Karadžić, Vuk Stefanović viii–xiv, 38, 94, 95, 100, 101, 118, 119
Kartoon Klowns 134
Kendrick, Lynne xv, 1, 3, 14, 30, 31, 51, 57, 60, 128, 129, 146, 154, 157, 169, 177, 208
Kene, Arinzé 117, 130, 131, 138, 150, 211
Kneehigh 26, 132, 154, 200
knowledge ix, 2, 6–13, 16, 18, 22, 24, 29, 32, 47, 48, 54, 56, 64, 94, 114, 120, 123, 161, 165, 174, 175, 176, 198; knowledge creation 13, 22, 26, 29, 31, 36, 37, 66, 163;
Kochhar-Lindgren, Kanta 109, 210
Kodwo, Eshun 140, 157
Kondo, Dorinne 29, 32, 33, 35–36, 50, 52, 57, 65, 66, 86, 172, 177
Kotarba, Joseph 122, 123, 135, 136, 157, 166, 177

Lacan, Jacques (Lacanian) 21, 79, 80
Language viii–xiii, 3, 5, 7, 11, 14, 19, 20, 21, 24, 38, 47, 50, 56, 65, 66, 70, 77, 79, 80, 86, 101, 109, 133, 137, 145, 159, 170, 172, 198, 209
Latour, Bruno 10, 11, 17, 35, 37, 57, 67, 89, 128, 157, 165, 168, 177
layers 74, 108, 118, 134, 168, 184, 201; dramaturgy of layering 40, 167–168; layering 40, 45, 71, 73, 75, 92, 93, 108, 168, 171
Lech, Kasia xvi, 70, 81, 89, 97, 109, 119, 210, 214
Lecoq, Jacques 5, 150
lecture performance 78, 161, 174, 178
Lehmann, Hans-Thies 14, 15, 27, 47, 49, 57, 86, 87, 111, 112, 114, 119, 128, 146, 157, 165, 166, 169, 177
Lepage, Robert 5, 53, 160, 174
Lend Me Your Ears (LMYE) xvi, 2, 35, 38–39, 41, 45, 46, 53, 62, 80, 107, 117, 165, 167, 173, 174, 175, 206–214; *see also* aural, www.auralia.space
liminality 25, 26, 32, 40, 45, 50, 161, 165, 172–174, 176
listening 3, 4, 5, 14, 15, 17, 18, 26, 32, 33, 42, 56, 59, 64, 66, 72, 73, 77, 81, 82, 89, 90, 114, 118, 127, 143, 144, 149, 155, 158, 168, 169, 170, 173, 177
Little Bulb 52, 125, 128, 154, 211
Littlewood, Joan 63, 138
live art 41, 160, 194, 195, 196
liveness 50, 54, 127, 128, 129, 154, 156; refracted liveness 114
looping 77, 78, 93, 108, 166, 168
Lord, Albert ix, 19, 23, 57, 170

Mac, Taylor 150, 203–205
Mars, Rachel 112, 189–190
Martin, Carol 5, 57, 61, 64, 81, 89
material 13, 14, 21, 45, 53, 62, 65, 71, 72, 73, 74, 75, 76, 77, 78, 79, 82, 87, 88, 90, 92, 108, 111, 126, 133, 140, 143, 145, 152, 166, 167, 179, 180, 186, 187, 188, 191, 204; materiality 2, 14, 35, 51, 87, 88
Mattson, Kevin 135, 136, 142, 158, 169, 177
McAuley, Gay xvi, 32, 33, 40, 44, 52, 57, 163, 177, 209
McBurney, Simon 5, 160, 174
McCormack, Jess 61, 70, 74, 75, 89
McCormick, Lucy 39, 133–134, 172, 194–195, 196–197, 207
McLuhan, Marshall 19, 20, 21, 49, 58
Mercuriali, Silvia xvi, 41, 52, 114, 162, 164, 208, 214
Merlin, Bella 72, 89, 90
media 19, 20, 44, 50, 54, 56, 58, 64, 87, 92, 104, 116, 118, 119, 120, 128, 139, 176, 189, 198; intermediality 14, 16, 41, 54, 55, 157, 162, 163, 174; mediatisation 54, 64, 83, 86, 113, 128, 156, 166, 175, 176; multimedia 5, 118, 173; new media dramaturgy 2, 14, 55
Memon, Maimuna 142, 145, 200, 211
memory x, 22, 34, 50, 75, 85, 128, 148, 154, 183, 186, 187
metaphor 15, 59, 62, 71, 74, 79, 81, 89, 90, 133, 166, 177, 179, 182
metatheatricality 79, 112, 186
Meteyard, James xvi, 125, 128, 142, 143, 200, 211,
methexis 168–170
methodology 19, 42, 44, 48, 50, 52, 62, 64, 65, 74, 78, 82, 86, 88, 132, 138,

155, 175; *see also* Smith, Anna Deavere, Anna Deavere Smith's methodology; research methodology
microphones 40, 93, 113, 121, 122, 130, 145, 168, 187, 192, 197, 198
Middle Child 5, 126, 127, 128, 139–140, 143, 154, 155, 158
Mignollo, Walter 153, 158
Mimesis 67, 170, 171
Mirčev, Andrej 71, 158, 208
Mitchell, Katie 160, 174
montage 67, 73, 77, 93, 106, 123, 147, 162
Montenegro 104, 105; Montenegrin 102, 103
Moon, Tony 136, 142
Moten, Fred 71, 83, 89, 106, 119, 166, 177
mouth xii, 3, 21, 80, 128, 208, 209
MTV xiii, 123, 195
Muldoon, Ronald 134, 138, 158; CAST 134, 138; Hackney Empire 138, 155, 158; *see also* Kartoon Klowns
multimodality 17, 103, 109, 112, 115, 118, 119, 120, 124, 132, 134, 146, 166, 171, 172, 174
multiprofessionalisation 51; *see also* deprofessionalisation
Murray, Conrad 102, 118, 123, 137, 150, 155, 156, 167, 175, 197, 208
music xiii, 5, 16, 18, 27, 38, 40, 54, 58, 69, 71, 72, 77, 81, 84, 87, 88, 90, 93, 96, 97, 101, 102, 104, 105, 108, 110, 116, 117, 119, 121–159, 160, 164, 165, 167, 172, 173, 177, 180, 185, 186, 187, 188, 194, 196, 197, 198, 200, 201, 202, 203–225, 211; music theatre 14, 15, 128, 160, 194; music video 39, 102–104, 105, 107, 123; musical 63, 87, 90. 128, 133, 136, 138, 150, 154, 158, 160; musical instrument 84, 94, 97, 105, 117; *see also* genre
musicality 14, 15, 54, 66, 69, 70, 71, 72, 74, 77, 87, 90, 133, 156, 159, 160, 176, 187

nabokov 139, 198–199
Nancy, Jean-Luc 15, 36, 47, 52, 58, 72, 82, 89, 129, 149, 158, 168, 169, 177
narrative 19, 80, 89, 92, 93, 94, 95, 97, 98, 102, 103, 104, 107–114, 117, 119, 120, 123, 137, 145, 157, 165, 176, 186, 189, 194, 195, 198, 199
network 13, 27, 37, 39, 52, 85, 95, 124, 136, 157, 160, 170, 174, 177; *see also* ANT

New Materialism 10, 17, 55, 16
Ngũgĩ Wa Thiong'o 23, 31, 32, 58, 95, 119, 177

Oades, Roslyn 64, 86
O'Briain, Donnacadh 143, 144, 145, 146, 156, 171, 211
O'Kelly, Donal 125, 126
Ong, Walter 20, 21, 25, 51, 58, 173, 177, Ontroerend Goed 26, 46, 51, 112, 113, 175, 185, 190–191
orality 18, 20, 21, 23, 30, 47, 49, 57, 58, 59, 160, 169, 170, 173, 177, 178
oratory 51, 181
orature 23, 32, 39, 58, 93, 95, 99, 100, 101, 102, 105, 109, 117, 118, 119, 169; cyberture 23, 95; oral literature ix, 6, 23, 95

Paget, Derek 63, 64, 65, 67, 74, 86, 89, 124, 158
Parry, Milman ix, 19, 23, 95, 170
participation 17, 30, 43, 51, 53, 54, 56, 60, 83, 100, 145, 150, 168, 170, 175, 180, 189, 204; participatory xi, 17, 23, 51, 67, 71, 83, 95, 129, 150, 154
Pattie, David 133, 136, 144, 145, 155, 158
performance art 77, 133, 134, 172, 176, 196, 205, 207
performance idiom 26, 27, 37, 41, 42, 46, 50, 77, 83, 88, 104, 110, 122, 123, 130, 134, 139, 151, 154, 163, 201
performance studies xi, 1, 2, 6, 7, 8, 9, 12, 29, 30, 32, 47, 48, 51, 55, 95; performativity 13, 56, 57, 59, 97, 105, 116, 172, 173, 175; *see also* ethnography, performative ethnography
performance-making 4, 8, 14, 27, 33, 37, 47, 73, 74, 78, 79, 83, 110, 121, 167
Pettitt, Thomas 19, 49, 58, 119
phenomenology 7, 8, 15, 16, 35, 47, 50, 71
philosophy x, 7, 8, 9, 21, 22, 36, 48, 55, 58, 79, 88, 98, 114, 119, 129, 176, 184
physical theatre 5, 6
Pitrolo, Flora xv, 41, 43, 46, 59, 131, 150, 158, 161, 176, 177, 178, 207, 213, 214
playwriting 4, 47, 80, 121, 130, 139, 201
policy 49, 51, 136, 137
politicity 17; politicity of form 82, 84, 160, 169
politics xiii, 3, 11–12, 15, 17, 28, 30, 33, 36, 49, 50, 53, 54, 55, 56, 58, 61, 67, 68, 73, 75, 77–78, 81, 85, 87, 88, 90, 92, 93, 102, 104, 113, 119, 123, 135, 136, 137, 138, 139, 141, 142, 148, 149,

150, 155, 156, 157, 158, 159, 168, 169, 170, 176, 177, 196, 204, 208, 213; political speeches 73, 77, 78, 88; political theatre 85
polyphony 39, 69, 70, 71, 72, 77, 81, 87, 90, 92, 95, 97, 109, 153, 161, 166
polysubjectivity 69, 70, 98, 99, 100, 105, 112, 145, 165, 169; see also intersubjectivity
popular culture/pop culture xiii, 78, 93, 102, 115, 122, 127, 131, 140, 155, 167, 174; popular music 38, 58, 105, 110, 116, 119, 121, 122, 123, 124, 131, 137, 139, 149, 150, 151, 153, 155, 156, 158, 165, 167, 172, 203, 204
post-critique 10, 11, 12, 35, 54
postdramatic 5, 14, 15, 40, 49, 54, 57, 58, 69, 71, 81, 86, 88, 92, 100, 112, 119, 128, 144, 146, 157, 166, 169, 176, 177
posthumanism 12, 13, 22, 17, 165
poststructuralism 47, 67, 70
practice 5, 7, 9, 11, 13, 16, 18, 19, 28, 33, 35, 37, 40, 42, 43, 47, 48, 53, 55, 56, 59, 60, 62, 63, 65, 66, 69, 72, 82, 83, 88, 90, 92, 95, 98, 100–102, 105, 108, 109, 110, 115, 117, 118, 120, 128, 130, 135, 140, 148, 158, 160, 164, 167, 175, 177, 178, 202, 206, 208; practice research /Practice as Research (PaR) 9, 10, 17, 26, 36, 45, 48, 50, 57, 58, 72, 153, 157, 173; see also research methodology
privileging 3, 9, 11–12, 15, 30, 32, 33, 43, 77, 81, 82, 92
process ix, xii, 1, 4, 5, 6, 8, 9, 12, 13, 14, 18, 19, 22, 24, 25, 26, 28, 31, 32, 33, 34, 35, 37, 39, 40–46, 50, 52, 53, 56, 57, 64, 65, 66, 69, 71, 72, 74, 75, 76, 77, 78, 81, 82, 83, 84, 85, 86, 92, 93, 94, 97, 99, 104, 108, 110, 112, 113, 114, 128, 129, 132, 136, 137, 143, 144, 145, 146, 147, 148, 161, 162, 163, 165, 167, 168, 169, 170, 171, 177, 184, 186, 191, 192, 203, 204, 214; see also artistic process
prosody 66, 101
punk 123, 124, 129–134, 134, 135, 148, 149, 150, 151, 153, 156, 157, 158, 177, 187, 211; k-punk 141–142; post-punk xiii, 124, 140–142, 153, 167; punk rock 128, 135–136, 142

Q Brothers (JQ) 123, 207
queer 8, 133, 148, 150, 204, 213
Quote Unquote 93, 108, 112, 114, 115, 123, 167, 210

race 57, 65, 115, 135, 157, 177, 178; anti-racist 12, 135, 137; racial 20, 68, 87, 133, 136, 155, 180; racism 134–139, 158, 160
radio 2, 17, 20, 63, 64, 112, 138, 144, 152, 156, 160, 187, 188, 189, 209, 213
Rambo Amadeus (Pušić, Antonije) 39, 102–107, 109, 117, 118, 123, 152, 165, 172
Rancière, Jacques 51, 58, 100, 120
Rao, Maya Krishna 82, 168, 207, 214
rap ix, 117, 123, 136, 137, 150, 197, 198
RashDash 5, 125, 129, 140, 142, 150, 155, 194, 200–201, 206, 208
Rau, Milo 81, 89, 183–185
rave 110, 124, 130, 147–151, 153, 157, 162, 164, 187, 188, 213
Raynolds, Simon 123, 141, 153, 158
reception 27, 33, 51, 54, 64, 70, 71, 76, 96, 97, 109, 147, 168, 169, 171, 172, 204
recording ix, xii, 17, 33, 39, 42, 52, 53, 64, 95, 102, 122, 127, 145, 151, 168, 172, 174, 206, 207
reggae 18, 56, 135, 149, 157, 176
rehearsal 33, 34, 36, 37, 40, 41, 44, 52, 53, 55, 56, 57, 59, 86, 111, 154, 156, 163, 177, 186, 189, 198, 209
relationality 12, 13, 15, 16, 22, 25, 29, 30, 31, 34, 38, 47, 50, 51, 60, 114, 144, 155, 168, 169, 178; relational aesthetics 30, 54; relational dramaturgy 4, 30, 37, 47, 112, 129, 174; relational epistemology 31, 94, 165; relational ethnography 32–35, 55, 160, 163, 176; relational ontology 15, 17; relational research methodology 36, 37, 165
Renton, David 134, 135, 155, 158
reparative 29, 35, 36; reparative critique 35; reparative reading 10; reparative research methodology 36, 165
representation 12, 18, 21, 34, 40, 66, 68, 79, 87, 91, 92, 152, 168, 171, 182, 198
research methodology 6–13, 16, 17, 22, 24–40, 47, 49, 55, 59, 110, 120, 122, 128, 136, 160, 161, 171, 178, 162–165; see also practice research
reversed engineering 46
rhetoric 16, 18, 25, 27, 28, 56, 64, 75, 77, 104, 134, 151
rhizomatic 64, 170–171
rhythm ix, 66, 71, 74, 75, 77, 82, 101, 105, 117, 133, 151, 153, 156, 177, 186, 199, 212
ritual xi, 117, 148, 151, 190, 205

rock music 102, 103, 121, 122, 123, 124, 128, 129, 131, 134, 151, 155, 158; Rock Against Racism 134–139; rock'n'roll 123, 133, 135, 187; *see also* genre; popular music
Roesner, David xvi, 14, 59, 60, 70, 72, 87, 90, 132, 154, 156, 158, 160, 166, 177, 211
Romanticism xii, 70; Romantic 70, 95, 98, 99, 100, 101, 105, 116, 122, 137, 155
Rotozaza 52, 189
Russian 47, 104, 117, 193, 203

Saldaña, Johnny 65, 66, 90
sampling 40, 46, 93, 103, 108, 123, 138, 187
Saunders, Red 134; *see also* rock music, Rock Against Racism
scenography 79, 155, 160, 172
Scotland 153, 187; Scottish 110, 130, 153, 188
semantic 2, 25, 27, 42, 70, 73, 74, 75, 87, 101, 104, 108, 109, 131, 132, 134, 145, 166, 168; semantic closure 133, 169, 170, 172, 175; semantic gap 72, 103, 171
Serbia viii, xiv, xvi, 94, 95, 109, 116, 119, 157; Serbian viii–xvi, 39, 93, 95, 96, 100, 101, 102, 104, 105, 107, 115, 116, 119, 152, 169
She Goat 108, 161, 168, 174, 212
site-specific 8, 41, 154, 162
SK Shlomo xvi, 41, 93, 108, 117, 122, 123, 147, 149, 150, 162, 164, 168, 175, 210, 211
SKaGeN Theatre 78–79, 181–182
Slattnë, Hanna 174, 175, 178, 212
Sleepwalk Collective xvi, 113, 161, 163, 164, 168, 174, 208, 212, 214
Smith, Anna Deavere 32, 39, 62, 63, 65, 66, 67, 68, 69, 73, 76, 80, 82, 86, 89, 90, 164, 179–181; Anna Deavere Smith's methodology 62, 65–68, 82, 179
sociology 28, 32, 58, 122; sociological 33, 35, 81, 105, 133, 135, 148, 149, 183
software 40, 45, 53, 88, 93, 94, 108, 167
Soleimanpour, Nassim 112, 189
sonic 3, 16, 17, 18, 38, 45, 55, 56, 58, 60, 75, 77, 87, 88, 104, 154, 157, 176, 178, 208, 210, 212, 213; sonic cues 43; sonic dominance 149, 150, 172
sound 1, 4, 13–23, 30, 31, 32, 35, 36, 39, 42, 44, 47, 51, 54, 55, 56, 58, 59, 60, 64, 77, 78, 81, 82, 87, 88, 104, 108, 109, 110, 112, 117, 118, 120, 129, 149, 153, 154, 157, 160, 161, 165–174, 176, 177, 178, 187, 188, 199, 206, 207, 210, 212, 214; sound art 41; sound design 14; sound effect 18, 47, 55, 154, 186, 210; sound object 16, 49, 59; sound ontology 32, 144, 169; sound studies 16, 56, 59, 64, 177; sound system 18, 56, 148, 149, 157, 176; sound technology 93, 108, 113, 122; soundscape 17, 55, 57, 59, 153, 183, 187, 190, 197
space 15, 18, 23, 33, 34, 37, 38, 39, 40, 42, 45, 49, 54, 60, 61, 68, 72, 74, 75, 77, 81, 85, 87, 88, 97, 105, 107, 108, 111, 143, 150, 160, 161, 163, 171, 173, 184, 186; spatiality 2, 32, 87, 88, 112, 154, 170; *see also* aural, www.auralia.space
speaking 15, 32, 33, 38, 45, 49, 61, 66, 68, 73, 78, 81, 83, 85, 88, 95, 104, 109, 145, 168, 170, 184, 192; spoken word 18, 41, 51, 73, 137, 166, 197; *see also* speech; voice
spectatorship 30, 50, 51, 54, 100
speech 3, 4, 5, 6, 13–23, 24, 32, 36, 37, 38, 39, 42, 43, 44, 45, 47, 49, 51, 64, 66, 68, 69, 70, 73, 74, 82, 84, 86, 88, 91–92, 109, 110, 112, 149, 154, 161, 165–176, 180; speeches 51, 73, 77, 78, 84, 88, 91, 181, 186; *see also* speaking
stand-up comedy 131, 134, 195
Steinby, Liisa 69–70, 90, 98, 99, 100, 120
Sterne, Jonathan 16, 19, 20, 23, 25, 49, 59, 166, 178
Stiegler, Bernard 4, 21, 22, 23, 50, 59, 92, 152
story xii, xiv, 64, 66, 74, 80, 84, 85, 92, 101, 104, 110, 114, 118, 127, 129, 132, 133, 136, 137, 140, 142, 143, 144, 145, 153, 156, 184, 185, 187, 188, 189, 195, 196, 197, 199, 200, 204

Taylor, Amy 126, 127, 156, 159
Taylor, S.W. 28, 153; Taylorism 122, 148
techne 9, 18, 22, 48; technicity 4, 21, 22, 24, 36, 39, 50, 54, 60, 63, 69, 79, 81, 83, 90, 93, 95, 101, 107, 161, 167, 171, 173, 212; technique 18, 56, 64, 68, 77, 81, 83, 86, 87, 88, 89, 101, 157, 176, 186
techno 147
techno-determinism 19, 49, 50, 92
technology 4, 12, 17, 20, 22, 35, 38, 39, 46, 49, 50, 54, 56, 62, 64, 73, 80, 82, 87, 88, 91, 92, 93, 94, 105, 107, 108,

109, 112, 113, 114, 115, 121, 122, 149, 152, 158, 161, 165, 168, 174, 184, 188, 191, 193, 198, 214
(tele)phone 17, 83, 93, 127, 161, 180, 197
text xii, 2, 5, 6, 12, 13, 14, 16, 22, 25, 32, 39, 49, 54, 58, 61, 70, 71, 74, 75, 76, 77, 79, 83, 88, 95, 97, 98, 99, 102, 108, 109, 111, 115, 120, 131, 143, 144, 145, 166, 167, 173, 174, 177, 181, 182, 192, 197; textocentrism 32, 33, 67, 68; textuality 21, 170
The Fall Collective 85, 209
The Unspoken Project 39, 91–92, 115, 168, 210
theatre in the dark 160, 175
Theatre Royal Stratford East 138, 153
theatre studies 16, 47, 50, 54,
theatre-making 1, 3–7, 9, 25–27, 28, 32, 36, 39, 42, 47, 50, 51, 52, 58, 59, 60, 65, 66, 69, 70, 72, 80, 85, 87, 90, 92, 93, 102, 122, 128, 140, 142, 150, 156, 158, 160, 161, 167, 169, 177, 181, 191
Thomaidis, Konstantinos 6, 47, 59, 73, 173, 209
training 7, 8, 9, 20, 24, 25, 29, 42, 46, 47, 51, 65, 70, 79, 82, 83, 85, 132, 140, 141, 142, 156, 165, 167, 206, 213
translation x, 21, 25, 27, 53, 70, 74, 88, 89, 96, 147, 152, 171
Trueman, Matt 61, 62, 86, 90, 155, 159
turbofolk 105, 151–152; *Turbofolk* 151–152, 211

Ultz 138, 156
Unfolding Theatre 150, 202–203, 211
United Kingdom 5, 8, 9, 10, 25, 28, 29, 41, 46, 50, 52, 63, 64, 65, 113, 121, 123, 124, 127, 132, 135, 137, 139, 142, 147, 148, 151; *see also* British
United States *see* American
university 7, 8, 9, 11, 28, 33, 47, 48, 51, 140, 141, 155, 174, 200, 201

Vaughan, Megan 75
verbatim 5, 39, 42, 53, 61–62, 62–66, 70, 72, 73–75, 77, 78, 81, 85, 86, 87, 89, 90, 124, 144, 164, 171, 179, 180, 181, 182; post-verbatim 5, 39, 62, 69, 73, 76, 78, 79, 80, 81–86, 124, 166, 171; *see also* headphones, headphone verbatim

video 34, 39, 42, 52, 102, 103, 109, 117, 147, 151, 173, 181, 184, 206, 207, 214; *see also* music, music video
Voegelin, Salomé 15, 35, 60, 172, 178
voice 5, 6, 15, 21, 30, 41, 46, 51, 55, 57, 58, 59, 60, 64, 70, 73, 74, 77, 85, 87, 89, 91, 96, 97, 113, 115, 116, 117, 135, 150, 163, 165, 168, 171, 176, 181, 182, 187, 189, 192, 193, 198, 202, 206, 209, 210, 212, 213, 214; vocal assemblage 73; voice training 46, 47; *see also* decolonisation, Decolonising the Voice

Wake, Caroline 61, 64, 66, 72, 82, 86, 90
West xiii, 70, 102, 169; Western ix, xiii, 2, 5, 6, 7, 9, 13, 14, 15, 17, 18, 20, 21, 22, 29, 31, 36, 50, 51, 85, 92, 94, 95, 100, 101, 105, 109, 110, 114, 115, 129, 137, 151, 168; non-Western 17, 20, 94, 152, 167, 169
West End 124, 130, 138, 150, 184, 198
Widgery, David 135
Wildcard Theatre 40, 142, 143, 146, 199–200, 211
Williams, Holly 126, 127, 128, 153, 154, 159
Williams, Raymond 8, 48
Wilson, Melanie 93, 108, 112, 114, 167, 174, 210
Wilson, Michael 93, 94, 112, 115, 120, 122, 124, 130, 153, 159
Worthen, W.B. 4, 22, 23, 51, 60, 62, 63, 79, 90, 92, 99, 120, 173, 212
writing viii–xiv, 1–3, 5, 10, 11, 20, 21, 22, 24, 27, 37, 38, 42, 44, 45, 47, 51, 53, 68, 89, 92, 93, 102, 106, 108, 109, 111, 112, 114, 115, 122, 126, 130, 139, 143, 155, 161, 165, 167, 172, 173, 175, 189, 193, 203, 207

Xia, Matthew 117, 123, 138, 147, 150, 156, 164, 167, 211

Yee, Shannon 174, 212
Yugoslavia viii–xiv, 19, 50, 101, 102, 103, 105, 123, 152

Zahn, Oliver 44, 161, 168, 173, 212
Zephaniah, Benjamin 135, 138
Zoom 41–46, 52, 53, 82, 161, 173, 206
ZU-UK 93, 108, 109, 112, 113, 114, 210